FILM THEORY

Critical Concepts in Media and Cultural Studies

Other titles in this series:

Television
Edited with a new introduction by Toby Miller
4 volume set

Hollywood
Edited with a new introduction by Thomas G. Schatz
4 volume set

FILM THEORY

Critical Concepts in Media and Cultural Studies

Edited by
Philip Simpson, Andrew Utterson and K. J. Shepherdson

Volume II

Routledge
Taylor & Francis Group
LONDON AND NEW YORK

First published 2004
by Routledge
11 New Fetter Lane, London EC4P 4EE

Simultaneously published in the USA and Canada
by Routledge
29 West 35th Street, New York, NY 10001

Routledge is an imprint of the Taylor & Francis Group

Typeset in Times by RefineCatch Limited, Bungay, Suffolk
Printed and bound in Great Britain by
TJ International Ltd, Padstow, Cornwall

British Library Cataloguing in Publication Data
A catalogue record for this book is available from the British Library

Library of Congress Cataloging in Publication Data
A catalog record for this book has been requested

ISBN 0–415–25971–1 (Set)
ISBN 0–415–25973–8 (Volume II)

Publisher's note
References within each chapter are as they appear in the original complete work

CONTENTS

VOLUME II

ACKNOWLEDGEMENTS

The publishers would like to thank the following for permission to reprint their material:

Cahiers du Cinéma for permission to reprint François Truffaut, 'A certain tendency of the French cinema', translator not specified, *Cahiers du Cinema in English*, 1, January 1966, pp. 30–41. (Originally published as 'Une certaine tendance du cinéma français', *Cahiers du Cinéma*, 31, January 1954, pp. 15–29.)

Anthology Film Archives for permission to reprint Andrew Sarris, 'Notes on the *auteur* theory in 1962', *Film Culture*, 27, Winter 1962, pp. 1–8.

bfi Publishing for permission to reprint Geoffrey Nowell-Smith, '*Luchino Visconti*: Introduction', in *Luchino Visconti*, London: Secker & Warburg in association with the British Film Institute, 1967, pp. 7–13.

bfi Publishing for permission to reprint Peter Wollen, 'The *auteur* theory', in *Signs and Meaning in the Cinema*, London: Secker & Warburg in association with the British Film Institute, 1969, pp. 74–115.

bfi Publishing for permission to reprint Peter Wollen, '*Signs and Meaning in the Cinema*: Conclusion', in *Signs and Meaning in the Cinema*, revised edition, London: Secker & Warburg in association with the British Film Institute, 1972, pp. 155–175.

Routledge for permission to reprint John Caughie, 'Fiction of the author/author of the fiction', in John Caughie, ed., *Theories of Authorship: A Reader*, London: Routledge & Kegan Paul in association with the British Film Institute, 1981, pp. 199–207.

Timothy Corrigan, 'Auteurs and the new Hollywood', in John Lewis, ed., *The New American Cinema*, Durham, NC: Duke University Press, pp. 38–63. Copyright 1998, Duke University Press. All rights reserved. Used by permission of the publisher.

Routledge for permission to reprint Steve Neale, 'Definitions of genre', in *Genre and Hollywood*, London: Routledge, 2000, pp. 9–29.

University of California Press for permission to reprint André Bazin, 'The western: or the American film *par excellence*', translated by Hugh Gray, in *What is Cinema? Vol. II*, Berkeley, CA: University of California Press, 1972, pp. 140–148. (Originally published as 'Le western ou le cinéma américain par excellence', preface to J.-L. Rieupeyrout, *Le western ou le cinéma américain par excellence*, 7e Art, Éditions du Cerf, 1953, pp. 5–13.)

Alain Silver for permission to reprint Nino Frank, 'A new kind of police drama: the criminal adventure', translated by Alain Silver, in Alain Silver and James Ursini, eds, *Film Noir Reader 2*, New York: Limelight Editions, 1999, pp. 15–19. © 1999. (Originally published as 'Un nouveau genre "policier": 'l'aventure criminelle', *L'Ecran Français*, 61, 28 August 1946, pp. 8–9 and p. 14.)

Alain Silver for permission to reprint Jean-Pierre Chartier, 'Americans also make *noir* films', translated by Alain Silver, in Alain Silver and James Ursini, eds, *Film Noir Reader 2*, New York: Limelight Editions, 1999, pp. 21–23. © 1999. (Originally published as 'Les Américains aussi font des films "noirs" ', *La Revue du Cinéma*, 1, 2, November 1946, pp. 67–70.)

Partisan Review for permission to reprint Robert Warshow, 'The gangster as tragic hero', *Partisan Review*, February 1948, pp. 240–244.

Film Comment for permission to reprint Paul Schrader, 'Notes on *film noir*', *Film Comment*, 8, 1, Spring 1972, pp. 8–13. (Originally published in 1971 as a pamphlet to accompany a short season of films programmed by Schrader for the Los Angeles Film Festival.)

Routledge Inc. for permission to reprint Jim Collins, 'Genericity in the nineties: eclectic irony and the new sincerity', in Jim Collins, Hilary Radner and Ava Preacher Collins, eds, *Film Theory Goes to the Movies: Cultural Analysis of Contemporary Film*, New York: Routledge Inc., 1993, pp. 242–263.

Routledge for permission to reprint Steve Neale, 'Issues, conclusions and questions', in *Genre and Hollywood*, London: Routledge, 2000, pp. 251–255.

Julia Lesage for permission to reprint Julia Lesage, '*S/Z* and *Rules of the Game*', *Jump Cut: A Review of Contemporary Cinema*, 12–13, Winter 1976–77, pp. 45–51.

University of California Press for permission to reprint Will Wright, 'The structure of myth' [extract], 'Myth as a narrative of social action' [and] 'Individuals and values: the classical plot', in *Sixguns and Society: A Structural Study of the Western*, Berkeley, CA: University of California Press, 1977, pp. 16–28 (Extract: pp. 25–28), pp. 124–129 and pp. 130–153.

David Bordwell, 'Principles of narration', in *narration in the Fiction Film*, Madison, WI: University of Wisconsin Press, 1985, pp. 48–62. © 1985. Reprinted by permission of The University of Wisconsin Press.

Bill Nichols, 'Form wars: the political unconscious of formalist theory', *South Atlantic Quarterly*, 88, 2, Spring 1989, pp. 487–515. Copyright 1989, Duke University Press. All rights reserved. Used by permission of the publisher.

University of Illinois Press for permission to reprint Tom Gunning, 'Theory and history: narrative discourse and the narrator system', in *D. W. Griffith and the Origins of American Narrative Film: The Early Years at Biograph*, Urbana, IL: University of Illinois Press, 1991, pp. 10–30.

Routledge for permission to reprint Edward Branigan, 'Levels of narration', in *Narrative Comprehension and Film*, London: Routledge, 1992, pp. 86–124.

Disclaimer

INTRODUCTION TO VOLUME II

'Authorship', 'Genre', 'Narrative and Narration'

Authorship

From the middle of the twentieth century the concepts of authorship, genre, and narrative and narration have been significant in film theory. While it may be true that authorship is now less popular than genre or narrative as a critical approach to film, it remains a concept implicit in much analysis of the reception and marketing of popular films.

François Truffaut is conventionally identified as the originator of modern authorship studies and the essay included here crystallises his approach. Though it can now be seen as a polemic about the perceived limitations of French cinema of the time, and as clearing a space for the directorial ambitions of Truffaut and his contemporaries, the implications of 'A Certain Tendency of the French Cinema' were far reaching. Following the work of André Bazin, it confirmed Hollywood Cinema as a serious object of critical attention by suggesting that artefacts issuing from an industrial system might nonetheless be created by individual authors. This perspective was taken up in the United States by Andrew Sarris who translated Truffaut's *politique des auteurs* as 'auteur theory' and used it as a means to bolster the standing of American cinema in relation to its European counterpart, and to create a pantheon of favoured American directors.

Structuralist linguistics, mediated by French literary theorists like Roland Barthes and the anthropologist Claude Lévi-Strauss, impacted upon ideas of authorship in the 1960s. Peter Wollen's influential essay, 'The *Auteur* Theory', countered the tendency of Truffaut and Sarris to see the director as an individual creative genius analogous to a novelist or dramatist. Wollen and Geoffrey Nowell-Smith propose a distinction between the historical figure of Alfred Hitchcock or Howard Hawks and what Nowell-Smith calls 'a structural hard-core of basic and often recondite motifs' discernible retrospectively through the analysis of their respective oeuvres and attached to their names. This appropriation of structuralist theory in relation to authorship was itself challenged, particularly with regard to its methodology (see Henderson 1973).

In the late 1960s, Barthes and Michel Foucault also questioned the idea of authorship in widely quoted essays. Barthes' theorising about readers 'constructing' writers contributed to the movement, in the 1980s and 1990s, away from theories of authorship towards those of genre and narrative where the emphasis is more upon the reception of a text. However, John Caughie, aware of 'the birth of the reader', contended that it may not necessarily be, as Barthes argues, 'at the cost of the death of the Author', though the author may be 'an effect of the text', his or her presence in a film may add to the meanings and experiences available to the reader (Barthes 1977). Timothy Corrigan locates the significance of authorship less in the expressivity of the director or the activity of the audience and more with the commercial significance of the director as author. With the decline of the Hollywood studio system, the name of the author can become, however briefly, a marketing device to facilitate audience identification of a product. Far from being dead, authors 'may be more alive than at any point in film history'.

Genre

As with authorship, genre has become a theoretical concept primarily associated with the study of popular cinema. Indian popular cinema, as one example, may be as generic as American popular cinema but most theoretical work in this context, so far, concerns Hollywood.

As the first of Steve Neale's essays indicates, the definition of genre has been the subject of shifting emphases since early formulations which tended to rely upon circular arguments: the criteria for establishing the genre of a film were derived from the films under examination. Some of the earlier writers, like Bazin and Robert Warshow, eschew theoretical questions about definition and attempt to indicate how the formal qualities of two popular genres demonstrate genre's distinctive potential for reflecting moral or social issues in American society and beyond. Essays included here also suggest directions in which genre criticism has been deployed to explain the formal operation of genres. The essays by Nino Frank and Jean-Pierre Chartier, in contrast, imply that the origin of *film noir* lies in the critical viewing in post-war France of the backlog of Hollywood films rather than as a studio production cycle or as a process of identification by audiences. Paul Schrader's subtle identification of mood and tone in such films raises doubts about their generic status in the absence of precise definition.

The essays by Jim Collins and Neale examine the explanatory potential of genre in relation to contemporary Hollywood cinema. Collins raises questions about the application of genre as a critical category through a discussion of two 'hybrid' films made in 1989 and 1990. Since 1980, Neale has argued against the overly simplistic ascription of genre in theorising the production, marketing and reception of Hollywood cinema. While endorsing the relevance of some of the genre theory and criticism summarised in the opening essay of this section, Neale nonetheless calls for further detailed research. He proposes more extensive viewing and historically based analyses of studio production and marketing in relation to film cycles and genres and the identification of 'unrecognised genres' and 'cross-generic cycles'.

Narrative and narration

As with genre, narrative theory of the past three decades has drawn upon the work of literary theorists. The influence of Barthes, Gérard Genette, Lévi-Strauss and Tzvetan Todorov is discernible in many of the essays included here. Furthermore, Will Wright and David Bordwell make reference to Vladimir Propp and the Russian Formalists who theorised narrative function in the 1920s and 1930s. The collection as a whole attempts to acknowledge the influence of these theorists as well as give some indication of their relevance to narration in the fiction film.

Julia Lesage's essay adapts Barthes' deconstructive analysis of a Balzac novella, *Sarrasine* (1974), to the narrative of Jean Renoir's *La Règle du Jeu/The Rules of the Game* (1939) with what she sees as a radical and liberating potential. Similarly, the passages from *Sixguns and Society* represent Wright's attempt to understand how the images and actions of narrative function cognitively in commercially successful Westerns structured like myths.

The perceptual and cognitive aspects of viewing the narration of Hollywood films are a central concern for Bordwell, whose influence on narrative study in this field has been paramount. Though not studying audiences empirically, Bordwell is nevertheless interested in how films encourage, sustain or block viewing operations and he evokes the Formalist ideas of *fabula* (story) and *syuzhet* (plot) to explain these narrational processes. For Bill Nichols, Bordwell's analysis, though valuable, is too Formalist in that it poses questions about viewing in isolation from questions of subjectivity, desire and power that Nichols sees as inescapable even in cognitive and perceptual activities. Tom Gunning is included here for his elaboration of important ideas introduced in the extract from Bordwell. Gunning suggests that Bordwell gives insufficient recognition to a conception of the narrator.

The chapter from Edward Branigan's *Narrative Comprehension and Film* links with the texts on authorship and language by placing both in the context of narrative comprehension. Its chief value lies in its demonstration of the density of the activities which the narrative of an unexceptional Hollywood film relies upon if the viewer is to fully engage with it. As Bordwell observes in *Narration in the Fiction Film*: 'Watching a movie may seem as effortless as riding a bicycle but both draw on a range of practised acts' (1985: 30).

References

Barthes, R. (1977) 'The Death of the Author', English translation by Stephen Heath. From *Image-Music-Text*, London: Fontana. (First published in 1968.)

Balzac, H. de (1974) *Sarrasine*, reprinted in R. Barthes, *S/Z*. English translation by Richard Miller, New York: Hill & Wang.

Bordwell, D. (1985) *Narration in the Fiction Film*, London: Routledge.

Foucault, M. (1977) 'What is an Author?', English translation by Donald F. Bouchard and Sherry Simon. From Donald F. Bouchard, ed., *Language, Counter-Memory, Practice*, Oxford: Basil Blackwell.

Henderson, B. (1973) 'Critique of Cine-Structuralism', *Film Quarterly*, Vol. 27, No. 1, Fall.

Philip Simpson

Part 4

AUTHORSHIP

25

A CERTAIN TENDENCY OF THE FRENCH CINEMA

François Truffaut

Source: Translator not specified, *Cahiers du Cinéma in English*, 1, January 1966, pp. 30–41. (Originally published as 'Une certaine tendance de cinéma français', *Cahiers du Cinéma*, 31, January 1954, pp. 15–29.)

These notes have no other object than to attempt to define a certain tendency of the French cinema—a tendency called "psychological realism"—and to sketch its limits.

Ten or twelve films

If the French cinema exists by means of about a hundred films a year, it is well understood that only ten or twelve merit the attention of critics and cinéphiles, the attention, therefore of "Cahiers."

These ten or twelve films constitute what has been prettily named the "Tradition of Quality"; they force, by their ambitiousness, the admiration of the foreign press, defend the French flag twice a year at Cannes and at Venice where, since 1946, they regularly carry off medals, golden lions and *grands prix*.

With the advent of "talkies," the French cinema was a frank plagiarism of the American cinema. Under the influence of *Scarface*, we made the amusing *Pèpé Le Moko*. Then, the French scenario is most clearly obliged to Prévert for its evolution; *Quai Des Brumes* (*Port Of Shadows*) remains the masterpiece of *poetic realism.*

The war and the post-war period renewed our cinema. It evolved under the effect of an internal pressure and for *poetic realism* — about which one might say that it died closing *Les Portes De La Nuit* behind it—was substituted *psychological realism*, illustrated by Claude Autant-Lara, Jean Delannoy, René Clement, Yves Allegret and Marcel Pagliero.

Scenarists' films

If one is willing to remember that not so long ago Delannoy filmed *Le Bossu* and *La Part De L'Ombre*, Clauda Autant-Lara *Le Plombier Amoureux* and *Lettres D'Amour*, Yves Allégret *La Boite Aux Reves* and *Les Démons De L'Aube*, that all these films are justly recognized as strictly commercial enterprises, one will admit that, the successes or failures of these cinéastes being a function of the scenarios they chose, *La Symphonie Pastorale*, *Le Diable Au Corps* (*Devil In The Flesh*), *Jeux Interdits* (*Forbidden Games*), *Manèges*. *Un Homme Marche Dans La Ville*, are essentially *scenarists' films*.

Today no one is ignorant any longer . . .

After having sounded out directing by making two forgotten shorts, Jean Aurenche became a specialist in adaptation. In 1936, he was credited, with Anouilh, with the dialogue for *Vous N'Avez Rien A Déclarer* and *Les Dégourdis De La Ile*.

At the same time Pierre Bost was publishing excellent little novels at the N.R.F.

Aurenche and Bost worked together for the first time while adapting and writing dialogue for *Douce*, directed by Claude Autant-Lara.

Today, no one is ignorant any longer of the fact that Aurenche and Bost rehabilitated adaptation by upsetting old preconceptions of being faithful to the letter and substituting for it the contrary idea of being faithful to the spirit—to the point that this audacious aphorism has been written: "An honest adaptation is a betrayal" (Carlo Rim, "Traveling And Sex-Appeal").

In adaptation there exists filmable scenes and unfilmable scenes, and that instead of omitting the latter (as was done not long ago) it is necessary to invent *equivalent* scenes, that is to say, scenes as the novel's author would have written them for the cinema.

"Invention without betrayal" is the watchword Aurenche and Bost like to cite, forgetting that one can also betray by omission.

The system of Aurenche and Bost is so seductive, even in the enunciation of its principles, that nobody even dreamed of verifying its functioning close-at-hand. I propose to do a little of this here.

The entire reputation of Aurenche and Bost is built on two precise points:

1. *Faithfulness* to the spirit of the works they adapt;
2. The talent they use.

That famous faithfulness . . .

Since 1943 Aurenche and Bost have adapted and written dialogue for: *Douce* by Michel Davet, *La Symphonie Pastoral* by Gide, *Le Diable Au Corps* by

Radiguet, *Un Recteur à l'Ile de Sein* (*Dieu A Besoin Des Hommes—God Needs Men*) by Queffelec, *Les Jeux Inconnus* (*Jeux Interdits*) by François Boyer, *Le Blé En Herbe* by Colette.

In addition, they wrote an adaptation of *Journal D'Un Curé De Campagne* that was never filmed, a scenario on *Jeanne D'Arc* of which only one part has been made (by Jean Delannoy) and, lastly, scenario and dialogue for *L'Auberge Rouge* (*The Red Inn*) (directed by Claude Autant-Lara).

You will have noticed the profound diversity of inspiration of the works and authors adapted. In order to accomplish this tour de force which consists of remaining faithful to the spirit of Michael Davet, Gide, Radiguet, Queffelec, Francois Boyer, Colette and Bernanos, one must oneself possess, I imagine, a suppleness of spirit, a habitually geared-down personality as well as singular eclecticism.

You must also consider that Aurenche and Bost are led to collaborate with the most diverse directors; Jean Delannoy, for example, sees himself as a mystical moralist. But the petty meanness of *Garcon Sauvage* (*Savage Triangle*), the shabbiness of *La Minute De Vérite*, the insignificance of *La Route Napoleon* show rather clearly the intermittent character of that vocation.

Claude Autant-Lara, on the contrary, is well known for his nonconformity, his "advanced" ideas, his wild anti-clericalism; let us recognize in this cinéaste the virtue of always remaining, in his films, honest with himself.

Pierre Bost being the technician in tandem; the spiritual element in this communal work seems to come from Jean Aurenche.

Educated by the Jesuits, Jean Aurenche has held on to nostaglia and rebellion, both at the same time. His flirtation with surrealism seemed to be out of sympathy for the anarchists of the thirties. This tells how strong his personality is, also how apparently incompatible it was with the personalities of Gide, Bernanos, Queffelec, Radiguet. But an examination of the works will doubtless give us more information.

Abbot Amédee Ayffre knew very well how to analyzse *La Symphonie Pastoral* and how to define the relationship between the written work and the filmed work:

"Reduction of Faith to religious psychology in the hands of Gide, now becomes a reduction to psychology, plain and simple . . . with this qualitative abasement we will now have, according to a law well-known to aestheticians, a corresponding quantitative augmentation. New characters are added: Piette and Casteran, charged with representing certain sentiments. Tragedy becomes drama, melodrama." (Dieu Au Cinema, p. 131).

What annoys me . . .

What annoys me about this famous process of equivalence is that I'm not at all certain that a novel contains unfilmable scenes, and even less certain that these scenes, decreed unfilmable, would be so for everyone.

Praising Robert Bresson for his faithfulness to Bernanos, André Bazin ended his excellent article "La Stylistique de Robert Bresson," with these words. "After *The Diary Of A Country Priest*, Aurenche and Bost are no longer anything but the Viollet-Leduc of adaptation."

All those who admire and know Bresson's film well will remember the admirable scene in the confessional when Chantal's face "began to appear little by little, by degrees" (Bernanos).

When, several years before Bresson, Jean Aurenche wrote an adaptation of *Diary*, refused by Bernanos, he judged this scene to be unfilmable and substituted for it the one we reproduce here.

> "Do you want me to listen to you here?" He indicates the confessional.
>
> "I never confess."
>
> "Nevertheless, you must have confessed yesterday, since you took communion this morning?"
>
> "I didn't take communion."
>
> He looks at her, very surprised.
>
> "Pardon me, I gave you communion."
>
> Chantal turns rapidly towards the pri-Dieu she had occupied that morning.
>
> "Come see."
>
> The curé follows her. Chantal indicates the missal she had left there.
>
> "Look in this book, Sir. Me, I no longer, perhaps, have the right to touch it."
>
> The curé, very intrigued, opens the book and discovers, between two pages, the host that Chantal had spit out. His face is stupified and confused.
>
> "I spit out the host," says Chantal.
>
> "I see," says the curé, with a neutral voice.
>
> "You've never seen anything like that, right?" says Chantal, harsh almost triumphant.
>
> "No, never," says the curé, very calmly.
>
> "Do you know what must be done?"
>
> The curé closes his eyes for a brief instant. He is thinking or praying, he says, "It is very simple to repair, Miss. But it's very horrible to commit."
>
> He heads for the altar, carrying the open book. Chantal follows him.
>
> "No, it's not horrible. What is horrible is to receive the host in a state of sin."
>
> "You were, then, in a state of sin?"
>
> "Less than the others, but then—it's all the same to them."

> "Do not judge."
> "I do not judge, I condemn," says Chantal with violence.
> "Silence in front of the body of Christ!"
> He kneels before the altar, takes the host from the books and swallows it.

In the middle of the book, the curé and an obtuse atheist named Arsène are opposed in a discussion on Faith. This discussion ends with this line by Arsène, "When one is dead, everything is dead." In the adaptation, this discussion takes place on the very tomb of the curé, between Arsène and another curé, and *terminates the film*. This line, "When one is dead, everything is dead," carries, perhaps the only one retained by the public. Bernanos did not say, for conclusion, "When one is dead, everything is dead," but "What does it matter, all is grace."

"Invention without betrayal," you say—it seems to me that it's a question here of little enough invention for a great deal of betrayal. One or two more details. Aurenche and Bost were unable to make *The Diary Of A Country Priest* because Bernanos was alive. Bresson declared that were Bernanos alive he would have taken more liberties. Thus, Aurenche and Bost are annoyed because someone is alive, but Bresson is annoyed because he is dead.

Unmask

From a simple reading of that extract, there stands out:

1. A constant and deliberate care to be *unfaithful* to the spirit as well as the letter;
2. A very marked taste for profanation and blasphemy.

This unfaithfulness to the spirit also degrades *Le Diable Au Corps*—a love story that becomes an anti-militaristic, anti-bourgeois film, *La Symphonie Pastorale*—a love story about an amorous pastor—turns Gide into a Béatrix Beck, *Un Recteur à l'ile de Sein* whose title is swapped for the equivocal one of *Dieu A Besoin Des Hommes* in which the islanders are shown like the famous "cretins" in Buñuel's *Land Without Bread*.

As for the taste for blasphemy, it is constantly manifested in a more or less insidious manner, depending on the subject, the *metteur-en-scène*, nay, even the star.

I recall from memory the confessional scene from *Douce*, Marthe's funeral in *Le Diable*, the profaned hosts in that adaptation of *Diary* (scene carries over to *Dieu A Besoin Des Hommes*), the whole scenario and the character played by Fernandel in *L'Auberge Rouge*, the scenario *in toto* of *Jeux Interdits* (joking in the cemetery).

Thus, everything indicates that Aurenche and Bost are the authors of *frankly* anti-clerical films, but, since films about the cloth are fashionable, our authors have allowed themselves to fall in with that style. But as it suits them—they think—not to betray their convictions, the theme of profanation and blasphemy, dialogues with double meanings, turn up here and there to prove to the guys that they know the art of "cheating the producer," all the while giving him satisfaction, as well as that of cheating the "great public," which is equally satisfied.

This process well deserves the name of "alibi-ism"; it is excusable and its use is necessary during a time when one must ceaselessly feign stupidity in order to work intelligently, but if it's all in the game to "cheat the producer," isn't it a bit scandalous to re-write Gide, Bernanos and Radiguet?

In truth, Aurenche and Bost work like all the scenarists in the world, like pre-war Spaak and Natanson.

To their way of thinking, every story includes characters A, B, C, and D. In the interior of that equation, everything is organized in function of criteria known to them alone. The sun rises and sets like clockwork, characters disappear, others are invented, the script deviates little by little from the original and becomes a whole, formless but brilliant; a new film, step by step makes its solemn entrance into the "Tradition of Quality."

So be it, they will tell me . . .

They will tell me, "Let us admit that Aurenche and Bost are unfaithful, but do you also deny the existence of their talent . . .?" Talent, to be sure, is not a function of fidelity, but I consider an adaptation of value only when written by a *man of the cinema*. Aurenche and Bost are essentially literary men and I reproach them here for being contemptuous of the cinema by underestimating it. They behave, *vis-a-vis* the scenario, as if they thought to reeducate a delinquent by finding him a job; they always believe they've "done the maximum" for it by embellishing it with subtleties, out of that science of nuances that make up the slender merit of modern novels. It is, moreover, only the smallest caprice on the part of the exegetists of our art that they believe to honor the cinema by using literary jargon. (Haven't Sarte and Camus been talked about for Pagliero's work, and phenomenology for Allégret's?)

The truth is, Aurenche and Bost have made the works they adapt insipid, for *equivalence* is always with us, whether in the form of treason or timidity. Here is a brief example: in *Le Diable Au Corps*, as Radiguet wrote it, Francois meets Marthe on a train platform with Marthe jumping from the train while it is still moving; in the film, they meet in the school which has been transformed into a hospital. What is the point of this *equivalence?* It's a decoy for the anti-militarist elements added to the work, in concert with Claude Autant-Lara.

Well, it is evident that Radiguet's idea was one of *mise en scène*, whereas the scene invented by Aurenche and Bost is *literary*. One could, believe me, multiply these examples infinitely.

One of these days . . .

Secrets are only kept for a time, formulas are divulged, new scientific knowledge is the object of communications to the Academy of Sciences and since, if we will believe Aurenche and Bost, adaptation is an exact science, one of these days they really could apprise us in the name of what criterion, by virtue of what system, by what mysterious and internal geometry of the work, they abridge, add multiply, devise and "rectify" these masterpieces.

Now that this idea is uttered, the idea that these equivalences are only timid astuteness to the end of getting around the difficulty, of resolving on the soundtrack problems that concern the image, plundering in order to no longer obtain anything on the screen but scholarly framing, complicated lighting-effects, "polished" photography, the whole keeping the "Tradition of Quality" quite alive—it is time to come to an examination of the ensemble of these films adapted, with dialogue, by Aurenche and Bost, and to research the permanent nature of certain themes that will explain, without justifying, the constant *unfaithfulness* of two scenarists to works taken by them as "pre-text" and "occasion."

In a two line résumé, here is the way scenarios treated by Aurenche and Bost appear:

La Symphonie Pastorale: He is a pastor, his is married. He loves and has no right to.

Le Diable Au Corps: They make the gestures of love and have no right to.

Dieu A Besoin Des Hommes: He officiates, gives benedictions, gives extreme unction and has no right to.

Jeux Interdits: They bury the dead and have no right to.

Le Blé En Herbe: They love each other and have no right to.

You will say to me that the book also tells the same story, which I do not deny. Only, I notice that Gide also wrote *La Porte Etroite*, Radiguet *La Bal Du Comte d'Orgel*, Colette *La Vagabonde* and that each one of these novels did not tempt Delannoy or Autant-Lara.

Let us notice also that these scenarios, about which I don't believe it useful to speak here, fit into the sense of my thesis: *Au Delà Des Grilles, Le Château De Verre, L'Auberge Rouge* . . .

One sees how competent the promoters of the "Tradition of Quality" are in choosing only subjects that favor the misunderstandings on which the whole system rests.

Under the cover of literature—and, of course, of quality—they give the public its habitual dose of smut, non-conformity and facile audacity.

The influence of Aurenche and Bost is immense . . .

The writers who have come to do film dialogue have observed the same imperatives; Anouillh, between the dialogues for *Dégourdis de la Ile* and *Un Caprice De Caroline Chérie* introduced into more ambitious films his universe with its affection of the bizarre with a background of nordic mists transposed to Brittany (*Pattes Blanches*). Another writer Jean Ferry, made sacrifices for fashion, he too, and the dialogue for *Manon* could just as well have been signed by Aurenche and Bost: "He believed me a virgin and, in private life, he is a professor of psychology!" Nothing better to hope for from the young scenarists. They simply work their shift, taking good care not to break any taboos.

Jacques Sigurd, one of the last to come to "scenario and dialogue," teamed up with Yves Allégret. Together, they bequeathed the French cinema some of its blackest masterpieces: *Dêdée D'Anvers, Manèges, Une Si Jolie Petite Plage, Les Miracles N'Ont Jeu Qu'une Fois, La Jeune Folle*. Jacques Sigurd very quickly assimilated the recipe; he must be endowed with an admirable spirit of synthesis, for his scenarios oscillate ingeniously between Aurenche and Bost, Prêvert and Clouzot, the whole lightly modernized. Religion is never involved, but blasphemy always makes its timid entrance thanks to several daughters of Mary or several good sisters who make their way across the field of vision at the moment when their presence would be least expected (*Manèges, Une Si Jolie Petite Plage*).

The cruelty by which they aspire to "rouse the trembling of the bourgeois" finds its place in well-expressed lines like: "he was old, he could drop dead" (*Manèges*). In *Une Si Jolie Petite Plage*, Jane Marken envies Berck's prosperity because of the tubercular cases found there: *Their family comes to see them and that makes business good!* (One dreams of the prayer of the rector of Sein Island).

Roland Laudenbach, who would seem to be more endowed than most of his colleagues, has collaborated on films that are most typical of that spirit: *La Minute De Vérité, Le Bon Dieu Sans Confession, La Maison Du Silence*.

Robert Scipion is a talented man of letters. He has only written one book; a book of pastiches. Singular badges: the daily frequenting of the Saint-Germain-des-Prés cafês, the friendship of Marcel Pagliero who is called the Sartre of the cinema, probably because his films resemble the articles in "Temps Modernes." Here are several lines from *Amants De Brasmort*, a populist film in which sailors are "heroes," like the dockers were in *Un Homme Marche Dans La Ville*:

"The wives of friends are made to sleep with."

"You do what agrees with you; as for that, you'd mount anybody, you might well say."

In one single reel of the film, towards the end, you can hear in less than ten minutes such words as: *prostitute, whore, slut* and *bitchiness*. Is this realism?

Prévert is to be regretted . . .

Considering the uniformity and equal filthiness of today's scenarios, one takes to regretting Prévert's scenarios. He believed in the Devil, thus in God, and if, for the most part, his characters were by his whim alone charged with all the sins in creation, there was always a couple, the new Adam and Eve, who could end the film, so that the story could begin again.

Psychological realism, neither real nor psychological . . .

There are scarcely more than seven or eight scenarists working regularly for the French cinema. Each one of these scenarists has but one story to tell, and, since each only aspires to the success of the "two greats," it is not exaggerating to say that the hundred-odd French films made each year tell the same story: it's always a question of a victim, generally a cuckold. (The cuckold would be the only sympathetic character in the film if he weren't always infinitely grotesque: Blier-Vilbert, etc. . . .) The knavery of his kin and the hatred among the members of his family lead the "hero" to his doom; the injustice of life, and for local color, the wickedness of the world (the curés, the concierges, the neighbors, the passers-by, the rich, the poor, the soldiers, etc . . .)

For distraction, during the long winter nights, look for titles of French films that do not fit into this framework and, while you're at it, find among these films those in which this line or its equivalent does not figure, spoken by the most abject couple in the film: "It's always they that have the money (or the luck, or love, or happiness. It's too unjust, in the end."

This school which aspires to realism destroys it at the moment of finally grabbing it, so careful is the school to lock these beings in a closed world, barricaded by formulas, plays on words, maxims, instead of letting us see them for ourselves, with our own eyes. The artist cannot always dominate his work. He must be, sometimes, God and, sometimes, his creature. You know that modern play in which the principal character, normally constituted when the curtain rises on him, finds himself crippled at the end of the play, the loss of each of his members punctuating the changes of acts. Curious epoch when the least flash-in-the-pan performer uses Kafkaesque words to qualify his domestic avatars. This form of cinema comes straight from modern literature—half-Kafka, half-Bovary!

A film is no longer made in France that the authors do not believe they are re-making Madame Bovary.

For the first time in French literature, an author adopted a distant, exterior attitude in relation to his subject, the subject becoming like an insect under the entomologist's microscope. But if, when starting this enterprise, Flaubert could have said, "I will roll them all in the same mud—and be right" (which today's authors would voluntarily make their exergue), he could declare afterwards "I am Madame Bovary" and I doubt that the same authors could take up that line and be sincere!

Mise-en-scène, metteur en scène, texts

The object of these notes is limited to an examination of a certain form of cinema, from the point of view of the scenarios and scenarists only. But it is appropriate, I think, to make it clear that the *metteurs-en-scène* are and wish to be responsible for the scenarios and dialogues they illustrate.

Scenarist' films, I wrote above, and certainly it isn't Aurenche and Bost who will contradict me. When they hand in their scenario, the film is done; the *metteur-en-scène*, in their eyes, is the gentleman who adds the pictures to it and it's true, alas! I spoke of the mania for adding funerals everywhere. And, for all that, death is always juggled away. Let us remember Nana's admirable death, or that of Emma Bovary, presented by Renoir; in *La Pastorale*, death is only a make-up job and an exercise for the camera man: compare the close-ups of Michèle Morgan in *La Pastorale*, Dominique Blanchar in *Le Sécret De Mayerling* and Madeleine Sologne in *L'Eternel Retour*: it's the same face! Everything happens *after* death.

Let us cite, lastly, that declaration by Delannoy that we dedicate, with perfidy, to the French scenarists: "When it happens that authors of talent, whether in the spirit of gain or out of weakness, one day let themselves go to "write for the cinema," they do it with the feeling of lowering themselves. They deliver themselves rather to a curious temptation towards mediocrity, so careful are they to not compromise their talent and certain that, to write for the cinema, one must make oneself understood by the lowliest. ("*La Symphonie Pastorale* ou L'Amour Du Métier," revue Verger, November 1947).

I must, without further ado, denounce a sophism that will not fail to be thrown at me in the guise of argument: "This dialogue is spoken by abject people and it is in order to better point out their nastiness that we give them this hard language. It is our way of being moralists."

To which I answer: it is inexact to say that these lines are spoken by the most abject characters. To be sure, in the films of "psychological realism" there are nothing but vile beings, but so inordinate is the authors' desire to be superior to their characters that those who, perchance, are not infamous are, at best, infinitely grotesque.

Well, as for these abject characters, who deliver these abject lines—I know a handful of men in France who would be INCAPABLE of conceiving them, several cinéastes whose world-view is at least as valuable as that of Aurenche and Bost, Sigurd and Jeanson. I mean Jean Renoir, Robert Bresson, Jean Cocteau, Jacques Becker, Abel Gance, Max Ophuls, Jacques Tati, Roger Leenhardt; these are, nevertheless, French cinéastes and it happens—curious coincidence—that they are *auteurs* who often write their dialogue and some of them themselves invent the stories they direct.

They will still say to me . . .

"But why," they will say to me, "why couldn't one have the same admiration for all those cinéastes who strive to work in the bosom of this "Tradition of Quality" that you make sport of so lightly? Why not admire Yves Allégret as much as Becker, Jean Delannoy as much as Bresson, Claude Autant-Lara as much as Renoir?" ["Taste is made of a thousand distastes"—Paul Valéry.]

Well—I do not believe in the peaceful co-existence of the "Tradition of Quality" and an "*auteur's* cinema."

Basically, Yves Allégret and Delannoy are only caricatures of Clouzot, of Bresson.

It is not the desire to create a scandal that leads me to depreciate a cinema so praised elsewhere. I rest convinced that the exaggeratedly prolonged existence of *psychological realism* is the cause of the lack of public comprehension when faced with such new works as *Le Carrosse D'Or* (*The Golden Coach*), *Casque D'or*, not to mention *Les Dames Du Bois De Boulogne* and *Orphée*.

Long live audacity, to be sure, still it must be revealed as it is. In terms of this year, 1953, if I had to draw up a balance-sheet of the French cinema's audacities, there would be no place in it for either the vomiting in *Les Orgueilleux* (*The Proud And The Beautiful*) or Claude Laydu's refusal to be sprinkled with holy water in *Le Bon Dieu Sans Confession* or the homosexual relationships of the characters in *Le Salaire De La Peur* (*The Wages Of Fear*), but rather the gait of *Hulot*, the maid's soliloquies in *La Rue De L'Estrapade*, the *mise-en-scène* of *La Carosse D'Or*, the direction of the actors in *Madame de* (*The Earrings Of Madame De*), and also Abel Gance's studies in polyvision. You will have understood that these audacities are those of *men of the cinema* and no longer of scenarists, directors and literatéurs.

For example, I take it as significant that the most brilliant scenarists and *metteur-en-scène* of the "Tradition of Quality" have met with failure when they approach comedy: Ferry-Clouzot *Miguette Et Sa Mère*, Sigurd-Boyer *Tous Les Chemins Mènent A Rome*, Scipion-Paglicro *La Rose Rouge*. Laudenbach-Delannoy *La Route Napoleon*. Auranche-Bost-Autant-Lara *L'Auberge Rouge* or, if you like, *Occupe-toi d'Amélie*.

Whoever has tried, one day, to write a scenario wouldn't be able to deny that comedy is by far the most difficult genre, the one that demands the most work, the most talent, also the most humility.

All bourgeois . . .

The dominant trait of psychological realism is its anti-bourgeois will. But what are Aurenche and Bost, Sigurd, Jeanson, Autant-Lara, Allégret, if not bourgeois, and what are the fifty thousand new readers, who do not fail to see each film from a novel, if not bourgeois?

What then is the value of an anti-bourgeois cinema made by the bourgeois for the bourgeois? Workers, you know very well, do not appreciate this form of cinema at all even when it aims at relating to them. They refused to recognize themselves in the dockers of *Un Homme Marche Dans La Ville*, or in the sailors of *Les Amants De Brasmort*. Perhaps it is necessary to send the children out on the stairway landing in order to make love, but their parents don't like to hear it said, above all at the cinema, even with "benevolence." If the public likes to mix with low company under the alibi of literature, it also likes to do it under the alibi of society. It is instructive to consider the programming of films in Paris, by neighborhoods. One comes to realize that the public-at-large perhaps prefers little naive foreign films that show it men "as they should be" and not in the way that Aurenche and Bost believe them to be.

Like giving oneself a good address . . .

It is always good to conclude, that gives everyone pleasure. It is remarkable that the "great" *metteurs-en-scène* and the "great" scenarists have, for a long time, all made minor films, and the talent they have put into them hasn't been sufficient to enable one to distinguish them from others (those who don't put in talent). It is also remarkable that they all came to "Quality" at the same time, as if they were giving themselves a good address. And then, a producer—even a director—earns more money making *Le Blé En Herbe* than by making *Le Plombier Amoureux*. The "courageous" films are revealed to be very profitable. The proof: someone like Ralph Habib abruptly renounces demi-pornography, makes *Les Compagnes De La Nuit* and refers to Cayatte. Well, what's keeping the André Tabets, Companeer, the Jean Guittons, the Pierre Vérys, the Jean Lavirons, the Ciampis, the Grangiers, from making, from one day to the next, intellectual films, from adapting masterpieces (there are still a few left) and, of course, adding funerals, here, there and everywhere?

Well, on that day we will be in the "Tradition of Quality" up to the neck and the French cinema, with rivalry among "psychological realism," "violence," "strictness," "ambiguity," will no longer be anything but one vast funeral that will be able to leave the studio in Billancourt and enter the cemetery directly—it seems to have been placed next door expressly, in order to get more quickly from the producer to the grave-digger.

Only, by dint of repeating to the public that it identified with the "heroes" of the films, it might well end by believing it, and on the day that it understands that this fine big cuckold whose misadventures it is solicited to sympathize with (a little) and to laugh at (a lot), is not, as had been thought, a cousin or neighbor down the hall but ITSELF, that abject family ITS family, that scoffed-at religion ITS religion—well, on that day it may show itself to be ungrateful to a cinema that will have labored so hard to show it life as one sees it on the fourth floor in Saint-German-desPrès.

To be sure, I must recognize it, a great deal of emotion and taking-sides are the controlling factors in the deliberately pessimistic examination I have undertaken of a certain tendency of the French cinema. I am assured that this famous "school of psychological realism" had to exist in order that, in turn, *The Diary Of A Country Priest, La Carrosse D'Or, Orpheus, Casque D'Or, Mr. Hulot's Holiday* might exist.

But our authors who wanted to educate the public should understand that perhaps they have strayed from the primary paths in order to become involved with the more subtle paths of psychology; they have passed on to that sixth grade so dear to Jouhandeau, but it isn't necessary to repeat a grade indefinitely!

Notes

1 *La Symphonie Pastorale*. Characters added to the film : Piette, Jacques' fiancée; Casteran, Piette's father. Characters omitted: the Pastor's three children. In the film, no mention is made of what happens to Jacques after Gertrude's death. In the book, Jacques enters an order.

Operation *Symphonie Pastorale*: a. Gide himself writes an adaptation of his book; b. This adaptation is judged "unfilmable"; c. Jean Aurenche and Jean Delannoy, in turn, write an adaptation; d. Gide refuses it; e. Pierre Bost's entry on the scene conciliates everyone.

2 *Le Diable Au Corps*. On the radio, in the course of a program by André Parinaud devoted to Radiguet, Claude Autant-Lara declared in substance, "*What led me to make a film out of Le Diable Au Corps was that I saw it as an anti-war novel.*"

On the same program, Francois Poulenc, a friend of Radiguet's, said he had found nothing of the book on seeing the film.

3 To the proposed producer of *The Diary Of A Country Priest*, who was astonished to see the character of Doctor Delbende disappear in the adaptation, Jean Aurenche (who had signed the script) answered, "*Perhaps, in ten years, a scenarist will be able to retain a character who dies midway through the film but, as for me, I don't feel capable of it.*" Three years later, Robert Bresson retained Doctor Delbende and allowed him to die in the middle of the film.

4 Aurenche and Bost never said they were "faithful." This was the critics.

5 *Le Blé En Herbe*. There was an adaptation of Colette's novel as early as 1946. Claude Autant-Lara accused Roger Leenhardt of having plagiarized Colette's *Le Blé En Herbe* with his *Les Dernieres Vacances*. The arbitration of Maurice Garcon went against Claude Autant-Lara. With Aurenche and Bost the intrigue imagined by Colette was enriched by a new character, that of Dick, a lesbian who lived with the "White Lady." This character was suppressed, several weeks before the film was shot, by Madame Ghislaine Auboin, who "reviewed" the adaptation with Claude Autant-Lara.

6 The characters of Aurenche and Bost speak, at will, in maxims. Several examples: *La Symphonie Pastorale*: "Ah! It would be better if children like that were never born." "Not everyone has the luck to be blind." "A cripple is someone who pretends to be like everyone else."

Le Diable Au Corps (a soldier has lost a leg): "He is perhaps the last of the wounded." "That makes a fine leg for him."

Jeux Interdits: Francis: "What does this mean—'to put the cart before the horse?' " Berthe: "Oh, it's what we're doing." (They are making love.) Francois: "I didn't know that's what it was called."

7 Jean Aurenche was on the crew of *Les Dames Du Bois De Boulogne*, but he had to leave Bresson because of incompatibility of inspiration.

8 An extract from the dialogue Aurenche and Bost wrote for *Jeanne D'Arc* was published in "La Revue Du Cinéma;" #8, page 9.

9 In fact, "psychological realism" was created parallel to "poetic realism," which had the tandem Spaak-Feyder. It really will be necessary, one day, to start an ultimate quarrel with Feyder, before he has dropped definitively into oblivion.

26

NOTES ON THE *AUTEUR* THEORY IN 1962

Andrew Sarris

Source: *Film Culture*, 27, Winter 1962, pp. 1–8.

> *I call these sketches Shadowgraphs, partly by the designation to remind you at once that they derive from the darker side of life, partly because like other shadowgraphs they are not directly visible. When I take a shadowgraph in my hand, it makes no impression on me, and gives me no clear conception of it. Only when I hold it up opposite the wall, and now look not directly at it, but at that which appears on the wall, am I able to see it. So also with the picture which I wish to show here, an inward picture which does not become perceptible until I see it through the external. This external is perhaps quite unobtrusive but not until I look through it, do I discover that inner picture which I desire to show you an inner picture too delicately drawn to be outwardly visible, woven as it is of the tenderest moods of the soul.*
>
> *Soren Kierkegaard, Either/Or*

An exhibitor once asked me if an old film I had recommended was *really* good or good only according to the *auteur* theory. I appreciate the distinction. Like the alchemists of old, *auteur* critics are notorious for rationalizing leaden clinkers into golden nuggets. Their judgments are seldom vindicated because few spectators are conditioned to perceive in individual works the organic unity of a director's career. On a given evening, a film by John Ford must take its chances as if it were a film by Henry King. Am I implying that the weakest Ford is superior to the strongest King? Yes! This kind of unqualified affirmation seems to reduce the *auteur* theory to a game of aesthetic solitaire with all the cards turned face up. By *auteur* rules, the Fords will come up aces as invariably as the Kings will come up deuces. Presumably we can all go home as soon as the directorial signature is flashed on the screen. To those who linger, *The Gunfighter* (King 1950) may appear worthier than *Flesh* (Ford 1932). (And how deeply one must burrow to undermine Ford!) No matter. The *auteur* theory is unyielding. If, by definition, Ford is invariably superior to King, any evidence to the contrary is merely an optical illusion. Now what could be sillier than this inflexible attitude? Let us abandon the absurdities of the *auteur* theory so that we may return to the chaos of common sense.

My labored performance as devil's advocate notwithstanding, I intend to praise the *auteur* theory, not to bury it. At the very least, I would like to grant the condemned system a hearing before its execution. The trial has dragged on for years, I know, and everyone is now bored by the abstract reasoning involved. I have little in the way of new evidence or new arguments, but I would like to change some of my previous testimony. What follows is consequently less a manifesto than a credo, a somewhat disorganized credo, to be sure, expressed in formless notes rather than in formal brief.

I. *Aimez-vous* Brahms?

> "Goethe? Shakespeare? Everything signed with their names is considered good, and one wracks one's brains to find beauty in their stupidities and failures, thus distorting the general taste. All these great talents, the Goethes, the Shakespeares, the Beethovens, the Michelangelos, created, side by side with their masterpieces, works not merely mediocre, but quite simply frightful."
>
> Tolstoy, Journal, 1895–1899

The preceding quotation prefaces the late Andre Bazin's famous critique of *la politique des auteurs* which appeared in the *Cahiers du Cinema* of April 1957. Because no comparably lucid statement opposing the *politique* has appeared since that time, I would like to discuss some of Bazin's arguments with reference to the current situation. (I except, of course, Richard Roud's penetrating article, *The French Line*, which dealt mainly with the post-*nouvelle vague* situation when the *politique* had degenerated into McMahonism.)

As Tolstoy's observation indicates, *la politique des auteurs* antedates the cinema. For centuries, the Elizabethan *politique* has decreed the reading of every Shakespearean play before any encounter with the Jonsonian repertory. At some point between *Timon of Athens* and *Volpone*, this procedure is patently unfair to Jonson's reputation. But not really. On the most superficial level of artistic reputations, the *auteur* theory is merely a figure of speech. If the man in the street could not invoke Shakespeare's name as an identifiable cultural reference, he would probably have less contact with all things artistic. The Shakespearean scholar, by contrast, will always be driven to explore the surrounding terrain with the result that all the Elizabethan dramatists gain more rather than less recognition through the pre-eminence of one of their number. Therefore on balance, the *politique* as a figure of speech does more good than harm.

Occasionally, some iconoclast will attempt to demonstrate the fallacy of this figure of speech. We will be solemnly informed that *The Gambler* was a potboiler for Dostoevski in the most literal sense of the word. In Jacques Rivette's *Paris nous appartient*, Jean-Claude Brialy asks Betty Schneider if she would still admire *Pericles* if it were not signed by Shakespeare. Zealous musicologists have played *Wellington's Victory* so often as an example of inferior Beethoven that I have grown fond of the piece, atrocious as it is. The trouble with such iconoclasm is that it presupposes an encyclopedic awareness of the *auteur* in question. If one is familiar with every Beethoven composition, *Wellington's Victory*, in itself, will hardly tip the scale toward Mozart, Bach or Schubert. Yet, that is the issue raised by the *auteur* theory. If not Beethoven, who? And why? Let us say that the politique for composers went Mozart, Beethoven, Bach and Schubert. Each composer would represent a task force of compositions, arrayed by type and quality with the mighty battleships and aircraft carriers flanked by flotillas of cruisers, destroyers and minesweepers. When the Mozart task force collides with the Beethoven task force, symphonies roar against symphonies, quartets maneuver against quartets, and it is simply no contest with the operas. As a single force, Beethoven's nine symphonies outgun any nine of Mozart's forty-one symphonies, both sets of quartets are almost on a par with Schubert's, but *The Magic Flute, The Marriage of Figaro* and *Don Giovanni* will blow poor *Fidelio* out of the water. Then, of course, there is Bach with an entirely different deployment of composition and instrumentation. The Haydn and Handel cultists are moored in their inlets ready to join the fray, and the moderns with their nuclear noises are still mobilizing their forces.

It can be argued that any exact ranking of artists is arbitrary and pointless. Arbitrary up to a point, perhaps, but pointless, no. Even Bazin concedes the polemical value of the *politique*. Many film critics would rather not commit themselves to specific rankings ostensibly because every film should be judged on its own merits. In many instances, this reticence masks the critic's condescension to the medium. Since it has not been firmly established that the cinema is an art at all, it requires cultural audacity to establish a pantheon for film directors. Without such audacity, I see little point in being a film critic. Anyway, is it possible to honor a work of art without honoring the artist involved? I think not. Of course, any idiot can erect a pantheon out of hearsay and gossip. Without specifying any work, the Saganesque seducer will ask quite cynically, "Aimez-vous Brahms?" The fact that Brahms is included in the pantheon of high-brow pick-ups does not invalidate the industrious criticism which justifies the composer as a figure of speech.

Unfortunately, some critics have embraced the *auteur* theory as a short-cut to film scholarship. With a "you-see-it-or-you-don't" attitude toward the reader, the particularly lazy *auteur* critic can save himself the drudgery of communication and explanation. Indeed, at their worst, *auteur* critiques are less meaningful than the straightforward plot reviews which pass for criticism in America. Without the necessary research and analysis, the *auteur* theory can degenerate into the kind of snobbish racket which is associated with the merchandising of paintings.

It was largely against the inadequate theoretical formulation of *la politique des auteurs* that Bazin was reacting in his friendly critique. (Henceforth, I will abbreviate *la politique des auteurs* as the *auteur* theory to avoid confusion.) Bazin introduces his arguments within the context of a family quarrel over the editorial policies of *Cahiers*. He fears that by assigning reviews to admirers of given directors, notably Alfred Hitchcock, Jean Renoir, Roberto Rossellini, Fritz Lang, Howard Hawks and Nicholas Ray, every work, major and minor, of these exalted figures is made to radiate the same beauties of style and meaning. Specifically, Bazin notes a distortion when the kindly indulgence accorded the imperfect work of a Minnelli is coldly withheld from the imperfect work of Huston. The inherent bias of the *auteur* theory magnifies the gap between the two films.

I would make two points here. First, Bazin's greatness as a critic, (and I believe strongly that he was the greatest film critic who ever lived,) rested in his disinterested conception of the cinema as a universal entity. It follows that he would react against a theory which cultivated what he felt were inaccurate judgments for the sake of dramatic paradoxes. He was, if anything, generous to a fault, seeking in every film some vestige of the cinematic art. That he would seek justice for Huston vis-a-vis Minnelli on even the secondary levels of creation indicates the scrupulousness of his critical personality.

However, my second point would seem to contradict my first. Bazin was wrong in this instance insofar as any critic can be said to be wrong in retrospect. We are dealing here with Minnelli in his *Lust for Life* period and Huston in his *Moby Dick* period. Both films can be considered failures on almost any level. The miscasting alone is disastrous. The snarling force of Kirk Douglas as the tormented Van Gogh, the brutish insensibility of Anthony Quinn as Gauguin, and the nervously scraping tension between these two absurdly limited actors, deface Minnelli's meticulously objective decor, itself inappropriate for the mood of its subject. The director's presentation of the paintings themselves is singularly unperceptive in the repeated failure to maintain the proper optical distance from canvases which arouse the spectator less by their detailed draughtsmanship than by the shock of a *gestalt* wholeness. As for *Moby Dick*, Gregory Peck's Ahab deliberates long enough to let all the demons flee the *Pequod*, taking Melville's Lear-like fantasies with them. Huston's epic technique with its casually shifting camera viewpoint then drifts on an intellectually becalmed sea toward a fitting rendezvous with a rubber whale. These two films are neither the best nor the worst of their time. The question is which deserves the harder review. And there's the rub. At the time, Huston's stock in America was higher than Minnelli's. Most critics expected Huston to do "big" things, and, if they thought about it all, expected Minnelli to stick to "small" things like musicals. Although neither film was a critical failure, audiences stayed away in large enough numbers to make the cultural respectability of the projects suspect. On the whole, *Lust for Life* was more successful with the audiences it did reach than was *Moby Dick*.

In retrospect, *Moby Dick* represents the turning downward of Huston as a director to be taken seriously. By contrast, *Lust for Life* is simply an isolated episode in the erratic career of an interesting stylist. The exact size of Minnelli's talent may inspire controversy, but he does represent something in the cinema today. Huston is virtually a forgotten man with a few actors' classics behind him surviving as the ruins of a once-promising career. Both Eric Rohmer, who denigrated Huston in 1957, and Jean Domarchi, who was kind to Minnelli that same year, somehow saw the future more clearly on an *auteur* level than did Bazin. As Santayana has remarked: "It is a great advantage for a system of philosophy to be substantially true." If the *auteur* critics of the Fifties had not scored so many coups of clairvoyance, the *auteur* theory would not be worth discussing in the Sixties. I must add that, at the time, I would have agreed with Bazin on this and every other objection to the *auteur* theory, but subsequent history, that history about which Bazin was always so mystical, has substantially confirmed most of the principles of the *auteur* theory. Ironically, most of the original supporters of the *auteur* theory have now abandoned it. Some have discovered more useful *politiques* as directors and would-be directors. Others have succumbed to a European-oriented pragmatism where intention is now more nearly equal to talent in critical relevance. Luc Moullet's belated discovery that Samuel Fuller was, in fact, fifty years old, signaled a reorientation of *Cahiers* away from the American cinema. (The handwriting was already on the wall when Truffaut remarked recently that where he and his colleagues had "discovered" *auteurs*, his successors have "invented" them.)

Bazin then explores the implications of Giraudoux' epigram: "There are no works; there are only authors." Truffaut has seized upon this paradox as the battle-cry of *la politique des auteurs*. Bazin casually demonstrates how the contrary can be argued with equal probability of truth or error. He subsequently dredges up the equivalents of *Wellington's Victory* for Voltaire, Beaumarchais, Flaubert and Gide to document his point. Bazin then yields some ground to Rohmer's argument that the history of art does not confirm the decline with age of authentic geniuses like Titian, Rembrandt, Beethoven, or nearer to us, Bonnard, Matisse and Stravinsky. Bazin agrees with Rohmer that it is inconsistent to attribute senility only to aging film directors while at the same time honoring the gnarled austerity of Rembrandt's later style. This is one of the crucial propositions of the *auteur* theory because it refutes the popular theory of decline for aging giants like Renoir and Chaplin, and asserts instead that as a director becomes older, he is likely to become more profoundly personal than most audiences and critics can appreciate. However, Bazin immediately retrieves his lost ground by arguing that whereas the senility of directors is no longer at issue, the evolution of an art-form is. Where directors fail and fall is in the realm not of psychology but of history. If a director fails to keep pace with the development of his medium, his work will become obsolescent. What seems like senility is in reality a disharmony between the subjective inspiration of the director and the objective evolution of the medium. By making this distinction between the subjective capability of an *auteur* and the objective value of a work in film history, Bazin reinforces the popular impression that the Griffith of *Birth of a Nation* is superior to the Griffith of *Abraham Lincoln* in the perspective of timing which similarly distinguishes the Eisenstein of *Potemkin* from the Eisenstein of *Ivan the Terrible*, the Renoir of *La Grande Illusion* from the Renoir of *Picnic in the Grass* and the Welles of *Citizen Kane* from the Welles of *Arkadin*.

I have embroidered Bazin's actual examples for the sake of greater contact with the American scene. In fact, Bazin implicitly denies a decline in the later works of Chaplin and Renoir, and never mentions Griffith. He suggests circuitously that Hawks' *Scarface* is clearly superior to Hawks' *Gentlemen Prefer Blondes* although the *auteur* critics would argue the contrary. Bazin is particularly critical of Rivette's circular reasoning on *Monkey Business* as the proof of Hawks' genius. "One sees the danger," Bazin warns, "which is an aesthetic cult of personality."

Bazin's taste, it should be noted, was far more discriminating than that of American film historians. Films Bazin cites as unquestionable classics are still quite debatable here in America. After all, *Citizen Kane* was originally panned by James Agee, Richard Griffith and Bosley Crowther, and *Scarface* has never been regarded as one of the landmarks of the American cinema by native critics. I would say that the American public has been ahead of its critics on both *Kane* and *Scarface*. Thus to argue against the *auteur* theory in America is to assume that we have anyone of Bazin's sensibility and dedication to provide an alternative, and we simply don't.

Bazin finally concentrates on the American cinema which invariably serves as the decisive battleground of the *auteur* theory whether over *Monkey Business* or *Party Girl*. Unlike most "serious" American critics, Bazin likes Hollywood films, but not solely because of the talent of this or that director. For Bazin, the distinctively American comedy, western and gangster genres have their own mystiques apart from the personalities of the directors concerned. How can one review an Anthony Mann western, Bazin asks, as if it were not an expression of the genre's conventions. Not that Bazin dislikes Anthony Mann's western. He is more concerned with otherwise admirable westerns which the *auteur* theory rejects because their directors happen to be unfashionable. Again, Bazin's critical generosity comes to the fore against the negative aspects of the *auteur* theory.

Some of Bazin's arguments tend to overlap each other as if to counter rebuttals from any direction. He argues in turn that the cinema is less individualistic an art than painting or literature, that Hollywood is less individualistic than other cinemas, and that even so, the *auteur* theory never really applies anywhere. In upholding historical determinism, Bazin goes so far as to speculate that if Racine had lived in Voltaire's century, it is unlikely that Racine's tragedies would have been any more inspired than Voltaire's. Presumably the Age of Reason would have stifled Racine's Neoclassical impulses. Perhaps. Perhaps not. Bazin's hypothesis can hardly be argued to a verifiable conclusion, but I suspect somewhat greater reciprocity between an artist and his *Zeitgeist* than Bazin would allow. He mentions more than once, and in other contexts, capitalism's influence on the cinema. Without denying this influence, I still find it impossible to attribute X directors and Y films to any particular system or culture. Why should the Italian cinema be superior to the German cinema after one war when the reverse was true after the previous one? As for artists conforming to the spirit of their age, that spirit is often expressed in contradictions whether of Stravinsky and Sibelius, Fielding and Richardson, Picasso and Matisse, Chateaubriand and Stendhal. Even if the artist does not spring from the idealized head of Zeus, free of the embryonic stains of history, history itself is profoundly affected by his arrival. If we cannot imagine Griffith's *October* or Eisenstein's *Birth of a Nation* because we find it difficult to transpose one artist's unifying conceptions of Lee and Lincoln to the other's dialectical conceptions of Lenin and Kerensky, we are nevertheless compelled to recognize other differences in the personalities of these two pioneers beyond their respective cultural complexes. It is with these latter differences that the *auteur* theory is most deeply concerned. If directors and other artists cannot be wrenched from their historical environments, aesthetics is reduced to a subordinate branch of ethnography.

I have not done full justice to the subtlety of Bazin's reasoning and to the civilized skepticism with which he propounds his own arguments as slight probabilities rather than absolute certainties. Contemporary opponents of the *auteur* theory may feel that Bazin himself is suspect as a member of the *Cahiers* family. After all, Bazin does express qualified approval of the *auteur* theory as a relatively objective method of evaluating films apart from the subjective perils of impressionistic and ideological criticism. Better to analyze the director's personality than the critic's nerve centers or politics. Nevertheless, Bazin makes his stand clear by concluding: "This is not to deny the role of the author, but to restore to him the preposition without which the noun is only a limp concept. "Author,' undoubtedly, but *of* what?"

Bazin's syntactical flourish raises an interesting problem in English usage. The French preposition "de" serves many functions, but among others, those of possession and authorship. In English, the preposition "by" once created a scandal in the American film industry when Otto Preminger had the temerity to advertise *The Man With the Golden Arm* as a film "by Otto Preminger." Novelist Nelson Algren and the Screen-writer's Guild raised such an outcry that the offending preposition was deleted. Even the noun "author" (which I cunningly mask as "*auteur*") has a literary connotation in English. In general conversation, an "author" is invariably taken to be a writer. Since "by" is a preposition of authorship and not of ownership like the ambiguous "de," the fact that Preminger both produced and directed *The Man With the Golden Arm* did not entitle him in America to the preposition "by." No one would have objected to the possessive form: "Otto Preminger's *The Man With the Golden Arm*." But even in this case, a novelist of sufficient reputation is usually honored with the possessive designation. Now this is hardly the case in France where *The Red and the Black* is advertised as "un film de Claude Autant-Lara." In America, "directed by" is all the director can claim when he is not also a well-known producer like Alfred Hitchcock or Cecil B. De Mille.

Since most American film critics are oriented toward literature or journalism rather than toward future film-making, most American film criticism is directed toward the script instead of toward the screen. The writer-hero in *Sunset Boulevard* complains that people don't realize that someone "writes a picture; they think the actors make it up as they go along." It would never occur to this writer or to most of his colleagues that people are even less aware of the director's function.

Of course, the much-abused man in the street has a good excuse not to be aware of the *auteur* theory even as a figure of speech. Even on the so-called classic level, he is not encouraged to ask aimez-vous Griffith or aimez-vous Eisenstein? Instead, it is which Griffith and which Eisenstein? As for less acclaimed directors, he is lucky to find their names in the fourth paragraph of the typical review. I doubt that most American film critics really believe that an indifferently directed film is comparable to an indifferently written book. However, there is little point in wailing at the Philistines on this issue, particularly when some progress is being made in telling one director from another, at least when the film comes from abroad. The Fellini, Bergman, Kurosawa and Antonioni promotions have helped push more directors up to the first paragraph of a review even ahead of the plot synopsis. So we mustn't complain.

Where I wish to redirect the argument is toward the relative position of the American cinema as opposed to the Foreign cinema. Some critics have advised me that the *auteur* theory only applies to a small number of artists who make personal films, not to the run-of-the-mill Hollywood director who takes whatever assignment is available. Like most Americans who take films seriously, I have always felt a cultural inferiority complex about Hollywood. Just a few years ago, I would have thought it unthinkable to speak in the same breath of a "commercial" director like Hitchcock and a "pure" director like Bresson. Even today, *Sight and Sound* uses different type-sizes for Bresson and Hitchcock films. After years of tortured revaluation, I am now prepared to stake my critical reputation, such as it is, on the proposition that Alfred Hitchcock is artistically superior to Robert Bresson by every criterion of excellence, and further, that, film for film, director for director, the American cinema has been consistently superior to that of the rest of the world from 1915 through 1962. Consequently, I now regard the *auteur* theory primarily as a critical device for recording the history of the American cinema, the only cinema in the world worth exploring in depth beneath the frosting of a few great directors at the top.

These propositions remain to be proven and, I hope, debated. The proof will be difficult because direction in the cinema is a nebulous force in literary terms. In addition to its own jargon, the director's craft often pulls in the related jargons of music, painting, sculpture, dance, literature, theatre, architecture, all in a generally futile attempt to describe the indescribable. What is it the old jazz man says of his art? If you gotta ask what it is, it ain't? Well, the cinema is like that. Criticism can only attempt an approximation, a reasonable preponderance of accuracy over inaccuracy. I know the exceptions to the *auteur* theory as well as anyone. I can feel the human attraction of an audience going one way when I am going the other. The temptations of cynicism, common sense and facile culture-mongering are always very strong, but somehow I feel that the *auteur* theory is the only hope for extending the appreciation of personal qualities in the cinema. By grouping and evaluating films according to directors, the critic can rescue individual achievements from an unjustifiable anonymity. If medieval architects and African sculptors are anonymous today, it is not because they deserved to be. When Ingmar Bergman bemoans the alienation of the modern artist from the collective spirit which rebuilt the Cathedral at Chartres, he is only dramatizing his own individuality for an age which has rewarded him handsomely for the travail of his alienation. There is no justification for penalizing Hollywood directors for the sake of collective mythology. So invective aside, aimez-vous Cukor?

II. What is the *auteur* theory?

As far as I know, there is no definition of the *auteur* theory in the English language, that is, by any American or British critic. Truffaut has recently gone to great pains to emphasize that the *auteur* theory was merely a polemical weapon for a given time and a given place, and I am willing to take him at his word. But lest I be accused of misappropriating a theory no one wants anymore, I give the *Cahiers* critics full credit for the original formulation of an idea which reshaped my thinking on the cinema. First of all, how does the *auteur* theory differ from a straightforward theory of directors. Ian Cameron's article, "Films, Directors and Critics" in *Movie* of September

1962, makes an interesting comment on this issue: "The assumption which underlies all the writing in *Movie* is that the director is the author of a film, the person who gives it any distinctive quality. There are quite large exceptions, with which I shall deal later." So far, so good, at least for the *auteur* theory which even allows for exceptions. However, Cameron continues: "On the whole we accept the cinema of directors, although without going to the farthest-out extremes of the *la politique des auteurs* which makes it difficult to think of a bad director making a good film and almost impossible to think of a good director making a bad one." We are back to Bazin again although Cameron naturally uses different examples. That three otherwise divergent critics like Bazin, Roud and Cameron make essentially the same point about the *auteur* theory suggests a common fear of its abuses. I believe there is a misunderstanding here about what the *auteur* theory actually claims, particularly since the theory itself is so vague at the present time.

First of all, the *auteur* theory, at least as I understand it and now intend to express it, claims neither the gift of prophecy nor the option of extracinematic perception. Directors, even *auteurs*, do not always run true to form, and the critic can never assume that a bad director will always make a bad film. No, not always, but almost always, and that is the point. What is a bad director, but a director who has made many bad films? What is the problem then? Simply this: the badness of a director is not necessarily considered the badness of a film. If Joseph Pevney directed Garbo, Cherkassov, Olivier, Belmondo, and Harriet Andersson in *The Cherry Orchard*, the resulting spectacle might not be entirely devoid of merit with so many subsidiary *auteurs* to cover up for Joe. In fact, with this cast and this literary property, a Lumet might be safer than a Welles. The realities of casting apply to directors as well as actors, but the *auteur* theory would demand the gamble with Welles, if he were willing.

Marlon Brando has shown us that a film can be made without a director. Indeed, *One-Eyed Jacks* is more entertaining than many films with directors. A director-conscious critic would find it difficult to say anything good or bad about direction which is non-existent. One can talk here about photography, editing, acting, but not direction. The film even has personality, but like *The Longest Day* and *Mutiny on the Bounty*, it is a cipher directorially. Obviously, the *auteur* theory cannot possibly cover every vagrant charm of the cinema. Nevertheless, the first premise of the *auteur* theory is the technical competence of a director as a criterion of value. A badly directed or undirected film has no importance in a critical scale of values, but one can make interesting conversation about the subject, the script, the acting, the color, the photography, the editing, the music, the costumes, the décor etc. That is the nature of the medium. You always get more for your money than mere art. Now by the *auteur* theory, if a director has no technical competence, no elementary flair for the cinema, he is automatically cast out from the pantheon of directors. A great director has to be at least a good director.

This is true in any art. What constitutes directorial talent is more difficult to define abstractly. There is less disagreement, however, on this first level of the *auteur* theory than there will be later.

The second premise of the *auteur* theory is the distinguishable personality of the director as a criterion of value. Over a group of films, a director must exhibit certain recurring characteristics of style which serve as his signature. The way a film looks and moves should have some relationship to the way a director thinks and feels. This is an area where American directors are generally superior to foreign directors. Because so much of the American cinema is commissioned, a director is forced to express his personality through the visual treatment of material rather than through the literary content of the material. A Cukor who works with all sorts of projects has a more developed abstract style than a Bergman who is free to develop his own scripts. Not that Bergman lacks personality, but his work has declined with the depletion of his ideas largely because his technique never equaled his sensibility. Joseph L. Mankiewicz and Billy Wilder are other examples of writer-directors without adequate technical mastery. By contrast, Douglas Sirk and Otto Preminger have moved up the scale because their miscellaneous projects reveal a stylistic consistency.

The third and ultimate premise of the *auteur* theory is concerned with interior meaning, the ultimate glory of the cinema as an art. Interior meaning is extrapolated from the tension between a director's personality and his material. This conception of interior meaning comes close to what Astruc defines as *mise-en-scene*, but not quite. It is not quite the vision of the world a director projects, nor quite his attitude toward life. It is ambiguous in any literary sense because part of it is imbedded in the stuff of the cinema and cannot be rendered in non-cinematic terms. Truffaut has called it the temperature of the director on the set, and that is a close approximation of its professional aspect. Dare I come out and say what I think it to be is an élan of the soul?

Lest I seem unduly mystical, let me hasten to add that all I mean by soul is that intangible difference between one personality and another, all other things being equal. Sometimes, this difference is expressed by no more than a beat's hesitation in the rhythm of a film. In one sequence of *La Règle du jeu*, Renoir gallops up the stairs, turns to his right with a lurching movement, stops in hop-like uncertainty when his name is called by a coquettish maid, and then, with marvelous post-reflex continuity, resumes his bearishly shambling journey to the heroine's boudoir. If I could describe the musical grace note of that momentary suspension, and I can't, I might be able to provide a more precise definition of the *auteur* theory. As it is, all I can do is point at the specific beauties of interior meaning on the screen, and later catalogue the moments of recognition.

The three premises of the *auteur* theory may be visualized as three concentric circles, the outer circle as technique, the middle circle personal style, and the inner circle interior meaning. The corresponding roles of the director may be designated as those of a technician, a stylist and an *auteur*. There is no prescribed course by which a director passes through the three circles. Godard once remarked that Visconti had evolved from a *metteur-en-scene* to an *auteur* while Rossellini had evolved from an *auteur* to a *metteur-en-scene*. From opposite directions, they emerged with comparable status. Minnelli began and remained in the second circle as a stylist; Bunuel was an *auteur* even before he had assembled the technique of the first circle. Technique is simply the ability to put a film together with some clarity and coherence. Nowadays it is possible to become a director without knowing too much about the technical side, even the crucial functions of photography and editing. An expert production crew could probably cover up for a chimpanzee in the director's chair. How do you tell the genuine director from the quasi-chimpanzee? After a given number of films, a pattern is established.

In fact, the *auteur* theory itself is a pattern theory in constant flux. I would never endorse a Ptolemaic constellation of directors in a fixed orbit. At the moment, my list of *auteurs* runs something like this through the first twenty: Ophuls, Renoir, Mizoguchi, Hitchcock, Chaplin, Ford, Welles, Dreyer, Rossellini, Murnau, Griffith, Sternberg, Eisenstein, Stroheim, Bunuel, Bresson, Hawks, Lang, Flaherty, Vigo. This list is somewhat weighted toward seniority and established reputations. In time, some of these *auteurs* will rise, some will fall, and some will be displaced by either new directors or rediscovered ancients. Again, the exact order is less important than the specific definitions of these and as many as two hundred other potential *auteurs*. I would hardly expect any other critic in the world to fully endorse this list, especially on faith. Only after thousands of films have been revaluated, will any personal pantheon have a reasonably objective validity. The task of validating the *auteur* theory is an enormous one, and the end will never be in sight. Meanwhile, the *auteur* habit of collecting random films in directorial bundles will serve posterity with at least a tentative classification.

Although the *auteur* theory emphasizes the body of a director's work rather than isolated masterpieces, it is expected of great directors that they make great films every so often. The only possible exception to this rule I can think of is Abel Gance, whose greatness is largely a function of his aspiration. Even with Gance, *La Roue* is as close to being a great film as any single work of Flaherty's. Not that single works matter that much. As Renoir has observed, a director spends his life on variations of the same film.

Two recent omnibus films — *Boccaccio 70* and *The Seven Capital Sins* — unwittingly reinforced the *auteur* theory by confirming the relative standing of the many directors involved. If I had not seen either film, I would have anticipated that the order of merit in *Boccaccio 70* would be Visconti, Fellini and De Sica, and in *The Seven Capital Sins*, Godard, Chabrol, Demy, Vadim, De Broca, Molinaro. (Dhomme, Ionesco's stage director and an unknown quantity in advance, turned out to be the worst of the lot.) There might be some argument about the relative badness of De Broca and Molinaro, but otherwise, the directors ran true to form by almost any objective criterion of value. However, the main point here is that even in these frothy, ultra-commercial servings of entertainment, the contribution of each director had less in common stylistically with the work of other directors on the project than with his own previous work.

Sometimes a great deal of corn must be husked to yield a few kernels of internal meaning. I recently saw *Every Night at Eight*, one of the many maddeningly routine films Raoul Walsh has directed in his long career. This 1935 effort featured George Raft, Alice Faye, Frances Langford and Patsy Kelly in one of those familiar plots about radio shows of the period. The film keeps moving along in the pleasantly unpretentious manner one would expect of Walsh until one incongruously intense scene with George Raft thrashing about in his sleep, revealing his inner fears in mumbling dream talk. The girl he loves comes into the room in the midst of his unconscious avowals of feeling, and listens sympathetically. This unusual scene was later amplified in *High Sierra* with Humphrey Bogart and Ida Lupino. The point is that one of the screen's most virile directors employed an essentially feminine narrative device to dramatize the emotional vulnerability of his heroes. If I had not been aware of Walsh in *Every Night at Eight*, the crucial link to *High Sierra* would have passed unnoticed. Such are the joys of the *auteur* theory.

27

LUCHINO VISCONTI: INTRODUCTION

Geoffrey Nowell-Smith

Source: *Luchino Visconti*, London: Secker & Warburg in association with the British Film Institute, 1967, pp. 7–13.

Luchino Visconti belongs, with Welles and Resnais, to a select company of major directors whose international reputation was established early in their careers and has been maintained, on the basis of a relatively small output, ever since. Among his Italian contemporaries he is unique. Unlike Antonioni or Fellini he did not have to wait for recognition. Unlike Rossellini he has never been a prolific director, and has managed to concentrate his energies over quarter of a century on less than a dozen meticulously prepared productions. Unlike De Sica he has not degenerated as a director with the decline of the movement which first thrust him into prominence. His early films are now classics, and each new film he makes is an eagerly awaited cultural event. And yet he has remained obstinately impervious to changes in intellectual fashions. A lonely and unassailable giant, his work has a devious consistency paralleled, on the world scale, only by Fritz Lang and Orson Welles.

There are signs recently, however, that his hitherto impregnable reputation is now beginning to suffer a decline, and that he is paying the seemingly inevitable penalty for his refusal to go any way but his own. His career has always been bound up, in the public mind, with the Italian neo-realist movement. His position with regard to the movement was in fact equivocal. But so long as critical discussion was centred round the problems of a realist aesthetic, Visconti's films were always a key point of reference. He has been seen, variously, as an embodiment of the committed and realist ideal, as its greatest betrayer, and as the man who most successfully transcended its limitations. Now that these problems no longer have the actuality they had ten, or even five years ago, Visconti's work has lost its particular exemplary role in the *Kulturkampf*. His latest films, though generally acknowledged, in a neutral fashion, as important and monumental works, have disappointed many people. They do not conform, somehow, to expectations built up on the basis of Visconti's past work. Nor do they break unexpectedly into the area where contemporary cultural battles are being fought.

What is happening to Visconti has happened before to other great directors. With Renoir in the 1940s it was a case of his films seeming to change and criticism being left behind. With John Ford, more recently, it could hardly be said that his films had changed, but the critical revolution brought about by the influence of *Cahiers du Cinéma* meant that he lost his place in the Pantheon in favour of different idols, from the same or from another generation. In both cases, however, a further turn of the wheel has restored them to their former position, though in a different guise. The liberal critique which put forward *La Grande Illusion* and *The Grapes of Wrath* as artistic and humanitarian ideals and neglected *French Can-Can* and *My Darling Clementine* has been superseded. The authors survive, but only on the basis of a thoroughgoing reappraisal of their work.

The principles which guided the revaluation of Ford and Renoir can now, I think, be legitimately and fruitfully applied to Visconti. It is not a question of reviving old polemics or laying down new dogmas, but of breaking down certain received ideas and establishing the basis of a more comprehensive interpretation. It is not possible to avoid polemic entirely, or even dogmatism. Misunderstandings still circulate, and demand to be contested. And, to a certain extent, the method of contesting them involves laying down, explicitly or implicitly, criteria of understanding which have to be taken as axiomatic.

The misunderstandings that require to be contested date back a long way, to the problems raised by the neo-realist aesthetic in the 1940s. One way of getting round these problems would be to disregard them. At twenty years' distance the arguments are beginning to look a bit threadbare and out of date. Two things make this easy solution impossible. One is the persistence of part of the general aesthetic of neo-realism, its naturalism-with-a-social-conscience, in the minds of many people. The other is the undeniable fact of Visconti's connection with the movement and the need to produce a responsible redefinition of this connection. Visconti without neo-realism is like Lang without Expressionism and Eisenstein without Formalism—and without the Russian Revolution.

At the same time the most important job to be done remains that of liberating Visconti from the heritage of past polemics; to free his early work from the conventional and stultifying image of masterpieces of realism and his later work from the charge of being a degeneration from his former ideals. This does not mean exalting the later work at the expense of the earlier, but making it one's primary concern to consider the work as a whole, as the product of a single intelligence, and to seek out the connections between each film at whatever level they are to be found. In Visconti's case the connections are multifarious, and can be traced in his choice of actors, his use of décors, his concern with certain historical questions, and so on. The development of each film out of the problems posed by the last can also be easily demonstrated. But there are further links within his work which exist at a deeper level, less easily discernible, and which are perhaps even more important. It is these hidden structural connections which bind his work together and which combine to form a picture of the author and his work which is far more complex and interesting, as well as more coherent, than is generally imagined.

It is necessary, at this point, to make clear certain assumptions about the concepts of authorship and of structure which have guided me in this work. The so-called *auteur* theory can be understood in three ways: as a set of empirical assertions to the effect that every detail of a film is the direct and sole responsibility of its author, who is the director; as a standard of value, according to which every film that is a *film d'auteur* is good, and every film that is not is bad; and as a principle of method, which provides a basis for a more scientific form of criticism than has existed hitherto. The first interpretation is manifestly absurd. Any proponent of the theory who puts it forward uncompromisingly in that form both trivialises the theory and commits himself to a statement that is demonstrably untrue. The second is simply gratuitous and leads only to a purposeless and anti-critical aesthetic dogmatism. It is only in the third interpretation that the theory has any validity. As a principle of method the theory requires the critic to recognise one basic fact, which is that the author exists, and to organise his analysis of the work round that fact. Whether one is trying to get to grips with a particular film or to understand the cinema in general, let alone when one is studying the development of an individual director, the concept of authorship provides a necessary dimension without which the picture cannot be complete.

But the principle of authorship does not stop short here. If it were simply a recommendation to look at films in terms of their directors it would hardly be an advance on what we know already. However, one essential corollary of the theory as it has been developed is the discovery that the defining characteristics of an author's work are not always those that are most readily apparent. The purpose of criticism becomes therefore to uncover behind the superficial contrasts of subject and treatment a structural hard core of basic and often recondite motifs. The pattern formed by these motifs, which may be stylistic or thematic, is what gives an author's work its particular structure, both defining it internally and distinguishing one body of work from another.

The structural approach, which has evolved, by a kind of necessary accident, out of the applications of the *auteur* theory and resolves many of the difficulties of the theory as originally put forward, brings with it, however, problems of its own. It narrows down the field of inquiry almost too radically, making the internal (formal and thematic) analysis of the body of work as a whole the only valid object of criticism. In so doing it is in danger of neglecting two other equally basic factors. One is the possibility of an author's work changing over time and of the structures being variable and not constant: the other is the importance of the non-thematic subject-matter and of sub-stylistic features of the visual treatment.

A completely structural approach to the work of a director seems to me at the present time unfeasible, except in very rare cases, of whom Visconti is not one. Despite the extreme formal and thematic consistency revealed in his films, the fact remains that he has changed and developed over the years. No single and comprehensive structure can be discerned, unchanging, underlying the whole of his work from *Ossessione* in 1942 to *Vaghe Stelle dell'Orsa* in 1965. Nor is he a director with whom the ostensible subject, in all its facticity, is a matter of no importance. He has carried over from *La Terra Trema* and the heritage of neo-realism, into his later films, a respect for the hard, intractable, documentary fact which cannot be assimilated into any simple analytic pattern. In most of his films the precise geographical and historical setting is as significant for our understanding of his work as the kind of themes that emerge from the story and the way it is told. Any analysis of his films, whatever its starting-point, is bound to take all these factors into account.

What I have preferred to do, therefore, rather than focus exclusively on elucidating the common underlying structures, is to consider the films singly, attempting in the analysis of each to bring out its relationship, hidden or overt, to the rest of Visconti's work. I have also dwelt at length, at the beginning of some chapters, on external factors: on the social and historical background in which the film is set; on the problems surrounding its production; and on the general "accidentalia" without which it would not have any substance. The arrangement of the book is dictated by these considerations. Basically it is chronological. But I have taken three films out of order so as to place them next to the work with which they most require to be compared—*Il Lavoro* with *Bellissima, The Leopard* with *Senso*, and *Vaghe Stelle dell'Orsa* with *White Nights*. The result of this shuffling exercise, as anyone who knows the order of Visconti's films will have realised, is to place at the end *Rocco and his Brothers*, Visconti's most ambitious and perhaps least satisfactory film. The reason for putting it last is partly negative; there didn't seem anywhere else to put it. But there is also another reason, which is that of all Visconti's films it is the one which most successfully defies analysis on purely internal criteria, and challenges the critic to look outside the narrow world of his private inquiry to problems which exist outside.

Postscript, 1972

Various changes have taken place since the above was written in 1967. In the first place, Visconti's reputation, so far from continuing to decline, is now once again, unaccountably, on the increase. In bringing the book up to date to include the three films—*Lo Straniero, The Damned*, and *Death in Venice*—completed by Visconti since 1966, I have decided to let the earlier part of the book stand exactly as it was originally written, despite the fact that the defence of Visconti's coherence as an *auteur*, which was part of the purpose of the original work, is no longer an urgent critical priority. It is also the case that his recent films have in a sense falsified part of my thesis on the relationship of realistic and melodramatic elements in his work. In these films certain features which had previously been kept in check emerge into the foreground, so that the overall trajectory of his career takes on a form different from the way I saw it five years ago. Meanwhile my own ideas have also changed. The new material included in this edition reflects both Visconti's change of direction and my change of vantage-point from which to view it. The revised judgement which I would now make of Visconti's work as a whole, together with the criticisms I have now of what I wrote in 1967, are implicit throughout the new section of the book and spelt out more explicitly at the end, on pp. 203–204.

28

THE *AUTEUR* THEORY

Peter Wollen

Source: *Signs and Meaning in the Cinema*, London: Secker & Warburg in association with the British Film Institute, 1969, pp. 74–115.

The *politique des auteurs*—the *auteur* theory, as Andrew Sarris calls it—was developed by the loosely knit group of critics who wrote for *Cahiers du Cinéma* and made it the leading film magazine in the world. It sprang from the conviction that the American cinema was worth studying in depth, that masterpieces were made not only by a small upper crust of directors, the cultured gilt on the commercial gingerbread, but by a whole range of authors, whose work had previously been dismissed and consigned to oblivion. There were special conditions in Paris which made this conviction possible. Firstly, there was the fact that American films were banned from France under the Vichy government and the German Occupation. Consequently, when they reappeared after the Liberation they came with a force—and an emotional impact—which was necessarily missing in the Anglo-Saxon countries themselves. And, secondly, there was a thriving ciné-club movement, due in part to the close connections there had always been in France between the cinema and the intelligentsia: witness the example of Jean Cocteau or André Malraux. Connected with this ciné-club movement was the magnificent Paris *Cinémathèque*, the work of Henri Langlois, a great *auteur*, as Jean-Luc Godard described him. The policy of the *Cinémathèque* was to show the maximum number of films, to plough back the production of the past in order to produce the culture in which the cinema of the future could thrive. It gave French *cinéphiles* an unmatched perception of the historical dimensions of Hollywood and the careers of individual directors.

The *auteur* theory grew up rather haphazardly; it was never elaborated in programmatic terms, in a manifesto or collective statement. As a result, it could be interpreted and applied on rather broad lines; different critics developed somewhat different methods within a loose framework of common attitudes. This looseness and diffuseness of the theory has allowed flagrant misunderstandings to take root, particularly among critics in Britain and the United States. Ignorance has been compounded by a vein of hostility to foreign ideas and a taste for travesty and caricature. However, the fruitfulness of the *auteur* approach has been such that it has made headway even on the most unfavourable terrain. For instance, a recent straw poll of British critics, conducted in conjunction with a Don Siegel Retrospective at the National Film Theatre, revealed that, among American directors most admired, a group consisting of Budd Boetticher, Samuel Fuller and Howard Hawks ran immediately behind Ford, Hitchcock and Welles, who topped the poll, but ahead of Billy Wilder, Josef Von Sternberg and Preston Sturges.

Of course, some individual directors have always been recognised as outstanding: Charles Chaplin, John Ford, Orson Welles. The *auteur* theory does not limit itself to acclaiming the director as the main author of a film. It implies an operation of decipherment; it reveals authors where none had been seen before. For years, the model of an author in the cinema was that of the European director, with open artistic aspirations and full control over his films. This model still lingers on; it lies behind the existential distinction between art films and popular films. Directors who built their reputations in Europe were dismissed after they crossed the Atlantic, reduced to anonymity. American Hitchcock was contrasted unfavourably with English Hitchcock, American Renoir with French Renoir, American Fritz Lang with German Fritz Lang. The *auteur* theory has led to the revaluation of the second, Hollywood careers of these and other European directors; without it, masterpieces such as *Scarlet Street* or *Vertigo* would never have been perceived. Conversely, the *auteur* theory has been sceptical when offered an American director whose salvation has been exile to Europe. It is difficult now to argue that *Brute Force* has ever been excelled by Jules Dassin or that Joseph Losey's recent work is markedly superior to, say, *The Prowler*.

In time, owing to the diffuseness of the original theory, two main schools of *auteur* critics grew up: those who insisted on revealing a core of meanings, of thematic motifs, and those who stressed style and *mise en scène*. There is an important distinction here, which I shall return to later. The work of the *auteur* has a semantic dimension, it is not purely formal; the work of the *metteur en scène*, on the other hand, does not go beyond the realm of performance, of transposing into the special complex of cinematic codes and channels a pre-existing text: a scenario, a book or a play. As we shall see, the meaning of the films of an *auteur* is constructed *a posteriori*; the meaning—semantic, rather than stylistic or expressive—of the films of a *metteur en scène* exists *a priori*. In concrete cases, of course, this distinction is not always clear-cut. There is controversy over whether some directors should be seen as *auteurs* or *metteurs en scène*. For example, though it is possible to make intuitive ascriptions, there have been no really persuasive accounts as yet of Raoul Walsh or William Wyler as *auteurs*, to take two very different directors. Opinions might differ about Don Siegel or George Cukor. Because of the difficulty of fixing the distinction in these concrete cases, it has often become blurred; indeed, some French critics have tended to value the *metteur en scène* above the *auteur*. MacMahonism sprang up, with its cult of Walsh, Lang, Losey and Preminger, its fascination with violence and its notorious text: 'Charlton Heston is an axiom of the cinema.' What André Bazin called 'aesthetic cults of personality' began to be formed. Minor directors were acclaimed before they had, in any real sense, been identified and defined.

Yet the *auteur* theory has survived despite all the hallucinating critical extravaganzas which it has fathered. It has survived because it is indispensable. Geoffrey Nowell-Smith has summed up the *auteur* theory as it is normally presented today:

> One essential corollary of the theory as it has been developed is the discovery that the defining characteristics of an author's work are not necessarily those which are most readily apparent. The purpose of criticism thus becomes to uncover behind the superficial contrasts of subject and treatment a hard core of basic and often recondite motifs. The pattern formed by these motifs . . . is what gives an author's work its particular structure, both defining it internally and distinguishing one body of work from another.

It is this 'structural approach', as Nowell-Smith calls it, which is indispensable for the critic.

The test case for the *auteur* theory is provided by the work of Howard Hawks. Why Hawks, rather than, say, Frank Borzage or King Vidor? Firstly, Hawks is a director who has worked for years within the Hollywood system. His first film, *Road to Glory*, was made in 1926. Yet throughout his long career he has only once received general critical acclaim, for his wartime film, *Sergeant York*, which closer inspection reveals to be eccentric and atypical of the main *corpus* of Hawks's films. Secondly, Hawks has worked in almost every genre. He has made westerns (*Rio Bravo*), gangsters (*Scarface*), war films (*Air Force*), thrillers (*The Big Sleep*), science fiction (*The Thing from Another World*), musicals (*Gentlemen Prefer Blondes*), comedies (*Bringing up Baby*), even a Biblical epic (*Land of the Pharaohs*). Yet all of these films (except perhaps *Land of the Pharaohs*, which he himself was not happy about) exhibit the same thematic preoccupations, the same recurring motifs and incidents, the same visual style and tempo. In the same way that Roland Barthes constructed a species of *homo racinianus*, the critic can construct a *homo hawksianus*, the protagonist of Hawksian values in the problematic Hawksian world.

Hawks achieved this by reducing the genres to two basic types: the adventure drama and the crazy comedy. These two types express inverse views of the world, the positive and negative poles of the Hawksian vision. Hawks stands opposed, on the one hand, to John Ford and, on the other hand, to Budd Boetticher. All these directors are concerned with the problem of heroism. For the hero, as an individual, death is an absolute limit which cannot be transcended: it renders the life which preceded it meaningless, absurd. How then can there be any meaningful individual action during life? How can individual action have any value—be heroic—if it cannot have transcendent value, because of the absolutely devaluing limit of death? John Ford finds the answer to this question by placing and situating the individual within society and within history, specifically within American history. Ford finds transcendent values in the historic vocation of America as a nation, to bring civilisation to a savage land, the garden to the wilderness. At the same time, Ford also sees these values themselves as problematic; he begins to question the movement of American history itself. Boetticher, on the contrary, insists on a radical individualism. 'I am not interested in making films about mass feelings. I am for the individual.' He looks for values in the encounter with death itself: the underlying metaphor is always that of the bull-fighter in the arena. The hero enters a group of companions, but there is no possibility of group solidarity. Boetticher's hero acts by dissolving groups and collectivities of any kind into their constituent individuals, so that he confronts each person face-to-face; the films develop, in Andrew Sarris's words, into 'floating poker games, where every character takes turns at bluffing about his hand until the final showdown'. Hawks, unlike Boetticher, seeks transcendent values beyond the individual, in solidarity with others. But, unlike Ford, he does not give his heroes any historical dimension, any destiny in time.

For Hawks the highest human emotion is the camaraderie of the exclusive, self-sufficient, all-male group. Hawks's heroes are cattlemen, marlin-fishermen, racing-drivers, pilots, big-game hunters, habituated to danger and living apart from society, actually cut off from it physically by dense forest, sea, snow or desert. Their aerodromes are fog-bound; the radio has cracked up; the next mail-coach or packet-boat does not leave for a week. The *élite* group strictly preserves its exclusivity. It is necessary to pass a test of ability and courage to win admittance. The group's only internal tensions come when one member lets the others down (the drunk deputy in *Rio Bravo*, the panicky pilot in *Only Angels Have Wings*) and must redeem himself by some act of exceptional bravery, or occasionally when too much 'individualism' threatens to disrupt the close-knit circle (the rivalry between drivers in *Red Line 7000*, the fighter pilot among the bomber crew in *Air Force*). The group's security is the first commandment: 'You get a stunt team in acrobatics in the air—if one of them is no good, then they're all in trouble. If someone loses his nerve catching animals, then the whole bunch can be in trouble.' The group members are bound together by rituals (in *Hatari!* blood is exchanged by transfusion) and express themselves univocally in communal sing-songs. There is a famous example of this in *Rio Bravo*. In *Dawn Patrol* the camaraderie of the pilots stretches even across the enemy lines: a captured German ace is immediately drafted into the group and joins in the sing-song; in *Hatari!* hunters of different nationality and in different places join together in a song over an intercom radio system.

Hawks's heroes pride themselves on their professionalism. They ask: 'How good is he? He'd better be good.' They expect no praise for doing their job well. Indeed, none is given except: 'The boys did all right.' When they die, they leave behind them only the most meagre personal belongings, perhaps a handful of medals. Hawks himself has summed up this desolate and barren view of life:

> It's just a calm acceptance of a fact. In *Only Angels Have Wings*, after Joe dies, Cary Grant says: 'He just wasn't good enough.' Well, that's the only thing that keeps people going. They just have to say: 'Joe wasn't good enough, and I'm better than Joe, so I go ahead and do it.' And they find out they're not any better than Joe, but then it's too late, you see.

In Ford films, death is celebrated by funeral services, an impromptu prayer, a few staves of 'Shall we gather at the river?'—it is inserted into an ongoing system of ritual institutions, along with the wedding, the dance, the parade. But for Hawks it is enough that the routine of the group's life goes on, a routine whose only relieving features are 'danger' (*Hatari!*) and 'fun'. Danger gives existence pungency: 'Every time you get real action, then you have danger. And the question, "Are you living or not living?" is probably the biggest drama we have.' This nihilism, in which 'living' means no more than being in danger of losing your life—a danger entered into quite gratuitously—is augmented by the Hawksian concept of having 'fun'. The word 'fun' crops up constantly in Hawks's interviews and scripts. It masks his despair.

When one of Hawks's *élite* is asked, usually by a woman, why he risks his life, he replies: 'No reason I can think of makes any sense. I guess we're just crazy.' Or Feathers, sardonically, to Colorado in *Rio Bravo*: 'You haven't even the excuse I have. We're all fools.' By 'crazy' Hawks does not mean psychopathic: none of his characters are like Turkey in Peckinpah's *The Deadly Companions* or Billy the Kid in Penn's *The Left-Handed Gun*. Nor is there the sense of the absurdity of life which we sometimes find in Boetticher's films: death, as we have seen, is for Hawks simply a routine occurrence, not a *grotesquerie*, as in *The Tall T* ('Pretty soon that well's going to be chock-a-block') or *The Rise and Fall of Legs Diamond*. For Hawks 'craziness' implies difference, a sense of apartness from the ordinary, everyday, social world. At the same time, Hawks sees the ordinary world as being 'crazy' in a much more fundamental sense, because devoid of any meaning or values. 'I mean crazy reactions—I don't think they're crazy, I think they're normal—but according to bad habits we've fallen into they seemed crazy.' Which is the normal, which the abnormal? Hawks recognises, inchoately, that to most people his heroes, far from embodying rational values, are only a dwindling band of eccentrics. Hawks's 'kind of men' have no place in the world.

The Hawksian heroes, who exclude others from their own *élite* group, are themselves excluded from society, exiled to the African bush or to the Arctic. Outsiders, other people in general, are perceived by the group as an undifferentiated crowd. Their role is to gape at the deeds of the heroes whom, at the same time, they hate. The crowd assembles to watch the showdown in *Rio Bravo*, to see the cars spin off the track in *The Crowd Roars*. The gulf between the outsider and the heroes transcends enmities among the *élite*: witness *Dawn Patrol* or Nelse in *El Dorado*. Most dehumanised of all is the crowd in *Land of the Pharaohs*, employed in building the Pyramids. Originally the film was to have been about Chinese labourers building a 'magnificent airfield' for the American army, but the victory of the Chinese Revolution forced Hawks to change his plans. ('Then I thought of the building of the Pyramids; I thought it was the same kind of story.') But the presence of the crowd, of external society, is a constant covert threat to the Hawksian *élite*, who retaliate by having 'fun'. In the crazy comedies ordinary citizens are turned into comic butts, lampooned and tormented: the most obvious target is the insurance salesman in *His Girl Friday*. Often Hawks's revenge becomes grim and macabre. In *Sergeant York* it is 'fun' to shoot Germans 'like turkeys'; in *Air Force* it is 'fun' to blow up the Japanese fleet. In *Rio Bravo* the geligniting of the badmen 'was very funny'. It is at these moments that the *élite* turns against the world outside and takes the opportunity to be brutal and destructive.

Besides the covert pressure of the crowd outside, there is also an overt force which threatens: woman. Man is woman's 'prey'. Women are admitted to the male group only after much disquiet and a long ritual courtship, phased round the offering, lighting and exchange of cigarettes, during which they prove themselves worthy of entry. Often they perform minor feats of valour. Even then though they are never really full members. A typical dialogue sums up their position:

> *Woman:* You love him, don't you?
> *Man* (embarrassed): Yes . . . I guess so . . .
> *Woman:* How can I love him like you?
> *Man:* Just stick around.

The undercurrent of homosexuality in Hawks's films is never crystallised, though in *The Big Sky*, for example, it runs very close to the surface. And he himself described *A Girl in Every Port* as 'really a love story between two men'. For Hawks men are equals, within the group at least, whereas there is a clear identification between women and the animal world, most explicit in *Bringing Up Baby, Gentlemen Prefer Blondes* and *Hatari!* Man must strive to maintain his mastery. It is also worth noting that, in Hawks's adventure dramas and even in many of his comedies, there is no married life. Often the heroes were married or at least intimately committed, to a woman at some time in the distant past but have suffered an unspecified trauma, with the result that they have been suspicious of women ever since. Their attitude is 'Once bitten, twice shy.' This is in contrast to the films of Ford, which almost always include domestic scenes. Woman is not a threat to Ford's heroes; she falls into her allotted social place as wife and mother, bringing up the children, cooking, sewing, a life of service, drudgery and subordination. She is repaid for this by being sentimentalised. Boetticher, on the other hand, has no obvious place for women at all; they are phantoms, who provoke action, are pretexts for male modes of conduct, but have no authentic significance in themselves. 'In herself, the woman has not the slightest importance.'

Hawks sees the all-male community as an ultimate; obviously it is very retrograde. His Spartan heroes are, in fact, cruelly stunted. Hawks would be a lesser director if he was unaffected by this, if his adventure dramas were the sum total of his work. His real claim as an author lies in the presence, together with the dramas, of their inverse, the crazy comedies. They are the agonised exposure of the underlying tensions of the heroic dramas. There are two principal themes, zones of tension. The first is the theme of regression: of regression to childhood, infantilism, as in *Monkey Business*, or regression to savagery: witness the repeated scene of the adult about to be scalped by painted children, in *Monkey Business* and in *The Ransom of Red Chief*. With brilliant insight, Robin Wood has shown how *Scarface* should be categorised among the comedies rather than the dramas: Camonte is perceived as savage, child-like, subhuman. The second principal comedy theme is that of sex-reversal and role-reversal. *I Was A Male War Bride* is the most extreme example. Many of Hawks's comedies are centred round domineering women and timid, pliable men: *Bringing Up Baby* and *Man's Favourite Sport*, for example. There are often scenes of male sexual humiliation, such as the trousers being pulled off the hapless private eye in *Gentlemen Prefer Blondes*. In the same film, the Olympic Team of athletes are reduced to passive objects in an extraordinary Jane Russell song number; big-game hunting is lampooned, like fishing in *Man's Favourite Sport*; the theme of infantilism crops up again: 'The child was the most mature one on board the ship, and I think he was a lot of fun.'

Whereas the dramas show the mastery of man over nature, over woman, over the animal and childish; the comedies show his humiliation, his regression. The heroes become victims; society, instead of being excluded and despised, breaks in with irruptions of monstrous farce. It could well be argued that Hawks's outlook, the alternative world which he constructs in the cinema, the Hawksian heterocosm, is not one imbued with particular intellectual subtlety or sophistication. This does not detract from its force. Hawks first attracted attention because he was regarded naïvely as an action director. Later, the thematic content which I have outlined was detected and revealed. Beyond the stylemes, semantemes were found to exist; the films were anchored in an objective stratum of meaning, a plerematic stratum, as the Danish linguist Hjelmslev would put it. Thus the stylistic expressiveness of Hawks's films was shown to be not purely contingent, but grounded in significance.

Something further needs to be said about the theoretical basis of the kind of schematic exposition of Hawks's work which I have outlined. The 'structural approach' which underlies it, the definition of a core of repeated motifs, has evident affinities with methods which have been developed for the study of folklore and mythology. In the work of Olrik and others, it was noted that in different folk-tales the same motifs reappeared time and time again. It became possible to build up a lexicon of these motifs. Eventually Propp showed how a whole cycle of Russian fairy-tales could be analysed into variations of a very limited set of basic motifs (or moves, as he called them). Underlying the different, individual tales was an archi-tale, of which they were all variants. One important point needs to be made about this type of structural analysis. There is a danger, as Lévi-Strauss has pointed out, that by simply noting and mapping resemblances, all the texts which are studied (whether Russian fairy-tales or American movies) will be reduced to one, abstract and impoverished. There must be a moment of synthesis as well as a moment of analysis: otherwise, the method is formalist, rather than truly structuralist. Structuralist criticism cannot rest at the perception of resemblances or repetitions (redundancies, in fact), but must also comprehend a system of differences and oppositions. In this way, texts can be studied not only in their universality (what they all have in common) but also in their singularity (what differentiates them from each other). This means of course that the test of a structural analysis lies not in the orthodox canon of a director's work, where resemblances are clustered, but in films which at first sight may seem eccentricities.

In the films of Howard Hawks a systematic series of oppositions can be seen very near the surface, in the contrast between the adventure dramas and the crazy comedies. If we take the adventure dramas alone it would seem that Hawks's work is flaccid, lacking in dynamism; it is only when we consider the crazy comedies that it becomes rich, begins to ferment: alongside every dramatic hero we are aware of a phantom, stripped of mastery, humiliated, inverted. With other directors, the system of oppositions is much more complex: instead of there being two broad strata of films there are a whole series of shifting variations. In these cases, we need to analyse the roles of the protagonists themselves, rather than simply the worlds in which they operate. The protagonists of fairy-tales or myths, as Lévi-Strauss has pointed out, can be dissolved into bundles of differential elements, pairs of opposites. Thus the difference between the prince and the goose-girl can be reduced to two antinomic pairs: one natural, male versus female, and the other cultural, high versus low. We can proceed with the same kind of operation in the study of films, though, as we shall see, we shall find them more complex than fairy-tales.

It is instructive, for example, to consider three films of John Ford and compare their heroes: Wyatt Earp in *My Darling Clementine*, Ethan Edwards in *The Searchers* and Tom Doniphon in *The Man Who Shot Liberty Valance*. They all act within the recognisable Ford world, governed by a set of oppositions, but their *loci* within that world are very different. The relevant pairs of opposites overlap; different pairs are foregrounded in different movies. The most relevant are garden versus wilderness, plough-share versus sabre, settler versus nomad, European versus Indian, civilised versus savage, book versus gun, married versus unmarried, East versus West. These antinomies can often be broken down further. The East, for instance, can be defined either as Boston or Washington and, in *The Last Hurrah*, Boston itself is broken down into the antipodes of Irish immigrants versus Plymouth Club, themselves bundles of such differential elements as Celtic versus Anglo-Saxon, poor versus rich, Catholic versus Protestant, Democrat versus Republican, and so on. At first sight, it might seem that the oppositions listed above overlap to the extent that they become practically synonymous, but this is by no means the case. As we shall see, part of the development of Ford's career has been the shift from an identity between civilised versus savage and European versus Indian to their separation and final reversal, so that in *Cheyenne Autumn* it is the Europeans who are savage, the victims who are heroes.

The master antinomy in Ford's films is that between the wilderness and the garden. As Henry Nash Smith has demonstrated, in his magisterial book *Virgin Land*, the contrast between the image of America as a desert and as a garden is one which has dominated American thought and literature, recurring in countless novels, tracts, political speeches and magazine stories. In Ford's films it is crystallised in a number of striking images. *The Man Who Shot Liberty Valance*, for instance, contains the image of the cactus rose, which encapsulates the antinomy between desert and garden which pervades the whole film. Compare with this the famous scene in *My Darling Clementine*, after Wyatt Earp has gone to the barber (who civilises the unkempt), where the scent of honeysuckle is twice remarked upon: an artificial perfume, cultural rather than natural. This moment marks the turning-point in Wyatt Earp's transition from wandering cowboy, nomadic, savage, bent on personal revenge, unmarried, to married man, settled, civilised, the sheriff who administers the law.

Earp, in *My Darling Clementine*, is structurally the most simple of the three protagonists I have mentioned: his progress is an uncomplicated passage from nature to culture, from the wilderness left in the past to the garden anticipated in the future. Ethan Edwards, in *The Searchers*, is more complex. He must be defined not in terms of past versus future or wilderness versus garden compounded in himself, but in relation to two other protagonists:

Scar, the Indian chief, and the family of homesteaders. Ethan Edwards, unlike Earp, remains a nomad throughout the film. At the start, he rides in from the desert to enter the log-house; at the end, with perfect symmetry, he leaves the house again to return to the desert, to vagrancy. In many respects, he is similar to Scar; he is a wanderer, a savage, outside the law: he scalps his enemy. But, like the homesteaders, of course, he is a European, the mortal foe of the Indian. Thus Edwards is ambiguous; the antinomies invade the personality of the protagonist himself. The oppositions tear Edwards in two; he is a tragic hero. His companion, Martin Pawley, however, is able to resolve the duality; for him, the period of nomadism is only an episode, which has meaning as the restitution of the family, a necessary link between his old home and his new home.

Ethan Edwards's wandering is, like that of many other Ford protagonists, a quest, a search. A number of Ford films are built round the theme of the quest for the Promised Land, an American re-enactment of the Biblical exodus, the journey through the desert to the land of milk and honey, the New Jerusalem. This theme is built on the combination of the two pairs: wilderness versus garden and nomad versus settler; the first pair precedes the second in time. Thus, in *Wagonmaster*, the Mormons cross the desert in search of their future home; in *How Green Was My Valley* and *The Informer*, the protagonists want to cross the Atlantic to a future home in the United States. But, during Ford's career, the situation of home is reversed in time. In *Cheyenne Autumn* the Indians journey in search of the home they once had in the past; in *The Quiet Man*, the American Sean Thornton returns to his ancestral home in Ireland. Ethan Edwards's journey is a kind of parody of this theme: his object is not constructive, to found a home, but destructive, to find and scalp Scar. Nevertheless, the weight of the film remains orientated to the future: Scar has burned down the home of the settlers, but it is replaced and we are confident that the homesteader's wife, Mrs Jorgensen, is right when she says: 'Some day this country's going to be a fine place to live.' The wilderness will, in the end, be turned into a garden.

The Man Who Shot Liberty Valance has many similarities with *The Searchers*. We may note three: the wilderness becomes a garden—this is made quite explicit, for Senator Stoddart has wrung from Washington the funds necessary to build a dam which will irrigate the desert and bring real roses, not cactus roses; Tom Doniphon shoots Liberty Valance as Ethan Edwards scalped Scar; a log-home is burned to the ground. But the differences are equally clear: the log-home is burned after the death of Liberty Valance; it is destroyed by Doniphon himself; it is his own home. The burning marks the realisation that he will never enter the Promised Land, that to him it means nothing; that he has doomed himself to be a creature of the past, insignificant in the world of the future. By shooting Liberty Valance he has destroyed the only world in which he himself can exist, the world of the gun rather than the book; it is as though Ethan Edwards had perceived that by scalping Scar, he was in reality committing suicide. It might be mentioned too that, in *The Man Who Shot Liberty Valance*, the woman who loves Doniphon marries Senator Stoddart. Doniphon when he destroys his log-house (his last words before doing so are 'Home, sweet home!') also destroys the possibility of marriage.

The themes of *The Man Who Shot Liberty Valance* can be expressed in another way. Ransom Stoddart represents rational-legal authority, Tom Doniphon represents charismatic authority. Doniphon abandons his charisma and cedes it, under what amount to false pretences, to Stoddart. In this way charismatic and rational-legal authority are combined in the person of Stoddart and stability thus assured. In *The Searchers* this transfer does not take place; the two kinds of authority remain separated. In *My Darling Clementine* they are combined naturally in Wyatt Earp, without any transfer being necessary. In many of Ford's late films—*The Quiet Man*, *Cheyenne Autumn, Donovan's Reef*—the accent is placed on traditional authority. The island of Ailakaowa, in *Donovan's Reef*, a kind of Valhalla for the homeless heroes of *The Man Who Shot Liberty Valance*, is actually a monarchy, though complete with the Boston girl, wooden church and saloon, made familiar by *My Darling Clementine*. In fact, the character of Chihuahua, Doc Holliday's girl in *My Darling Clementine*, is split into two: Miss Lafleur and Lelani, the native princess. One represents the saloon entertainer, the other the non-American in opposition to the respectable Bostonians, Amelia Sarah Dedham and Clementine Carter. In a broad sense, this is a part of a general movement which can be detected in Ford's work to equate the Irish, Indians and Polynesians as traditional communities, set in the past, counter-posed to the march forward to the American future, as it has turned out in reality, but assimilating the values of the American future as it was once dreamed.

It would be possible, I have no doubt, to elaborate on Ford's career, as defined by pairs of contrasts and similarities, in very great detail, though—as always with film criticism—the impossibility of quotation is a severe handi-cap. My own view is that Ford's work is much richer than that of Hawks and that this is revealed by a structural analysis; it is the richness of the shifting relations between antinomies in Ford's work that makes him a great artist, beyond being simply an undoubted *auteur*. Moreover, the *auteur* theory enables us to reveal a whole complex of meaning in films such as *Donovan's Reef*, which a recent filmography sums up as just 'a couple of Navy men who have retired to a South Sea island now spend most of their time raising hell'. Similarly, it throws a completely new light on a film like *Wings of Eagles*, which revolves, like *The Searchers*, round the vagrancy versus home an-tinomy, with the difference that when the hero does come home, after flying round the world, he trips over a child's toy, falls down the stairs and is completely paralysed so that he cannot move at all, not even his toes. This is the macabre *reductio ad absurdum* of the settled.

Perhaps it would be true to say that it is the lesser *auteurs* who can be defined, as Nowell-Smith put it, by a core of basic motifs which remain constant, without variation. The great directors must be defined in terms of shifting relations, in their singularity as well as their uniformity. Renoir once remarked that a director spends his whole life making one film; this film, which it is the task of the critic to construct, consists not only of the typical features of its variants, which are merely its redundancies, but of the principle of variation which governs it, that is its esoteric structure, which can only manifest itself or 'seep to the surface', in Lévi-Strauss's phrase, 'through the repetition process'. Thus Renoir's 'film' is in reality a 'kind of permutation group, the two variants placed at the far ends being in a symmetrical, though inverted, relationship to each other'. In practice, we will not find perfect symmetry, though as we have seen, in the case of Ford, some antinomies are completely reversed. Instead, there will be a kind of torsion within the permutation group, within the matrix, a kind of exploration of certain possibilities, in which some antinomies are foregrounded, discarded or even inverted, whereas others remain stable and constant. The important thing to stress, however, is that it is only the analysis of the whole *corpus* which permits the moment of synthesis when the critic returns to the individual film.

Of course, the director does not have full control over his work; this explains why the *auteur* theory involves a kind of decipherment, decryptment. A great many features of films analysed have to be dismissed as indecipherable because of 'noise' from the producer, the cameraman or even the actors. This concept of 'noise' needs further elaboration. It is often said that a film is the result of a multiplicity of factors, the sum total of a number of different contributions. The contribution of the director—the 'directorial factor', as it were—is only one of these, though perhaps the one which carries the most weight. I do not need to emphasise that this view is quite the contrary of the *auteur* theory and has nothing in common with it at all. What the *auteur* theory does is to take a group of films—the work of one director—and analyse their structure. Everything irrelevant to this, everything non-pertinent, is considered logically secondary, contingent, to be discarded. Of course, it is possible to approach films by studying some other feature; by an effort of critical ascesis we could see films, as Von Sternberg sometimes urged, as abstract light-show or as histrionic feasts. Sometimes these separate texts—those of the cameraman or the actors—may force themselves into prominence so that the film becomes an indecipherable palimpsest. This does not mean, of course, that it ceases to exist or to sway us or please us or intrigue us; it simply means that it is inaccessible to criticism. We can merely record our momentary and subjective impressions.

Myths, as Lévi-Strauss has pointed out, exist independently of style, the syntax of the sentence or musical sound, euphony or cacophony. The myth functions 'on an especially high level where meaning succeeds practically in "taking off" from the linguistic ground on which it keeps rolling'. *Mutatis mutandis*, the same is true of the *auteur* film. 'When a mythical schema is transmitted from one population to another, and there exist differences of language, social organisation or way of life which make the myth difficult to communicate, it begins to become impoverished and confused.' The same kind of impoverishment and confusion takes place in the film studio, where difficulties of communication abound. But none the less the film can usually be discerned, even if it was a quickie made in a fortnight without the actors or the crews that the director might have liked, with an intrusive producer and even, perhaps, a censor's scissors cutting away vital sequences. It is as though a film is a musical composition rather than a musical performance, although, whereas a musical composition exists *a priori* (like a scenario), an *auteur* film is constructed *a posteriori*. Imagine the situation if the critic had to construct a musical composition from a number of fragmentary, distorted versions of it, all with improvised passages or passages missing.

The distinction between composition and performance is vital to aesthetics. The score, or text, is constant and durable; the performance is occasional and transient. The score is unique, integrally itself; the performance is a particular among a number of variants. The score, in music, consists partly of a message to be translated from one channel to another (from 'the stream of ink' to the 'stream of air') and partly of a set of instructions. In some modern scores, by Lamonte Young or George Brecht, there are only instructions; others, by Cornelius Cardew, for instance, are literary texts, which have to be translated between codes (verbal and musical) as well as between channels. But the principle remains the same. Both messages and instructions must necessarily refer back to a common code, so that they are intelligible to the performer. The performance itself, however, is not coded; hence its ungeneralised particularity. The distinctive marks of a performance, like those of somebody's accent or tone of voice, are facultative variants. A coded text consists of discrete units; a performance is continuous, graded rather than coded. It works more like an analog computer than a digital one; it is similar to a clock rather than a calendar, a slide-rule rather than an abacus. The intelligibility of a performance of a piece of music is of a different kind to the intelligibility of a score. Here we confront the distinction made by Galvano della Volpe, referred to elsewhere in this book, between the realm in which *de jure* criticism is possible and the realm in which criticism can only be *de facto*, 'the kingdom of more or less', as Nicholas Ruwet has called it in his study of the semiology of music.

Linguists have often striven to restrict their field of study to the coded aspects of texts and to expel graded features, such as accents, grunts, rasps, chuckles, wails and so on. Charles F. Hockett, for example, has written that

> the embedding medium of linguistic messages . . . shows a continuous scale of dynamics, organised to some extent in any given culture;

> one may speak softly, or more loudly, or more loudly still, or anywhere in between—with no theoretic limit to the fineness of gradation. But . . . in general . . . if we find continuous-scale contrasts in the vicinity of what we are sure is language, we exclude them from language (though not from culture).

Other linguists have contested this epistemological asceticism. Thomas A. Sebeok, for instance, has argued against Hockett and others, and demanded a radical rethinking of the relationship between coded and graded features of language. His own work in zoo-linguistics, communication among animals, has led him to the conclusion that discrete units cannot be absolutely separated from their 'embedding medium'; if linguists expel continuous phenomena from their field of study they cannot then account, for instance, for linguistic change. Similar conclusions could be reached by considering the relations between composition and performance. There is no unbridged abyss between the two.

Painting provides a particularly interesting example. At one time, during the Renaissance and Mannerist periods, many paintings were initially composed and designed by an iconographic programmer, expert in mythology or Biblical studies, and then executed by the painter. Some of these programmes have survived. Thus, for example, the marvellous Farnese Palace at Caprarola was decorated throughout according to a scheme elaborated by three humanist scholars, Annibale Caro, Onophrio Panvinio and Fulvio Orsini. The scheme was extremely detailed. For the ceiling of the study, the Stanza della Solitudine, Caro outlined the following programme, in a letter to Panvinio:

> Thus in one of the large pictures of the middle I would show the solitude of Christians: and in the middle of this I would represent Christ Our Lord, and then on the sides in the following order, St Paul the Apostle, St John the Baptist, St Jerome, St Francis, and others if it can contain more, who would come out from the desert at different places and would go and meet the people to preach the evangelical doctrine, showing the desert on one side of the painting and the people on the other. In the opposite picture, I would show, as a contrast, the solitude of the pagans . . .

and so on. A letter also survives from Caro to Taddeo Zuccaro, the painter. Evidently, this kind of iconographic programming has its similarities with a scenario.

Gradually, however, the painter emancipated himself from the iconographic programmer. We can see the beginnings of this, indeed, even in the case of Caprarola; Caro complained to Panvinio that either the programme 'must be adapted to the disposition of the painter, or his disposition to your subjects, and since it is obvious that he has refused to adapt himself to you, we must, perforce, adapt ourselves to him to avoid disorder and confusion'. That was in 1575. Fourteen years later, in 1589, the sculptor Giovanni Bologna proved even more headstrong: he sent a bronze to his patron which, he remarked, 'might represent the Rape of Helen, or perhaps of Proserpine, or even one of the Sabines'. According to a contemporary, he made sculptures 'solely to show his excellence in art and without having any subject in mind'. This was unusual at the time. Most painters submitted to some kind of iconographical programming for many years after Giovanni Bologna made his break for freedom. During the seventeenth century, it was still widely felt that verbal language and Alciati's 'syntax of symbols' were mutually translatable. Shaftesbury, as late as 1712, was programming a complicated allegorical 'draught or tablature' of the Judgement of Hercules. This was to be painted by Paulo de Matthaeis, but it was made perfectly clear that he was to be the subordinate partner in the enterprise.

Shaftesbury came down clearly on the side of design and repeatedly diminished the importance of colouring, which he regarded as 'false relish, which is governed rather by what immediately strikes the sense, than by what consequentially and by reflection pleases the mind, and satisfies the thought and reason'. Painting, as such, gave no more pleasure than 'the rich stuffs and coloured silks worn by our ladies'. Elsewhere he wrote that

> the good painter (*quatenus* painter) begins by working first *within*. Here the imagery! Here the plastic work! First makes forms, fashions, corrects, amplifies, contracts, unites, modifies, assimilates, adapts, conforms, polishes, refines etc., forms his *ideas*: then his hand: his strokes.

Shaftesbury was trying to hold back a tide much too strong for him. Painting succumbed to

> the *je ne sais quoi* to which idiots and the ignorant of the art would reduce everything. 'Tis not the *dokei*, the I like and you like. But why do I like? And if not with reason and truth I will refuse to like, dislike my fancy, condemn the form, search it, discover its deformity and reject it.

Shaftesbury's platonising and allegorising was swept away by the full flood of Romanticism.

Yet even during the nineteenth century we can still see traces of the old attitudes. The Pre-Rephaelites worked from extremely detailed programmes; even Courbet painted what he called a 'real allegory'. Gauguin programmed his paintings but according to a system effectively opaque to anybody but himself. And, at the beginning of this century, Marcel Duchamp rebelled against what he called 'retinal' painting and the validation of the painter's touch—*la patte*, his 'paw'. The *Large Glass* was based upon the complicated notes and diagrams which Duchamp later published in the *Green Box*: 'It had to be planned and drawn as an architect would do it.' In a similar spirit, Laszlo Moholy-Nagy produced paintings by telephone, dictating instructions about the use of graph paper and standardised colours. Thus the wheel came full circle. The painter, after the long and successful struggle to emancipate himself from the iconographer, reacted against the outcome and strove to turn himself into a designer in his own right. One dimension of the history of painting lies in this shifting interaction between composition and performance.

However, it is not only in painting that the performer has made efforts to emancipate himself from the designer. Even in music, which seems the most stable art in this respect, there have been intermittent periods in which improvisation has been highly valued. And, of course, jazz provides a striking example. To begin with, jazz musicians improvised on tunes which they took from a repertory: march tunes, popular songs. Later they began to write their own tunes and use these as a basis for improvisation. Finally, they began to become primarily composers and only secondarily performers. The legal battle over whether Ornette Coleman should be categorised as a classical or a popular musician recalls the very similar battles which took place during the Renaissance over the disputed status of the painter, whether he was an artist or an artificer. Conversely, an opposite movement has taken place within legitimate music, allowing the performers much greater freedom to interpret and improvise. Thus the score of Cornelius Cardew's *Treatise* only partially and sporadically refers back to a common code; it oscillates between a discrete and continuous notation, between the coded and the graded.

Closer to the cinema has been the experience of the theatre. The polemic of Ben Jonson against Inigo Jones might well be that of a scriptwriter against a director more concerned with visual values:

> . . . O Showes! Showes! Mighty Showes!
> The Eloquence of Masques! What need of prose
> Or Verse, or Sense t'express Immortall you?
> You are the Spectacles of State! 'Tis true
> Court Hieroglyphicks! and all Artes affoord
> In the mere perspective of an Inch board!
> You aske noe more then certeyne politique Eyes,
> Eyes that can pierce into the Misteryes
> Of many Coulors! read them! and reveale
> Mythology there painted on slit deale!
> Oh, to make Boardes to speake! There is a taske!
> Painting and Carpentry are the Soule of Masque!

> Pack with your pedling Poetry to the State!
> This is the money-gett, Mechanick Age!

The accusation of commercialism and mechanicality is all too familiar. Ben Jonson's complaint is based on an assumption of the superiority of verbal language, the inadequacy of emblems and images. The theatre has oscillated between two modes of communication. A very similar impulse to that which motivated masque, a downgrading of the literary text, made itself felt at the end of the nineteenth and beginning of the twentieth centuries, springing in part from the theory and practice of Wagner, developed at Bayreuth. Edward Gordon Craig stressed the non-verbal dimensions of the theatre and the sovereignty of the director; his theories made a particular impact in Germany and in Russia, where he was invited to work. In Russia, we can trace a direct link from Craig, through Meyerhold to the work of Eisenstein, first at the Proletcult Theatre, then in the cinema. In Germany, Max Reinhardt was the analogue to Meyerhold; he had an equivalent kind of effect on the German Expressionist cinema: even Von Sternberg has acknowledged his admiration of Reinhardt. For Meyerhold, words were no longer sacrosanct, plays were ruthlessly altered and adapted; there was a counter-stress on the specifically theatrical modes of expression: mime, *commedia dell'arte*, set design, costume, acrobatics and the circus, the performing art *par excellence*. Meyerhold and Reinhardt insisted on full control. Ironically, when Reinhardt did make a film, *A Midsummer Night's Dream* in Hollywood, he was made to share the direction with an established cinema director, William Dieterle. None the less his work in theatre pointed forward to the cinema.

Even in literature, it should be said, the relationship between composition and performance occasionally varies. Most literary works used to be spoken aloud and this persisted, even with prose, until quite recently: Benjamin Constant read *Adolphe* aloud numerous times before it ever saw print; Dickens had immensely successful recital tours. There is still a strong movement in favour of reading poetry aloud. Of course, literacy and printing have diminished the social importance of this kind of performance. Ever since St Ambrose achieved the feat of reading to himself, the performance of literary works has been doomed to be secondary. Yet, during the nineteenth century, as literacy rose, the fall of public readings was accompanied by its converse, a rising interest in typography. The typographer has become, potentially, a kind of interpreter of a text, like a musician. Early instances of creative typography can be seen in *Tristram Shandy* and the work of Baroque poets, such as Quarles and Herbert. But the modern movement springs from the convergence of Morris's concern over typography and book design, spread through the Arts and Crafts guilds and Art Nouveau, with the innovations of Mallarmé. In the first decades of the century there was a great upsurge of interest in typography—Pound, Apollinaire, Marinetti, El Lissitsky, Picabia,

De Stijl, the Bauhaus—which is still bearing fruit today. A world-wide Concrete Poetry movement has grown up, in which poets collaborate with typographers.

The cinema, like all these other arts, has a composition side and a performance side. On the one hand, there is the original story, novel or play and the shooting-script or scenario. Hitchcock and Eisenstein draw sequences in advance in a kind of strip-cartoon form. On the other hand, there are the various levels of execution: acting, photography, editing. The director's position is shifting and ambiguous. He both forms a link between design and performance and can command or participate in both. Different directors, of course, lean in different directions. Partly this is the result of their backgrounds: Mankiewicz and Fuller, for instance, began as scriptwriters; Sirk as a set-designer; Cukor as a theatre director; Siegel as an editor and montage director; Chaplin as an actor; Klein and Kubrick as photographers. Partly too it depends on their collaborators: Cukor works on colour design with Hoyningen-Huene because he respects his judgement. And most directors, within limits, can choose who they work with.

What the *auteur* theory demonstrates is that the director is not simply in command of a performance of a pre-existing text; he is not, or need not be, only a *metteur en scène*. Don Siegel was recently asked on television what he took from Hemingway's short story for his film, *The Killers*; Siegel replied that 'the only thing taken from it was the catalyst that a man has been killed by somebody and he did not try to run away'. The word Siegel chose—'catalyst'—could not be bettered. Incidents and episodes in the original screenplay or novel can act as catalysts; they are the agents which are introduced into the mind (conscious or unconscious) of the *auteur* and react there with the motifs and themes characteristic of his work. The director does not subordinate himself to another author; his source is only a pretext, which provides catalysts, scenes which fuse with his own preoccupations to produce a radically new work. Thus the manifest process of performance, the treatment of a subject, conceals the latent production of a quite new text, the production of the director as an *auteur*.

Of course, it is possible to value performances as such, to agree with André Bazin that Olivier's *Henry V* was a great film, a great rendering, transposition into the cinema, of Shakespeare's original play. The great *metteurs en scène* should not be discounted simply because they are not *auteurs*: Vincente Minnelli, perhaps, or Stanley Donen. And, further than that, the same kind of process can take place that occurred in painting: the director can deliberately concentrate entirely on the stylistic and expressive dimensions of the cinema. He can say, as Josef Von Sternberg did about *Morocco*, that he purposely chose a fatuous story so that people would not be distracted from the play of light and shade in the photography. Some of Busby Berkeley's extraordinary sequences are equally detached from any kind of dependence on the screen-play: indeed, more often than not, some other director was entrusted with the job of putting the actors through the plot and dialogue. Moreover, there is no doubt that the greatest films will be not simply *auteur* films but marvellous expressively and stylistically as well: *Lola Montès*, *Shinheike Monogatari*, *La Règle du Jeu*, *La Signora di Tutti*, *Sansho Dayu*, *Le Carrosse d'Or*.

The *auteur* theory leaves us, as every theory does, with possibilities and questions. We need to develop much further a theory of performance, of the stylistic, of graded rather than coded modes of communication. We need to investigate and define, to construct critically the work of enormous numbers of directors who up to now have only been incompletely comprehended. We need to begin the task of comparing author with author. There are any number of specific problems which stand out: Donen's relationship to Kelly and Arthur Freed, Boetticher's films outside the Ranown cycle, Welles's relationship to Toland (and—perhaps more important—Wyler's), Sirk's films outside the Ross Hunter cycle, the exact identity of Walsh or Wellman, the decipherment of Anthony Mann. Moreover there is no reason why the *auteur* theory should not be applied to the English cinema, which is still utterly amorphous, unclassified, unperceived. We need not two or three books on Hitchcock and Ford, but many, many more. We need comparisons with authors in the other arts: Ford with Fenimore Cooper, for example, or Hawks with Faulkner. The task which the critics of *Cahiers du Cinéma* embarked on is still far from completed.

29

SIGNS AND MEANING IN THE CINEMA: CONCLUSION

Peter Wollen

Source: *Signs and Meaning in the Cinema*, revised edition, London: Secker & Warburg in association with the British Film Institute, 1972, pp. 155–175.

Looking back over this book, even after a short distance of time, it strikes me that it was written at the beginning of a transitional period which is not yet over. What marks this period, I think, is the delayed encounter of the cinema with the 'modern movement' in the arts. The great breakthroughs in literature, painting and music, the hammer-blows which smashed (or should have smashed) traditional aesthetics, took place in the years before the First World War, at a time when the cinema was in its infancy, a novelty in the world of vaudeville, peepshows and nickelodeons. This was the period of the first abstract paintings, the first sound poems, the first noise bands. It was also the period when the idea of semiology was launched by Saussure in his Geneva Course and when Freud was making the most important of his discoveries. Precisely because the cinema was a new art, it took time for any of this to have an effect on it.

The first impact of the 'modern movement' on the cinema took place in the twenties. The clearest example of this, of course, is Eisenstein. At the same time there was the work of the Parisian *avant-garde*—Léger, Man Ray, Buñuel—and of abstract film-makers like Eggeling and Richter. In Germany Expressionism fed into the cinema in the form of 'Caligarism', mainly under Eric Pommer's patronage. But looking back on it, we can see how superficial this first contact was and how it was completely obliterated during the thirties. In Russia, socialist realism was launched and the *avant-garde* cinema of the twenties cut short. In Germany, Pommer lost control of UFA after the financial disaster of *Metropolis* and soon, in any case, the Nazi regime was in power. The early experiments of Léger or Richter petered out. Buñuel went his own way. Fischinger was working for Disney in the thirties; Moholy-Nagy for Korda. If there was any kind of *avant-garde* in this period, it was to be found in the documentary movement, certainly the most conservative *avant-garde* imaginable.

The rise of the sound film and the rapid expansion of American economic and political power after the war led to the domination of Hollywood throughout most of the world. It is in this context that a director like Orson Welles could appear as an innovator, a dangerous experimentalist, Rossellini as a revolutionary, Humphrey Jennings a poet. Today these estimations seem absurd. There has been a complete change, a revaluation, a shift of focus which had made cinema history into something different. Eisenstein or Vertov look contemporary instead of antique. Welles or Jennings look hopelessly old-fashioned and dated. Yet this change has been very recent and its full effects are still to be felt. All the old landmarks are disappearing in the mists of time.

What has happened? Really, two things. First, the rise of the underground, particularly in America. This was a product of three factors: poets and painters taking up film-making, the arrival of European *avant-garde* artists like Richter as refugees, the peeling off of mavericks from Hollywood. There was also a crucial economic pre-condition: the availability of equipment and money to buy it. In the context of the underground, film-making was seen as an extension of the other arts. There was no attempt to compete with Hollywood by making feature films (except, as with Curtis Harrington, by becoming a Hollywood director). It took some time before the underground began to get into the cinemas, in fact only in the last few years when Warhol films began to bite into the sexploitation field. But it was more and more obvious that it was there to stay.

The second key development was the way that the French New Wave evolved, pushing back the conventional frontiers of the 'art' cinema. Godard has had an incalculable effect, and it was only right that this book should have built up towards a paean of praise for his films and an eager anticipation of what was to come. At the time I was writing, *Weekend* was the last Godard movie I had seen. It is now much clearer what the effect of May 1968 was on Godard. His films have increasingly been, so to speak, both politicised and semiologised. It is difficult not to think of directors like Makavejev, Skolimowski, Bertolucci, Kluge, Glauber Rocha and so on, simply as post-Godard directors. Yet none of them have gone the whole way with him, and some have tended to retreat from the adventurousness of their own early 'Godardian' work.

It seems to me now that I was wrong in what I expected of Godard. 'More than anybody else Godard has realised the fantastic possibilities of the cinema as a medium of communication and expression. In his hands, as in Peirce's perfect sign, the cinema has become an almost equal amalgam of the symbolic, the iconic and the indexical. His films have conceptual meaning, pictorial beauty and documentary truth.' In a sense, the programme I was outlining has been fulfilled, but more by others than by Godard. A film like Makavejev's *WR—Mysteries of The Organism* exploits the full semiological possibilities of film in its blend of documentary, *vérité*, library clips, Hollywood, montage, etc. But thinking back on it, credit for this should go to Kenneth Anger's *Scorpio Rising*, rather than to Godard. Anger was the first film-magician in this sense (*WR* can almost be read out of *Scorpio Rising* by substituting Crowley for Reich and Jesus Christ for Stalin). It is obvious now that what concerned Godard was an interrogation of the cinema rather than a fulfilment of its potential.

It is necessary at this point to make a digression, to sketch in the background against which Godard is working and against which the 'modern movement' in the other arts also emerged. The twentieth century witnessed an assault on traditional art and aesthetics which laid the foundations for a revolutionary art which has not yet been consolidated. It is possible that this consolidation cannot take place independently, apart from the movement of society and of politics. The heroic first phase of the *avant-garde* in the arts coincided, after all, with the political phase which led from 1905 to the October Revolution; Godard's films are clearly linked with the political upheavals which reached a climax in Europe in May 1968. But it is nevertheless possible, on a theoretical level, to try and explain what this potential break with the past involved, would involve if it were to be carried through. This raises problems about the nature of art, its place in intellectual production, the ideology and philosophy which underpin it.

Signs and meaning: contemporary Western thought, like its forerunners, sees the problem predominantly one way. Signs are used to communicate meanings between individuals. An individual constructs a message in his mind, a complex of meaning, an idea or thought-process, which he wishes to convey to someone else. Both individuals possess a common code or grammar which they have learned. Through the agency of this code, the first individual, the source, maps his message on to, for instance, its verbal representation, a sentence. He then re-maps this sentence on to a signal, a sequence of sounds which give it a physical form, and transmits this signal through a channel. It is picked up by the second individual, the receiver, who then decodes the signal and thus obtains the original message. An idea has been transferred from one mind to another. There is some disagreement among scholars about whether the original message is articulated in words or in some kind of non-articulated thought-process (the problem of semantics) but, given this reservation, the model outlined above holds good for most contemporary linguistics and semiotic: Weaver and Shannon, Jakobson, Chomsky, Prieto and their followers.

The common assumption of all these various views is that language, or any other system of transmitted signals, is an instrument, a tool. This assumption is quite explicit in Jakobson, for instance: 'These efforts (of the Prague School) proceed from a universally recognised view of language as a tool of communication.' Or the British linguist, Halliday: 'Language serves for the expression of "content": that is, of the speaker's expression of the real world, including the inner world of his own consciousness. We may call this the ideational function . . .' And Prieto: '. . . the instruments which are called signals and whose function consists of the transmission of messages. . . . These instruments permit man to exercise an influence on his environment: in this case, this involves the transmission of messages to other members of the social group.' Or, to strike out in a different direction, Stalin: 'Language is a medium, an instrument with the help of which people communicate with one another, exchange thoughts and understand each other. Being directly connected with thought, language registers and fixes in words, and in words combined into sentences, the results of thought and man's successes in his quest for knowledge, and thus makes possible the exchange of ideas in human society.' Both Jakobson and Halliday note additional functions of language, but both regard themselves primarily as 'functionalist' in approach. Prieto uses the term 'utilitarian' rather than 'functional' but the drift is the same.

Clearly this model of language rests on the notion of the thinking mind or consciousness which controls the material world. Matter belongs to the realm of instrumentality; thus, the consciousness makes use of the material signal as a tool. Behind every material signal is an ideal message, a kind of archi-signal. In essence, this view is a humanised version of the old theological belief that the material world as a whole comprised a signal which, when decoded, would reveal the message of the divine Logos. Like verbal language the material world was inadequate to express the Logos fully (it remained ineffable) but it could give a partial idea of the deity, who was, so to speak, pure Message. At the time of the Enlightenment, God was no longer envisaged as the author of the great book of the world, but the same semiotic model was transferred to human communication. Artists, in particular, were seen as quasi-divine authors who created a world in their imagination which they then expressed externally. Within a Romantic aesthetic, the signals were taken as symbols, to be decoded not by applying a common code but by intuition and empathy, projection into the artist's inner world. Porphyry's 'wise Theology wherein man indicated God and Divine Powers by images akin to sense and sketched invisible things in visible forms' was echoed in Coleridge's description of a symbol as characterised 'above all, by the translucence of the eternal through and in the temporal'. Within Classical aesthetics signals remained made up of conventional counters or tokens, as the Romantics contemptuously dubbed them.

In criticism, it was the Classical view which prevailed, not surprisingly, since Romanticism saw no need for critics. The function of criticism was seen as clarifying the decoding of signals in order to restore the original message as fully as possible. This was necessary because artistic messages were usually very complex, the signals were often ambiguous and a knowledge of the situation of the source, culturally and socially, could be helpful towards deciding on the most satisfactory decoding. Criticism thus comes to posit a 'content' of works of art, not immediately obvious from a rapid perusal of the work itself. Much might be missed by the casual or unsophisticated reader, which the critic could point out. Basically, there was one correct decoding, as though the work of art was the Rosetta Stone. Within a Romantic or symbolist aesthetic, on the other hand, decoded intuitively, there could be no 'right answer'; it was all a matter of sensitivity, of spiritual attunement, so that criticism ended up with Walter Pater's mood-recreations. Within the Classical model, as positivism gained strength, the 'content' of the work was interpreted not as a body of ideas or experiences, but as the expression of the artist's racial or geographical or social situation. Thus Taine's 'milieu' or the 'class background' of positivist Marxists. Another tradition saw content in terms of moral stance. Of course, a number of critics have always confused the different positions, switching from technical expertise to mystical intuition at will.

One of the main effects of the 'modern movement' was to discredit the ideas of 'intention' and of 'content'. An artist like Duchamp for example stressed the impersonality of the work, the role of chance and parody, and even left works deliberately unfinished. The Surrealists produced automatic writing; any number of modern artists stressed the importance of 'form'. The really important breakthrough, however, came in the rejection of the traditional idea of a work as primarily a representation of something else, whether an idea or the real world, and the concentration of attention on the text of the work itself and on the signs from which it was constructed. This was not exactly the same thing as 'abstraction' or 'formalism' though it was easily confused with it. An 'abstract' artist like Kandinsky for example saw himself as expressing spiritual realities, which could be grasped only through pure form. Kandinsky was really the end-product of symbolism. The same kind of aesthetic was developed by Hulme in England, who saw abstract art as representing timeless, suprahistorical values, in contrast with the history-bound, man-centred figurative art of the Renaissance and Romanticism.

The 'modern movement' made it possible for the artist to interrogate his own work for the first time, to see it as problematic, to put in the forefront the material character of the work. Again, this could easily slide into a kind of mystical naturalism, in which an artefact was equated with a natural object like a tree, thus seeking to eradicate its status as a sign entirely. Or, on the other hand, it could lead towards technicians, concentrating on the material aspects of art simply to perfect the work as an instrument. In a sense, modern art was searching for a semiology which would enable it to break with the Renaissance tradition, but which had still to be elaborated, and perhaps could not be elaborated until the need for it was felt. The aesthetic and 'philosophical' background to most of the works of the *avant-garde* was a dismal mixture of theosophy, Worringer, Frazer, bits of Bergson, even Bradley, and so on. The only exception to this is to be found in the early collaboration between the Russian linguists and Futurist poets. And later, of course, the Surrealists made an effort to understand Freud.

What was (and still is) needed was a semiology which reversed and transformed the usual terms of its problematic, which stopped seeing the signal, the text, as a means, a medium existing between human beings and the truth or meaning, whether the idealist transcendent truth of the Romantics or the immanent intentional meaning of the Classical aesthetic. Thus a text is a material object whose significance is determined not by a code external to it, mechanically, nor originally as a symbolic whole, but through its own interrogation of its own code. It is only through such an interrogation, through such an interior dialogue between signal and code, that a text can produce spaces within meaning, within the otherwise rigid straitjacket of the message, to produce a meaning of a new kind, generated within the text itself. To point out a parallel: this would be as if the dialogue of Freudian psychoanalysis, segregated as it is between the space of the signal (analysand) and that of the code (analyst), were to be compressed and condensed within one single space, that of the text.

The ideological effects of such a re-casting of the semiological foundations of art would be of the utmost importance. It would situate the consciousness of the reader or spectator no longer outside the work as receiver, consumer and judge, but force him to put his consciousness at risk within the text itself, so that he is forced to interrogate his own codes, his own method of interpretation, in the course of reading, and thus to produce fissures and gaps in the space of his own consciousness (fissures and gaps which exist in reality but which are repressed by an ideology, characteristic of bourgeois society, which insists on the 'wholeness' and integrity of each individual consciousness). All previous aesthetics have accepted the universality of art founded either in the universality of 'truth' or of 'reality' or of 'God'. The modern movement for the first time broke this universality into pieces and insisted on the singularity of every act of reading a text, a process of multiple decodings, in which a shift of code meant going back over signals previously 'deciphered' and vice versa, so that each reading was an open process, existing in a topological rather than a flat space, controlled yet inconclusive.

Classical aesthetics always posited an essential unity and coherence to every work, which permitted a uniform and exhaustive decoding. Modernism disrupts this unity; it opens the work up, both internally and externally, outwards. Thus there are no longer separate works, monads, each enclosed in its own individuality, a perfect globe, a whole. It produces works which are no longer centripetal, held together by their own centres, but centrifugal, throwing the reader out of the work to other works.

Thus, in the past, the difficulty of reading was simply to find the correct code, to clear up ambiguities or areas of ignorance. Once the code was known reading became automatic, the simultaneous access to the mind of signal and 'content', that magical process whereby ideas shone through marks on paper to enter the skull through the windows of the eyes. But modernism makes reading difficult in another sense, not to find the code or to grasp the ideas, the 'content', but to make the process of decoding itself difficult, so that to read is to work. Reading becomes problematic; the 'content' is not attached to the signal (so closely attached as to be inseparable from it) by any bond; it is deliberately, so to speak, detached, held in suspension, so that the reader has to play his own part in its production. And, at the same time, the text, through imposing this practice of reading, disrupts the myth of the reader's own receptive consciousness. No longer an empty treasure house waiting to receive its treasure, the mind becomes productive. It works. Just as the author no longer 'finds' the words, but must 'produce' a text, so the reader too must work within the text. The old image of the reader as consumer is broken.

The text is thus no longer a transparent medium; it is a material object which provides the conditions for the production of meaning, within constraints which it sets itself. It is open rather than closed; multiple rather than single; productive rather than exhaustive. Although it is produced by an individual, the author, it does not simply represent or express the author's ideas, but exists in its own right. It is not an instrument of communication but a challenge to the mystification that communication can exist. For interpersonal communication, it substitutes the idea of collective production; writer and reader are indifferently critics of the text and it is through their collaboration that meanings are collectively produced. At the same time, these 'meanings' have effects; just as the text, by introducing its own decoding procedures, interrogates itself, so the reader too must interrogate himself, puncture the bubble of his consciousness and introduce into it the rifts, contradictions and questions which are the problematic of the text.

The text then becomes the location of thought, rather than the mind. The text is the factory where thought is at work, rather than the transport system which conveys the finished product. Hence the danger of the myths of clarity and transparency and of the receptive mind; they present thought as prepackaged, available, given, from the point of view of the consumer. Whereas the producer of thought is then envisaged as the traditional philosopher, whose thought is the function of a pure consciousness, pure mental activity, externalised for others only when completed. It is to preserve this myth that notebooks and drafts are so rigidly separated from final versions, so that the process of thought as a dialectic of writing and reading (in the case even of 'individual' thought, as a dialogue with oneself) is obscured and is presented as an internal affair made public only when finished. In addition, drafts and notes, when they are made public, are seen as the raw material, itself still partly inchoate and incoherent, out of which the final, coherent version is fashioned. Thus incompatible elements have to be made compatible, and it is this general compatibility and consequentiality which marks the completion of a work. Within a modernist view, however, all work is work in progress, the circle is never closed. Incompatible elements in a text should not be ironed out but confronted.

This is the context in which Godard's films should be seen. Godard's work represents a continual examination and re-examination of the premises of film-making accepted by film-maker and by spectator. It is not simply a question of the juxtaposition of different styles or of different 'points of view', but of the systematic challenging of the assumptions underlying the adoption of a style or a point of view. In Godard's earliest films the narrative and dramatic structure is taken for granted, but the characters in the films question each other about the codes they use, about the sources of misunderstanding and incomprehension. Then, as his career continued, be began more and more to question, not the interpersonal communication of the characters, but the communication represented by the film itself. Finally he began to conceive of making a film, not as communicating at all, but as producing a text in which the problems of film-making were themselves raised. This is as political an aspect of Godard's cinema as the overtly political debate and quotation which also take place in it. For it is precisely by making things 'difficult' for the spectator in this way, by breaking up the flow of his films, that Godard compels the spectator to question himself about how he looks at films, whether as a passive consumer and judge outside the work, accepting the code chosen by the director, or whether within the work as a participant in a dialogue.

Godard's work is particularly important for the cinema, because there, more perhaps than in any other art-form, semiological mystification is possible. This is because of the predominantly indexical-iconic character of most films and the 'illusion of reality' which the cinema provides. The cinema seems to fulfil the age-old dream of providing a means of communication in which the signals employed are themselves identical or near-identical with the world which is the object of thought. Reality is, so to speak, filtered and abstracted in the mind, conceptualised, and then this conceptualisation of reality is mapped on to signals which reflect the original reality itself, in a way which words, for instance, can never hope to match. Thus the cinema is seen to give world-views in the literal sense of the term, world-conceptions which are literally world-pictures. The dross filtered out of the sensuous world by the process of abstraction and thought is restored in the process of communication. Hence the immense attraction of realist aesthetics for theorists of the cinema.

For realist aesthetics, the cinema is the privileged form which is able to provide both appearance and essence, both the actual look of the real world and its truth. The real world is returned to the spectator purified by its traverse through the mind of the artist, the visionary who both sees and shows. Non-realist aesthetics, as is pointed out elsewhere in this book, are accused of reducing or dehydrating the richness of reality; by seeking to make the cinema into a conventional medium they are robbing it of its potential as an alternative world, better, purer, truer, and so on. In fact, this aesthetic rests on a monstrous delusion: the idea that truth resides in the real world and can be picked out by a camera. Obviously, if this were the case, everybody would have access to the truth, since everybody lives all their life in the real world. The realism claim rests on a sleight-of-hand: the identification of authentic experience with truth. Truth has no meaning unless it has explanatory force, unless it is knowledge, a product of thought. Different people may experience the fact of poverty, but can attribute it to all kinds of different causes: the will of God, bad luck, natural dearth, capitalism. They all have a genuine experience of poverty, but what they know about it is completely different. It is the same with sunshine: everybody has experienced it but very few know anything scientifically about the sun. Realism is in fact, as it was historically, an outgrowth of Romanticism, typically Romantic in its distrust of or lack of interest in scientific knowledge.

Besides realism, the other main current in film theory has been the attempt to import into the cinema a traditional Romantic concept of the artist, the privileged individual with the faculty of imagination. Basically, the concept of imagination was the short-cut by which Romantic writers on aesthetics crammed the classical duality of thought plus expression, reason plus rhetoric, into one copious portmanteau. The imagination produced not concepts plus similes, but metaphors which fused concept and simile into a whole. Thus the artist in the cinema is able to produce visual metaphors, in which the act of thought and the act of filming are simultaneous and inseparable. This idea of the imaginative artist makes it possible to go beyond the old distinction of script-writer and director which divorced composition from execution. One of the problems that had always faced film aesthetics was how to get round this awkward division, which made it impossible to see a film as the creation of a single subjectivity. Gradually, in the acknowledged 'art' cinema first of all, the gap was bridged and the director was acknowledged to be the imaginative artist. A few critics, attached to the idea of the priority of the script-writer and of composition before execution, have held out against this trend, but not with much success. While it is possible to argue that the composer of a musical score envisages every note auditory or that the writer of a play has an idea of how it should be performed inherent in the text, because of the primacy of words in the bourgeois theatre, it is difficult to argue along similar lines about the script-writer.

At this point, it is necessary to say something about the *auteur* theory since this has often been seen as a way of introducing the idea of the creative personality into the Hollywood cinema. Indeed, it is true that many protagonists of the *auteur* theory do argue in this way. However, I do not hold this view and I think it is important to detach the *auteur* theory from any suspicion that it simply represents a 'cult of personality' or apotheosis of the director. To my mind, the *auteur* theory actually represents a radical break with the idea of an 'art' cinema, not the transplant of traditional ideas about 'art' into Hollywood. The 'art' cinema is rooted in the idea of creativity and the film as the expression of an individual vision. What the *auteur* theory argues is that any film, certainly a Hollywood film, is a network of different statements, crossing and contradicting each other, elaborated into a final 'coherent' version. Like a dream, the film the spectator sees is, so to speak, the 'film façade', the end-product of 'secondary revision', which hides and masks the process which remains latent in the film 'unconscious'. Sometimes this 'façade' is so worked over, so smoothed out, or else so clotted with disparate elements, that it is impossible to see beyond it, or rather to see anything in it except the characters, the dialogue, the plot, and so on. But in other cases, by a process of comparison with other films, it is possible to decipher, not a coherent message or world-view, but a structure which underlies the film and shapes it, gives it a certain pattern of energy cathexis. It is this structure which *auteur* analysis disengages from the film.

The structure is associated with a single director, an individual, not because he has played the role of artist, expressing himself or his own vision in the film, but because it is through the force of his preoccupations that an unconscious, unintended meaning can be decoded in the film, usually to the surprise of the individual involved. The film is not a communication, but an artefact which is unconsciously structured in a certain way. *Auteur* analysis does not consist of re-tracing a film to its origins, to its creative source. It consists of tracing a structure (not a message) within the work, which can then *post factum* be assigned to an individual, the director, on empirical grounds. It is wrong, in the name of a denial of the traditional idea of creative subjectivity, to deny any status to individuals at all. But Fuller or Hawks or Hitchcock, the directors, are quite separate from 'Fuller' or 'Hawks' or 'Hitchcock', the structures named after them, and should not be methodologically confused. There can be no doubt that the presence of a structure in the text can often be connected with the presence of a director on the set, but the situation in the cinema, where the director's primary task is often one of co-ordination and rationalisation, is very different from that in the other arts, where there is a much more direct relationship between artist and work. It is in this sense that it is possible to speak of a film *auteur* as an unconscious catalyst.

However, the structures discerned in the text are often attacked in another way. Robin Wood, for example, has argued that the '*auteur*' film is something like a Platonic Idea. It posits a 'real' film, of which the actual film is only a flawed transcript, while the archi-film itself exists only in the mind of the critic. This attack rests on a misunderstanding. The main point about the Platonic Idea is that it pre-dates the empirical reality, as an archetype. But the '*auteur*' film (or structure) is not an archi-film at all in this sense. It is an explanatory device which specifies partially how any individual film works. Some films it can say nothing or next-to-nothing about at all. *Auteur* theory cannot simply be applied indiscriminately. Nor does an *auteur* analysis exhaust what can be said about any single film. It does no more than provide one way of decoding a film, by specifying what its mechanics are at one level. There are other kinds of code which could be proposed, and whether they are of any value or not will have to be settled by reference to the text, to the films in question.

Underlying the anti-Platonic argument, however, there is often a hostility towards any kind of explanation which involves a degree of distancing from the 'lived experience' of watching the film itself. Yet clearly any kind of serious critical work—I would say scientific, though I know this drives some people into transports of rage—must involve a distance, a gap between the film and the criticism, the text and the meta-text. It is as though meteorologists were reproached for getting away from the 'lived experience' of walking in the rain or sun-bathing. Once again, we are back with the myth of transparency, the idea that the mark of a good film is that it conveys a rich meaning, an important truth, in a way which can be grasped immediately. If this is the case, then clearly all the critic has to do is to describe the experience of watching the film, reception of a signal, in such a way as to clear up any little confusions or enigmas which still remain. The most that the critic can do is to put the spectator on the right wavelength so that he can see for himself as clearly as the critic, who is already tuned in.

The *auteur* theory, as I conceive it, insists that the spectator has to work at reading the text. With some films this work is wasted, unproductive. But with others it is not. In these cases, in a certain sense, the film changes, it becomes another film—as far as experience of it is concerned. It is no longer possible to look at it 'with the same eyes'. There is no integral, genuine experience which the critic enjoys and which he tries to guide others towards. Above all, the critic's experience is not essentially grounded in or guaranteed by the essence of the film itself. The critic is not at the heart of the matter. The critic is someone who persists in learning to see the film differently and is able to specify the mechanisms which make this possible. This is not a question of 'reading in' or projecting the critic's own concerns in to the film; any reading of a film has to be justified by an explanation of how the film itself works to make this reading possible. Nor is it the single reading, the one which gives us the true meaning of the film; it is simply a reading which produces more meaning.

Again, it is necessary to insist that since there is no true, essential meaning there can therefore be no exhaustive criticism, which settles the interpretation of a film once and for all. Moreover, since the meaning is not contained integrally in any film, any decoding may not apply over the whole area of it. Traditional criticism is always seeking for the comprehensive code which will give the complete interpretation, covering every detail. This is a wild goose chase, in the cinema, above all, which is a collective form. Both Classical and Romantic aesthetics hold to the belief that every detail should have a meaning—Classical aesthetics because of its belief in a common, universal code;

Romantic aesthetics because of its belief in an organic unity in which every detail reflects the essence of the whole. The *auteur* theory argues that any single decoding has to compete, certainly in the cinema, with noise from signals coded differently. Beyond that, it is an illusion to think of any work as complete in itself, an isolated unity whose intercourse with other films, other texts, is carefully controlled to avoid contamination. Different codes may run across the frontiers of texts at liberty, meet and conflict within them. This is how language itself is structured, and the failure of linguistics, for instance, to deal with the problem of semantics, is exemplified in the idea that to the unitary code of grammar (the syntactic component of language) there must correspond a unitary semantic code, which would give a correct semantic interpretation of any sentence. Thus the idea of 'grammaticality' is wrongly extended to include a quite false notion of 'semanticity'. In fact, no headway can be made in semantics until this myth is dispelled.

The *auteur* theory has important implications for the problem of evaluation. Orthodox aesthetics sees the problem in predictable terms. The 'good' work is one which has both a rich meaning and a correspondingly complex form, wedded together in a unity (Romantic) or isomorphic with each other (Classical). Thus the critic, to demonstrate the value of a work, must be able to identify the 'content', establish its truth, profundity, and so forth, and then demonstrate how it is expressed with minimum loss or leakage in the signals of the text itself, which are patterned in a way which gives coherence to the work as a whole. 'Truth' of content is not envisaged as being like scientific truth, but more like 'human' truth, a distillation of the world of human experience, particularly inter-personal experience. The world itself is an untidy place, full of loose ends, but the artefact can tie all these loose ends together and thus convey to us a meaningful truth, an insight, which enables us to go back to the real world with a re-ordered and re-cycled experience which will enable us to cope better, live more fully and so on. In this way art is given a humanistic function, which guarantees its value.

All this is overthrown when we begin to see loose ends in works of art, to refuse to acknowledge organic unity or integral content. Moreover, we have to revise our whole idea of criteria, of judgement. The notion behind criteria is that they are timeless and universal. They are then applied to a particular work and it is judged accordingly. This rigid view is varied to the extent that different criteria may apply to different kinds of works or that slightly different criteria may reflect different points of view or kinds of experience, though all are rooted in a common humanity. But almost all current theories of evaluation depend on identifying the work first and then confronting it with criteria. The work is then criticised for falling short on one score or another. It is blemished in some way. Evidently, if we reject the idea of an exhaustive interpretation, we have to reject this kind of evaluation. Instead, we should concentrate on the *productivity* of the work. This is what the 'modern movement' is about. The text, in Octavio Paz's words, is something like a machine for producing meaning. Moreover, its meaning is not neutral, something to be simply absorbed by the consumer.

The meaning of texts can be destructive—of the codes used in other texts, which may be the codes used by the spectator or the reader, who thus finds his own habitual codes threatened, the battle opening up in his own reading. In one sense, everybody knows this. We know that *Don Quixote* was destructive of the chivalric romance. We know that *Ulysses* or *Finnegans Wake* are destructive of the nineteenth-century novel. But it seems difficult to admit this destructiveness into court when judgements are to be made. We have to. To go to the cinema, to read books or to listen to music is to be a partisan. Evaluation cannot be impartial. We cannot divorce the problem of codes from the problem of criteria. We cannot be passive consumers of films who then stand back to make judgements from above the fray. Judgements are made in the process of looking or reading. There is a sense in which to reject something as unintelligible is to make a judgement. It is to refuse to use a code. This may be right or wrong, but it is not the same thing as decoding a work before applying criteria. A valuable work, a powerful work at least, is one which challenges codes, overthrows established ways of reading or looking, not simply to establish new ones, but to compel an unending dialogue, not at random but productively.

This brings us back to Godard. The hostility felt towards Godard expresses precisely a reluctance to embark on this dialogue, a satisfaction with the cinema as it is. When, in *East Wind*, Godard criticises not only the work of other film-makers, but his own practice in the first part of the same film, he is at the same time asking us to criticise our own practice of watching his film. At the same time as he interrogates himself, we are interrogating ourselves. The place of his interrogation is the film, the text. This is not simply a question of self-consciousness. It is consciousness, first and foremost, of a text and the effect of this text is like the effect of an active intruder. It is this intrusion which sets up conflicts which cannot be settled by one (rational) part of consciousness surveying another part of its own past and then bringing it back into line. It is only natural that people should want to drive the intruder out, though it is difficult to see how a critic could justify this.

Godard represents the second wave of impact of the 'modern movement' on the cinema—the movement represented elsewhere by Duchamp, Joyce, and so on. During the twenties, Russian film-makers like Eisenstein and Vertov make up the first wave. It remains to be seen whether Godard will have any greater short-term effect than they had. But it is necessary to take a stand on this question and to take most seriously directors like Godard himself, Makavejev, Straub, Marker, Rocha, some underground directors. As I have suggested, they are not all doing the same thing, and it may be that a director like Makavejev is not really in the same camp as Godard at all. This remains to be seen. For this reason, I do not believe that development of *auteur* analyses of Hollywood films is any longer a first priority. This does not mean that the real advances of *auteur* criticism should not be defended and safeguarded. Nor does it mean that Hollywood should be dismissed out of hand as 'unwatchable'. Any theory of the cinema, any film-making must take Hollywood into account. It provides the dominant codes with which films are read and will continue to do so for the foreseeable future. No theorist, no *avant-garde* director can simply turn their back on Hollywood. It is only in confrontation with Hollywood that anything new can be produced. Moreover, while Hollywood is an implacable foe, it is not monolithic. It contains contradictions within itself, different kinds of conflicts and fissures. Hollywood cannot be smashed semiologically in a day, any more than it can economically. In this sense, there may be an aspect of 'adventurism' or Utopianism in Godard. There certainly is in a number of underground film-makers.

So, looking back over this book, I feel that its most valuable sections are those on Eisenstein and on semiology, even though I have now changed my views on the latter. I no longer think that the future of cinema simply lies in a full use of all available codes. I think codes should be confronted with each other, that films are texts which should be structured around contradictions of codes. The cinema had its origins in popular entertainment and this gave it great strength. It was able to resist the blandishments of traditional 'art'—novel, play, painting and so on. Nevertheless the period of the rise of Hollywood coincided in many respects with a move in Hollywood towards artistic respectability, personified for example by Irving Thalberg. This movement never really got beyond kitsch—Welles, who should have been its culmination, proved too much for it. At the same time, the popular side of Hollywood was never completely smothered by the cult of the Oscar and of fine film-making either. Now, for the second time—the first wave proved premature—the *avant-garde* has made itself felt in the cinema. Perhaps the fact that it is fighting mainly against Hollywood rather than against traditional 'art' will give it an advantage over the *avant-garde* in the other arts. It is possible that the transitional period we have now entered into could end with victories for the *avant-garde* which has emerged.

Booklist

Roland BARTHES, *Elements of Semiology*, Cape, London.
André BAZIN, *What is cinema*?, California, Los Angeles.
Robert J. CLEMENS, *Picta Poesis*, Edizioni di Storia e Letteratura, Rome.
Sergei M. EISENSTEIN, all his works, especially *Film Form* and *The Film Sense*, Faber, London.
Victor ERLICH, *Russian Formalism*, Mouton, Hague.
Sigmund FREUD, all his works, especially *The Interpretation of Dreams*, Hogarth, London.

Jean-Luc GODARD, *Godard on Godard*, Secker & Warburg, London; Viking Press, New York. Also the scripts of his films.

Peter GRAHAM (ed.), *The New Wave*, Secker & Warburg, London; Doubleday, New York.

Stephen HEATH, Colin MACCABE and Christopher PRENDERGAST (ed.), *Signs of the Times. Introductory Readings in Textual Semiotics*, Granta, Cambridge.

Göran HERMEREN, *Representation and Meaning in the Visual Arts*, Scandinavian University Books, Lund.

Roman JAKOBSON, various writings, especially 'The Metaphoric and Metonymic Poles' in *Fundamentals of Language*, Mouton, Hague; 'In Search of the Essence of Language' in *Diogenes* 51, Casalini, Montreal; 'Linguistics and Poetics' in *Style in Language* (ed. Sebeok), MIT, Boston.

Michael LANE (ed.), *Structuralism: a reader*, Cape, London.

L. T. LEMON and M. J. REIS (ed.), *Russian Formalist Criticism*, Nebraska, Lincoln.

Claude LEVI-STRAUSS, various writings, especially 'The Structural Study of Myth' in *Myth: a symposium* (ed. Sebeok), Indiana, Bloomington, and 'The Story of Asdiwal' in *The Structural Study of Myth and Totemism*, Tavistock, London.

Richard MACKSEY and Eugenio DONATO (ed.), *The Languages of Criticism and the Sciences of Man: the Structuralist Controversy*, Johns Hopkins, Baltimore.

Christian METZ, *Essais sur la signification au cinéma*, Klincksieck, Paris, shortly to be published in English and *Langage et cinéma*, Larousse, Paris.

Erwin PANOVSKY, various writings, especially 'Style and Medium in the Moving Pictures' in *Film: an Anthology* (ed. Talbot), California, Los Angeles.

Pier-Paolo PASOLINI, *Pasolini on Pasolini* (ed. Stack), Secker & Warburg, London; Indiana University Press, Bloomington, Ind.

C. S. PEIRCE, 'Speculative Grammar', 'Letters to Lady Welby' and 'Existential Graphs' in *Collected Papers*, Harvard, Boston.

Vladimir PROPP, *Morphology of the Russian Folktale*, Indiana, Bloomington.

Ferdinand de SAUSSURE, *Course in General Linguistics*, Peter Owen, London.

Josef von STERNBERG, *Fun in a Chinese Laundry*, Secker & Warburg, London; Macmillan, New York.

Andrew TUDOR, *Theories of Film*, Secker & Warburg, London; Viking Press, New York.

Peter WOLLEN (ed.), *Sociology and Semiology: Working Papers on the Cinema*, BFI, London.

A number of magazines are also of interest. See especially *Semiotica*, Mouton, Hague; *Screen*, SEFT, London; *Afterimage*, Narcis, London. *20th Century Studies* 3, Kent, Canterbury, is a special number on 'Structuralism'. The French review *Communications*, CECMAS, Paris, is invaluable, as are *Cahiers du Cinéma*, Paris, and *Cinéthique*, Paris.

30

FICTION OF THE AUTHOR/ AUTHOR OF THE FICTION

John Caughie

Source: John Caughie, ed., *Theories of Authorship: A Reader*, London: Routledge & Kegan Paul in association with the British Film Institute, 1981, pp. 199–207.

The text is a fetish object, and *this fetish desires me*. The text chooses me, by a whole disposition of invisible screens, selective baffles: vocabulary, references, readability, etc.; and, lost in the midst of a text (not *behind* it, like a *deus ex machina*) there is always the other, the author.

As institution, the author is dead, his civil status, his biographical person have disappeared; dispossessed, they no longer exercise over his work the formidable paternity whose account literary history, teaching, and public opinion had the responsibility of establishing and renewing; but in the text, in a way, *I desire* the author: I need his figure (which is neither his representation nor his projection), as he needs mine (except when 'prattling'[1]).

Roland Barthes[2]

Then perhaps the subject returns, not as illusion, but as *fiction*. A certain pleasure is derived from a way of imagining oneself as *individual*, of inventing a final rarest fiction: the fictive identity.

Roland Barthes[3]

So the subject of the statement should not be regarded as identical with the author of the formulation – either in substance, or in function. He is not in fact the cause, origin, or starting-point of the phenomenon of the written or spoken articulation of a sentence; nor is it that meaningful intention which, silently anticipating words, orders them like the visible body of its intuition; it is not the constant, motionless, unchanging focus of a series of operations that are

> manifested, in turn, on the surface of discourse through the statements. It is a particular vacant place that may in fact be filled by different individuals; but, instead of being defined once and for all, and maintaining itself as such throughout a text, a book, or an *oeuvre*, this place varies – or rather it is variable enough to be able either to persevere, unchanging, through several sentences, or to alter with each one. It is a dimension that characterizes a whole formulation *qua* statement. It is one of the characteristics proper to the enunciative function and enables one to describe it. If a proposition, a sentence, a group of signs can be called a 'statement', it is not therefore because, one day, someone happened to speak them or put them into some concrete form of writing; it is because the position of the subject can be assigned. To describe a formulation *qua* statement does not consist in analysing the relations between the author and what he says (or wanted to say, or said without wanting to); but in determining what position can and must be occupied by any individual if he is to be the subject of it.
>
> Michel Foucault[4]

> It seems to me . . . that the 'fiction' of the author enables us to locate an *author of the fiction* who is by no means dispersed but who in 'his' notional coherence provides the means for us to grasp the text in the moment of its production before us.
>
> Geoffrey Nowell-Smith[5]

The intervention of semiotics and psychoanalysis into the field of film theory has tended to shatter the unity of the author, scattering fragments over the whole terrain, calling into question the possibility of a theory of the author which is not also a theory of ideologies, of discourses, of commodities and, crucially, of the subject. If the *politique* and the theory of the *auteur* had seemed to hold out the promise of a coherency which would resolve the debate about authorship by explaining the role of the author as someone exterior and prior to the text, the present section is more concerned with how the text itself works, and with the author's place within a textual process which involves a shifting relationship with the spectator. The author, rather than standing behind the text as a source, becomes a term in the process of reading or spectating. At the same time, there is a reluctance to situate this new attention as a simple devaluation of the author (hence the hesitation implied by the title of this section). Rather, the attempt is to give the theory of authorship a context within a theory of textuality, of the subject, and of film as a discourse. There are two 'pulls' which have to be taken into account: on the one hand, there is 'John Ford', the author-function, the subject constituted in language; on the other hand, there is the insistence of the pleasure (and seduction) of the films identified by Ford's name and marked by his recognizable thematic and stylistic presence (we go to see John Ford movies). This section tries to hold the two pulls together.

At a certain level, it can seem that the shift within criticism and theory from the concept of the artist as a self-expressive personality to the concept of subject positions within the text is simply a strategy, a ploy to institute a materialist aesthetic, a decision by someone to replace an untidy humanism with the 'scientific' concept of an impersonal, non-individual subject. While it is true that the development of a theory of how subjects are constructed is closely bound up with developments in recent materialist and Marxist theory, it would nevertheless be wrong to see this as a simple voluntarist decision to re-adjust priorities. What a theory of the subject pursues is an account of the determinations and pressures which operate on individuals in terms of the places they come to occupy within the formations (social, textual, sexual, familial, discursive) which provide the sites of their activity. Such a theory is called for by the view that individuals are neither merely 'economic agents' nor simply 'free agents', but are formed as social, sexual, political subjects by a whole range of often contradictory discourses. Within film, a theory of the constructed spectating subject is called for by the quite generally held belief that film has ideological effects (that is to say, it positions its spectators as ideological subjects). But simply to produce a theory of the spectating subject is to suggest a stable, fixed relation, a one-way process in which the spectator is simply acted upon. What the conjunction of articles in this section is intended to suggest is the need for a theory of the subject of enunciation in film which involves an understanding of the shifting relation between enunciating subject and spectating subject, the subject of the enunciation being a position which can be occupied by either. Such a theory is in no way co-extensive with a theory of authorship; but, at the same time, such a theory cannot do without an understanding of the way in which the author-figure functions in the shifting relation. Much of the basis of this project was laid in work on language, and in the theorization (reinforced by Lacanian psychoanalysis) of the ways in which the subject was constituted within language.

The development of semiotics in France, principally in the writing of Barthes, Kristeva and the *Tel Quel* group,[6] offered a mode of analysis of signifying practices which was both precise and specific, opening itself, from its basis in Saussure's systematization of the sign, and his separation of the signifier and the signified,[7] to the specific operations by which literary language signified and was understood, and to the specificities of modes of signification other than spoken or written language. The introduction of semiotics to the analysis of film, broadly speaking, took two forms, which are at least methodologically separable. First, semiological work was concerned with the structures, codes and conventions by which film signified. The focus here was on the codes of narrative, it found its most developed form in the early work of Christian Metz,[8] and was inserted into

English-speaking film theory largely, and controversially, through a special issue of *Screen* in 1973.[9] When semiology is referred to casually it tends to be a reference to this area of work: work, that is, which was considerably marked by linguistic formalism (if that can be said without in any way dismissing the conjunctural and theoretical importance of the work).

Second (and in a sense necessarily – filling in the hole left by the formalism of a purely structural concentration), semiotics, as the science of specific signifying *practices*, was concerned with film as discourse; with the analysis, that is, of film not simply as a statement (something already formulated, 'given'), but also as an enunciating practice, an 'utterance' (something in process at the moment of projection). The distinction of 'statement' and 'enunciation' (product and producing activity) corresponds to the distinction in linguistics between *énoncé* and *énonciation*, which is elaborated here by Metz and Nowell-Smith in the context of Emile Benveniste's related distinction of *histoire* (history, story) and *discours* (discourse).[10] For such a distinction the functioning of the enunciating subject in the text is crucial: who is it who says 'I'? or what is the relationship of a concealed 'I' to the revealed 'he/she/it'? The position of the narrator, or the 'implied author' in the novel, and the relation of narrator to reader have been long-standing issues for literary theory.[11] For film, lacking the clearly marked 'persons' (first, second and third) which can indicate the terms of a novel's address, the issue is particularly difficult: how does a film say 'I', 'you', or 'dear reader'? The absence of those clear marks which Jakobson calls 'shifters',[12] which immediately show up the presence of someone speaking (the apparent absence in film of those incursions and digressions by the narrator, which, in the novel, continually play on our relation to the text), encourages the impression that film is simply narrative (the art of the story), offering a fixed and passive position to the spectator. The focus of a theory of authorship (almost, of narratorship) in this context becomes to retrace the marks of the enunciating subject, the marks which constitute the film as a discourse, an ideological address rather than 'just a story', and which determine the shifting positions and relations of the spectating subject within and to the text.

The distinction of discourse and story, or, in a way more appropriately, of discourse and history (the translation of '*histoire*' as 'history' being justified by the importance of the distinction between the 'presentness' of discourse and the 'pastness' of the story) is central to this section. It has to be insisted, though, that the distinction is not a mutual exclusion, with the text as either one or the other, but that it refers to two terms which continually jostle each other in the text, both, even, present at the same moment, the one masked by the other, or, more precisely, masquerading as the other. The object of the analysis is, in Metz's sense here of 'breaking open the toy to see how it works',[13] to open up the history to discover the terms of its discourse, to break the story as something which is already finished in order to discover the operation of its address and its relation to the spectator in the present. Metz's playful metaphor should not conceal the seriousness of such an analysis for an understanding of the production of ideology in films since it is precisely the masquerade of discourse in the form of story which allows the ideological and the historically specific to masquerade in the form of the natural and the everlasting. The film, since it is not 'authored', seems to proceed from nowhere, taking its 'truth' only from the 'real world'. The removal or suppression of the clear marks of 'authored discourse' transforms ideology from something produced out of a locatable, historical, determined position into something natural to the world. The strategies, techniques and rules of classical film-making are there to conceal construction and enunciation (invisible editing at natural points, eyeline match, camera movement justified by movement in the frame). The film seems to have an organic relation to the world: a story of what happened, rather than a discourse on it.

If on the contrary, we consider a film such as the Godard/Gorin *Letter to Jane*,[14] where the film is presented as an explicit discourse (precisely, a letter, addressed and signed), we find a text which not only admits an authorial position, but, more importantly, in the same moment renders itself problematic as ideology by constituting a subject outside the text (Jane Fonda, and, in her place, the spectator) who can object, forcing the spectating subject into a critical position ('critical' in every sense – the finding of a position in relation to what is being said becomes urgent). In the face of a discourse which *identifies itself*, which announces a subject of its enunciation, identification is made difficult, or impossible, for the spectator, and he/she is given a distance from the text. This is part of the strategy of Brecht, which is exemplified in didactic form in *Letter to Jane*.

Letter to Jane is an exceptional case, but a useful illustration. The contrary effect, in narrative, of the story's suppression of an authorial discourse is to leave a vacant space within the text, a vacant subject position into which the spectator can fall, identifying with (that is to say, finding his/her identity in) the coherent world of the fiction and its characters. In the absence of an enunciating subject the spectator becomes the subject of the enunciation, giving it its coherence.

But this only begins the question. What is frequently left insufficiently explicit is the extent to which films are not frozen as *either* discourse *or* history, but move continually between the two, filling and emptying the subject positions with enunciating subjects and spectating subjects, the spectators continually moving in and out of identification with the fictive world. More precisely, what is left inexplicit is the extent to which this movement of positions is not the exclusive privilege of the Brechtian film which has learned the lessons of distanciation, but is a movement characteristic also of classic narrative; the extent, that is, to which this movement in and out of the fictional space is involved as much in the pleasure of the text as in its disruption. Attention to film as a text has, perhaps, produced a lack of attention to film as a performance.

In a sense, performance is always an enunciation, and in so far as film is both a text and a performance of a text it can be seen as moving between statement and enunciation, activating a play of subjectivity. In those sequences of a film where the story seems to be suspended in a moment of pure performance, of visual delight, of an excess of style, one is aware of nothing so much as of spectating, of looking on. Think of Ophuls, or Sternberg, or Minnelli. There is an admiration of skill. In those moments, equally, where the film finds an image which contains and represents its dramas and its tensions, we are aware of being spoken to, of having things made clear. Geoffrey Nowell-Smith refers to the moment in *All That Heaven Allows* when Jane Wyman finds herself reflected back in the blank screen of her new television set. We are being addressed in the discourse of the film; we are aware of ourselves as spectators at a performance; the conception of a perpetually passive spectator, his/her identity helplessly given over to the unfolding of the story, has to be qualified.

This is not at all to say that such moments of enunciative performance constitute their films as in some way 'Brechtian'. Where the interruptions of the Brechtian performance work as dislocations, a discourse never entirely recuperated into the story, the play of subjectivity in the classic narrative is a play of relocations, most typically intensifying our pleasure in a moment of admiration and delight in performance. The argument which I am conducting here is with the view which sees the 'classic realist text' as a stability of subject positions from which enunciation can be discovered only by force. Such a view can understand the incursion of the enunciative instance into the smooth flow of the history only as a moment of 'disturbance' or 'threat' to the narrative, a break in the continuity of the spectator's identification, a crack in the coherence of the fictive world. Given enough cracks in the representation of the bourgeois world, the text is reconstituted for progressive criticism as radical. While stylistic excess can be disruptive, there is a danger of neglecting the ways in which disruptions are recuperated, and the extent to which performance and the play of positions which it involves is pleasurable.

Within this concept of the film as performance, the figure of the author seems to function in a complex but important way. It seems frequently to be the recognition of the marks of a supposed (or real) author which allows the spectator, in a moment of admiration (or, indeed, in an awareness of clumsiness), to give up his/her position within the fiction without losing possession of it. I admire (or criticize) from outside the fiction. The moment of admiration, in a sense, is one of dispossession. Paradoxically, by identifying with the fiction, by accepting the subject position which it gives me, by agreeing to forget my individual separateness in favour of the identity which the film has constructed for me, I seem to possess the film: it shows me what I want to see, it is my fantasy, I am at its centre, in the position of the subject. But in the moment of performance and admiration, someone else is performing the film: I am dislodged from the centre, a looker-on, and my pure possession of the film is challenged. This dispossession, however, is not experienced as a loss of pleasure, because it is accompanied by a recognition – a recognition of the figure of the author which I construct precisely to fill the subject position of the film's performance. The appearance of this new subject of the enunciation establishes me outside the fiction, but still within the textual space, still within a certain possession of the film (the performance is for me), and, where the performance is expert or familiar, my pleasure is intensified from a new position. In those films where the director does not operate as a recognizable figure, the 'performer' is as likely to be identified as the actor, the designer, or simply the film itself. In those films, on the other hand, where the director has a 'signature', my admiration and my pleasure is focused on the recognition of the author, whom I place, at least momentarily, as subject of the film's discourse. It's in this way that the presence or absence (presence *and* absence) of the marks of the enunciative authorial figure activates the play of subject positions.

Not to acknowledge the functioning of this recognition and the position which can be given to the author-figure in the film's performance is to leave out of account part of the movement of our pleasure and to leave a gap in any theory of subjectivity in the cinema. This question overlaps with questions of ideology. What is the relation between film's production of ideology and its production of pleasurable recognition? Given that I am a social subject with a very different ideological formation from John Ford, what is the relation between my pleasure (and emotional involvement) in Ford's films (in the scene, say, of John Wayne's retiral from the army in *She Wore a Yellow Ribbon*), and my recognition of the marks of a Fordian discourse? Where a film is so authored (and few are) it seems more important to account for the seductiveness of its pleasure than to deny that that pleasure had something to do with John Ford, the *auteur*.

Equally, in our reading of the film and in our construction of its sense, it seems clear that there are indeed continuities and consistencies in the films of certain directors, and that an awareness of these in the films in general comes into play as we watch a film in particular. While it is true that, as a critical term, the author is a figure constructed out of his films, and while it can be argued that he does not have an existence prior to those films, it does not follow that the figure does not have an existence prior to each individual film. In a sense, the continuities and consistencies which can be recognized in, and which identify, an authorial code or sub-code constitute another text which has to be read into the single film, determining our expectations and recognitions, breaking the pure self-containment of the singular, autonomous text, producing a kind of authorial intertextuality,[15] one text finding its meaning and effect in its relation to other texts. We are left happily conceding certain assumptions of *auteurism* – that there are consistencies – but instead of celebrating them as demonstrations of creativity, or finding in them the expression and values of a personality, we return them to the question of discourse, of how they produce an authorial subject for the discourse, and of how that production relates to the production, positioning and continual repositioning of spectating subjects.

The recognition of intertextuality is important. We are no longer dealing with a pure text which inhabits a 'noiseless' space, containing all its meanings and effects within its own edges, or with an ideal spectator who comes to the text innocently, cleansed of the contagion of other films and other practices. The crack in the singular text's self-containment is opened wider by questions of subjects other than the purely textual subject – social subjects, sexual subjects, historical subjects – subjects who are constituted in a plurality of discourses (in an intertextuality of other texts) of which the single text is only one moment. For authorship, just as the ideal spectator existing outside history and sociality is an illusory figure, so also the ideal author, existing only inside the text, will have to be questioned. Both of these figments have allowed theory to confront some problems by side-stepping others; but it is becoming increasingly clear that those other problems are now pressing. Feminist criticism, in particular, has to question the priorities which allowed the ideal author to be removed from sexuality, separated from a sexual look. This question is raised here by Sandy Flitterman;[16] and in his essay on Bresson, Oudart raises the question of the traces of the director's desire and its repression, and of his status as a social subject producing his discourse within and for a specific social group. Such questions are important if theory is to be related to different and specific practices, rather than to a monolithically conceived 'Cinema', and they are crucial for the understanding and development of alternative practices with different terms of address. Theory and analysis which remains within a pure semiotics, while it offers a theorization of the negotiation of subject positions within the textual process, and while it produces a rhetoric of the textual disposition, nevertheless finds it difficult to escape formalism. It's precisely this limitation which produces the need for semiotics (theory of the textual subject) to be joined with psychoanalysis (theory of the sexual, specular, divided subject) and historical materialism (theory of the social, political, historical subject, and the economic subject of exchange).

The author, then, both as a possible subject of the enunciation and as a sexual, social, historical subject, does indeed have a place within theory. The insistence on holding together the notion of the author as a subject position constructed in the film's performance, the notion of the authorial code as another text determining our reading and our recognition and the notion of the author as a subject of other practices and formations – that is to say, 'the fiction of the author' and 'the author of the fiction' – is precisely to break the autonomous coherence of each: to break the coherence of the text as a pure 'inside' (producing itself, for an empty spectator, out of its own internal operations), or as a pure 'outside' (given by an originating source), and to attempt to formulate the text, and its subjects, as a movement between the two, or as the involvement of the one in the other, destroying the purity of each.

Notes

1 '*Sauf à "babiller"*', 'except to "prattle"': I have altered the translation a little: Barthes has earlier referred to the 'prattle' of a text which is boring, which only satisfies the writer's desire to write, but carries no satisfaction for the reader.
2 Roland Barthes, *The Pleasure of the Text* (1973) (trans. R. Miller), New York, Hill & Wang, 1975, p. 27.
3 ibid., p. 62.
4 Michel Foucault, *The Archaeology of Knowledge* (1969) (trans. Sheridan Smith), London, Tavistock, 1972, pp. 95–6.
5 Geoffrey Nowell-Smith, 'Six authors in pursuit of *The Searchers*', see below, p. 223.
6 There is a useful introduction to the work of this group in Rosalind Coward and John Ellis, *Language and Materialism*, London, Routledge & Kegan Paul, 1977. The work is also represented in a collection of essays, *Théorie d'ensemble*, Paris, Editions du Seuil (collection *Tel Quel*), 1968.
7 See Appendix I, 'Notes on terms'.
8 Christian Metz, *Film Language*, New York/London, Oxford University Press, 1974; and *Language and Cinema*, Paris/The Hague, Mouton, 1974.
9 Double issue, 'Cinema semiotics and the work of Christian Metz', *Screen*, vol. 14, nos 1–2, Spring–Summer 1973; to be reprinted in *Screen Reader 2*.
10 Emile Benveniste, *Problems of General Linguistics*, Coral Gables, Florida, University of Miami Press, 1971; see also Appendix I, 'Notes on terms'.
11 Discussed particularly in Wayne Booth, *The Rhetoric of Fiction*, Chicago/London, University of Chicago Press, 1961; and in Gérard Genette, *Figures III*, Paris, Editions du Seuil, 1972.
12 See Appendix I, 'Notes on terms'.
13 Below, p. 227.
14 The film takes the form of a spoken letter, addressed to Jane Fonda, following her role in the Godard/Gorin *Tout va bien*. The 'writers' of the letter question the way in which the film star allows her image (specifically, a photograph of her talking to a group of Vietcong) to be appropriated by the media.
15 For Kristeva's use of the notion of intertextuality, see 'Problèmes de la structuration du texte', in *Théorie d'ensemble*, pp. 311 ff. See also Coward and Ellis, op. cit., pp. 52–3.
16 The question is also raised in Laura Mulvey, 'Visual pleasure and narrative cinema', *Screen*, vol. 16, no. 3, Autumn 1975, pp. 6–18; in Pam Cook and Claire Johnston, 'The place of women in the cinema of Raoul Walsh', in *Raoul Walsh*, ed. Phil Hardy, Edinburgh Film Festival, 1974, pp. 93–109; and in Constance Penley, 'The avant-garde and its imaginary', *Camera Obscura*, no. 2, Fall 1977.

31

AUTEURS AND THE NEW HOLLYWOOD

Timothy Corrigan

Source: Jon Lewis, ed., *The New American Cinema*, Durham, NC: Duke University Press, 1998, pp. 38–63.

As soon as you become that big, you get absorbed.

Francis Coppola

In the autumn of 1995 Quentin Tarantino celebrated his meteoric rise as Hollywood's latest artistic revolutionary with a guest-host appearance on "Saturday Night Live," a traditional television forum for cutting-edge personalities and entertainers. In one skit Tarantino played the host in a parody of a TV talk show called "Directors on Directing" in which he was joined by caricatures of some of Hollywood's other recent visionaries—Oliver Stone, Spike Lee, and Gus Van Sant. Despite such heady company, the discussion soon got to whether or not the directors sleep with the actresses in their films.

Alongside this somewhat lame parody of the American auteur today, the show featured a variety of other spoofs of Tarantino the auteur, including an episode of "This Is Your Life." In it, one guest recalled those critical formative days in the then 32-year-old director's life when Tarantino worked as a clerk in a video rental shop. On the one hand, the spotlighting of Tarantino here seems, if not premature, at least, for those of us who can associate this sort of personality probing of auteurs with Truffaut's famous conversations with Hitchcock, irreverently empty-headed. On the other hand, both the unabashed self-promotion of this appearance and its deliberate attempt to ironize Tarantino as auteur-celebrity tells us that if auteurism—as a description of movies being the artistic expression of a director—is still very much alive today, the artistic expression of contemporary directors is fully bound up with the celebrity industry of Hollywood.

Tarantino is in many ways the quintessential 1990s' American auteur. His stunning debut, *Reservoir Dogs* (1992), was considered by reviewers (and his legions of fans) to be no less than a reworking of the language of contemporary film. *Pulp Fiction* (1994), his following feature, succeeded in rearticulating the figures of violence, communication, and the ethics of (mostly male) relationship laid out in *Reservoir Dogs*. Indeed, almost mimicking his sudden auteurist celebrity status, Tarantino's characters are relentlessly caught in the strain of identity—too self-consciously, too theatrically, always too intently driven by what one character in *Pulp Fiction* calls "a moral test of oneself." Offscreen, Tarantino plays the same dangerous game with identity politics. He works with Miramax Films to spot, promote, and distribute marginal films,[1] directs for both television (where he shot an episode of *ER*, the TV show rated number one in 1997. He also has appeared in acting roles and cameos and in the mid-nineties was the subject of three biographies. In a brief span Tarantino has become, from one point of view, a confrontational individual succeeding in Hollywood despite an uncompromising trash-art vision, and, from another, a showman quickly cashing in on an image that may be gone tomorrow.

But, lest we become too cynical too quickly, let us keep this in mind: auteurs and theories and practices of auteurism have never been a consistent or stable way of talking about movies. When auteurs and auteuristic codes for understanding film spread from France to the United States and elsewhere in the sixties and seventies, these models were hardly the pure reincarnations (as critics sometimes urged us to believe) of literary notions of the author as the sole creator of the film or of Sartrean demands for "authenticity" in personal expression.[2] Rather, from its inception, auteurism has been bound up with changes in industrial desires, technological opportunities, and marketing strategies. In the United States, for instance, the industrial utility of auteurism from the late 1960s to the early 1970s had much to do with the waning of the American studio system and the subsequent need to find new ways to mark a movie other than with a studio's signature. One might likewise recognize the crucial contribution to auteurism made by the new social formation of movie audiences in the early sixties: the massive "teenaging" of audiences in Europe and America. In the late sixties the global encounter with traditional forms of authority on campuses and on the streets opened doors in academia to nontraditional disciplines like film studies, and this is turn helped create a crucial forum and platform for a new international art cinema identified with auteurs like Ingmar Bergman, Luis Buñuel, Michelangelo Antonioni, and Jean-Luc Godard, as well as American auteurs like Arthur Penn, Peter Bogdanovich, and Robert Altman.

Since the 1970s especially, the auteurist marketing of movies whose titles often proclaim the filmmaker's name, such as Michael Cimino's *Heaven's Gate* (1981) or Oliver Stone's *Nixon* (1995), aim to guarantee a relationship between audience and movie whereby an intentional and authorial agency governs, as a kind of brand-name vision whose aesthetic meanings and values have already been determined. This industrial model of auteurism (as a trademark of sorts) reverses the studio's attempt to regulate the way movies are seen and received. But, in contemporary film culture, such a project is fraught with all sorts of contradictions and obstacles.

Auteurs: from author to agent

One of the chief claims and mystifications within early theories and practices of auteurism has been a tendency to valorize one or another idea of expression, mostly disconnected from its marketing and commercial implications. Despite their large differences, theories and practices of auteurism from Alexandre Astruc and Peter Wollen to Michel Foucault and Stephen Heath, from John Ford to Jean-Luc Godard, share basic assumptions about the auteur as the voice or presence that accounts for how a film is organized.[3] These different positions might, for example, locate the auteur's presence and power in style or narrative consistencies and variations (such as in Peter Wollen's account of Howard Hawks's different but structurally consistent "male universes" in *To Have and Have Not* and *Bringing Up Baby*). Even when contemporary critics make claims for the irrelevance (and sometimes the figurative "death") of the actual author/auteur (as Roland Barthes outlines in "The Death of the Author"), the figure of the auteur/author remains an important construct, a principle of textual causality like genre or narrative which asks and insists that readers and audiences see the work as whole, complete, and beyond individual differences and inconsistencies.[4]

Auteurs in this sense fill in the gaps of understanding and misunderstanding. While David Lynch can proudly muse about his films (*Blue Velvet* and *Wild at Heart*), "I don't know what a lot of things mean," audiences, faced with the quirky opacities of his films, can both bond and transcend in the name of the auteur Lynch.[5] To view a film as the product of an auteur means to read it or respond to it as an expressive organization that precedes and forecloses the historical fragmentations and subjective distortions that can take over the reception of even the most classically coded movie. The often strained attempts to make consistent or evolutionary the British and American movies of Alfred Hitchcock or the German and Hollywood films of Fritz Lang, for example, are governed by some sense of a historically transsubjective and transcendent category—the auteur—which authorizes certain readings or understandings of specific movies. In David Bordwell's analysis of auteurism as an interpretative cue,

> the overt self-consciousness of the narration is often paralleled by an extratextual emphasis on the filmmaker as source. Within the art cinema's mode of production and reception, the concept of the author has a formal function it did not possess in the Hollywood studio system. Film journalism and criticism promote authors, as do film festivals, retrospectives, and academic film study. Directors' statements of intent guide comprehension of the film, while a body

> of work linked by an authorial signature encourages viewers to read each film as a chapter of an oeuvre. . . . More broadly, the author becomes the real-world parallel to the narrational presence who communicates (what is the filmmaker saying?) and who expresses (what is the author's personal vision?).[6]

Formalist and cognitive critiques of auteurism, such as Bordwell's, can vanquish most of the myths of expressivity in the cinema in favor of more formal and heuristic uses for the auteur. Yet, these too do not fully attend to the survival—and, in fact, increasing importance—of the auteur as a commercial strategy.

What I want to argue here is that today, even recent corrections, discussions, or deconstructions of the romantic roots of auteurism need to be taken another step toward recontextualizing them within contemporary industrial and commercial trajectories. Illustrating this need to investigate how "the author is constructed by and for commerce," John Caughie has noted that this question has mostly been overlooked since Brecht's 1931 account of *The Threepenny Opera* trial in which Brecht "brilliantly exposes the contradiction in cinema between the commercial need to maintain the ideology of the creative artist and the simultaneous need to redefine ownership in terms of capital, rather than creative investment."[7]

Certainly, such a reappraisal of auteurism—as more than just a way to account for artistic expression in a film or a category for interpretation—could and should take any national film history and industry into consideration. The international and commercial imperatives of contemporary culture have made it clear that commerce is now much more than just a contending discourse. If, in conjunction with the so-called international art cinema of the sixties and seventies, the auteur had been absorbed as a phantom presence, he or she has rematerialized in the eighties and nineties as an agent of a commercial performance of the business of being an auteur. To follow this move in contemporary culture, the practices of auteurism now must be reexamined in terms of the wider material strategies of social agency. Seen as a cultural agent, the auteur must now be described according to the conditions of a cultural and commercial inter-subjectivity, a social interaction distinct from an intentional causality or textual transcendence.

Models of agency are useful here precisely because they are models of intersubjectivity that aim to undermine the metaphysics and the authority of expression and intention, the cornerstones of a stable subjectivity. They delineate a model of action in which both expression and reception are conditioned and monitored by reflective postures toward their material conditions.[8] In the cinema, auteurism as agency thus becomes a place for encountering not so much a transcending expression but the different conditions through which expressive meaning is made by an auteur and reconstructed by an audience, conditions that involve historical and cultural motivations and rationalizations. Here, even exasperating auteurs like Tarantino may strategically embrace the more promising possibilities of the auteur as a commercial presence, since the commercial status of that presence now necessarily becomes part of an agency that culturally and socially monitors identification and critical reception.

Celebrity auteurs and the business of movies

The practice of the auteur as a particular brand of social agency appears most clearly and most ironically in the contemporary status of the auteur as celebrity. This idea of the auteur-star vaguely harks back to earlier versions of auteurism that ranked directors, from Orson Welles to Robert Bresson, in aesthetic and intellectual pantheons fitting the distinctions of their films. Today, however, American auteurs are, often and largely, defined by their commercial status and their ability to promote a film, sometimes regardless of its distinction.[9] In a twist on the tradition of certain movies being vehicles for certain stars, the auteur-star can potentially carry and redeem any sort of textual material, often to the extent of making us forget that material through the marvel of its agency.[10] In this sense, promotional technology and production feats become the new "camera-stylo,"[11] serving a new auteurism in which the making of a movie, like Oliver Stone's *Nixon* (1995), or its unmaking, like Stone's *JFK* (1991), foreground an agency that preempts and forecloses the value of the film in and of itself. As Godard has parodied so incisively in films like *King Lear* (1987), in today's commerce we want to know what our authors and auteurs look like or how they act; it is the text and not its author that now may be dead.

At this point, Michael Cimino and his film *Heaven's Gate* (1980) become an ideal example of this new phenomenon, a director and "his" event dramatizing the major points and counterpoints that have defined celebrity auteurism and its place in American film culture in recent years. Partly as a result of the takeover of United Artists by Transamerica Corporation, both Cimino and *Heaven's Gate* sprang from the urgency, especially in Hollywood after 1970, to make blockbuster movies. In a particularly resonant transformation of United Artists history—the studio originating with independent artists such as Charles Chaplin and D. W. Griffith and traditionally associated with independent productions like *Last Tango in Paris* (1972)—Transamerica decided that the studio should adjust to its parent company's financial logic and, in keeping with the economic potential that spurred the takeover, Transamerica urged the pursuit of blockbuster films and audiences. *Heaven's Gate* was to be one of the newly reorganized studio's grandest efforts.

In this particular case, Transamerica-United Artists recruited Cimino and in doing so anointed him as an auteur-artist: part epic genius and part promotional commodity. Perhaps because he was, paradoxically, a relatively unknown quantity with a background, significantly, in advertising, Cimino became the conglomerate image of the blockbuster auteur solely on the basis of the massive *potential* of his Vietnam film, *The Deer Hunter* (1978)—which many of the studio executives had not yet seen.

United Artists signed Cimino to the *Heaven's Gate* deal for a $7.8 million projected cost and gave him almost unprecedented directorial freedom. As is commonly reported, the budget ultimately exceeded $40 million, and the film became one of the most notorious financial and (undeservedly perhaps) critical disappointments in movie history. Just as the studio attempted to produce or exploit a new celebrity auteur, the film ultimately appealed to no one because of its blockbuster goal of appealing to everyone. At least as an indirect result, Kirk Kerkorian's MGM would purchase United Artists; this merger, in turn, would founder, and the studio would next end up in the hands of Giancarlo Parretti and Pathé Communications and then, following foreclosure, a French bank, Crédit Lyonnais. A telling by-product of these conglomerate quick changes would be the formation of a more specialized major studio, Orion, by a number of UA executives who moved out and reorganized in the wake of Transamerica's new agendas.

In the almost universal bashings that the film suffered, Cimino would become the scapegoat for "auteurism-out-of-control." Yet, in the end, the image of the auteur would survive the conglomerate formulas of the new Hollywood through the home video market; there, the film would be reissued in the form of a "director's cut," and it would return rental figures sufficient to make it a financial success. Both Cimino and *Heaven's Gate* would act out the often repeated contemporary formula of redemption through the extended market of home video where the making of successful movies and identifiable auteurs falls outside the promotional formulas of the studios and the critical pronouncements of the Establishment.[12]

Cimino's case and this particular episode are not, I want to argue, an eccentric or isolated event in modern American film history, but rather they form a central image and metaphor for what distinguishes film culture today. To clarify these historical and cultural contours and how they shape the contemporary auteur, I plan to use the example of Cimino to identify three related shifts in current film culture: (1) the blockbuster productions of the conglomerate studios, (2) the alternative films of Hollywood's mini-majors (like Orion), and (3) the importance of VCR technology in sustaining both kinds of moviemaking. Needless to say, other forces are at work in contemporary movie culture, but these three seem to me to shed the most light on the peculiar power and look of today's auteur.

The historical transition point for these industrial, sociological, and aesthetic changes within movie culture is the late 1960s, when the impending birth of the contemporary blockbuster would appear to encourage (almost in a contradictory fashion) the invasion of VCRS, satellite dishes, and cable networks. Although the movie industry had been moving in this direction since 1946,[13] the economics had operated, up to this point, according to the fairly lucid logic of profitable investment: a successful movie invests efficient and controllable resources such as actors, technicians, and a director to meet the demands and desires of a hopefully predictable and relatively stable audience. During the period after 1965, however, that logic lost much of its antiquated clarity as the industry moved full force into an age of inflation and conglomeration. The most dramatic indicators of this shift are the acquisition of the major studios by multinational corporations attracted by growing movie profits. Universal was taken over by MCA (1962), Paramount by Gulf & Western (1966), United Artists by Transamerica Corporation (1967), Warner Bros. by Kinney National Services (1969), and MGM by Las Vegas businessman Kirk Kerkorian (1969).

The general consequences of these new production structures follow from their economic attractions. Responding to the inflation of costs—such as those caused by the new computer and laser technologies, better-organized union labor, and hugely inflated star salaries, a Marlon Brando or Jack Nicholson could command more than $5 million for a film in the early 1970s; Sylvester Stallone commanded $20 million per film in 1997—the corporate conglomerates became simply the next, and perhaps necessary, step in the economic expansion of the studios. Within this conglomerate structure, however, the movie industry became one of many products, albeit one with the special attraction of offering the extremely large and relatively fast turnovers that blockbuster movies like *The Godfather* (1972) or *Jaws* (1975) or *Batman* (1989) could provide. Despite failures and nods to other kinds of movies, this blockbuster vision—which during the early stages of film history was something between the exception and the accident that *The Birth of a Nation* was in 1915—would decisively guide the American movie industry through and beyond the seventies. While in the 1960s, only five American movies made profits of at least $40 million, four movies would make that much in 1979 alone (*Superman, Every Which Way But Loose, Rocky II*, and *Alien*). According to the revised logic of Hollywood economics, a movie attracts audiences through the excess of its investment in capital and technology; even a high-priced auteur, manufactured or real, might be justified and recuperated by an enormous payback. In the late 1970s the conglomerates had every reason to be encouraged. The value of George Lucas's *Star Wars*, for example, could be understood empirically. Some $27 million was invested in 1977 ($11 million of it in the shooting budget), and well over $500 million in revenues were generated by 1980—a 1,855 percent profit in three years.

As investments grew astronomically, the studios did much more than simply increase the size of the stakes that once were invested in film stars in the 1940s, 3-D technology in the fifties, or the productions of artistically acclaimed directors in the early sixties. The studios transformed the fundamental nature of the film product by forcing massive alternations in the relation of a film to an audience, since to return those massive investments meant appealing to and aiming at not just the largest possible audience (the more modest strategy of classical films or the alternative art-house audiences of early auteur film culture) but *all* audiences. No longer is investment capital directed at differentiating one audience, however dominant, from another. Instead, those investments must aim to "undifferentiate" the character and desires of different audiences, usually by emphasizing the importance of that investment as a universal value in and of itself—for example, the presence and use of computer animation or of an expensive star or director. With blockbusters, what begins as an attempt to target the teenage audience quickly becomes an attempt to absorb as many other groups as possible within that mass; it becomes the only methodology that makes sense to a conglomerate's bottom line. Contemporary movie culture thus necessarily aligns itself with advertising, not only as a method to abate costs (by advertising other people's products on the screen: cars, soft drinks, and so on), but because blockbuster movies can themselves succeed only as an advertisement of a product that, in appealing to everyone, can never possibly satisfy an audience of different individuals.

The deleterious effects of this conglomerate and blockbuster perspective have all too often been remarked upon.[14] The most obvious result of this new corporate mind-set is the postmodern "high-concept film," a clear offshoot of the blockbuster phenomenon of the 1970s. Justin Wyatt and R. L. Rutsky argue that high-concept movies like *Top Gun* (1986) and *9½ Weeks* (1986) rely "less on a well-developed story and characters than on a big-name star, a commercial musical score, and high visual impact." High-concept movies, from *Saturday Night Fever* (1978) to *Rambo III* (1988), become advertisements that can be abstracted to easily assimilable images and regenerated through multiple viewings and the ancillary sales of various tie-ins (records, T-shirts, and other paraphernalia). "In a postmodern world," this position contends, "high concept is the 'rational' conclusion of those processes of capitalism which tend toward the abstraction and fetishization of the image, and to the increasingly rapid movements of fashion and style."[15] Not surprisingly, one of the most effective and common high-concept strategies today is the use of the name of the deserving or undeserving director/auteur as a foregrounded and often bombastic piece of advertisement. Not surprisingly, three of Hollywood's most successful auteurs in the seventies and eighties were Michael Cimino, Adrian Lyne, and Ridley Scott, all with backgrounds in the advertising business.

Contemporary film culture is not, however, a single story. Indeed, directly related to grandiose visions and projects of the conglomerate blockbuster are the more idiosyncratic, modest, and riskier movies produced by semi-independent companies or mini-majors such as Orion and TriStar. An immediate consequence of the corporate studio system that alienated and often cut loose former studio executives (such as Arthur Krim's departure from United Artists to form Orion), these groups represent smaller enterprises than both the conglomerates and, in many cases, the studios that existed before the takeovers. Many of these satellites are refashioned production houses that, because of more circumscribed ambitions, have been more able and willing to take risks (significantly in TriStar's case because of a financial arrangement with the HBO cable network). Others such as Robert Redford's Sundance Institute, whose successes include *The Milagro Beanfield War* (1988), Miramax Films with *sex, lies, and videotape* (1989),[16] or Avenue Pictures with *Drugstore Cowboy* (1989) have positioned themselves as alternatives to the blockbuster mentality. Offering purportedly more serious, "specialized" movies, these companies often produce films for well under the average price of a usual studio production, raise their funds by putting together packages from a variety of investors, and then make deals to have studios distribute their finished products. But just as the origin and success of these companies remains bound to the aspirations and limitations of the conglomerates, successful auteurs found here will relocate there tomorrow.

The third shift in this movie culture and one that in many ways is the linchpin between the first two is VCR technology (and other viewer-oriented, home box-office technologies such as cable and satellite dishes). These, I believe, have changed the nature and structure of the film industry as few other technologies have ever even approximated, reshuffling both classical and modernist relations between filmmaker and film audience, creating viewer-movie relations as impulsive and contingent as the contemporary production process. By January 1995, 81 percent of U.S. homes had VCRS capable of showing movies on videocassette. About two-thirds of U.S. households subscribed to basic cable TV service, while one out of three take pay cable (which includes such film channels as Cinemax, HBO, The Movie Channel, and Showtime). According to the Associated Press, there are 27,000 video rental stores in business, many of which have more than 30,000 "theatrical/entertainment" titles available. As it continues to permeate all cultures, this spectator-oriented technology becomes the bridge between the two dominant trends of corporate and semi-independent production, as well as the many films that might straddle the middle ground between blockbusters and specialty films. Both small and large movies now figure on advances and expectations from video sales and rentals; the lag time between a commercial theatrical release and its video reappearance decreases every year. The ability of a movie, even the most marginal, to find an audience or audiences—however large or small, discriminating or not—becomes a bankable likelihood. If the conglomerate blockbusters might be said to have created an empty advertisement at the center of contemporary film culture, this dispersal of movies through VCR technology has de-authorized them by opening up, according to more individualistic and private patterns, the possibilities of what is seen and how it is seen.

"Shareability" becomes a technological and economic imperative, as well as a textual, production, and financial strategy for addressing audiences outside the walls of traditional theatrical cinema and outside its traditional ways of viewing and making meaning of the movies. If auteurism was one of those traditional ways, it is no wonder that the most celebrated American auteur in the mid-1990s, Quentin Tarantino, received a good part of his training in a video rental shop where hierarchies are (potentially) always in question.

If in this new film/video culture, auteurs have been recuperated as promotional stars, the process is fairly indiscriminate. Placed before, after, and outside a film, and in effect usurping the work of that film and its reception, today's auteurs—from Spielberg to Tarantino—are agents who, whether they wish it or not, are always on the verge of being self-consumed by their status as stars. I am not suggesting merely some brand of egotism or self-marketing posture. Instead, institutional and commercial agencies now work, whatever the filmmaker's intentions, to define auteurism as publicity and advertisement or as the dispersal of the control of the auteur into the total flow of television monitors. A large part of auteurism has become, that is, both a provocative and empty display of material surface, subject to almost indiscriminate circulation, befuddling those more traditional auteurist relations based on models of writer/text/reader. Meaghan Morris has noted (in language similar to Richard Dyer's description of on-screen stars) that today "the primary modes of film and auteur packaging are advertising, review snippeting, trailers, magazine profiles—always already in appropriation as the precondition, and not the postproduction of meaning."[17]

To respond to a movie as primarily or merely a Spielberg film, for example, is, after all, the pleasure of refusing an evaluative relation to it—a tendency that he interestingly has tried to reverse with his mimicking of a European art film, *Schindler's List* (1993). Much of that pleasure lies in being able to already know, not read, the meaning of the film as a product of the public image of its creator. An auteur film today seems to aspire more and more to a critical tautology, capable of being understood and consumed without being seen. Like an Andy Warhol movie, it can communicate a great deal for a large number of audiences who know the maker's reputation but have never seen the films themselves.

Of the several tacks within the commerce of the auteur-star, let me isolate two broad, central, and ultimately interactive groupings: the commercial auteur and the auteur of commerce. The first category could include a vast range of stars who also direct (Mel Gibson, Jodie Foster, Robert Redford, Kevin Costner, and Clint Eastwood), as well as star directors like Steven Spielberg, George Lucas, Brian De Palma, and, with different agendas and at different periods in their careers, John Sayles and Woody Allen. My argument so far would assimilate most of these names since what defines this group is a recognition, either foisted upon them or chosen by them, that the celebrity of their agency produces and promotes a text that invariably exceeds the movie itself, both before and after its release. That this category seems not to distinguish between actors and directors as controlling agents is telling since the commercial auteur is far more a product of the magnitude of the image that anchors a movie or group of movies than a text of ideas, styles, or nuances of expression.

With the commercial auteur, the Hollywood agent becomes essential to and emblematic of the mix. Movies are often created by the packaging of one or more dominant images (such as Dustin Hoffman, Robin Williams, Julia Roberts, and Steven Spielberg for *Hook*). One of the ironies here is that Michael Ovitz, the former agent of the William Morris Agency who later founded Creative Artists Agency (CAA), became one of the most powerful commercial auteurs in Hollywood because so many high-concept stars, directors, and scriptwriters were under contract to his agency. In this context, it becomes completely logical that Ovitz would later be recognized as such when he briefly signed on as president of Disney.

If auteurism can be used to promote a movie, filmmakers now run the commerce of the auteurist and autonomous self up against its textual expression in a way that shatters the coherence of both authorial expression and stardom. Motivations, desires, and historical developments—which are frequently dramatized in critical readings of films as at least semiautobiographical—now become destabilized and usually with a purpose. To what extent, for instance, has Spike Lee simply taken advantage of his image and name (commercialized and advertised by Air Jordan and beyond) to consolidate his power; to what extent has he used that image and name as a critical wedge to question his own and others' authority and power? A film like *Do the Right Thing* (1989) seems to me to place itself on the line between these two questions. Casting himself as the central character Mookie, Lee here questions, with some implicit self-criticism, the relation of fame, power, and responsibility within the commerce of a public sphere. While a more traditional auteurist position would want to describe these changes in perspective and expression according to some coherent notion of evolution, an evaluation of many contemporary film-makers—like Lee—must admit fissures and discrepancies that consciously employ the public image of the auteur in order to then confront and fragment its expressive coherency.[18]

As a specific example of the contemporary auteur's construction and promotion of a self, I will now turn to one director at the historical heart of this dilemma and to one "semi-textual" strategy that is often taken for granted in the relation between a filmmaker, his or her films, and an audience—namely, the interview, which is one of the few extratextual spaces that can be documented where the auteur, in addressing fans and critical viewers, engages and disperses his or her own organizing agency as an auteur. Here, the standard directorial interview might be described according to the action of promotion and explanation; it is the writing and explaining of a film through the promotion of a certain intentional self, and it is frequently the commercial dramatization of self as the motivating agent of textuality. But it is this image of the auteur that the contemporary auteur necessarily troubles, confuses, or subverts through the agency of commerce.

The economics of self-sacrifice: Francis Coppola as American auteur

Certainly Francis Coppola is one of the more celebrated and bewildering examples of auteurism as it has evolved through the 1970s and 1980s. In an essay on the evolution of Coppola's career, Richard Macksey astutely made the connection between Orson Welles and the more recent child prodigy of Hollywood, Welles connected to Coppola across the heyday of auteurism as Romantic expression and independent (if not transgressive) vision. Yet, as Macksey observes, distinctions between the two filmmakers are even more compelling. On the one hand, "Welles has been a presiding model of Romantic genius, the myth of the explosive, comprehensive talent challenging corporate power and ultimately becoming the victim of its own genius." On the other hand, there is Coppola's marketing of that myth. As Macksey argues:

> If he has inherited something of the Romantic artist's impatience with the system, his powers of persuasion and need to take risks have led him toward the boardroom rather than the garret, back toward the old putative center of power in Hollywood (and the financial centers off-camera) rather than toward exile and "independent film-making." His perilous if uncanny power to enlist bankers probably depends upon his temperamental inability to fold in a poker game; movie-making and risk-taking are synonymous for him.[19]

As a Romantic entrepreneur, Coppola becomes a self-exiled and stridently independent auteur who claims in one sentence, "I need to be a solo guy," and then for *Tucker* humbly surrenders the film to George Lucas's "marketing sense of what people want."[20] Straddling the margins of European art cinema and the center of commercial Hollywood, he is one of the original directors of the contemporary blockbuster, *The Godfather* (1972), and the one whose experimental goals seem most threatened by the financial and commercial exigencies of his blockbuster successes. Jon Lewis explains that as "far back as 1968, four years before *The Godfather* made him the best-known director in America, Coppola predicted that his generation of film school-educated *auteurs* would someday trigger significant change in the movie business"; yet, with the needed special emphasis on finances in Coppola's version of this paradox, the

> dazzling box office success of expensive *auteurist* movies like *The Godfather, Jaws*, and *Star Wars*—the very sort of movies Coppola had once believed would foster a new American *auteur* industry—led

> to an industrywide focus on blockbuster box office revenues. The success of *auteur* films in the 1970s did not, as Coppola had hoped it would, give *auteur* directors increased access to film financing. Instead, directors became increasingly dependent on studio financing to produce and distribute such "big" films.[21]

Indeed, this ambivalent double image as the auteur-star of gigantic productions and the auteur-creator victimized by the forces of those productions defines Coppola's central place within the commerce of auteurism, characterizing him, in Andrew Sarris's offhand portrait, as a "modern dissonant auteur."[22]

Coppola's career has followed an almost allegorical path. It begins confidently as a commercial talent with *Finian's Rainbow* (1968), transforms itself through the commerce of auteurism with *The Godfather I* and *II* and *The Conversation* (1974), suffers the contradictions of that position with *Apocalypse Now* and *One from the Heart* (1982), and more recently settles uncomfortably into the aims of the commercial auteur with *Tucker: The Man and His Dream, The Godfather, Part III*, and *Bram Stoker's Dracula*. Jeffrey Chown has described these commercial pressures and contradictions, beginning with Coppola's first appearance as the auteur-creator of *The Godfather*. "It is curious," Chown writes, "that the film that put Coppola on the celebrity map, that gave him the magic adjective 'bankable,' is also extremely problematic in terms of authorship. . . . Coppola coordinated diverse creative agents in this production, he was clearly the catalyst for the film's success, but, in a career view, his creative control and originality are far less than in other films that bear his directorial signature" (p. 59). Even Coppola's most arty and individual film, *The Conversation*, demonstrates major industrial complications within auteurism, at least as it is applied to the control of the filmmaker. For many critics, Walter Murch, who engineered the brilliant soundtrack and much of the editing of that movie, can claim the most important part in the film's creation. With *Apocalypse Now*, moreover, this most celebrated of contemporary American auteurs surrenders the choice of three different endings to a battery of advisers and miles of computer printouts that surveyed the expectations and desires of different audiences (including then-President Jimmy Carter). In the most industrial and textual sense, then, Coppola has become the willing victim of his successful name. As Chown observes of the critical slaughter that greeted *One from the Heart, The Outsiders* (1983), and *Rumble Fish* (1983): "The name Francis Ford Coppola connotes spectacles, Hollywood entertainment combined with artistic sensibility, Italian weddings, and napalm in the morning. Coppola the individual seems stifled by those expectations."[23] As with his capitulations to U.S. Army censors over *Gardens of Stone* (1987), self-destruction seems part of his "creative compromises" with the contemporary terms of auteurism.

More exactly, his commercial compromises with the agency of auteurism mean a kind of sacrificing of that self as a form of spending and expending. In 1975 Coppola summed up his perspective on auteurism:

> The auteur theory is fine, but to exercise it you have to qualify, and the only way you can qualify is by having earned the right to have control, by having turned out a series of really incredibly good films. Some men have it and some men don't. I don't feel that one or two beautiful films entitle anyone to that much control. A lot of very promising directors have been destroyed by it. It's a big dilemma, of course, because, unfortunately, the authority these days is almost always shared with people who have no business being producers and studio executives. With one or two exceptions, there's no one running the studios who's qualified, either, so you have a vacuum, and the director has to fill it.[24]

Coppola's emphasis on "earned" is especially significant, since for him the expressionistic privileges of auteurism are directly related to financial actualities of investment and risk; an auteur earns his status by spending himself, and both gestures involve the aggrandizing, demeaning, and "expending" of oneself through a primary identification with the agency and exchange of money. Thus, the complement of a self that is constructed as a financial agency is degradation of that self as merely a financial product. For Coppola, "the artist's worst fear is that he'll be exposed as a sham,"[25] namely, that an audience's financial investment in his agency will be revealed as only commercial advertisement.

The image of the divided self curiously mirrors the obsessive geniuses found in Coppola's liturgical and operatic narratives. From the first two *Godfather* films through *Apocalypse Now* and *Tucker*, his visionary characters invariably pursue grandiose spectacles that reflect their desires but that either literally or metaphorically then serve to destroy them. While these spectacles frequently echo their nineteenth-century origins (lavish visuals and operatic soundtracks), the more exact terms of their agency as cinematic characters are the contemporary spectacles of industrial technology as a financial investment (for war, for corporate industry, for the business of the family). *The Conversation* is the most appropriate example. Driven by the passions of the protagonist, Harry Caul, it is a conversation through technology that leads to the absolute collapse of a sacrosanct individuality. Coppola's description of Harry, the devout and tortured Catholic, could indeed describe Coppola himself as auteur: "he's a man who has dedicated his existence to a certain kind of activity, to technology, and who in a part of his life experiences regrets and realizes that the weapon he uses for others in a certain fashion is destroying the man himself. . . . the single reason for which he is destroyed is perhaps that he has started to question all that."[26] If

Hollywood's commercial industry is the financial agency that makes and unmakes Coppola the auteur, Coppola remains driven to invest and lose that self in ever-grander forms of its technological spectacle. Perhaps the most extraordinary and thus indicative example of this tendency are his technological dream projects: a giant domed theater in the Rocky Mountains, or an imagined film megalopolis where four elaborate video films would draw on Goethe's *Elective Affinities* to tell the story of Japanese-U.S. relations.[27]

Not coincidently, I think, an interview with Coppola becomes a media performance focused on the technology and the business that define and threaten him. Worried about the casual setting of his meeting with this Coppola, for instance, one interviewer found relief in Coppola's immediate identification with the technology of performance. "I needn't have worried. The minute I switched on my tape recorder, Coppola came to life. This was work. First, he corrected the position of the machine, then he fiddled with the volume and tone controls till he had them set to his satisfaction. Finally, he allowed me to question him."[28] During the interview, Coppola constructed himself as both an entrepreneur orchestrating the forces of technology and as a character lost in the improvisations of Hollywood business. He describes his expectations and frustrations about the Academy Awards, his struggles with Paramount executives to cast Marlon Brando in *The Godfather*, and he acknowledges that this most famous vehicle for his agency as an auteur had less to do with his control of the film than with submission of self and the loss of energy. "A lot of the energy that went into the film went into simply trying to convince the people who held the power to let me do the film my way."[29]

Ultimately, of course, the expenditure of energy and the loss of self are the contradictory measures of Coppola as auteur. Evaluating the ratio of his position as artist against his possible decision to actually assume the full agency of a studio (which he would do with the phoenixlike Zoetrope Studios), he casts himself according to the finances of running a large piece of technology:

> if I were running a studio, it might take me 100 B.T.U.S worth of energy to bend something a quarter inch; if I stay independent and use my own resources, those 100 B.T.U.S could bend something a foot. . . . But look: The average executive of a movie studio may make $150,000 a year, and have a corresponding power, over his company. As a film artist I make much, much more than that and, consequently, have that much more power over my company. . . . Perhaps the wisest thing to do is to use all my energies to make a film that grosses some stupendous amount, then go out and buy a major company and change it from the top.[30]

Appropriately, for this elaborate characterization of himself at the turning point in his commercial career, Coppola begins this 1975 interview by claiming, "this is my last interview."[31] Within this glossy, high-tech conversation with an interviewer for the glossy high-tech magazine *Playboy*, he must naturally be given up from the start.[32]

Attempting to synthesize his relation to his movies in the manner of the Big Picture, Coppola becomes the presiding genius of the film of himself. However, this genius is represented not in expression or productive control but in expenditure and loss: loss of control, loss of money, loss of vision, and loss of self. His renowned posture as a risk-taker thus becomes a bombastic effacement of any distinguishing differences between his intentions and the films. In 1982 Jonathan Cott asked Coppola about the publicity gained from adopting this posture of loss during the production of *One from the Heart:*

> The real answer, from my point of view, is that I just say what the facts are; in this case, that I'm working on a film, I'm told that the money's gone, and that if I want to go ahead, I'll have to risk something of my own. And by that point, I'm so far into it that I say okay. . . . And then that tends to be the story that the people who write about me want to go for. If they ask me, "If the picture's a flop, will the company go out of business?" and if I say yes, it's because that seems to be the case. But it's not the idea that I want to push out into the public. In fact, I regret that I'm treated more as a charlatan or a con man than as a professional person, and to be honest, my feelings are hurt. I feel that I'm not reckless or crazy. It's just that I'm primarily interested in making films more than amassing money, which is just a tool. If someone suddenly gave me a billion dollars, for instance, I'd only invest it in my work. I will say yes to anything that seems reasonable to me, and sometimes I get in a little deep because I want to participate so much.[33]

A key moment in this interview, as with other Coppola interviews, is the appeal for sympathy, not the distance of authority. It elicits a kind of social and psychological identification between Coppola and an imagined interlocutor, like that between a spectator and an actor-victim in an epic movie. For Coppola, the auteur communicates from one heart to another. For him, specifically, his is a self-portrait of the auteur as persecuted and dismissed by the operatic conglomerates who have made him a powerless vehicle in their success. "I've done so much for them, and yet they resent even putting me in a position where I don't have to go to one of them with my hat in my hand and have them tell me what movies I can or cannot make."[34] At other times, with astonishing dexterity, he rhetorically moves between an image of himself as the powerful agent of a financial and technological machine and an image of the completely insignificant individuality that inhabits that agency:

> You know what I think? I think people are afraid of me, basically. They're afraid if I ever got like too much power, I'd change their lives, and they're right! . . . I'm only a minor representative of the times. I may be a schmuck, but you can be sure that some other people somewhere are going to start doing the same kind of stuff, and the world is going to change. . . . As for myself, I'm not worried. What the hell! If I don't do it with this film, I'll go and invent some little gadget that will make billions![35]

The sympathetic enlistment of an audience has become the path for locating multiple subjectivities ("other people somewhere") within an agency that disallows the authority or stability of any single organizing perspective. In this action, Coppola puts into play the central problem of contemporary auteurism as an interpretive category; while it remains a more powerful figure and agency than ever, it is invariably forced to disperse its authority in terms of its commercial agency.

In the end, Coppola within the commerce of auteurism remains a most utopian figure, for whom the spectacle of self-destruction becomes a way back to self-expression. For him, the destruction of the authority of the auteur can mean the resurrection of a world of private auteurs, an intimate yet expansive network of electronic communication. Speculating on the future of new technologies that regenerate themselves through money made and money spent on them, he proclaims a home-video exchange that somehow retains the aura of auteurist agency, the expressive "I" becoming a third-person plural: "Everybody will use it, everybody will make films, everybody will make dreams. That's what I think is gonna happen. You'll ship 'em over to your friend, and he'll ship one back. . . . I think that, very shortly, there's going to be a whole new approach to things, and the designers and the architects and philosophers and artists are going to be the ones to help lead the society."[36]

The age and aging of auteurs

There are many kinds of auteurs in contemporary film culture. And there are many strategies through which a moviemaker can employ the agency of auteurism and by which audiences can use it as a way of understanding films. Both European and Asian filmmakers, for instance, have complicated this category for many years, and one only has to look to German or British filmmakers such as Rainer Werner Fassbinder or Peter Greenaway to get a sense of the range of such revisions of auteurist practices. In the United States the "displaced Hollywood auteur," more so than ever before, raises questions and issues that need to be addressed. From Wim Wenders to Peter Weir, this group of global filmmakers situated in Hollywood suggests contradictions and alternative descriptions to the history and coherence of auteurism. Even in my emphasis on the massive role that television has had in redefining auteurist practice today, I feel that I have only sketched the first stages of its impact.

In "The Unauthorized Auteur Today," Dudley Andrew has added another dimension to auteurism that my model does not—or I think cannot—take into account. Following Gilles Deleuze's suggestions about the relation between an auteur's signature and a temporal "duration," Andrew puts forward the idea that the largely spatial description of the commerce of auteurism laid out here—one which plays across public and private space—forgets or is asked to forget about a crucial dimension of temporality as a figure of the auteur. "The signature," Andrew posits, "embeds within it—as a hypertext—a genuine fourth dimension, the temporal process that brought the text into being in the first place. . . . The auteur marks the presence of temporality and creativity in the text, including the creativity of emergent thought contributed by the spectator."[37] One common characteristic of new American auteurs like Tarantino or David Lynch is the instantaneity of their careers. The brief duration of auteur celebrity these days parallels the rapid turnover of postmodern consumerism. Without being nostalgic, I would at least like to follow Andrew and urge this notion of duration as the missing element in the account of the modern American auteur.

Duration is a distinguishing characteristic of another sort of auteur today—the auteur who creates a figure of time as enduring, evolving within the commerce of its expression. Coppola ultimately might belong and be reclaimed here, as certainly do Martin Scorsese and Robert Altman.[38] These temporal auteurs demand that we encounter them across the historical vicissitudes of a commercial agency in which they have sometimes triumphed and sometimes faltered, temporal vicissitudes that, in today's climate, take on a variety of shapes and figures. Contemporary auteurs appear "immediately"; they "historically remake" themselves; there are "futuristic" auteurs and "nostalgic" auteurs; some auteurs become identified with the histories of different nationalities and some with the temporalities of different genders. In the final analysis, the achievement of auteurs today will reflect far more than their individual films and be found in a figure of temporality that their work dramatizes.

In whatever shape and in whatever agency, then, auteurs are far from dead. In fact, they may be more alive than at any other point in film history. This particular interpretive category has of course never addressed audiences in simple or singular ways. Yet, within the commerce of contemporary culture, auteurism has become, as both a production and interpretive position, something quite different from what it may have been in the 1950s or 1960s. Since the early 1970s, the commercial conditioning of this figure has successfully evacuated it of most of its expressive power and textual coherency; simultaneously, this commercial conditioning has called renewed attention to the layered pressures of auteurism as an agency that establishes different modes of identification with its audiences. However vast some of their differences as filmmakers may be, they each, it seems to me, willingly or not, have had to give up their authority as authors and begin to communicate as figures within the commerce of that image. For viewers, this should mean the pleasure of engaging and adopting one more image of, in, and around a movie without, perhaps, the pretenses of its traditional authorities and mystifications.

Notes

1 Tarantino's best-known effort as an executive producer is probably *Killing Zoe* (1994).

2 See Jim Hillier's introduction to *Cahiers du Cinema: The 1950s*, ed. Jim Hillier (Cambridge, Mass.: Harvard University Press, 1985), pp. 1–17.

3 A collection of the major debates and documents about auteurism can be found in *Theories of Authorship*, ed. John Caughie (London: Routledge, 1981).

4 See Roland Barthes, *Image-Music-Text* (New York: Hill and Wang, 1977), pp. 142–48.

5 This point suggests, I believe, one way to discuss the way that cult followings of certain directors and films has become increasingly popular. In some cases a kind of identification and appropriation of the image of the film or filmmaker can replace the need for interpretive meaning.

6 David Bordwell, *Narration in the Fiction Film* (Madison: University of Wisconsin Press, 1985), p. 211.

7 *Theories of Authorship*, ed. Caughie, p. 2. See also Ben Brewster's "Brecht and the Film Industry," *Screen* 16 (Winter 1976–77): 16–33.

8 Charles Taylor, for instance, has argued a model of human agency that foregrounds "second-order desires" where the "reflective self-evaluation" of "the self-interpreting subject" has as its object "the having of certain first-order desires." Similarly, Anthony Giddens suggests a materialist model of expression as self-reflexive action: the motivation of expressive action, the rationalization of that action, and the reflective monitoring of action concomitantly interact to map the structure of expression as a reflective social discourse that necessarily calls attention to the material terms of its communication. In both cases, agency becomes a mode of expression (or more exactly enunciation) that describes an active and monitored engagement with its own conditions as the subjective expresses itself through the socially symbolic. See Charles Taylor, *Human Agency and Language: Philosophical Papers* (Cambridge: Cambridge University Press, 1985), pp. 43, 28, 15; and Anthony Giddens, *Central Problems in Social Theory: Action, Structure, and Contrast in Social Analysis* (Berkeley: University of California Press, 1983).

9 A direct and oversimplified example of this position, which responds to the contemporary status of the auteur but fails to reflect on its larger cultural and critical implications, is Joseph Gelmis's *The Film Director as Superstar* (Garden City, N.Y.: Doubleday, 1970). "Over half the movie tickets sold today," he notes, "are bought by moviegoers between the ages of sixteen and twenty-five. They know what a director is, what he does, and what he's done" (p. xvii).

10 Steven Bach's *Final Cut: Dreams and Disasters* (New York: William Morrow, 1985) is a particularly graphic and detailed account of the contemporary auteur as a self-promoting celebrity. A sophisticated analysis of this tendency around the globe (specifically in Germany) is Sheila Johnston's "A Star is Born: Fassbinder

and the New German Cinema," *New German Critique* 24–25 (Fall/Winter 1981–82): 57–72.

11 The phrase "camera stylo" is from Alexandre Astruc's "The Birth of a New Avant-Garde: *le camera-stylo*," *Ecran Français* 144 (1948).

12 According to Robert Sklar, the uncut version of the movie was "rescued by home video from the limbo of lost films." "Homevideo," *Cineaste* 14, no. 4 (1987): 29.

13 In "The New Hollywood," Thomas Schatz lays out the different stages that describe Hollywood's evolution toward blockbuster production. See *Film Theory Goes to the Movies*, ed. Jim Collins, Hilary Radner, and Ava Collins (New York: Routledge, 1993), pp. 8–36.

14 Mark Crispin Miller states the negative view most strongly in his "Hollywood: The Ad," *Atlantic*, April 1990, pp. 41–54.

15 Justin Wyatt and R. L. Rutsky, "High Concept: Abstracting the Postmodern," *Wide Angle* 10, no. 4 (1988): 42.

16 Disney's 1993 purchase of Miramax is one of several indicators that this industrial field remains very much in flux, showing that independent voices can become quickly assimilated while new ones appear on the horizon.

17 Meaghan Morris, "Tooth and Claw: Tales of Survival and *Crocodile Dundee*," in *Universal Abandon?: The Politics of Postmodernism*, ed. Andrew Ross (Minneapolis: University of Minnesota Press, 1988), pp. 122–23. See also Richard Dyer, *Stars* (London: British Film Institute, 1979).

18 David Bordwell recognizes this fragmentation of the auteur but sees it more as simply a variation on the traditional auteur-narrator: "The popularity of R. W. Fassbinder . . . may owe something to his ability to change narrational personae from film to film so that there is a 'realist' Fassbinder, a 'literary' Fassbinder, a 'pastiche' Fassbinder, and so on" (*Narration in the Fiction Film*, p. 210). I believe that mobilizing these different agencies within an auteurist category has important implications.

19 Richard Macksey, " 'The Glitter of the Infernal Stream': The Splendors and Miseries of Francis Coppola," *Bennington Review* **15** (1983): 2, 3.

20 Robert Lindsay, "Francis Ford Coppola: Promises to Keep," *New York Times Magazine*, July 24, 1988, pp. 23–27.

21 Jon Lewis, *Whom God Wishes to Destroy* (Durham, N.C.: Duke University Press, 1993), pp. 21, 22.

22 Andrew Sarris, "O Hollywood!, Oh Mores!" *Village Voice*, 5 March 1985, p. 5.

23 Jeffrey Chown, *Hollywood Auteur: Francis Coppola* (New York: UMI Research Press, 1981), p. 175.

24 William Murray, "*Playboy* Interview: Francis Ford Coppola," *Playboy*, July 1975, p. 68.

25 Ibid., p. 65.

26 Gabria Belloni and Lorenzo Codelli, "Conversation avec Francis Ford Coppola," *Positif* 161 (1974): 51.

27 Not surprisingly, the ambivalent identification of the artistic self within the commerce of auteurism and its promise of the great spectacle of self becomes fraught with all the religious guilt of sin and the weight of self-sacrifice: "I am more interested in technology than I am in content. This, in some circles, is the same as admitting one is a child molester and likes it. The truth is that I am interested in a content I can't get at. I yearn to be able to move into a world where story and content is available to me; where my ideas connect into a pattern that could be identified as a story. But I truly cannot get there." Francis Coppola, "The Director on Content," *Washington Post*, August 29, 1982, p. 3D.

28 Murray, "*Playboy* Interview: Francis Ford Coppola," p. 54.

29 Ibid., p. 59.
30 Ibid., p. 68.
31 Ibid., p. 54.
32 Jon Lewis's comparative discussion of Coppola's Zoetrope studios and George Lucas's Lucasfilm studios suggests how one's failure and the other's success reveals two distinct and different philosophies of the New Hollywood. *Whom God Wishes to Destroy*, pp. 38–40. I would add that in many other ways Lucas seems much more directed toward what I call commercial auteurism than toward the strains of working within the commerce of auteurism.
33 Jonathan Cott, "Francis Coppola," *Rolling Stone*, March 18, 1982, p. 24.
34 Ibid., p. 76.
35 Ibid.
36 Ibid.
37 Dudley Andrew, "The Unauthorized Auteur Today," in *Film Theory Goes to the Movies*, ed. Collins, Collins, and Radner, p. 83.
38 Altman's *The Player* (1992) is one of the most incisively bitter and lucid depictions of today's production and auteurist practice as I have described it.

Part 5

GENRE

32

DEFINITIONS OF GENRE

Steve Neale

Source: *Genre and Hollywood*, London: Routledge, 2000, pp. 9–29.

'Genre' is a French word meaning 'type' or 'kind'. As we shall see, it has occupied an important place in the study of the cinema for over thirty years, and is normally exemplified (either singly or in various combinations) by the western, the gangster film, the musical, the horror film, melodrama, comedy and the like. On occasion, the term 'sub-genre' has also been used, generally to refer to specific traditions or groupings within these genres (as in 'romantic comedy', 'slapstick comedy', 'the gothic horror film' and so on). And sometimes the term 'cycle' is used as well, usually to refer to groups of films made within a specific and limited time-span, and founded, for the most part, on the characteristics of individual commercial successes: the cycle of historical adventure films made in the wake of *Treasure Island* (1934) and *The Count of Monte Cristo* (1934), for instance (Behlmer 1979: 12; Taves 1993a: 68–9), or the cycle of 'slasher' or 'stalker' films made in the wake of *The Texas Chainsaw Massacre* (1974) and *Halloween* (1978) (Clover 1992; Dika 1990).

As these examples illustrate, the definition and discussion of genre and genres in the cinema has tended to focus on mainstream, commercial films in general and Hollywood films in particular. Sometimes, indeed, genre and genres have been exclusively identified with these kinds of films. 'Stated simply', writes Barry Keith Grant, 'genre movies are those commercial feature films which, through repetition and variation, tell familiar stories with familiar characters in familiar situations.' 'They have been exceptionally significant', he adds, 'in establishing the popular sense of cinema as a cultural and economic institution, particularly in the United States, where Hollywood studios early on adopted an industrial model based on mass production' (1986b: ix). However, if (for the moment at least) we accept that genres are simply types or kinds of films, there is no logical reason for excluding either such non-American instances as the Indian mythological, the Japanese samurai film, or the Hong Kong *wu xia pan* or swordplay film, or such 'non-commercial' or non-feature length instances as the documentary, the animated short, the avant-garde film or the art film. Although writing can be found which considers these types of film from a generic point of view, most of the writing on genre and genres in the cinema has focused on the commercial feature film and on Hollywood.[1]

There are a number of reasons for this. Most can be found either in the history of the study of the cinema, or in the history of genre as a concept within the fields of written fiction and drama. Given that this book will also concentrate on the feature film and on Hollywood, it is important to highlight these reasons at the outset, and to expose some of the limitations and problems to which they have given rise.

Genre criticism and genre theory in the 1960s and 1970s

In her survey of writing on genre in *The Cinema Book*, Christine Gledhill (1985a: 58) points out that books and articles on individual Hollywood genres began to be published in the US and in Europe (especially in France) in the 1940s and 1950s, notably by Bazin (1971a, 1971b), Chabrol ([1955] 1985), Rieupeyrout (1953) and Warshow ([1948] 1975a, [1954] 1975b). However, it was not until the late 1960s and early 1970s that the study of genre and genres began to establish itself more fully in Britain and in the US, in tandem with the establishment of Film Studies as a formal, academic discipline. As Gledhill goes on to indicate, there were two main reasons for the appearance of genre and genres on the agenda of theorists, critics, and teachers of film at this time. One was a desire to engage in a serious and positive way with popular cinema in general and with Hollywood in particular. The other was a desire to complement, temper or displace altogether the dominant critical approach used hitherto – auteurism.

There had always existed reviewers and critics (like James Agee, Manny Farber and Parker Tyler) who had discussed Hollywood films with some sympathy, intelligence and insight. But they had also always been the exception among those who wrote about film in the US and Britain. For the most part, intellectuals, critics and reviewers had been at best patronizing and at worst overtly hostile to Hollywood and its films – on the grounds that they were commercially produced, that they were aimed at a mass market, that they were ideologically or aesthetically conservative, or that they were imbued with the values of entertainment and fantasy rather than those of realism, art or serious aesthetic stylization.

During the late 1950s, the 1960s, and the early 1970s, a generation of intellectuals who had grown up with and who for various reasons liked and valued elements of commercial popular culture in general, and American popular culture in particular, began to debate and to re-assess its value.[2] By then the French film journal *Cahiers du cinéma* had pioneered an approach to the cinema that François Truffaut called 'la politique des auteurs' (Truffaut [1954] 1976), and that came in the US and in Britain to be known either as 'the auteur theory' (Sarris 1968) or else, more simply, as auteurism. *Cahiers*' auteurism was founded on three basic premisses. The first was that despite the ostensibly collective and impersonal nature of film production, the cinema could be, and often was, a realm of individual and personal expression. The second was that in the cinema, the figure equivalent to the artist or author (*auteur*) in painting or in literature was – or could be – the director. And the third, and by far the most radical, was that directorial artistry and cinematic authorship were to be found not just within the culturally respectable realms of international art cinema (a common idea at that time), nor even, as far as Hollywood was concerned, solely within the realms of the occasional prestige or maverick project (another common idea), but also, perhaps especially, within the realms of its routine output (Hillier 1985b: 7).

Adapted, modified, reworked in various ways, these premisses were adopted by Andrew Sarris, film critic for *The Village Voice* in the USA, and by *Movie* magazine, and later *The Brighton Film Review, Monogram* and *Cinema*, in Britain (Caughie 1981). The impact of auteurism on film criticism in general and on the criticism and appreciation of Hollywood films in particular was immense. It enabled both a systematic charting of a great deal of Hollywood's output, and much detailed discussion of form, style, theme and *mise-en-scène*. It thus provided those wishing to analyse – and validate – Hollywood cinema with a valuable critical stance and with a valuable set of critical tools. However, given its evaluative base (auteurs were preferred to non-auteurs and to mere '*metteurs-en-scène*'), and given its commitment to individual directors and hence to individualized corpuses of films, auteurism was of little help in dealing with the range of Hollywood's output overall, or in charting broader trends and developments within it. Moreover, the third of *Cahiers*'s premisses in particular required the adoption of a 'perverse' attitude to Hollywood, a way of looking at and thinking about its films which neither Hollywood itself nor society at large encouraged. (Hence the tendency of *Cahiers* in particular and of auteurism in general to lapse into cultishness.) It thus encouraged an approach to Hollywood films which either ignored or defamiliarized their institutional status, their institutional conventions and the audiences to whom they were principally addressed. It is precisely for these reasons that the auteurism of *Cahiers, Movie*, Sarris and *Monogram* was – and is – of interest. However, it was for these reasons too that those interested in identifying these conventions and in taking account of the institution and its audiences found untrammelled auteurism unhelpful. Towards the end of the 1960s, they began to turn their attention instead to issues of genre.

As Gledhill has pointed out, an American art critic, Lawrence Alloway (1963, 1971), had already made the case for paying more attention to genres and cycles, arguing that they were fundamental not just to Hollywood cinema but to popular art as a whole. 'Alloway . . . resists the temptation to establish "classic" timeless dimensions in popular forms', she writes. 'He insists on the transitional and ephemeral character of genres, of cycles, and of any individual popular film (1985a: 59–60). In an overview of the writing on genre that followed, Tom Ryall restates the case against auteurism and reiterates Alloway's point about the nature of popular art: 'The auteur theory, though important and valuable during the 1950s and 1960s for drawing attention to the importance of the American cinema, nevertheless tended to treat popular art as if it were "high art" ' (1975/6: 28). He also makes explicit the importance and the role of the audience. And he offers a definition of genre itself. 'The master image for genre criticism', he writes, 'is a triangle composed of artist/film/audience. Genres may be defined as patterns/forms/styles/structures which transcend individual films, and which supervise both their construction by the film maker, and their reading by an audience' (ibid.).

I shall return to this definition in a moment. However, at this point it is worth stressing the extent to which Ryall is critical of some of the writing on genre that immediately preceded his own. 'By and large', he writes, 'genre criticism has confined itself to producing taxonomies on the basis of "family resemblances", allocating films to their position within the generic constellation, stopping short of what are the interesting and informative questions about generic groupings'. (1975/6: 27). To a degree these remarks are well-founded. Some of the writing that preceded (and followed) Ryall's article was indeed taxonomic, devoted to the discovery and analysis of the components of individual genres rather than to the pursuit of theoretical questions about the nature of genre as such. However, while writing of this kind has its limitations, it also has its uses, providing as it does an initial means of 'collating the range of cultural knowledge . . . genres assumed' (Gledhill 1985a: 61).

Moreover, not all the writing on genre in the late 1960s and early 1970s was taxonomic in kind. Both Buscombe (1970) and McArthur (1972), for instance, were concerned, among other things, to demonstrate the active role played by genre conventions in shaping the form and the meaning of individual Hollywood films. Here, for example, is Buscombe on *Guns in the Afternoon* (a.k.a. *Ride the High Country*) (1962), a western:

> Knowing the period and location, we expect at the beginning to find a familiar western town. In fact, the first few minutes of the film brilliantly disturb expectations. As the camera moves around the town, we discover a policeman in uniform, a car, a camel, and Randolph Scott, dressed up as Buffalo Bill. Each of these images performs a function. The figure of the policeman conveys that the law has become institutionalised; the rough and ready frontier days are over. The car suggests . . . that the west is no longer isolated from modern technology and its implications. Significantly, the camel is racing against a horse; such a grotesque juxtaposition is painful. A horse in a western is not just an animal but a symbol of dignity, grace

> and power. These qualities are mocked by it competing with a camel; and to add insult to injury, the camel wins.
>
> (Buscombe 1970: 44)

He later continues:

> the essential theme of *Guns in the Afternoon* is one that, while it could be put into other forms is ideally suited to the one chosen. The film describes the situation of men who have outlived their time . . .
>
> The cluster of images and conventions that we call the western genre is used by Peckinpah [the film's director] to define and embody this situation, in such a way that we know what the West was and what it has become. The first is communicated through images that are familiar, the second through those that are strange. And together they condition his subject matter. Most obviously, because the film is a western, the theme is worked out in terms of violent action. If it were a musical, the theme might be similar in some way, but because the conventions would be different, it would probably not involve violence . . . And if it were a gangster picture, it seems unlikely that the effect of the film's ending, its beautifully elegiac background of autumn leaves, would be reproduced, suggesting as it does that the dead Judd is at one with nature, the nature which seems at the beginning of the film to have been overtaken by 'civilization'.
>
> (Buscombe 1970: 44–5)

In this particular essay, Buscombe attempts also to advance a general theory about the aesthetic characteristics of popular genres. He borrows the concepts of 'inner' and 'outer' form from Warren and Welleck, who argued that 'Genres should be conceived as a grouping of literary works based, theoretically, upon both outer form (specific metre or structure) and also upon inner form (attitude, tone, purpose – more crudely, subject and audience)' (1956: 260). These particular concepts were not taken up by subsequent writers. But in illustrating the idea of 'outer form', Buscombe talked about 'visual conventions'. His work here thus drew on and fed into a concept that was to become much more influential – the concept of iconography.

Iconography

Along with its twin, 'iconology', the term 'iconography' derives from art history, and in particular from the work of Erwin Panofsky. Panofsky himself discussed the application of these terms to popular cinema ([1934] 1974), but it was Lawrence Alloway who sought to apply them in a systematic way to the analysis of genres and cycles (1963).

In 'Iconography and Iconology: An Introduction to the Study of Renaissance Art', first published in 1938 and reprinted in his *Meaning in the Visual Arts*, Panofsky distinguishes between three possible levels or stages in the analysis of Renaissance paintings, corresponding to three possible 'strata' of meaning (1970: 51–81). The first involves the identification and description of what he calls 'motifs' (essentially, the objects and events depicted through lines, colours and volumes). The second involves the identification and description of what he calls 'images' (the 'secondary or conventional' meanings conveyed by these motifs, as determined in particular by reference to the Bible and to other written sources. This for Panofsky is the realm of iconography). And the third involves the interpretation of these images. (This for Panofsky is the realm of iconology.)

In arguing for the application of the concept of iconography to the cinema, Alloway writes that

> The meaning of a single movie is inseparable from the larger pattern of content-analysis of other movies. And the point is, that this knowledge, of concepts and themes, is the common property of the regular audience of the movies. It comes from 1) exposure to runs of related movies (soap opera, westerns) and from the fact that 2) the movies connect with other topical interests and activities of the audience. Such themes as kitchen technology and domestic leisure in soap opera and male outdoor leisure clothes, as well as attitudes towards violence in westerns, exist outside the movies, but aid identification with the movies once you are inside the cinema.
>
> (Alloway 1963: 5)

He precedes this passage with another example, and with another facet of this argument:

> iconography is not to be isolated from other aspects of film making. For instance, *The Thousand Eyes of Dr Mabuse* and *Rear Window* can be related to a persistent theme of American movies since World War II. There were the F.B.I. movies in which the Department of Justice kept spies under observation with a battery of voyeuristic electronic devices. Since *The Glass Web* television monitor devices of every kind have been brilliantly handled in urban films: for instance, a telephone wired with a bomb, as in *The Case Against Brooklyn* or the difficulties of telephone tapping in the '30s in *The Scarface Mob*.
>
> (Alloway 1963: 4–5)

It should be noted that 'iconography' here tends to mean the objects, events and figures in films, as well as their identification and description. It should also be noted that Alloway tends to avoid interpretation. Partly for this reason, iconology does not even figure as a term. (It tends to disappear altogether in subsequent writing on genre. Only McArthur, in an unpublished paper written in 1973, briefly resurrects both the term and the conceptual distinction Panofsky originally designed it to make.) Finally, it should be pointed out that although Alloway discusses and exemplifies iconography in relation to genres and cycles, he also discusses its application to stars and to star personae.

The concept of iconography was widely used by genre theorists and critics during the course of the next decade. There were two main reasons for this. One was the extent to which, in Alloway's formulation at least, it dovetailed with a sympathetic interest in popular films. The other was the extent to which it could be used to stress the visual aspects of popular films (in keeping with the stress placed on style and *mise-en-scène* by auteurism, and in contrast to the emphasis placed on character, plot and theme by more literary-minded theorists and critics). Hence Buscombe's synonym for iconography – 'visual conventions'. Hence his insistence on the argument that 'Since we are dealing with a visual medium we ought surely to look for our defining criteria on the screen' (1970: 36). And hence the stress placed on 'visual conventions' as well as on the 'relationship between genre and audience' in the chapter on the iconography of the 'gangster film/thriller' in McArthur's *Underworld USA*:

> In *Little Caesar* (1930) a police lieutenant and two of his men visit a night-club run by gangsters. All three wear large hats and heavy coats, are grim and sardonic and stand in triangular formation, the lieutenant in front, his two men flanking him in the rear. The audience knows immediately what to expect of them by their physical attributes, their dress and deportment. It knows, too, by the disposition of the figures, which is dominant, which subordinate. In *The Harder They Fall* (1956) a racketeer and two of his men go to a rendezvous in downtown New York. As they wait for the door of the building to be opened they take up the same formation as the figures in the earlier film, giving the same information to the audience by the same means . . . In *On the Waterfront* (1954) and *Tony Rome* (1967) there are carefully mounted scenes in which the central figure is walking down a dark and deserted street. In each case an automobile drives swiftly towards him; and the audience, drawing on accumulated experience of the genre, realises that it will be used as a murder weapon against the hero. Both these examples indicate the continuity over several decades of patterns of visual imagery, of recurrent objects and figures in dynamic relationship. These repeated patterns might be called the iconography of the genre.
>
> (McArthur 1972: 23)

McArthur goes on to categorize the genre's iconography, subdividing the patterns of its imagery into three basic types: 'those surrounding the physical presence, attributes and dress of the actors and the characters they play; those emanating from the milieux within which the characters operate; and those connected with the technology at the characters' disposal' (ibid.: 24). However, it is unclear as to whether this taxonomy is meant to be applicable to other genres as well. It is also unclear as to whether iconography is to be thought of as one of the defining features of a genre.

There are certainly traces of such a position in McArthur's book. He says at one point, for instance, that the iconographic patterns of a genre 'set it off visually from other types of film and are the means by which primary definitions are made' (1972: 24). However, he himself does not elaborate, and it is Buscombe who comes closest to arguing a position of this kind. Although stressing that not all generic conventions are visual in kind, he argues nevertheless that 'the major defining characteristics of a genre will be visual: guns, cars, clothes in the gangster film; clothing and dancing in musical (apart from the music, of course!); castles, coffins and teeth in horror movies' (1970: 41). This argument occurs during the course of a much more detailed discussion of the western. Nevertheless, the paucity of these examples (together with the taxonomic tendencies both of genre criticism in general and of iconographic analysis in particular) is strikingly apparent. One of the major reasons for this is that the possible connections between the items (or icons) listed is unclear. Another, more important, reason is that it is actually very difficult to list the defining visual characteristics of more than a handful of genres, for the simple reason that many genres – among them the social problem film, the biopic, romantic drama and the psychological horror film – lack a specific iconography.

It is no accident, therefore, that the genres discussed at some length by Buscombe and McArthur are the western and the gangster film, two of the genres which (along with the gothic horror film and the biblical epic) the concept of generic iconography seems to fit rather well. The failure to apply the concept productively to other genres suggests on the one hand that the defining features of Hollywood's genres may be heterogeneous in kind (some visual, others not). It suggests on the other that a number of fundamental questions – to do with definition, to do with identification, and to do with the nature and role of genre theory – still needed to be asked. They began to be asked first by Tudor (1974a: 131–52, 1974b: 180–220) and then by Ryall. They were displaced during the decade that followed as attention was turned to structuralism, to semiotics and to psychoanalysis – to general theories of method and meaning (Stam, Burgoyne and Flitterman-Lewis 1992). Structuralism, in particular, played a part in work on individual genres like the western (notably by Kitses 1969 and Wright 1975). However, although some or all of these theories were to have an impact on writing on genre in the 1980s, notably by Neale (1980) and Altman ([1984] 1986, 1987), and although feminist inflections and reworkings of these approaches were to find an important place in writing on hitherto neglected genres like the woman's film (see Doane 1987), issues and theories of genre as such were largely put to one side. Hence some of these questions remained unanswered and had to be re-raised, firstly by Alan Williams (1984), and then by Neale (1990a).

Theoretical questions

The questions raised by Ryall derive from a distinction he draws between two types of analytical activity:

> The key to understanding the theoretical foundations of the concept of genre lies in pushing beyond . . . classificatory exercises and confronting the crucial distinction between, on the one hand suggesting that a film is a Western; and, on the other, suggesting that a film is a genre film. The former simply involves observing similarities between films, while the latter urges us towards a more generalised theoretical activity in which our conclusions would not merely link one film with another under some category such as 'Western'; but rather, would link the established genres (Westerns, gangster films, musicals, etc) under the more general concepts of 'convention' and 'expectation', and would explore the variety of questions associated with the area of 'reading' film.
>
> (Ryall 1975/6: 27)

Ryall goes on to note the multi-dimensional aspects of genre, insisting on the importance of audience knowledge and audience expectation on the one hand, and of the industry and film reviewers on the other. It is clear, therefore, that for Ryall genres are not simply groups of films linked by common characteristics. He argues in addition that the problem of defining genre as a term is exacerbated by its pervasiveness: 'its widespread usage by film distributors, by reviewers and critics, and by popular audiences, poses problems for criticism insofar as ordinary usage carries with it the implication that the concept of genre is clear and well-defined, non-problematic' (1975/6: 27).

Similar points are made by Tudor (1974a), who tends both to pursue them further and to raise other issues as well. He begins by raising questions about genre identification and genre recognition:

> most writers tend to assume that there is some body of films we can safely call the western and then move on to the real work – the analysis of the crucial characteristics of the already recognized *genre* . . . These writers, and almost all writers using the term *genre*, are caught in a dilemma. They are defining a western on the basis

> of analyzing a body of films that cannot possibly be said to be westerns until after the analysis . . . To take a *genre* such as the western, analyze it, and list its principal characteristics is to beg the question that we must first isolate the body of films that are westerns. But they can only be isolated on the basis of the 'principal characteristics', which can only be discovered from the films themselves after they have been isolated. That is, we are caught in a circle that first requires that the films be isolated, for which purpose a criterion is necessary, but the criterion is, in turn, meant to emerge from the empirically established common characteristics of the films. This 'empiricist dilemma' has two solutions. One is to classify films according to a priori criteria depending on the critical purpose. This leads back to the earlier position in which the special *genre* term is redundant. The second is to lean on a common cultural consensus as to what constitutes a western and then go on to analyze it in detail.
>
> (Tudor 1974a: 135–8)

This is a fundamental point. It raises questions about the nature and purpose of genre criticism. And, implicitly at least, it raises questions as to how 'a common cultural consensus' is established. What agencies and institutions are involved? What is the role of the film industry? What is the role of film critics, film reviewers and the like? On the one hand it helps underline Ryall's point about the importance of distributors, reviewers and critics. On the other it helps stress the culturally relative, and therefore the culturally contingent, nature of genres themselves:

> In short to talk about the western is (arbitrary definitions apart) to appeal to a common set of meanings in our culture. From a very early age most of us have built up a picture of the western. We feel that we know a western when we see one, though the edges may be rather blurred. Thus in calling a film a western a critic is implying more than the simple statement 'This film is a member of a class of films (westerns) having in common x, y, and z.' The critic is also suggesting that such a film would be universally recognized as such in our culture. In other words, the crucial factors that distinguish a *genre* are not only characteristics inherent in the films themselves; they also depend on the particular culture with which we are operating. And unless there is a world consensus on the subject (which is an empirical question), there is no basis for assuming that a western will be received in the same way in every culture. The way in which the *genre* term is applied can quite conceivably vary from case to case. *Genre* notions – except in the case of arbitrary definition – are not critics' classifications made for special purposes;

> they are sets of cultural conventions. *Genre* is what we collectively believe it to be.
>
> (Tudor 1974a: 139)

The stress here on culture and cultures, rather than just on films, leads Tudor, like Ryall, to stress the role and the importance of audiences too. And this leads him in turn (and for the first time in work on genre and genres in the cinema) not just outside the realm of Hollywood but outside the realms of mainstream cinema altogether:

> the genre concept is indispensable in more strictly social and psychological terms as a way of formulating the interplay between culture, audience, films and filmmakers. For example, there is a class of films thought by a relatively highly educated middle-class group of filmgoers as 'art movies' [Tudor goes on to cite *The Seventh Seal* (1956), *L'Aventura* (1960) and *La Dolce Vita* (1959) as examples]. Now for the present purposes *genre* is a conception existing in the culture of any particular group or society; it is not a way in which a critic classifies films for methodological purposes, but the much looser way in which an audience classifies its films. According to this meaning of the term, 'art movies' is a *genre*.
>
> (Tudor 1974a: 145)

Thus, to reiterate, 'there does not seem to me to be any crucial difference between the most commonly applied *genre* term – the western – and the art-movie that I have been discussing. They are both conceptions held by certain groups about certain films' (ibid.: 147).

It is here, in including art films under the rubric of genre, and in defining genres as 'conceptions', that Tudor departs most radically from most of the ideas and definitions of genre in the cinema advanced hitherto. The questions he asks are radical ones. They challenge conventional notions as to the cinematic and cultural site of genre and genres. They open up the issue of groupings and classification. And they place spectatorial and audience activity and the cultural and institutional contexts within which that activity takes place firmly at the centre of theoretical debate. To that extent they are echoed not just by Williams and Neale, but also by a number of linguists, philosophers and literary theorists who have written on genre in recent years.

Literature, linguistics and genre

On a number of occasions in the 1960s and 1970s, writers on genre in the cinema referred to definitions and theories of genre in literature. Some, like Cawelti (1976), made use of particular literary theories (in Cawelti's case, those of Frye 1957). However, while the existence of literary theory was explicitly acknowledged, it was in practice usually ignored. One of the reasons for this, as Ryall points out, was the apparent discrepancy between generic terms and 'divisions' in literature, and the terms and divisions familiar to critics and theorists of the cinema:

> As well as the widespread usage within film, the critic also has to contend with the term as it occurs in the discussion of other arts, notably literature where genre divisions have been made on the basis of formal distinctions (the novel, drama, poetry) compared with the subject or content divisions more usual in film criticism. The term, therefore, while having an apparent stability within the discussion of film becomes somewhat confusing in the context of, for example, genre definitions in literature.
>
> (Ryall 1975/6: 27)

Hence while Buscombe, for instance, referred in passing to the divisions in Aristotle's *Poetics* between 'tragedy, epic, lyric, and so forth' (1970: 33), they were effectively forgotten by the time he turned to the gangster film, the western and the musical.

It was not until 1984 that this discrepancy was re-raised and discussed as an issue, during the course of Williams's review of Schatz's *Hollywood Genres* (1981):

> Perhaps the biggest problem with genre or genre criticism in the field of the cinema is the word *genre*. Borrowed, as a critical tool, from literary studies (or at least having resonances from that area – the word does have a life of its own in the film industry) the applicability of 'genre' as a concept in film studies raises some fairly tough questions. Sample genres are held to be Westerns, Science Fiction Films, more recently Disaster Films, and so on. What do these loose groupings of works – that seem to come and go, for the most part, in ten- and twenty-year cycles – have to do with familiar genres such as tragedy, comedy, romance, or (to mix the pot up a bit) the epistolary novel or the prose poem?
>
> (A. Williams 1984: 121)

Williams continues:

> For the phrase 'genre films', referring to a general category, we can frequently, though not always, substitute 'film narrative'. Perhaps *that* is the real genre. Certainly there is much more difference between *Prelude to Dog Star Man* and *Star Wars* than there is between the latter and *Body Heat*. It's mainly a question of terminology, of course, but I wonder if we ought to consider the principal

film genres as being the narrative film, experimental/avant-garde film, and documentary. Surely these are the categories in film studies that have among themselves the sorts of significant differences that one can find between, say, epic and lyric poetry.

(A. Williams 1984: 121)

The first point to make in response to this is to highlight the extent to which genres and genre categories in literature are by no means always as systematically coherent or long-lived as Williams – or Ryall – seem to suggest. Comedy, romance and tragedy are long-lived as terms, but the criteria that define them, along with the types of work they encompass, have in each case changed over time (see Beer 1970 on romance, and Koelb 1975 on tragedy). Moreover, comedy and romance, at least, are familiar as terms and as genres to critics and theorists of film. In addition, the criteria that define, say, the epistolary novel and epic poetry on the one hand and comedy and romance on the other are very different in kind, varying from the purely formal (in the case of the epistolary novel), to a mix of criteria involving form, content and tone (in the case of most of the others). And to switch the focus of the argument, the western and science fiction are both literary genres as well as cinematic ones. Even the disaster film of the late 1960s and early 1970s has its analogue – indeed its origins – in contemporary novels written by Arthur Hailey, Paul Gallico, Richard Martin Stern, and others.

This leads me to a second point, a point that is crucial for understanding why genre and genres have so often been identified with Hollywood (rather than, say, the art film), and hence why some of the contradictions and discrepancies to which Williams points have arisen. Within a great deal of modern writing on literature, the kind of fiction exemplified by disaster novels and science fiction is often the only kind labelled as generic. The rest is 'literary fiction' or simply 'literature' proper. The latter is the province of 'genuine' literary art and 'authentic' authorial expression. The former, by contrast, is usually considered formulaic, stereotypical, artistically anonymous, and therefore artistically worthless. Hence the following, from Sutherland's *Fiction and the Fiction Industry*:

> Another feature of the increasingly 'packaged' nature of all fiction – including the quality novel – is the advance of 'genre' or the categorised product. By 'genre' is meant such forms as Science Fiction, the detective novel, Gothic, etc . . .
>
> Genre incorporates a high ration of familiar to strange elements. Habitually it eliminates the bewilderment associated with avant garde and experimentalism. It specialises in books without shock. If, as Ezra Pound says, the modernist's motto is 'make it new' then the genre author's motto is 'make it the same' . . . Genre fiction is, characteristically, convention-governed . . . There is a soothing

> quality to much genre fiction; a high incidence of what Q.D. Leavis calls 'living at the novelist's expense' . . . generally the material is bland, despite its claims to unbearable excitement. Similarly genre may have a superficially impressive specialised knowledge . . . But in the end there will be nothing to task the reader's capacities.
> (Sutherland 1978: 192–4. For a very different view, see Bloom 1996.)

It will be readily apparent that those writing on Hollywood's genres in the 1960s and 1970s decisively rejected – indeed often symmetrically inverted – the values and judgement evident in a passage like this McArthur for instance, argues that genre conventions can play a positive role in curbing authorial 'excess and self-indulgence' (1972: 94). However, the point to emphasize here is that they share its definitions and its terms, and that these definitions and terms, along with the values and judgements of someone like Sutherland, have a distinct and particular history. As Kress and Threadgold have pointed out:

> *Genre* is valorised very differently in different contexts. From the Romantics through modernism to postmodernism, *genre* is a devalued term in the dominant literary/aesthetic discourse. To be 'generic' is to be predictable and clichéd; within that ideology, literature and art generally has to be free, creative, individual . . . hence literature cannot be generic . . .
>
> In classical periods, for example the English Neo-classical period in the late seventeenth and early eighteenth centuries, or even before then in the Renaissance, the reverse was the case. Literature had to be generic to be considered literature (consider Dryden's famous essay on Dramatic Poesy), and notions of genre were so intimately tied up with what was to be literature that they overtly and in very conscious ways affected both the reading and writing of literary texts.
>
> (Kress and Threadgold 1988: 219–20)

Threadgold reiterates these points elsewhere, stressing the role of conceptions of genre within and across the cultural divisions in artistic practice, in particular those between 'high' and 'low', 'popular' and 'elite':

> Before Romanticism what was Generic was Literature. The rest, the 'popular culture' of political pamphlets, ballads, romances, chapbooks, was not only *not* generic; it escaped the law of genre, was excluded by that law, suffering a kind of rhetorical exclusion by inclusion in the classical distinction between high, middle, and low styles. It was seen as a kind of anarchic, free area, unconstrained by the rules of polite society and decorum, by *genre* in fact.
>
> (Threadgold 1989: 121–2)

Thus genre has undergone 'a fundamental shift of positioning' (ibid.: 120). And this shift runs parallel with shifts both in cultural and aesthetic production and consumption, and in the history of the term 'genre' itself. As Cohen has pointed out, the use of the term in English to refer to aesthetic practices and products is a nineteenth-century phenomenon (1986: 203). Thus although the concept is clearly much older, the term itself emerges with industrialization, mass production, new technologies, new capital, new means of distribution (notably postal systems and the railways), the formation of a relatively large literate (or semi-literate) population – and hence a potential market – at a point of profound transformation in the conditions governing cultural production and the discourses and debates with which it was accompanied.[3] Now it is the new popular culture, the new mass culture that is marked – with a new term – as 'generic'. Repetitive patterns, ingredients and formulae are now perceived by many cultural commentators not as the law of Culture, but as the law of the market. It is therefore hardly surprising that genre was – and still is – principally associated with an industrial, commercial and mechanically based art like the cinema, and with its most obviously industrial, commercial and popular sectors like Hollywood in particular. And it is thus particularly important to consider ideas, definitions and theories of genre which challenge conventional conceptions.

One source of and for such ideas is the literary critic E. D. Hirsch (a surprising source, perhaps, given his commitment to traditional literary values). Hirsch insists on the fundamental role played by genre – not just in the framing and interpretation of works of art but also in the framing and interpretation of any kind of utterance. He also insists on the fact that genres centrally include – even consist of – a set of expectations. A reader's or interlocutor's 'preliminary generic conception', he writes, 'is constitutive of everything that he subsequently understands, . . . and this [always] remains the case unless and until that generic conception is altered' (1967: 74). In elaborating this view at greater length, Hirsch makes clear that genre in this sense is as much a phenomenon of everyday discourse as it is of literary texts:

> quite apart from the speaker's choice of words, and, even more remarkably, quite aside from the context in which the utterance occurs, the details of meaning that an interpreter understands are powerfully determined and constituted by his meaning expectation. And these expectations arise from the interpreter's conception of the type of meaning that is being expressed.
>
> By 'type of meaning' I do not, of course, intend to imply merely a type of message or theme or anything so simple as content. The interpreter's expectations embrace far more than that. They include a number of elements that may not even be explicitly given in the utterance or its context, such as the relationship assumed to exist

> between the speaker and the interpreter, thc type of vocabulary and syntax that is used, the type of attitude adopted by the speaker, and the type of inexplicit meanings that go with explicit ones. Such expectations are always necessary to understanding, because only by virtue of them can the interpreter make sense of the words he experiences along the way. He entertains the notion that 'this is a certain type of meaning,' and his notion of the meaning as a whole grounds and helps determine his understanding of details. This fact reveals itself whenever a misunderstanding is suddenly recognized. After all, how could it have been recognized unless the interpreter's expectations had been thwarted? How could anything surprising or puzzling occur to force a revision of his past understanding unless the interpreter had expectations that could be surprised or thwarted? Furthermore, these expectations could have arisen only from the genre idea: 'In this type of utterance, we expect these types of traits.'
>
> (Hirsch 1967: 72–3)

During the course of his discussion of genre, Hirsch draws in particular on the structural linguistics of Saussure ([1959] 1974). Issues of genre and parallels with Hirsch's position have been more apparent, however, in speech act theory and pragmatics. Speech-act theory and pragmatics are branches of linguistics and of analytical philosophy, respectively. They are both concerned with language in use, and in particular with the rules and conventions that govern the production, reception and comprehension of specific kinds of linguistic utterance in specific kinds of context.[4] Mary Louise Pratt (1977), for instance, has written a pioneering book on speech-act theory and literature stressing the generic aspects of all forms of discourse, indeed of 'literature' as such. More recently, in an essay on the short story, she highlights the role, importance and ubiquity of genre in literary and in non-literary discourse alike. 'Genre is not solely a literary matter', she writes. 'The concept of genres applies to all verbal behavior, in all realms of discourse. Genre conventions are in play in any speech situation, and any discourse belongs to a genre, unless it is a discourse explicitly designed to flaunt the genre system' (1981: 176).

Speech-act-oriented theories of genre have recently been drawn on (and sometimes modified, extended or criticized, though always from within a recognizable similar ambit of concerns) by Derrida (1992), Freadman (1988), Hunter (1989), Reid (1989) and Ryan (1981). Derrida criticizes speech-act theories of genre on the grounds that texts can always exceed specific expectations, contexts and labels. He would therefore contest Pratt's notion that texts 'belong' to genres. He would also deny, though, that any text or instance of discourse could ever escape being generic. A text or an instance of discourse might be able to 'flaunt' a particular 'genre system', but they could never flaunt the 'law of genre' as such, for the simple reason that all texts, all utterances, all instances of discourse are always encountered in some kind of context, and are therefore always confronted with expectations, with systems of comprehension, and in all probability with labels and names. Freadman gives a good example of this:

> When the title 'Untitled' started appearing beneath paintings, it corresponded to the claim of abstract painting to be non-representational: to be 'painting', simply . . . It is a title that represents the non-representational. Now, since the titles of paintings – place-names, personal names, the names of historical or legendary events, or kinds of subjects – designate not only their represented subjects but also, through the naming conventions themselves, their genres, the title 'Untitled' claims above all to transcend genre. Reflect on this. For 'untitled' paintings are themselves a genre; and the title 'Untitled' points to genre in the very act of its denial.
>
> (Freadman 1988: 67)

A less spectacular example from the cinema would be a film like *Un Chien Andalou* (1928), which certainly flaunted the genre system predominant in Europe at the time it was made. It also flaunted the genre 'narrative feature film', and the genres of the contemporary European art film. One of its makers, Luis Buñuel, claimed it was not even an instance of avant-garde film-making, but rather 'a desperate appeal to murder' (Aranda 1975: 63). However, it is precisely for all these reasons that it is usually now understood, and now usually labelled generically, as an exemplary instance of Surrealism. Hence, to return to Derrida, 'Every text participates in one or several genres, there is no genreless text.' Although 'participation never amounts to belonging', 'there is always a genre or genres' (1992: 230).

Derrida's use of the phrase 'one or several genres', his stress on the possible plurality of generic participation, may not resolve the discrepancies between some of the genre terms used in literary studies and the terms that tend to dominate the study of the cinema. (Such discrepancies are historical in origin, and are thus not entirely susceptible to logical or conceptual resolution.) But it does point to a way of resolving Williams' dilemma about 'real' genres, and the validity of categories like the western and science fiction on the one hand, and 'narrative film, experimental/avant-garde film, or documentary' on the other. For from a Derridean perspective, this dilemma is ultimately false. Any film (like any text, utterance or instance of representation) can participate in several genres at once. In fact, it is more common than not for a film to do so. Thus, without trying to be too exhaustive (and leaving aside for the moment the issue of overt generic hybrids), both *Star Wars* (1977) and *Body Heat* (1981), to use two of Williams' (1984) examples, participate in the genres 'film', 'fiction film', 'Hollywood film' and 'narrative feature film'. The former also participates in the genre 'science fiction', and the latter in the genre 'thriller' (and possibly also 'neo-*noir*'). *Prelude to Dog Star Man* (1965), meanwhile, participates in the genres 'film' and 'avant-garde/experimental film' – and also, for some of its viewers at least, the genres 'mythopoeic' and/or 'visionary film', categories first suggested by the influential critic and historian of American avant-garde film, P. Adams Sitney (1979).

While challenging traditional definitions of genre, it is worth noting that there remains a degree of common ground between speech-act-oriented theorists like Pratt, Hirsch and Derrida and theorists like Tudor and Ryall. All agree that genre is a multi-dimensional phenomenon and that its dimensions centrally include systems of expectation, categories, labels and names, discourses, texts and corpuses of texts, and the conventions that govern them all. Some stress the primacy of expectations, others the primacy of texts, still others the primacy of categories, corpuses, the norms they encompass, the traditions they embody and the formulae that mark them. What seems clear is that all these dimensions need to be taken into account. What also seems clear is that they need to be distinguished one from another.

However, the argument that genre is ubiquitous, a phenomenon common to all instances of discourse, ignores or collapses the distinction between those instances which are relatively formulaic, relatively predictable, relatively conventional, and those which are not, between those produced in accordance with the conventions of a pre-signalled genre or genre system and those designed to flaunt them. It also ignores or collapses the boundaries between different ways of categorizing texts and of grouping expectations. The expectations triggered by the name of a star or director are as generic as those triggered by terms like 'western', 'thriller' or 'horror film'. One would normally want, though, to distinguish between the two.

These boundaries and distinctions underlie a great deal of traditional thinking about genres. They have often been tied, as we have seen, to issues of evaluation. They have often been linked to the establishment of aesthetic and cultural hierarchies. And they have often inhibited the development of genre theory. However, while it is important to question traditional thinking and to expand the definition, the meaning and the field of application of genre as a term, it is also important to recognize the differences these boundaries and distinctions serve to mark.

Genre and the genre film

One way of acknowledging some of these differences without falling into the usual conceptual or cultural traps is to note that they apply to high art as well as to low: a sonnet is formulaic in a way that free verse is not; a Restoration comedy is conventional in a way that a modernist novel is not; and so on. In addition, it should be noted that when Warshow talked about the pleasures and characteristics of aesthetic 'types', he was referring to

Restoration comedy and Elizabethan tragedy as well as to westerns and gangster films: 'For a type to be successful', he wrote

> its conventions have imposed themselves upon the general consciousness and become the vehicle of a particular set of attitudes and a particular aesthetic effect. One goes to any individual example of the type with very definite expectations, and originality is to be welcomed only in the degree that it intensifies the expected experience without fundamentally altering it.
>
> (Warshow [1948] 1975a: 129–30)

Within the realms of cinema, numerous movements or trends in art cinema and in avant-garde film-making are or become as predictable (and as typically pleasurable) as any Hollywood western. However, and conversely, there is a difference between academic or programmatic aesthetic formulae and formulae which arise as a result of commercial conditions. And there is a difference between films which are designed to conform, however broadly, to pre-existing categories, expectations and models, and those, like *Un Chien Andalou*, which are not. The latter may encounter expectations and those expectations may be based on previous films or on the tenets of a movement or a group. They may conform to labels or descriptions circulated in advance by critics, distributors, reviewers, perhaps even film-makers themselves. And they may all establish their own internal norms and hence become more familiar – and more predictable – as they unfold. But many of these norms are often unique to the films themselves. Thus the films are less predictable in advance, and at more or less every level. That does not necessarily make them better. But it does make them different.

Altman makes a further distinction. He points out that

> not all films engage spectators' generic knowledge in the same way and to the same extent. While some films simply borrow devices from established genres, others foreground their generic characteristics to the point where the genre concept itself plays a major role in the film
>
> (Altman 1996a: 279)

Parodies are an obvious instance of the latter, as Altman goes on to indicate. So too are films like *Silverado* (1985), *Chinatown* (1974), *Scarface* (1983) and *Back to the Future III* (1990), films which pastiche, rework or in other ways foreground particular generic traditions, norms and conventions. Altman, following Schatz (1981: 16–18), goes on to propose two different terms, 'film genre' and 'genre film,' in order to mark this particular distinction:

> By definition, all films belong to some genre(s) . . . but only certain films are self-consciously produced and consumed according to (or

> against) a specific generic model. When the notion of genre is limited to descriptive uses, as it commonly is when serving . . . classification purposes, we speak of 'film genre'. However, when the notion of genre takes on a more active role in the production and consumption process, we appropriately speak instead of 'genre film', thus recognizing the extent to which generic identification becomes a formative component of film viewing.
>
> (Altman 1996a: 277)

While these terms and definitions are useful, Altman here tends to conflate genre as a category and genre as a corpus of films: *Stagecoach* (1939) is both a singular instance of the category 'western' and part of an expanding corpus that includes films like *Hell's Hinges* (1916), *Riders of the Range* (1923), *Bend of the River* (1952), *El Dorado* (1967) and *Tombstone* (1993). The two are distinct. He also tends, through the term 'self-conscious', to conflate routine generic production and routine generic consumption, both of which entail specific generic models and in both of which such models are 'active', with special and particular instances like parody and pastiche. In addition, he tends to imply that the activation of a generic model necessarily entails conformity or participation. But a model may be invoked in order to be reworked or rejected altogether, as is arguably the case with some of the 'revisionist' films of the late 1960s and early 1970s – films like *Chinatown, The Long Goodbye* (1973) and *Buffalo Bill and the Indians* (1976) – which rework or reject existing models of the detective film and the western, and as is certainly the case with *Un Chien Andalou*, which both invokes and decisively rejects the model of the contemporary narrative film. For all these reasons, the proposed term 'genre film' tends to evoke traditional definitions, thereby potentially reducing the multiplicity and scope of the phenomenon of genre itself. In order to avoid some of these problems, and in order to take some account of speech-act-oriented thinking, terms like 'generically marked film' and 'generically modelled film' might be preferable. The former would indicate films which rely on generic identification by an audience – and hence specific forms of audience knowledge – in order to make sense. (This would include parody, pastiche and other forms of self-consciousness. But it would also include less specialized instances as well.) The latter would indicate films which draw on and conform to existing generic traditions, conventions and formulae. In practice, of course, the two often overlap. But the former refers more to the moment of reception, and may include instances of generic reworking and generic rejection as well as instances of generic conformity. The latter refers to the moment of production, and by definition excludes generic rejection. Both remain distinct from genre as a category, and genre as a group or corpus of films.

What emerges from this overview is that genre as a term has been used in different ways in different fields, and that many of its uses have been governed by the history of the term within these fields – and by the cultural factors at play within them – rather than by logic or conceptual consistency. The questions raised by Ryall, Tudor and Williams are important ones, as are the questions raised by speech-act theory and pragmatics. The answers to these questions require thinking of genres as ubiquitous, multifaceted phenomena rather than as one-dimensional entities to be found only within the realms of Hollywood cinema or of commercial popular culture. Only then can some of the pitfalls identified by Ryall, by Tudor, by Williams and by others be avoided. And only then can the nature, the functions, and the general topic of genre in Hollywood itself be examined in more detail.

Notes

1 On the Indian mythological, see Barnouw and Krishnaswarmy (1980: 11–23), and on the Hong Kong swordplay film, see Mo-ling (1981). On the documentary, see Barnouw (1974), Corner (1996), Guynn (1990), Nichols (1991), Renov (1993), and Winston (1995). On art cinema and art films, see Bordwell (1979, 1985), Neale (1981a) and Siska (1976).

2 See, for instance, Hall and Whannel (1964). On some of the reasons for a more positive response in Britain at this time to American popular culture in general and to Hollywood films in particular, see Bennett (1981), Nowell-Smith (1987b) and Strinati (1993).

3 On the growth and forms of industrial mass culture in the West in the ninteenth century, see among others, Allen (1981), Altick (1957), Barth (1980), Bianchi (1986), Birch (1987), Bold (1987, 1991), Denning (1987), Fullerton (1979), Gedin (1977), Hart (1963), McConachie and Freedman (1988), Mates (1985), Noel (1954), Pryluck (1986), Purcell (1977), Radway (1984), Reynolds (1955), Snyder (1970), Somers (1971), Sterne (1980), Toll (1976) and Wilson (1973).

4 On pragmatics and speech-act theory, see Blakemore (1992), Davis (1991), Leech (1983), Levinson (1983), Lyons (1981) and Mey (1993).

References

(Most references to newspapers, magazines and trade journals are given in full in the text or the notes.)

Allen, J. S. (1981) *Popular French Romanticism: Authors, Readers and Books in the 19th Century*, Syracuse: Syracuse University Press.

Alloway, L. (1963) 'On the Iconography of the Movies', *Movie* 7: 4–6.

—— (1971) *Violent America: The Movies 1946–1964*, New York: Museum of Modern Art.

Altick, R. (1957) *A Social History of the Mass Reading Public*, Chicago: Chicago University Press.

Altman, R. (ed.) (1981a) *Genre: The Musical*, London: RKP/British Film Institute.
([1978] 1981b) 'The American Film Musical: Paradigmatic Structure and Mediatory Function', in Altman 1981a, 197–207.

—— ([1984] 1986) 'A Semantic/Syntactic Approach to Film Genre', in Grant 1986a, 26–39.

—— (1987) *The American Film Musical*, Bloomington: Indiana University Press.
—— (1996a) 'Cinema and Genre', in Nowell-Smith 1996, 276–85.
Aranda, F. (1975) *Luis Buñuel: A Critical Biography*, London: Secker and Warburg.
Barnouw, E. (1974) *Documentary: A History of the Non-Fiction Film*, Oxford: Oxford University Press.
Barnouw, E. and Krishnaswarmy, S. (1980) *Indian Film*, Oxford: Oxford University Press.
Barth, G. (1980) *City People: The Rise of Modern City Culture in Nineteenth Century America*, Oxford: Oxford University Press.
Bazin, A. (1971a) 'The Western, or the American Film par excellence', in *What is Cinema?*, vol. 2, trans. and ed. H. Gray, Berkeley: University of California Press, 140–8.
—— (1971b) 'The Evolution of the Western', in *What is Cinema?*, vol. 2, 149–57.
Beer, G. (1970) *The Romance*, London: Methuen.
Behlmer, R. (1979) 'Introduction: From Legend to Film', in R. Behlmer (ed.), *The Adventures of Robin Hood*, Wisconsin: Wisconsin University Press, 11–41.
Bennett, T. (1981) 'Popular Culture and Hegemony in Post-War Britain', in *Politics, Ideology and Popular Culture*, Milton Keynes: Open University.
Bianchi, A. (1986) 'Le Roman Feuilleton en Italie', in R. Guise and H.-J. Neuschafer (eds), *Richesses du Roman Populaire*, Nancy: Centre de Recherches sur le Roman Populaire, 389–97.
Birch, M. J. (1987) 'The Popular Fiction Industry: Market, Formula, Ideology', *Journal of Popular Culture* 21, 3: 79–102.
Blakemore, D. (1992) *Understanding Utterances: An Introduction to Pragmatics*, Oxford: Blackwell.
Bloom, C. (1996) *Cult Fiction: Popular Reading and Pulp Theory*, Houndmills: Macmillan.
Bold, C. (1987) *Selling the Wild West: Popular Western Fiction, 1860–1960*, Bloomington: Indiana University Press.
—— (1991) 'Popular Forms 1', in Elliott 1991, 285–305.
Bordwell, D. (1979) 'Art Cinema as a Mode of Film Practice', *Film Criticism* 4, 1: 56–64.
—— (1985) *Narration and the Fiction Film*, London: Methuen.
Buscombe, E. (1970) 'The Idea of Genre in the American Cinema', *Screen* 11/2: 33–45.
Caughie, J. (ed.) (1981) *Theories of Authorship*, London: Routledge.
Cawelti, J. (1970) *The Six-Gun Mystique*, Bowling Green: Bowling Green University Press.
—— (1976) *Adventure, Mystery and Romance: Formula Stories as Art and Popular Culture*, Chicago: Chicago University Press.
Chabrol, C. ([1955] 1985) 'The Evolution of the Thriller', trans. L. Heron, in Hillier 1985a, 158–64.
Clover, C. J. (1992) *Men, Women and Chainsaws: Gender in the Modern Horror Film*. London: British Film Institute.
Cohen, R. (1986) 'History and Genre', *New Literary History* 17, 2: 203–18.
Cook, P. (1978) 'Duplicity in *Mildred Pierce*', in Kaplan 1978a, 68–82.
—— (ed.) (1985) *The Cinema Book*, London: British Film Institute.

Corner, J. (1996) *The Art of Record: A Critical Introduction to Documentary*, Manchester: Manchester University Press.
Davis, S. (ed.) (1991) *Pragmatics: A Reader*, Oxford: Oxford University Press.
Denning, M. (1987) *Mechanic Accents: Dime Novels and Working-Class Culture in America*, New York: Verso.
Derrida, J. (1992) 'The Law of Genre', in *Acts of Literature*, ed. D. Attridge, New York: Routledge, 221–52.
Dika, V. (1990) *Games of Terror*: Halloween, Friday the Thirteenth *and the Films of the Stalker Cycle*, London: Associated University Presses.
Doane, M.-A. (1987) *The Desire to Desire: The Woman's Film of the 1940s*, Basingstoke: Macmillan.
Elliott, E. (ed.) (1991) *The Columbia History of the American Novel*, New York: Columbia University Press.
Freadman, A. (1988) 'Untitled (On Genre)', *Cultural Studies* 2, 1: 67–99.
Frye, N. (1957) *Anatomy of Criticism: Four Essays*, Princeton: Princeton University Press.
Fullerton, R. (1979) 'Creating a Mass Book Market in Germany: The Story of the "Colporteur Novel", 1870–1890', *Journal of Social History* 2, 4: 489–511.
Gedin, P. (1977) *Literature in the Marketplace*, London: Faber.
Gledhill (1978) '*Klute* Part I: A Contemporary Film Noir and Feminist Criticism', in Kaplan 1978a, 6–21.
—— (1985a) 'History of Genre Criticism', in Cook 1985, 58–64.
—— (ed.) (1987a) *Home is Where The Heart Is: Studies in Melodrama and the Woman's Film*, London: British Film Institute.
Grant, B. K. (ed.) (1984) *Planks of Reason: Essays on the Horror Film*, Metuchen: Scarecrow Press.
—— (ed.) (1986a) *Film Genre Reader*, Austin: University of Texas Press.
—— (1986b) 'Introduction' to Grant 1986a, ix–xvi.
Guynn, W. (1990) *A Cinema of Nonfiction*, London: Associated University Presses.
Hall, S. and Whannel, P. (1964). *The Popular Arts*, London: Hutchinson.
Hart, J. D. (1963) *The Popular Book: A History of America's Literary Taste*, Berkeley: University of California Press.
Hillier, J. (ed.) (1985a) *Cahiers du Cinéma, The 1950s: New-Realism, Hollywood, New Wave*, Cambridge, Mass.: Harvard University Press.
—— (1985b) 'Introduction' to Hillier 1985a, 1–27.
Hirsch, E. D. (1967) *Validity in Interpretation*, New Haven: Yale University Press.
Hunter, I. (1989) 'Providence and Profit: Speculation in the Genre Market', *Southern Review* 22: 211–23.
Kaplan, E. A. (1978a) *Women in Film Noir*, London: British Film Institute.
Kitses, J. (1969) *Horizons West*, London: Thames and Hudson.
Koelb, C. (1975) 'The Problem of Tragedy as a Genre', *Genre* 8, 3: 248–66.
Kress, G. and Threadgold, T. (1988) 'Towards a Social Theory of Genre', *Southern Review* 21, 3: 215–43.
Leech, G. (1974) *Semantics*, Harmondsworth: Penguin.
—— (1983) *The Principles of Pragmatics*, London: Longman.
Levinson, S. C. (1983) *Pragmatics*, Cambridge: Cambridge University Press.
Lyons, J. (1977) *Semantics*, 2 vols, Cambridge: Cambridge University Press.
—— (1981) *Language, Meaning and Context*, London: Fontana.

McArthur, C. (1972) *Underworld USA*, London: Secker and Warburg.
—— (1973) 'Iconography and Iconology', unpublished paper.
McConachie, B. A. and Freedman, D. (eds) (1988) *Theatre for Working-Class Audiences in the United States, 1830–1980*, Westport: Greenwood Press.
Mates, J. (1985) *America's Musical Stage: Two Hundred Years of Musical Theatre*, New York: Praeger.
Mey, J. L. (1993) *Pragmatics: An Introduction*, Oxford: Blackwell.
Mo-ling, L. (ed.) (1981) *A Study of the Hong Kong Swordplay Film*, Hong Kong: The Fifth Hong Kong International Film Festival.
Neale, S. (1980) *Genre*, London: British Film Institute.
—— (1981a) 'Art Cinema as Institution', *Screen* 22, 1: 11–39.
—— (1990a) 'Questions of Genre', *Screen* 31, 1: 45–66.
Nichols, B. (1991) *Representing Reality: Issues and Concepts in Documentary*, Bloomington: Indiana University Press.
Noel, M. (1954) *Villains Galore . . . The Heyday of the Popular Story Weekly*, New York: Macmillan.
Nowell-Smith, G. ([1977] 1987a) 'Minnelli and Melodrama', in Gledhill 1987a, 70–9.
—— (1987b) 'Popular Culture', *New Formations* 2: 79–90.
—— (ed.) (1996) *The Oxford History of World Cinema*, Oxford: Oxford University Press.
Panofsky, I. (1970) *Meaning in the Visual Arts*, Harmondsworth: Penguin.
—— ([1934] 1974) 'Style and Medium in the Motion Pictures', in G. Mast and M. Cohen (eds), *Film Theory and Criticism: Introductory Readings*, New York: Oxford University Press.
Pratt, M. L. (1977) *Towards a Speech Act Theory of Literary Discourse*, Bloomington: Indiana University Press.
—— (1981) 'The Short Story: The Long and the Short of It', *Poetics* 10: 175–94.
Pryluck, C. (1986) 'Industrialization of Entertainment in the United States', in B. A. Austin (ed.), *Current Research in Film: Audiences, Economics, and Law*, vol. 2, Norwood: Ablex, 117–35.
Purcell, L. E. (1977) '*Trilby* and *Trilby*-Mania: The Beginnings of the Bestseller System', *Journal of Popular Culture* 11, 1: 62–76.
Radway, J. (1984) *Reading the Romance: Women, Patriarchy, and Popular Literature*, Chapel Hill: University of North Carolina Press.
Reid, I. (1989) 'When is an Epitaph Not an Epitaph? A Monumental Generic Problem and a Jonsonian Instance', *Southern Review* 22: 198–208.
Renov, M. (1988) *Hollywood's Wartime Women: Representation and Ideology*, Ann Arbor: UMI Research Press.
—— (ed.) (1993) *Theorizing Documentary*, New York: Routledge.
Reynolds, Q. (1955) *The Fiction Factory, or From Pulp Row to Quality Street*, New York: Random House.
Rieupeyrout, J. L. (1953) *Le Western, ou le Cinema Américain par Excellence*, Paris: Editions du Cerf.
Ryall, T. (1975/6) 'Teaching through Genre', *Screen Education* 17: 27–33.
Ryan, M.-L. (1981) 'Introduction: On the Why, What and How of Generic Taxonomy', *Poetics* 10: 127–47.
Sarris, A. (1968) *The American Cinema: Directors and Directions 1929–1968*, New York: Dutton.

Saussure, F. de ([1959] 1974) *Course in General Linguistics*, trans. W. Baskin, London: Collins.

Schatz, T. (1981) *Hollywood Genres: Formulas, Filmmaking and the Studio System*, New York: Random House.

Siska, W. (1976) 'Modernism in the Narrative Cinema: The Art Film as Genre', Unpublished Ph.D. thesis, Northwestern University.

Sitney, P. A. (1979) *Visionary Film: The American Avant-Garde 1943–1978*, New York: Oxford University Press.

Snyder, F. E. (1970) 'American Vaudeville – Theater in a Package – Origins of Mass Entertainment', Unpublished Ph.D. thesis, Yale University.

Somers, D. A. (1971) 'The Leisure Revolution: Recreation in America', *Journal of Popular Culture* 1, 1: 125–47.

Stam, R., Burgoyne, R. and Flitterman-Lewis, S. (1992) *New Vocabularies in Film Semiotics: Structuralism, Post-Structuralism and Beyond*, London: Routledge.

Sterne, M. (ed.) (1980) *Publishers for Mass Entertainment in Nineteenth Century America*, Boston: G. K. Hall.

Strinati, D. (1993) 'The Taste of America: Americanization and Popular Culture in Britain', in D. Strinati and S. Wragg (eds), *Come on Down? Popular Media Culture in Post-War Britain*, London: Routledge, 46–81.

Sutherland, J. A. (1978) *Fiction and the Fiction Industry*, London: Athlone Press.

Taves, B. (1993a) *The Romance of Adventure: The Genre of Historical Adventure Movies*, Jackson: University of Mississippi Press.

Threadgold, T. (1989) 'Talking about Genre: Ideologies and Incompatible Discourse', *Cultural Studies* 3, 1: 101–26.

Toll, R. C. (1976) *On With The Show: The First Century of Show Business in America*, New York: Oxford University Press.

Truffaut, F. ([1954] 1976) 'A Certain Tendency of the French Cinema', trans. uncredited, in B. Nichols (ed.), *Movies and Methods: Anthology*, vol. 1, Berkeley: University of California Press, 224–37.

Tudor, A. (1974a) *Theories of Film*, London: Secker and Warburg.

—— (1974b) *Image and Influence: Studies in the Sociology of Film*, London: Allen and Unwin.

Warren, A. and Welleck, R. (1956) *Theory of Literature*, New York: Harcourt, Brace.

Warshow, R. ([1948] 1975a) 'The Gangster as Tragic Hero', in *The Immediate Experience: Movies, Comics, Theatre and Other Aspects of Popular Culture* [1962], New York: Atheneum, 127–33.

—— ([1954] 1975b) 'Movie Chronicle: The Westerner', in *The Immediate Experience: Movies, Comics, Theatre and Other Aspects of Popular Culture* [1962], New York: Atheneum, 135–54.

Williams, A. (1984) 'Is a Radical Genre Criticism Possible?', *Quarterly Review of Film Studies* 9, 2: 121–5.

Wilson, G. B. (1973) *Three Hundred Years of American Drama and Theatre*, Englewood Cliffs: Prentice-Hall.

Winston, B. (1995) *Claiming the Real: The Documentary Film Revisited*, London: British Film Institute.

Wright, W. (1975) *Six-Guns and Society: A Structural Study of the Western*, Berkeley: University of California Press.

33

THE WESTERN: OR THE AMERICAN FILM *PAR EXCELLENCE*

André Bazin

Source: Translated by Hugh Gray, in *What is Cinema? Vol. 2*, Berkeley CA: University of California Press, 1972, pp. 140–148. (Originally published as 'Le western ou le cinéma américain par excellence', Preface to J.-L. Rieupeyrout, *Le western ou le cinéma américain par excellence*, 7e Art, Éditions du Cerf, 1953, pp. 5–13.)

The western is the only genre whose origins are almost identical with those of the cinema itself and which is as alive as ever after almost half a century of uninterrupted success. Even if one disputes the quality of its inspiration and of its style since the thirties, one is amazed at the steady commercial success which is the measure of its health. Doubtless the western has not entirely escaped the evolution of cinema taste—or indeed taste, period. It has been and will again be subjected to influences from the outside—for instance the crime novel, the detective story, or the social problems of the day—and its simplicity and strict form have suffered as a result. We may be entitled to regret this, but not to see in it a state of decay. These influences are only felt in a few productions of relatively high standing and do not affect the low-budget films aimed principally at the home market. Furthermore, it is as important for us to marvel at the western's capacity to resist them as to deplore these passing moments of contamination. Every influence acts on them like a vaccine. The microbe, on contact, loses its deadly virulence. In the course of fifteen years, the American comedy has exhausted its resources. If it survives in an occasional success, it is only to the extent that, in some way, it abandons the rules that before the war made for successful comedy. From *Underworld* (1927) to *Scarface* (1932) the gangster film had already completed the cycle of its growth. The scenarios of detective stories have developed rapidly, and if it is still possible to rediscover an aesthetic of violence within the framework of the criminal adventure which they share with *Scarface*, we would be hard put to see in the private eye, the journalist, or the G-man the reflection of the original hero. Furthermore, if there is such a genre as the American detective film one cannot attribute to it the independent identity of the western; the literature which preceded it has continued to influence it, and the latest interesting variants of the crime film derive directly from it.

On the contrary, the durability of the western heroes and plots has been demonstrated recently by the fabulous success on television of the old Hopalong Cassidy films. The western does not age.

Its world-wide appeal is even more astonishing than its historical survival. What can there possibly be to interest Arabs, Hindus, Latins, Germans, or Anglo-Saxons, among whom the western has had an uninterrupted success, about evocations of the birth of the United States of America, the struggle between Buffalo Bill and the Indians, the laying down of the railroad, or the Civil War!

The western must possess some greater secret than simply the secret of youthfulness. It must be a secret that somehow identifies it with the essence of cinema.

It is easy to say that because the cinema is movement the western is cinema *par excellence*. It is true that galloping horses and fights are its usual ingredients. But in that case the western would simply be one variety of adventure story. Again, the continuous movement of the characters, carried almost to a pitch of frenzy, is inseparable from its geographical setting and one might just as well define the western by its set—the frontier town and its landscapes; but other genres and schools of filmmaking have made use of the dramatic poetry of the landscape, for example the silent Swedish film, but although it contributed to their greatness it did not insure their survival. Better still, sometimes, as in *The Overlanders*, a western theme is borrowed—in this case the traditional cattle drive—and set in a landscape, central Australia, reasonably like the American West. The result, as we know, was excellent. But fortunately no attempt was made to follow up this paradoxical achievement, whose success was due to an unusual combination of circumstances. If in fact westerns have been shot in France against the landscapes of the Camargue, one can only see in this an additional proof of the popularity and healthiness of a genre that can survive counterfeiting, pastiche, or even parody.

It would be hopeless to try to reduce the essence of the western to one or other of these manifest components. The same ingredients are to be found elsewhere but not the same benefits that appear to go with them. Therefore, the western must be something else again than its form. Galloping horses, fights, strong and brave men in a wildly austere landscape could not add up to a definition of the genre nor encompass its charms.

Those formal attributes by which one normally recognizes the western are simply signs or symbols of its profound reality, namely the myth. The western was born of an encounter between a mythology and a means of expression: the saga of the West existed before the cinema in literary or folklore form, and the multiplication of western films has not killed off western literature which still retains its public, and continues to provide screenwriters with their best material. But there is no common measure between the limited and national audience for western stories and the world-wide audience for the films which they inspire. Just as the miniatures of the *Books of Hours* served as models for the statuary and the stained-glass windows of the cathedrals, this western literature, freed from the bonds of language, finds a distribution on the screen in keeping with its size—almost as if the dimensions of the image had become one with those of the imagination.

This book [J.-L. Rieupeyrout's *La Grande adventure du western 1894–1964*, for which Bazin was here writing the Preface] will emphasize a little-known aspect of the western: its faithfulness to history. This is not generally recognized—primarily, doubtless, because of our ignorance, but still more because of the deeply rooted prejudice according to which the western can only tell extremely puerile stories, fruits of a naïve power of invention that does not concern itself with psychological, historical, or even material verisimilitude. True, few westerns are explicitly concerned with historical accuracy. True, too, these are not the only ones of any value. It would be absurd to judge the character of Tom Mix—still more of his magic white horse—or even of William Hart or Douglas Fairbanks, all of whom made lovely films in the great primitive period of the western, by the yardstick of archeology.

After all, many current westerns of honorable standing—I am thinking of *Beyond the Great Divide, Yellow Sky,* or *High Noon*—have only a tenuous relation to historical fact. They are primarily works of imagination. But one would be as much in error not to recognize the historical references in the western as to deny the unabashed freedom of its screenplays J.-L. Rieupeyrout gives a complete account of the birth of its epic-like idealization, based on comparatively recent history, yet it could be that his study, concerned to recall to us what is ordinarily forgotten, or even not known, and confining itself to films that justify his thesis, discards by implication the other side of the aesthetic reality. Still, this would show him to be doubly right. For the relations between the facts of history and the western are not immediate and direct, but dialectic. Tom Mix is the opposite of Abraham Lincoln, but after his own fashion he perpetuates Lincoln's cult and his memory. In its most romantic or most naïve form, the western is the opposite of a historical reconstruction. There is no difference between Hopalong Cassidy and Tarzan except for their costume and the arena in which they demonstrate their prowess. However, if one wanted to take the trouble to compare these delightful but unlikely stories and to superimpose on them, as is done in modern physiognomy, a number of negatives of faces, an ideal western would come through, composed of all the constants common to one and to the other: a western made up solely of unalloyed myth. Let us take one example, that of the woman.

In the first third of the film, the good cowboy meets the pure young woman—the good and strong virgin, let us call her—with whom he falls in love. Despite its chasteness we are able to guess this love is shared. However, virtually insurmountable obstacles stand in its way. One of the most significant and most frequent comes from the family of the beloved—for example, her brother is a sinister scoundrel and the good cowboy is forced to rid society of him, man to man. A modern Chimène, our heroine refuses to see in her brother's assassin any sort of a fine fellow. In order to redeem himself in his charmer's eyes and merit forgiveness, our knight must now pass through a series of fabulous trials. He ends by saving his elected bride from a danger that could be fatal to her person, her virtue, her fortune, or all three at once. Following which, since we are now near the end of the film, the damsel would indeed be ungrateful if she did not feel that her suitor had repaid his debt, and allow him to start dreaming of lots of children.

Up to this point, this outline into which one can weave a thousand variants—for example, by substituting the Civil War for the Indian threat, cattle rustlers—comes close to reminding us of the medieval courtly romances by virtue of the preeminence given to the woman and the trials that the finest of heroes must undergo in order to qualify for her love.

But the story is often complicated by a paradoxical character—the saloon B-girl—who as a rule, is also in love with the cowboy. So there would be one woman too many if the god of the screenwriter was not keeping watch. A few minutes before the end, the prostitute with the heart of gold rescues the man she loves from some danger or another, sacrificing her life and her hopeless love for the happiness of her cowboy. This also serves to redeem her in the eyes of the spectators.

There is food for thought here. Note, first of all, that the distinction between good and bad applies only to the men. Women, all up and down the social scale, are in every case worthy of love or at least of esteem or pity. The least little prostitute is redeemed by love and death—although she is spared the latter in *Stagecoach* with its resemblance to de Maupassant's *Boule de Suif*. It is true that the good cowboy is more or less a reformed offender so that henceforth the most moral of marriages with his heroine becomes possible.

Furthermore, in the world of the western, it is the women who are good and the men who are bad, so bad that the best of them must redeem themselves from the original sin of their sex by undergoing various trials. In the Garden of Eden, Eve led Adam into temptation. Paradoxically Anglo-Saxon puritanism, under the pressure of historical circumstances, reverses the Biblical situation. The downfall of the woman only comes about as a result of the concupiscence of men.

Clearly, this theory derives from the actual sociological conditions obtaining in primitive western society which, because of the scarcity of women and the perils of a too harsh existence in this burgeoning world, make it imperative to safeguard its female members and its horses. Hanging was considered enough punishment for stealing a horse. To engender respect for women more was needed than the fear of a risk as trifling as the loss of one's life, namely the positive power of a myth. The myth of the western illustrates, and both initiates and confirms woman in her role as vestal of the social virtues, of which this chaotic world is so greatly in need. Within her is concealed the physical future, and, by way of the institution of the family to which she aspires as the root is drawn to the earth, its moral foundation.

These myths, of which we have just examined what is perhaps the most significant example (the next is the myth of the horse) may themselves doubtless be reduced to an even more essential principle. Basically each of these particularize, by way of an already specific dramatic plot, the great epic Manicheism which sets the forces of evil over against the knights of the true cause. These immense stretches of prairie, of deserts, of rocks to which the little wooden town clings precariously (a primitive amoeba of a civilization), are exposed to all manner of possible things. The Indian, who lived in this world, was incapable of imposing on it man's order. He mastered it only by identifying himself with its pagan savagery. The white Christian on the contrary is truly the conqueror of a new world. The grass sprouts where his horse has passed. He imposes simultaneously his moral and his technical order, the one linked to the other and the former guaranteeing the latter. The physical safety of the stagecoaches, the protection given by the federal troops, the building of the great railroads are less important perhaps than the establishment of justice and respect for the law. The relations between morality and law, which in our ancient civilization are just a subject for an undergraduate paper, were half a century ago the most vital thing confronting the youthful United States. Only strong, rough, and courageous men could tame these virgin lands. Everyone knows that familiarity with death does not keep alive the fear of hell, nor do scruples or moral debate. Policemen and judges are of most help to the weak. It was the force of this conquering humanity that constituted its weakness. Where individual morality is precarious it is only law that can impose the order of the good and the good of order.

But the law is unjust to the extent that it pretends to guarantee a moral society but ignores the individual merits of those who constitute that society. If it is to be effective, this justice must be dispensed by men who are just as strong and just as daring as the criminals. These virtues, as we have said, are in no way compatible with virtue in the absolute sense. The sheriff is not always a better person than the man he hangs. This begets and establishes an inevitable and necessary contradiction. There is often little moral difference between the outlaw and the man who operates within the law. Still, the sheriff's star must be seen as constituting a sacrament of justice, whose worth does not depend on the worthiness of the man who administers it. To this first contradiction a second must be added, the administration of justice which, if it is to be effective, must be drastic and speedy—short of lynching, however—and thus must ignore extenuating circumstances, such as alibis that would take too long to verify. In protecting society, such a form of justice runs the risk of unkindness to the most turbulent though not perhaps the least useful nor even the least deserving of its children.

Although the need for law was never more clearly allied to the need for morality, at the same time never was their antagonism more concrete and more evident. It is this which provides a basis, within a slapstick framework, for Charlie's *Pilgrim*, at the conclusion of which we see our hero riding his horse along the borderline between good and evil, which also happens to be the Mexican border.

John Ford's *Stagecoach*, which is a fine dramatic illustration of the parable of the pharisee and the publican, demonstrates that a prostitute can be more respectable than the narrow-minded people who drove her out of town and just as respectable as an officer's wife; that a dissolute gambler knows how to die with all the dignity of an aristocrat; that an alcoholic doctor can practice his profession with competence and devotion; that an outlaw who is being sought for the payment of past and possibly future debts can show loyalty, generosity, courage, and refinement, whereas a banker of considerable standing and reputation runs off with the cashbox.

So we find at the source of the western the ethics of the epic and even of tragedy. The western is in the epic category because of the superhuman level of its heroes and the legendary magnitude of their feats of valor. Billy the Kid is as invulnerable as Achilles and his revolver is infallible. The cowboy is a knight-at-arms. The style of the *mise en scène* is in keeping with the character of the hero. A transformation into an epic is evident in the set-ups of the shots, with their predilection for vast horizons, all-encompassing shots that constantly bring to mind the conflict between man and nature. The western has virtually no use for the closeup, even for the medium shot, preferring by contrast the traveling shot and the pan which refuse to be limited by the frameline and which restore to space its fullness.

True enough. But this epic style derives its real meaning only from the morality which underlies and justifies it. It is the morality of a world in which social good and evil, in their simplicity and necessity, exist like two primary and basic elements. But good in its natal state engenders law in all its primitive rigor; epic becomes tragedy, on the appearance of the first conflict between the transcendence of social justice and the individual character of moral justice, between the categorical imperative of the law which guarantees the order of the future city, and the no less unshakeable order of the individual conscience.

The Corneille-like simplicity of western scripts has often been a subject for parody. It is easy to see the analogy between them and the text of *Le Cid*: there is the same conflict between love and duty, the same knightly ordeals on the completion of which the wise virgin will consent to forget the insult to her family; the same chaste sentiments which are based on a concept of love subordinated to respect for the laws of society and morality. But this comparison is double-edged: to make fun of the western by comparing it to Corneille is also to draw attention to its greatness, a greatness near perhaps to the child-like, just as childhood is near to poetry.

Let there be no doubt about it. This naïve greatness is recognized in westerns by simple men in every clime—together with the children—despite differences of language, landscape, customs, and dress. The epic and tragic hero is a universal character. The Civil War is part of nineteenth century history, the western has turned it into the Trojan War of the most modern of epics. The migration to the West is our Odyssey.

Not only is the historicity of the western not at odds with the no less evident penchant of the genre for outlandish situations, exaggerations of fact and the use of the *deus ex machina* (in short, everything that makes for improbability); it is, on the contrary, the foundation of its aesthetic and its psychology. The history of film has only known one other epic cinema and that too is a historical cinema. Our purpose here is not to compare epic form in the Russian and in the American film, and yet an analysis of their styles would shed an unexpected light on the historical meaning of the events reconstructed in the two of them. Our only purpose is to point out that it is not their closeness to the facts that has given them their styles. There are legends that come into being almost instantaneously, that half a generation suffices to ripen into an epic. Like the conquest of the West, the Soviet revolution is a collection of historical events which signal the birth of a new order and a new civilization. Both have begotten the myths necessary for the confirmation of history, both had to reinvent a morality to rediscover at their living source and before mixture or pollution took place, the foundation of the law which would make order out of chaos, separate heaven from earth. But perhaps the cinema was the only language capable of expressing this, above all of giving it its true aesthetic dimension. Without the cinema the conquest of the West would have left behind, in the shape of the western story, only a minor literature, and it is neither by its painting nor its novels that Soviet art has given the world a picture of its grandeur. The fact is that henceforth the cinema is the specifically epic art.

34

A NEW KIND OF POLICE DRAMA: THE CRIMINAL ADVENTURE

Nino Frank

Source: Translated by Alain Silver, in Alain Silver and James Ursini, eds, *Film Noir Reader 2*, New York: Limelight Editions, 1999, pp. 15–19. (Originally published as 'Un nouveau genre "policier": l'aventure criminelle', *L'Ecran Français*, 61, August 1946, pp. 8–9 and p. 14.)

Here we are one year after a series of poor quality American movies made it seem that Hollywood was finished. Today another conclusion is needed, because the appearance of half a dozen fine works made in California compels us to write and affirm that American cinema is better than ever. Our filmmakers are decidedly manic depressive.

Seven new American films are particularly masterful: *Citizen Kane, The Little Foxes, How Green Was My Valley*, plus *Double Indemnity, Laura*, and, to a certain extent, *The Maltese Falcon* and *Murder, My Sweet*. The first three are exceptional; but we cannot consider them if we want to focus on typical Hollywood productions. Instead let's look at the other four.

They belong to a class that we used to call the crime film, but that would best be described from this point on by a term such as criminal adventures or, better yet, such as criminal psychology. This is a major class of films which has superseded the *Western*: and there are wry conclusions to be drawn from the displacement of an on-screen dynamic involving chases on horseback and idylls in coaches by the dynamic of violent death and dark mysteries, as well as the change in background from a vast and novelistic treatment of nature to a "fantastic" social order.

This sort of film has now notably changed in the U.S. following the course of popular literature where the preeminence of S.S. Van Dine has ceded to that of Dashiell Hammett. Since Poe, since Gaboriau, and since Conan Doyle, we've become familiar with the formula for detective stories: an unsolved crime, some suspects, and in the end the discovery of the guilty party through the diligence of an experienced observer. This formula had long been perfected: the detective novel (and film) have substituted for the Sunday crossword puzzle and become overshadowed by boring repetition. I don't know of any enlightened devotees of the genre who could not nowadays plumb the mystery from the first fifty pages or the first two reels . . .

In motion pictures this handicap was heavier. First problem: long explications coming at the end of the narrative, at the exact moment when a film, its action being over, no longer interests the viewer. Another problem: if most of the characters could be lively and imaginative, the hero—that is to say, the detective—was merely a thinking machine and, even under the best of circumstances ([such as Simenon's,] Maigret), a thinking machine while sniffing and stuffing his pipe. One would consider the scenery, a moment of levity, other crimes, anything to spark one's interest.

We are witnessing the death of this formula. Of the four works cited earlier, only *Laura* belongs to this outdated genre; but Otto Preminger and his collaborators forced themselves to renew the formula by introducing a charming study of the furnishings and faces, a complicated narrative, a perverse writer who is prosaic but amusing, and foremost a detective with an emotional life. To sum up, the result is a film lacking in originality but perfectly distracting and, one can say, successful.

For the other three, the method is different. They are to the traditional crime drama what the novels of Dashiell Hammett are to those of Van Dine or Ellery Queen. They are as what one might call "true to life." The detective is not a mechanism but a protagonist, that is the character most important to us: accordingly the heroes of *Maltese Falcon* and *Murder, My Sweet* practice this strange profession of private detective, which (in the U.S.) has nothing to do with bureaucratic function but, by definition, puts them on the fringe of the law—the law as represented by the police and the codes of gangsters as well. The essential question is no longer "who-done-it?" but how does this protagonist act? It's not even required to comprehend all the twists and turns of the action in which he is caught up (I would never be able to sum up coherently the sequence of events of which these two films are composed), only the uncertain psychology of one and the other, at once friend and foe. Still more significantly neither the punch in the face nor the gunshot play a major role until the end. And it cannot be by accident that the two films end in the same manner, the cruelest way in the world with the heroines paying full price. These final scenes are harsh and misogynistic, as is most of contemporary American literature.

I would not go so far as to say these films are completely successful. While *Maltese Falcon* is quite exciting (and is taken from a novel by Dashiell Hammett), *Murder, My Sweet* is very uneven and at times vacuous (despite the excellent reputation of the Raymond Chandler novel from which it is adapted).

We rediscover this hardness, this misogyny, in *Double Indemnity*. There is no mystery here, we know everything from the beginning, and we follow the preparation for the crime, its execution, and its aftermath (just as in *Suspicion* which Alfred Hitchcock adapted from a remarkable novel by

Francis Iles with poor results). Consequently our interest is focused on the characters, and the narrative unfolds with a striking clarity that is sustained throughout. This is because the director, Billy Wilder, has done more than merely transpose the narrative structure offered by the James Cain novel from which the film is adapted. He started by creating, with Raymond Chandler, a peremptorily precise script which deftly details the motives and reactions of its characters. The direction is a faithful rendering of this script.

In this manner these "noir" films no longer have any common ground with run-of-the-mill police dramas. Markedly psychological plots, violent or emotional action, have less impact then facial expressions, gestures, utterances—rendering the truth of the characters, that "third dimension" of which I have already spoken. This is a significant improvement: after films such as these the figures in the usual cop movie seem like mannequins. There is nothing remarkable in the fact that today's viewers are more responsive to this stamp of verisimilitude, of "true to life," and, why not, to the kind of gross cruelties which actually exist and the past concealment of which has served no purpose: the struggle to survive is not a new story.

Concurrently with this internal development, there is another, purely formal, change in expository style, the intervention of a narrator or commentator permits a fragmentation of the narrative, to quickly gloss over the traditional plot elements and to accentuate the "true-to-life" side. It's clear that this method permits the story to be rapidly engaged, but it also permits the insertion of a dynamic element into an otherwise static, psychological portrait.

Sacha Guitry was the first to utilize this technique in *Le Roman d'un Tricheur*. The makers of the films which I have mentioned (except for *The Maltese Falcon*) utilized it also and revealed both its flexibility and the enhanced possibility of adding a deeper layer to the narrative style. I must note, however, that Preminger in *Laura* has the story explained in the beginning by a character who cannot know the succeeding events nor, reason dictates, their conclusion.

Has Hollywood definitively outclassed Paris?

It seems to me that we shouldn't rush precipitously to this conclusion. Doubtless after this sort of film, it won't be easy to construct police stories in the usual manner. Doubtless we'll have to work harder, assiduously refine our scripts, and give up beautiful images, camera tricks, and other technical razzle-dazzle which diminish that "third dimension" on screen by creating visual falsehood and "going Hollywood" (in the bad sense of the term). Certainly we've witnessed the emergence of a new class of authors, the Billy Wilders, the Premingers, the Chandlers, the John Hustons, who promise to leave behind the old guard and the old school, the John Fords, the Wylers, and even the Capras.

But from this, to conclude that French filmmakers should fold up their tents . . .

There is one point, however, that deserves to be underscored for our own filmmakers: the primacy of the script, and the fact that a film is first and foremost a sober story well constructed and presented in an original manner. I read exactly the opposite of what I've just said from my old friend Georges Charensol writing about *How Green Was My Valley*. Charensol and other reviewers seemed to be nostalgic for the silent movie and to judge a film by the quantity of pretentious flourishes it displays. I'm afraid it would be useless to contradict them: the relentless evolution of motion pictures will settle their case-motion pictures, the creation of which are more and more a function of the screenplay and where today one can find more dramatic energy in a static shot than in a majestic panorama.

The proof? Admirable films such as *How Green Was My Valley* and *The Letter*, admirable and profoundly boring. On the one hand, production value written in capital letters, graphic beauty, paternalistic traveling shots, and dullness precisely distilled by the camera. On the other hand, filmed theater in all its splendor made possible by a special lens, a ballet going nowhere, magnificently rendered, prodigiously breathed to life, that one follows with a yawn. Both are devoid of life, of truth, of depth, of charm, of vitality, of real energy–of that "third dimension" that I prefer. Trompe-l'oeil and filmed theater, these two antiquated and antithetical formulas come together and compel us to assert, sadly, that such magnificent gentlemen as John Ford and William Wyler are already museum pieces. The meaningful glances in *Laura* or *Double Indemnity*—it's sad to say, but it must be said—are more moving than the eloquent compositions of the former or the skilled touch of the latter.

Above all, don't make me say that the future belongs to crime movies told in the first person . . .

Translated from the French by Alain Silver

35

AMERICANS ALSO MAKE *NOIR* FILMS

Jean-Pierre Chartier

Source: Translated by Alain Silver, in Alain Silver and James Ursini, eds, *Film Noir Reader 2*, New York: Limelight Editions, 1999, pp. 21–23. (Originally published as 'Les Américans aussi font des films "noirs"; *La Revue du Cinéma*, 1, 2, November 1946, pp. 67–70.)

"She kisses him so that he'll kill for her." Emblazoned on the movie posters, over a blood stain, is that description of Billy Wilder's *Double Indemnity*. The same line would work just as well for Edward Dmytryk's *Murder, My Sweet*. It would hold true again for *The Postman Always Rings Twice* which is currently a big hit in the U.S. We understood why the Hays Office had previously forbidden film adaptations of James M. Cain's two novels from which *Double Indemnity* and *The Postman Rings Twice* are drawn. It is harder to understand, given this censor's moral posture, why this interdiction was lifted, as it's hard to imagine story lines with a more pessimistic or disgusted point of view regarding human behavior.

Doubtless the crime film has its genre conventions: one needs a dead victim, and no society condones murder. But with a detective as protagonist and a few innocent bystanders in support, human nature's tendency to do right can still be reaffirmed. In *Double Indemnity*, as in *Murder, My Sweet*, all the characters are more or less venal. And while there is a pure young girl in both films, which permits some hope about future generations, the females are particularly monstrous. Practically every scene reveals a new evil created by Barbara Stanwyck portraying Phyllis Dietrichson in *Double Indemnity*. As the film opens, she flirts with the young insurance salesman who has come to close a deal with her husband; two meetings later she asks him to kill her husband after insuring his life; she cold-bloodedly takes part in the murder; we then learn that she had previously poisoned Dietrichson's first wife; when things gets complicated, she tries to kill her insurance agent accomplice; and the film hasn't yet reached its climax before we further learn that, while all this was going on, she was having an affair with her step-daughter's fiancé.

Claire Trevor in *Murder, My Sweet* has no less charming a role. Despite having married into respectability, she acts like a cheap hooker: after committing murder to cover up her sordid past, the least she can do, as naturally as drawing breath, is to offer her favors to a private detective in exchange for helping with a second killing.

We can see how significant sexual attraction is in the through line of these narratives. It's a sort of contradiction that, from convention, the film censors, insensitive to the pessimism and despair which radiates from these characters, forbids putting the real emphasis on the sexual drive that dooms them. The result is that the actions of all these figures seems conditioned by an obsessive and fatal attraction to the crime itself. The sexual expropriation that Phyllis Dietrichson exercises over the free will of Walter Neff (Fred MacMurray), if it were underscored even more, would make his character even more hapless, as he actually is while under her spell, and this would be a sort of relief for the viewer.

As with many new films from the U.S., *Double Indemnity* and *Murder, My Sweet* are told in the first person. This choice of a specific point of view is used in both films but with very different results.

The narrator of *Murder, My Sweet* is a private detective. He is catapulted into a shadowy scheme without knowing either the principals nor their intentions. The confusion of the film, that the viewer is immersed in an imbroglio, these are the desired effects. *Murder, My Sweet* is no ordinary crime drama where from scene to scene more of the mystery is revealed: the script is not a whodunit designed to draw the viewer into guessing the outcome, it aims not to intrigue but to create an atmosphere of fright. Precisely because we don't understand them, we sense the menace of unknown dangers. *Murder, My Sweet* genuinely deserves the label of thriller, as the first person narrative is used to make the viewer shudder with the thrill of fear. This forced perspective is uncompromising. Several times in the course of the film, the detective is rendered unconscious, and each time the screen tries to render the experience of someone being knocked out: a play of twisted shapes, which makes us think of the experiments of "pure cinema," of the presentation of a nightmare and disturbed vision in the manner of the old school of avant-garde filmmakers. *Double Indemnity* used the narrative progression for psychological ends: as the guilty man is telling the story, there is no formal mystery; on the contrary, it is the psychological mechanism by which Walter Neff is dragged unrelentingly into the criminal action that unwinds before our eyes. The action doesn't spring from exterior causes: the seduction of law-abiding young man by a calculating bitch, the appeal of the perfect crime, the gauntlet thrown down to the friend in charge of investigating fraud have a verisimilitude that draws us personally into this sordid tale.

Raymond Chandler is the author of the source material for *Murder, My Sweet* and the co-screenwriter of *Double Indemnity*; and one can sense the same influence on both films. *Double Indemnity* doubtless owes its superiority to the source material of James Cain. But the hand of director Billy Wilder is clearly evident, particularly in the first person narrative which is used as well in his other "*noir*" film *The Lost Weekend.* In that film, the development of the story is extremely stylized and Wilder's success is even more telling: Ray Milland, who portrays the protagonist, is in every frame and often alone. It's almost a case study: as per its tag line, the film is "the diary of an alcoholic." The entire story is restricted to the memories of a pathological drunk. Usually in the care of his brother, Milland, left alone for a weekend takes a drink and starts to talk, takes another drink and resumes his monologue, sleeps for awhile and then drinks some more. The impressions of insanity, of a senseless void, left by the drama of a young man in the grip of singular addiction, makes *the Lost Weekend* one of the most depressing movies I have ever seen. Certainly a charming young lady helps our alcoholic hero sober up and permits the film to end with a kiss. But the impression of extreme despair persists despite this upbeat ending.

Women as insatiable as the Empress Messalina, animalistic or senile husbands, young guys ready to kill for the sexual favors of a femme fatale, unrepentant alcoholics, these are the charming types from the films we've discussed. There's been talk of a French school of *film noir*, but *Le Quai des Brumes* and *L'Hotel du Nord* contain some glimmer of resistance to the dark side, where love provides at least the mirage of a better world, where some re-vindication of society opens the door for hope, and even though the characters may despair they retain our pity and our sympathy. There is none of that in the films before us now: these are monsters, criminals and psychopaths without redemptive qualities who behave according to the preordained disposition to evil within themselves.

Translated from the French by Alain Silver

36

THE GANGSTER AS TRAGIC HERO

Robert Warshow

Source: *Partisan Review*, February 1948, pp. 240–244.

America, as a social and political organization, is committed to a cheerful view of life. It could not be otherwise. The sense of tragedy is a luxury of aristocratic societies, where the fate of the individual is not conceived of as having a direct and legitimate political importance, being determined by a fixed and supra-political—that is, non-controversial—moral order or fate. Modern equalitarian societies, however, whether democratic or authoritarian in their political forms, always base themselves on the claim that they are making life happier; the avowed function of the modern state, at least in its ultimate terms, is not only to regulate social relations, but also to determine the quality and the possibilities of human life in general. Happiness thus becomes the chief political issue—in a sense, the only political issue—and for that reason it can never be treated as an issue at all. If an American or a Russian is unhappy, it implies a certain reprobation of his society, and therefore, by a logic of which we can all recognize the necessity, it becomes an obligation of citizenship to be cheerful; if the authorities find it necessary, the citizen may even be compelled to make a public display of his cheerfulness on important occasions, just as he may be conscripted into the army in time of war.

Naturally, this civic responsibility rests most strongly upon the organs of mass culture. The individual citizen may still be permitted his private unhappiness so long as it does not take on political significance, the extent of this tolerance being determined by how large an area of private life the society can accommodate. But every production of mass culture is a public act and must conform with accepted notions of the public good. Nobody seriously questions the principle that it is the function of mass culture to maintain public morale, and certainly nobody in the mass audience objects to having his morale maintained.[1] At a time when the normal condition of the citizen is a state of anxiety, euphoria spreads over our culture like the broad smile of an idiot. In terms of attitudes towards life, there is very little difference between a "happy" movie like *Good News*, which ignores death and suffering, and a "sad" movie like *A Tree Grows in Brooklyn*, which uses death and suffering as incidents in the service of a higher optimism.

But, whatever its effectiveness as a source of consolation and a means of pressure for maintaining "positive" social attitudes, this optimism is fundamentally satisfying to no one, not even to those who would be most disoriented without its support. Even within the area of mass culture, there always exists a current of opposition, seeking to express by whatever means are available to it that sense of desperation and inevitable failure which optimism itself helps to create. Most often, this opposition is confined to rudimentary or semi-literate forms: in mob politics and journalism, for example, or in certain kinds of religious enthusiasm. When it does enter the field of art, it is likely to be disguised or attenuated: in an unspecific form of expression like jazz, in the basically harmless nihilism of the Marx Brothers, in the continually reasserted strain of hopelessness that often seems to be the real meaning of the soap opera. The gangster film is remarkable in that it fills the need for disguise (though not sufficiently to avoid arousing uneasiness) without requiring any serious distortion. From its beginnings, it has been a consistent and astonishingly complete presentation of the modern sense of tragedy.[2]

In its initial character, the gangster film is simply one example of the movies' constant tendency to create fixed dramatic patterns that can be repeated indefinitely with a reasonable expectation of profit. One gangster film follows another as one musical or one Western follows another. But this rigidity is not necessarily opposed to the requirements of art. There have been very successful types of art in the past which developed such specific and detailed conventions as almost to make individual examples of the type interchangeable. This is true, for example, of Elizabethan revenge tragedy and Restoration comedy.

For such a type to be successful means that its conventions have imposed themselves upon the general consciousness and become the accepted vehicles of a particular set of attitudes and a particular aesthetic effect. One goes to any individual example of the type with very definite expectations, and originality is to be welcomed only in the degree that it intensifies the expected experience without fundamentally altering it. Moreover, the relationship between the conventions which go to make up such a type and the real experience of its audience or the real facts of whatever situation it pretends to describe is of only secondary importance and does not determine its aesthetic force. It is only in an ultimate sense that the type appeals to its audience's experience of reality; much more immediately, it appeals to previous experience of the type itself: it creates its own field of reference.

Thus the importance of the gangster film, and the nature and intensity of its emotional and aesthetic impact, cannot be measured in terms of the place of the gangster himself or the importance of the problem of crime in

American life. Those European movie-goers who think there is a gangster on every corner in New York are certainly deceived, but defenders of the "positive" side of American culture are equally deceived if they think it relevant to point out that most Americans have never seen a gangster. What matters is that the experience of the gangster *as an experience of art* is universal to Americans. There is almost nothing we understand better or react to more readily or with quicker intelligence. The Western film, though it seems never to diminish in popularity, is for most of us no more than the folklore of the past, familiar and understandable only because it has been repeated so often. The gangster film comes much closer. In ways that we do not easily or willingly define, the gangster speaks for us, expressing that part of the American psyche which rejects the qualities and the demands of modern life, which rejects "Americanism" itself.

The gangster is the man of the city, with the city's language and knowledge, with its queer and dishonest skills and its terrible daring, carrying his life in his hands like a placard, like a club. For everyone else, there is at least the theoretical possibility of another world—in that happier American culture which the gangster denies, the city does not really exist; it is only a more crowded and more brightly lit country—but for the gangster there is only the city; he must inhabit it in order to personify it: not the real city, but that dangerous and sad city of the imagination which is so much more important, which is the modern world. And the gangster—though there are real gangsters—is also, and primarily, a creature of the imagination. The real city, one might say, produces only criminals; the imaginary city produces the gangster: he is what we want to be and what we are afraid we may become.

Thrown into the crowd without background or advantages, with only those ambiguous skills which the rest of us—the real people of the real city—can only pretend to have, the gangster is required to make his way, to make his life and impose it on others. Usually, when we come upon him, he has already made his choice or the choice has already been made for him, it doesn't matter which: we are not permitted to ask whether at some point he could have chosen to be something else than what he is.

The gangster's activity is actually a form of rational enterprise, involving fairly definite goals and various techniques for achieving them. But this rationality is usually no more than a vague background; we know, perhaps, that the gangster sells liquor or that he operates a numbers racket; often we are not given even that much information. So his activity becomes a kind of pure criminality: he hurts people. Certainly our response to the gangster film is most consistently and most universally a response to sadism; we gain the double satisfaction of participating vicariously in the gangster's sadism and then seeing it turned against the gangster himself.

But on another level the quality of irrational brutality and the quality of rational enterprise become one. Since we do not see the rational and routine aspects of the gangster's behavior, the practice of brutality—the quality of unmixed criminality—becomes the totality of his career. At the same time, we are always conscious that the whole meaning of this career is a drive for success: the typical gangster film presents a steady upward progress followed by a very precipitate fall. Thus brutality itself becomes at once the means to success and the content of success—a success that is defined in its most general terms, not as accomplishment or specific gain, but simply as the unlimited possibility of aggression. (In the same way, film presentations of businessmen tend to make it appear that they achieve their success by talking on the telephone and holding conferences and that success *is* talking on the telephone and holding conferences.)

From this point of view, the initial contact between the film and its audience is an agreed conception of human life: that man is a being with the possibilities of success or failure. This principle, too, belongs to the city; one must emerge from the crowd or else one is nothing. On that basis the necessity of the action is established, and it progresses by inalterable paths to the point where the gangster lies dead and the principle has been modified: there is really only one possibility—failure. The final meaning of the city is anonymity and death.

In the opening scene of *Scarface*, we are shown a successful man; we know he is successful because he has just given a party of opulent proportions and because he is called Big Louie. Through some monstrous lack of caution, he permits himself to be alone for a few moments. We understand from this immediately that he is about to be killed. No convention of the gangster film is more strongly established than this: it is dangerous to be alone. And yet the very conditions of success make it impossible not to be alone, for success is always the establishment of an *individual* pre-eminence that must be imposed on others, in whom it automatically arouses hatred; the successful man is an outlaw. The gangster's whole life is an effort to assert himself as an individual, to draw himself out of the crowd, and he always dies *because* he is an individual; the final bullet thrusts him back, makes him, after all, a failure. "Mother of God," says the dying Little Caesar, "is this the end of Rico?"—speaking of himself thus in the third person because what has been brought low is not the undifferentiated *man*, but the individual with a name, the gangster, the success; even to himself he is a creature of the imagination. (T. S. Eliot has pointed out that a number of Shakespeare's tragic heroes have this trick of looking at themselves dramatically; their true identity, the thing that is destroyed when they die, is something outside themselves—not a man, but a style of life, a kind of meaning.)

At bottom, the gangster is doomed because he is under the obligation to succeed, not because the means he employs are unlawful. In the deeper layers of the modern consciousness, *all* means are unlawful, every attempt to succeed is an act of aggression, leaving one alone and guilty and defenseless among enemies: one is *punished* for success. This is our intolerable dilemma: that failure is a kind of death and success is evil and dangerous, is—ultimately—impossible. The effect of the gangster film is to embody this dilemma in the person of the gangster and resolve it by his death. The dilemma is resolved because it is *his* death, not ours. We are safe; for the moment, we can acquiesce in our failure, we can choose to fail.

Notes

1 In her testimony before the House Committee on Un-American Activities, Mrs. Leila Rogers said that the movie *None But the Lonely Heart* was un-American because it was gloomy. Like so much else that was said during the unhappy investigation of Hollywood, this statement was at once stupid and illuminating. One knew immediately what Mrs. Rogers was talking about; she had simply been insensitive enough to carry her philistinism to its conclusion.

2 Efforts have been made from time to time to bring the gangster film into line with the prevailing optimism and social constructiveness of our culture; *Kiss of Death* is a recent example. These efforts are usually unsuccessful; the reasons for their lack of success are interesting in themselves, but I shall not be able to discuss them here.

37

NOTES ON *FILM NOIR*

Paul Schrader

Source: *Film Comment*, 8, 1, Spring 1972, pp. 8–13. (Originally published in 1971 as a pamphlet to accompany a short season of films programmed by Schrader for the Los Angeles Film Festival.)

In 1946 French critics, seeing the American films they had missed during the war, noticed the new mood of cynicism, pessimism and darkness which had crept into the American cinema. The darkening stain was most evident in routine crime thrillers, but was also apparent in prestigious melodramas.

The French cineastes soon realized they had seen only the tip of the iceberg: as the years went by, Hollywood lighting grew darker, characters more corrupt, themes more fatalistic and the tone more hopeless. By 1949. American movies were in the throes of their deepest and most creative funk. Never before had films dared to take such a harsh uncomplimentary look at American life, and they would not dare to do so again for twenty years.

Hollywood's *film noir* has recently become the subject of renewed interest among moviegoers and critics. The fascination *film noir* holds for today's young filmgoers and film students reflects recent trends in American cinema: American movies are again taking a look at the underside of the American character, but compared to such relentlessly cynical films noir as KISS ME DEADLY or KISS TOMORROW GOODBYE, the new self-hate cinema of EASY RIDER and MEDIUM COOL seems naïve and romantic. As the current polical mood hardens, filmgoers and filmmakers will find the *film noir* of the late Forties increasingly attractive. The Forties may be to the Seventies what the Thirties were to the Sixties.

Film noir is equally interesting to critics. It offers writers a cache of excellent, little-known films (*film noir* is oddly both one of Hollywood's best periods and least known), and gives *auteur*-weary critics an opportunity to apply themselves to the newer questions of classification and transdirectorial style. After all, what is a *film noir*?

Film noir is not a genre (as Raymond Durgnat has helpfully pointed out over the objections of Higham and Greenberg's *Hollywood in the Forties*). It is not defined, as are the western and gangster genres, by conventions of setting and conflict, but rather by the more subtle qualities of tone and mood. It is a *film "noir,"* as opposed to the possible variants of film gray or film off-white.

Film noir is also a specific period of film history, like German Expressionism or the French New Wave. In general, *film noir* refers to those Hollywood films of the Forties and early Fifties which portrayed the world of dark, slick city streets, crime and corruption.

Film noir is an extremely unwieldy period. It harks back to many previous periods: Warner's Thirties gangster films, the French "poetic realism" of Carné and Duvivier, Sternbergian melodrama, and, farthest back, German Expressionist crime films (Lang's MABUSE cycle). *Film noir* can stretch at its outer limits from THE MALTESE FALCON (1941) to TOUCH OF EVIL (1958), and most every dramatic Hollywood film from 1941 to 1953 contains some *noir* elements. There are also foreign offshoots of *film noir*, such as THE THIRD MAN, BREATHLESS and LE DOULOS.

Almost every critic has his own definition of *film noir*, and a personal list of film titles and dates to back it up. Personal and descriptive definitions, however, can get a bit sticky. A film of urban nightlife is not necessarily a *film noir*, and a *film noir* need not necessarily concern crime and corruption. Since *film noir* is defined by tone rather than genre, it is almost impossible to argue one critic's descriptive definition against another's. How many *noir* elements does it take to make a *film noir noir*?

Rather than haggle definitions, I would rather attempt to reduce *film noir* to its primary colors (all shades of black), those cultural and stylistic elements to which any definition must return.

At the risk of sounding like Arthur Knight, I would suggest that there were four conditions in Hollywood in the Forties which brought about the *film noir*. (The danger of Knight's *Liveliest Art* method is that it makes film history less a matter of structural analysis, and more a case of artistic and social forces magically interacting and coalescing). Each of the following four catalytic elements, however, can define the film noir, the distinctly *noir* tonality draws from each of these elements.

War and post-war disillusionment. The acute downer which hit the U.S. after the Second World War was, in fact, a delayed reaction to the Thirties. All through the Depression, movies were needed to keep people's spirits up, and, for the most part, they did. The crime films of this period were Horatio Algerish and socially conscious. Toward the end of the Thirties a darker crime film began to appear (YOU ONLY LIVE ONCE, THE ROARING TWENTIES) and, were it not for the War, *film noir* would have been at full steam by the early Forties.

The need to produce Allied propaganda abroad and promote patriotism at home blunted the fledgling moves toward a dark cinema, and the *film noir* thrashed about in the studio system, not quite able to come into full prominence. During the War the first uniquely *film noir* appeared: THE MALTESE FALCON, THE GLASS KEY, THIS GUN FOR HIRE, LAURA, but these films lacked the distinctly *noir* bite the end of the war would bring.

As soon as the War was over, however, American films became markedly more sardonic—and there was a boom in the crime film. For fifteen years the pressures against America's amelioristic cinema had been building up, and, given the freedom, audiences and artists were now eager to take a less optimistic view of things. The disillusionment many soldiers, small businessmen and housewife/factory employees felt in returning to a peacetime economy was directly mirrored in the sordidness of the urban crime film.

This immediate post-war disillusionment was directly demonstrated in films like CORNERED, THE BLUE DAHLIA, DEAD RECKONING and RIDE A PINK HORSE, in which a serviceman returns from the war to find his sweetheart unfaithful or dead, or his business partner cheating him, or the whole society something less than worth fighting for. The war continues, but now the antagonism turns with a new viciousness toward the American society itself.

Post-war realism. Shortly after the War every film-producing country had a resurgence of realism. In America it first took the form of films by such producers as Louis de Rochemont (HOUSE ON 92ND STREET, CALL NORTHSIDE 777) and Mark Hellinger (THE KILLERS, BRUTE FORCE), and directors like Henry Hathaway and Jules Dassin. "Every scene was film on the actual location depicted," the 1947 de Rochemont-Hathaway KISS OF DEATH proudly proclaimed. Even after de Rochemont's particular "March of Time" authenticity fell from vogue, realistic exteriors remained a permanent fixture of *film noir*.

The realistic movement also suited America's post-war mood; the public's desire for a more honest and harsh view of America would not be satisfied by the same studio streets they had been watching for a dozen years. The post-war realistic trend succeeded in breaking *film noir* away from the domain of the high-class melodrama, placing it where it more properly belonged, in the streets with everyday people. In retrospect, the pre-de Rochemont *film noir* looks definitely tamer than the post-War realistic films. The studio look of films like THE BIG SLEEP and THE MASK OF DIMITRIOS blunts their sting, making them seem polite and conventional in contrast to their later, more realistic counterparts.

The German influence. Hollywood played host to an influx of German expatriates in the Twenties and Thirties, and these filmmakers and technicians had, for the most part, integrated themselves into the American film establishment. Hollywood never experienced the "Germanization" some civic-minded natives feared, and there is a danger of over-emphasizing the German influence in Hollywood.

But when, in the late Forties, Hollywood decided to paint it black, there were no greater masters of chiaroscuro than the Germans. The influence of expressionist lighting has always been just beneath the surface of Hollywood films, and it is not surprising, in *film noir*, to find it bursting out full bloom.

Neither is it surprising to find a larger number of Germans and East Europeans working in *film noir*: Fritz Lang, Robert Siodmak, Billy Wilder, Franz Waxman, Otto Preminger, John Brahm, Anatole Litvak, Karl Freund, Max Ophuls, John Alton, Douglas Sirk, Fred Zinnemann, William Dieterle, Max Steiner, Edgar G. Ulmer, Curtis Bernhardt, Rudolph Maté.

On the surface the German expressionist influence, with its reliance on artificial studio lighting, seems incompatible with post-war realism, with its harsh unadorned exteriors; but it is the unique quality of *film noir* that it was able to weld seemingly contradictory elements into a uniform style. The best *noir* technicians simply made all the world a sound stage, directing unnatural and expressionistic lighting onto realistic settings. In films like UNION STATION, THEY LIVE BY NIGHT, THE KILLERS there is an uneasy, exhilarating combination of realism and expressionism.

Perhaps the greatest master of *noir* was Hungarian-born John Alton, an expressionist cinematographer who could relight Times Square at noon if necessary. No cinematographer better adapted the old expressionist techniques to the new desire for realism, and his black-and-white photography in such gritty *film noir* as T-MEN, RAW DEAL, I THE JURY, THE BIG COMBO equals that of such German expressionist masters as Fritz Wagner and Karl Freund.

The hard-boiled tradition. Another stylistic influence waiting in the wings was the "hard-boiled" school of writers. In the Thirties, authors such as Ernest Hemingway, Dashiell Hammett, Raymond Chandler, James M. Cain, Horace McCoy and John O'Hara created the "tough," a cynical way of acting and thinking which separated one from the world of everyday emotions—romanticism with a protective shell. The hard-boiled writers had their roots in pulp fiction or journalism, and their protagonists lived out a narcissistic, defeatist code. The hardboiled hero was, in reality, a soft egg compared to his existential counterpart (Camus is said to have based *The Stranger* on McCoy), but he was a good deal tougher than anything American fiction had seen.

When the movies of the Forties turned to the American "tough" moral understrata, the hardboiled school was waiting with preset conventions of heroes, minor characters, plots, dialogue and themes. Like the German expatriates, the hard-boiled writers had a style made to order for *film noir*; and, in turn, they influenced *noir* screenwriting as much as the Germans influenced *noir* cinematography.

The most hard-boiled of Hollywood's writers was Raymond Chandler himself, whose script of DOUBLE INDEMNITY (from a James M. Cain story) was the best written and most characteristically *noir* of the period. DOUBLE INDEMNITY was the first film which played *film noir* for what it essentially was: small-time, unredeemed, unheroic; it made a break: from the romantic *noir* cinema of MILDRED PIERCE and THE BIG SLEEP.

(In its final stages, however, *film noir* adapted and then bypassed the hard-boiled school. Manic, neurotic post-1948 films such as KISS TOMORROW

GOODBYE, D.O.A., WHERE THE SIDEWALK ENDS, WHITE HEAT, and THE BIG HEAT are all post-hard-boiled: the air in these regions was even too thin for old-time cynics like Chandler.)

STYLISTICS. There is not yet a study of the stylistics of *film noir*, and the task is certainly too large to be attempted here. Like all film movements *film noir* drew upon a reservoir of film techniques, and given the time one could correlate its techniques, themes and casual elements into a stylistic schema. For the present, however, I'd like to point out some of *film noir*'s recurring techniques.

■ The majority of scenes are lit for night. Gangsters sit in the offices at midday with the shades pulled and the lights off. Ceiling lights are hung low and floor lamps are seldom more than five feet high. One always has the suspicion that if the lights were all suddenly flipped on the characters would shriek and shrink from the scene like Count Dracula at sunrise.

■ As in German expressionism, oblique and vertical lines are preferred to horizontal. Obliquity adheres to the choreography of the city, and is in direct opposition to the horizontal American tradition of Griffith and Ford. Oblique lines tend to splinter a screen, making it restless and unstable. Light enters the dingy rooms of *film noir* in such odd shapes—jagged trapezoids, obtuse triangles, vertical slits—that one suspects the windows were cut out with a pen knife. No character can speak authoritatively from a space which is being continually cut into ribbons of light. The Anthony Mann/John Alton T-MEN is the most dramatic but far from the only example of oblique *noir* choreography.

■ The actors and setting are often given equal lighting emphasis. An actor is often hidden in the realistic tableau of the city at night, and, more obviously, his face is often blacked out by shadow as he speaks. These shadow effects are unlike the famous Warner Brothers lighting of the Thirties in which the central character was accentuated by a heavy shadow; in *film noir*, the central character is likely to be standing *in* the shadow. When the environment is given an equal or greater weight than the actor it, of course, creates a fatalistic, hopeless mood. There is nothing the protagonist can do; the city will outlast and negate even his best efforts.

■ Compositional tension is preferred to physical action. A typical *film noir* would rather move the scene cinematographically around the actor than have the actor control the scene by physical action. The beating of Robert Ryan in THE SET-UP, the gunning down of Farley Granger in THEY LIVE BY NIGHT, the execution of the taxi driver in THE ENFORCER and of Brian Donlevy in THE BIG COMBO are all marked by measured pacing, restrained anger and oppressive compositions, and seem much closer to the *film noir* spirit than the rat-tat-tat and screeching tires of SCARFACE twenty years before or the violent, expressive actions of UNDERWORLD U.S.A. ten years later.

■ There seems to be an almost Freudian attachment to water. The empty *noir* streets are almost always glistening with fresh evening rain (even in Los Angeles), and the rainfall tends to increase in direct proportion to the drama. Docks and piers are second only to alleyways as the most popular rendezvous points.

■ There is a love of romantic narration. In such films as THE POSTMAN ALWAYS RINGS TWICE, LAURA, DOUBLE INDEMNITY, THE LADY FROM SHANGHAI, OUT OF THE PAST and SUNSET BOULEVARD the narration creates a mood of *temps perdu*: an irretrievable past, a predetermined fate and an all-enveloping hopelessness. In OUT OF THE PAST Robert Mitchum relates his history with such pathetic relish that it is obvious there is no hope for any future: one can only take pleasure in reliving a doomed past.

■ A complex chronological order is frequently used to reinforce the feelings of hopelessness and lost time. Such films as THE ENFORCER, THE KILLERS, MILDRED PIERCE, THE DARK PAST, CHICAGO DEADLINE, OUT OF THE PAST and THE KILLING use a convoluted time sequence to emerse the viewer in a time-disoriented but highly stylized world. The manipulation of time, whether slight or complex, is often used to reinforce a *noir* principle: the how is always more important than the what.

THEMES. Raymond Durgnat has delineated the themes of *film noir* in an excellent article in the British *Cinema* magazine ("The Family Tree of *Film Noir*," August, 1970), and it would be foolish for me to attempt to redo his thorough work in this short space. Durgnat divides *film noir* into eleven thematic categories, and although one might criticize some of his specific groupings, he does cover the whole gamut of *noir* production (thematically categorizing over 300 films).

In each of Durgnat's *noir* themes (whether Black Widow, killers-on-the-run, *dopplegangers*) one finds that the upwardly mobile forces of the Thirties have halted; frontierism has turned to paranoia and claustrophobia. The small-time gangster has now made it big and sits in the mayor's chair, the private eye has quit the police force in disgust, and the young heroine, sick of going along for the ride, is taking others for a ride.

Durgnat, however, does not touch upon what is perhaps the over-riding *noir* theme: a passion for the past and present, but also a fear of the future. The *noir* hero dreads to look ahead, but instead tries to survive by the day, and if unsuccessful at that, he retreats to the past. Thus *film noir*'s techniques emphasize loss, nostalgia, lack of clear priorities, insecurity; then submerge these self-doubts in mannerism and style. In such a world style becomes paramount; it is all that separates one from meaninglessness. Chandler described this fundamental *noir* theme when he described his own fictional world: "It is not a very fragrant world, but it is the world you live in, and certain writers with tough minds and a cool spirit of detachment can make very interesting patterns out of it."

Film noir can be subdivided into three broad phases. The first, the wartime period, 1941–'46 approximately, was the phase of the private eye and the lone wolf, of Chandler, Hammett and Greene, of Bogart and Bacall, Ladd and Lake, classy directors like Curtiz and Garnett, studio sets, and, in general, more talk than action. The studio look of this period was reflected in such pictures as THE MALTESE FALCON, CASABLANCA, GASLIGHT, THIS GUN FOR HIRE, THE LODGER, THE WOMAN IN THE WINDOW, MILDRED PIERCE, SPELLBOUND, THE BIG SLEEP, LAURA, THE LOST WEEKEND, THE STRANGE LOVE OF MARTHA IVERS, TO HAVE AND HAVE NOT, FALLEN ANGEL, GILDA, MURDER MY SWEET, THE POSTMAN ALWAYS RINGS TWICE, DARK WATERS, SCARLET STREET, SO DARK THE NIGHT, THE GLASS KEY, THE MASK OF DIMITRIOS, and THE DARK MIRROR.

The Wilder/Chandler DOUBLE INDEMNITY provided a bridge to the post-War phase of *film noir*. The unflinching *noir* vision of DOUBLE INDEMNITY came as a shock in 1944, and the film was almost blocked by the combined efforts of Paramount, the Hays Office and star Fred MacMurray. Three years later, however, DOUBLE INDEMNITYS were dropping off the studio assembly lines.

The second phase was the post-War realistic period from 1945–'49 (the dates overlap and so do the films; these are all approximate phases for which there are many exceptions). These films tended more toward the problems of crime in the streets, political corruption and police routine. Less romantic heroes like Richard Conte, Burt Lancaster and Charles McGraw were more suited to this period, as were proletarian directors like Hathaway, Dassin and Kazan. The realistic urban look of this phase is seen in such films as THE HOUSE ON 92ND STREET, THE KILLERS, RAW DEAL, ACT OF VIOLENCE, UNION STATION, KISS OF DEATH, JOHNNY O'CLOCK, FORCE OF EVIL, DEAD RECKONING, RIDE THE PINK HORSE, DARK PASSAGE, CRY OF THE CITY, THE SET-UP, T-MEN, CALL NORTHSIDE 777, BRUTE FORCE, THE BIG CLOCK, THIEVES' HIGHWAY, RUTHLESS, PITFALL, BOOMERANG!, and THE NAKED CITY.

The third and final phase of *film noir*, from 1949–'53, was the period of psychotic action and suicidal impulse. The *noir* hero, seemingly under the weight of ten years of despair, started to go bananas. The psychotic killer, who had in the first period been a subject worthy of study (Olivia de Havilland in THE DARK MIRROR), in the second a fringe threat (Richard Widmark in KISS OF DEATH), now became the active protagonist (James Cagney in KISS TOMORROW GOODBYE). There were no excuses given for the psychopathy in GUN CRAZY—it was just "crazy." James Cagney made a neurotic comeback and his instability was matched by that of younger, actors like Robert Ryan and Lee Marvin. This was the phase of the "B" *noir* film, and of psychoanalytically-inclined directors like Ray and Walsh. The forces of personal disintegration are reflected in such films as WHITE HEAT, GUN CRAZY, D.O.A, CAUGHT, THEY LIVE BY NIGHT, WHERE THE SIDEWALK ENDS, KISS TOMORROW GOODBYE, DETECTIVE STORY, IN A LONELY PLACE, I THE JURY, ACE

IN THE HOLE, PANIC IN THE STREETS, THE BIG HEAT, ON DANGEROUS GROUND, and SUNSET BOULEVARD.

This third phase is the cream of the *film noir* period. Some critics may prefer the early "gray" melodramas, others the post-War "street" films, but *film noir's* final phase was the most aesthetically and sociologically piercing. After ten years of steadily shedding romantic conventions, the later *noir* films finally got down to the root causes of the period: the loss of public honor, heroic conventions, personal integrity, and, finally, psychic stability. The third-phase films were painfully self-aware; they seemed to know they stood at the end of a long tradition based on despair and disintegration and did not shy away from that fact. The best and most characteristically *noir* films—GUN CRAZY, WHITE HEAT, OUT OF THE PAST, KISS TOMORROW GOODBYE, D.O.A., THEY LIVE BY NIGHT, and THE BIG HEAT—stand at the end of the period and are the results of self-awareness. The third phase is rife with end-of-the-line *noir* heroes: THE BIG HEAT and WHERE THE SIDEWALK ENDS are the last stops for the urban cop, ACE IN THE HOLE for the newspaper man, the Victor Saville-produced Spillane series (I THE JURY, THE LONG WAIT, KISS ME DEADLY) for the private eye, SUNSET BOULEVARD for the Black Widow, WHITE HEAT and KISS TOMORROW GOODBYE for the gangster, D.O.A. for the John Doe American.

Appropriately, the masterpiece of *film noir* was a straggler, KISS ME DEADLY, produced in 1955. Its time delay gives it a sense of detachment and thoroughgoing seediness—it stands at the end of a long sleazy tradition. The private eye hero, Mike Hammer, undergoes the final stages of degradation. He is a small-time "bedroom dick," and makes no qualms about it because the world around him isn't much better. Ralph Meeker, in his best performance, plays Hammer, a midget among dwarfs. Robert Aldrich's teasing direction carries *noir* to its sleaziest and most perversely erotic. Hammer overturns the underworld in search of the "great whatsit," and when he finally finds it, it turns out to be—joke of jokes—an exploding atomic bomb. The inhumanity and meaningless of the hero are small matters in a world in which The Bomb has the final say.

By the middle Fifties *film noir* had ground to a halt. There were a few notable stragglers, KISS ME DEADLY, the Lewis/Alton THE BIG COMBO, and *film noir*'s epitaph, TOUCH OF EVIL, but for the most part a new style of crime film had become popular.

As the rise of McCarthy and Eisenhower demonstrated, Americans were eager to see a more bourgeois view of themselves. Crime had to move to the suburbs. The criminal put on a grey flannel suit and the footsore cop was replaced by the "mobile unit" careening down the expressway. Any attempt at social criticism had to be cloaked in ludicrous affirmations of the American way of life. Technically, television, with its demand for full lighting and close-ups, gradually undercut the German influence, and color cinematography was, of course, the final blow to the "*noir*" look.

New directors like Seigel, Fleischer, Karlson and Fuller, and TV shows like *Dragnet, M-Squad, Lineup* and *Highway Patrol* stepped in to create the new crime drama. This transition can be seen in Samuel Fuller's 1953 PICKUP ON SOUTH STREET, a film which blends the black look with the red scare. The waterfront scenes with Richard Widmark and Jean Peters are in the best *noir* tradition, but a later, dynamic fight in the subway marks Fuller as a director who would be better suited to the crime school of the middle and late Fifties.

Film noir was an immensely creative period—probably the most creative in Hollywood's history—at least, if this creativity is measured not by its peaks but by its median level of artistry. Picked at random, a *film noir* is likely to be a better made film than a randomly selected silent comedy, musical, western and so on. (A Joseph H. Lewis "B" *film noir* is better than a Lewis "B" western, for example.) Taken as a whole period, *film noir* achieved an unusually high level of artistry.

Film noir seemed to bring out the best in everyone: directors, cameramen, screenwriters, actors. Again and again, a *film noir* will make the high point on an artist's career graph. Some directors, for example, did their best work in *film noir* (Stuart Heisler, Robert Siodmak, Gordon Douglas, Edward Dymtryk, John Brahm, John Cromwell, Raoul Walsh, Henry Hathaway); other directors began in *film noir* and, it seems to me, never regained their original heights (Otto Preminger, Rudolph Maté, Nicholas Ray, Robert Wise, Jules Dassin, Richard Fleischer, John Huston, Andre de Toth, and Robert Aldrich): and other directors who made great films in other molds also made great *film noir* (Orson Welles, Max Ophuls, Fritz Lang, Elia Kazan, Howard Hawks, Robert Rossen, Anthony Mann, Joseph Losey, Alfred Hitchcock, and Stanley Kubrick). Whether or not one agrees with this particular schema, its message is irrefutable: *film noir* was good for practically every director's career. (Two interesting exceptions to prove the case are King Vidor and Jean Renoir.)

Film noir seems to have been a creative release for everyone involved. It gave artists a chance to work with previously forbidden themes, yet had conventions strong enough to protect the mediocre. Cinematographers were allowed to become highly mannered, and actors were sheltered by the cinematographers. It was not until years later that critics were able to distinguish between great directors and great *noir* directors.

Film noir's remarkable creativity makes its long-time neglect the more baffling. The French, of course, have been students of the period for some time (Borde and Chaumenton's *Panorama du Film Noir* was published in 1955), but American critics until recently have preferred the western, the musical or the gangster film to the *film noir*.

Some of the reasons for this neglect are superficial; others strike to the heart of the *noir* style. For a long time *film noir*, with its emphasis on corruption and despair, was considered an aberation of the American character.

The western, with its moral primitivism, and the gangster film, with its Horatio Alger values, were considered more American than the *film noir*.

This prejudice was reinforced by the fact that *film noir* was ideally suited to the low budget "B" film, and many of the best *noir* films were "B" films. This odd sort of economic snobbery still lingers on in some critical circles: high-budget trash is considered more worthy of attention than low-budget trash, and to praise a "B" film is somehow to slight (often intentionally) an "A" film.

There has been a critical revival in the U.S. over the last ten years, but *film noir* lost out on that too. The revival was *auteur* (director) oriented, and *film noir* wasn't. *Auteur* criticism is interested in how directors are different; *film noir* criticism is concerned with what they have in common.

The fundamental reason for *film noir*'s neglect, however, is the fact that it depends more on choreography than sociology, and American critics have always been slow on the uptake when it comes to visual style. Like its protagonists, *film noir* is more interested in style than theme, whereas American critics have been traditionally more interested in theme than style.

American film critics have always been sociologists first and scientists second: film is important as it relates to large masses, and if a film goes awry it is often because the theme has been somehow "violated" by the style. *Film noir* operates on opposite principles: the theme is hidden in the style, and bogus themes are often flaunted ("middle-class values are best") which contradict the style. Although, I believe, style determines the theme in *every* film, it was easier for sociological critics to discuss the themes of the western and gangster film apart from stylistic analysis than it was to do for *film noir*.

Not surprisingly it was the gangster film, not the *film noir*, which was canonized in *The Partisan Review* in 1948 by Robert Warshow's famous essay, "The Gangster as Tragic Hero." Although Warshow could be an aesthetic as well as a sociological critic, in this case he was interested in the western and gangster film as "popular" art rather than as style. This sociological orientation blinded Warshow, as it has many subsequent critics, to an aesthetically more important development in the gangster film—*film noir*.

The irony of this neglect is that in retrospect the gangster films Warshow wrote about are inferior to *film noir*. The Thirties gangster was primarily a reflection of what was happening in the country, and Warshow analyzed this. The *film noir*, although it was also a sociological reflection, went further than the gangster film. Toward the end *film noir* was engaged in a life-and-death struggle with the materials it reflected, it tried to make America accept a moral vision of life based on style. That very contradiction—promoting style in a culture which valued themes—forced *film noir* into artistically invigorating twists and turns. *Film noir* attacked and interpreted its sociological conditions, and, by the close of the *noir* period, created a new artistic world which went beyond a simple sociological reflection, a nightmarish world of American mannerism which was by far more a creation than a reflection.

Because *film noir* was first of all a style, because it worked out its conflicts visually rather than thematically, because it was aware of its own identity, it was able to create artistic solutions to sociological problems. And for these reasons films like KISS ME DEADLY, KISS TOMORROW GOODBYE and GUN CRAZY can be works of art in a way that gangster films like SCARFACE, PUBLIC ENEMY and LITTLE CAESAR can never be.

38

GENERICITY IN THE NINETIES: ECLECTIC IRONY AND THE NEW SINCERITY

Jim Collins

Source: Jim Collins, Hilary Radner and Ava Preacher Collins, eds, *Film Theory Goes to the Movies: Cultural Analysis of Contemporary Film*, New York: Routledge Inc., 1993, pp. 242–263.

Perhaps the most useful way to begin discussion of "genre film" in the early 1990s is to look at representative scenes in two quite recent Westerns, each representing in its own way how "genericity" works in contemporary American culture. In *Back to the Future III* (1990) Marty and Doc ride through the desert in what is supposed to be 1885, charging across the landscape in their disabled DeLorean time machine, sitting side-by-side atop the car, drawn by a team of horses. This configuration of drivers, horses and desert is made to resemble not just any stagecoach in any old Western, but *the* stagecoach, namely John Ford's *Stagecoach* (1939) — a parallel made explicit by replicating one of the most famous shots of Ford's film almost exactly. The DeLorean "stagecoach" is pulled through Monument Valley, framed in a high angle shot, moving diagonally through the frame, accompanied by soundtrack music that is remarkably similar to the "original." The second scene comes from *Dances With Wolves* (1990). After John Dunbar has taken part in a buffalo hunt and begun his initiation into the tribe, he contemplates the Sioux tribe moving across the horizon, silhouetted against a spectacular sunset, a picturesque vision of an unspoiled West. Dunbar says in a voice-over that he had never encountered a people so completely connected to their environment—"The only word that came to mind was harmony"—at which point we see not the Sioux, but Dunbar framed perfectly in the midst of a magnificent sunset, situated just as heroically and just as harmoniously within that landscape.

I choose these scenes because they represent two divergent types of genre film that co-exist in current popular culture. One is founded on dissonance, on eclectic juxtapositions of elements that very obviously don't belong together, while the other is obsessed with recovering some sort of missing harmony, where everything works in unison. Where the former involves an ironic hybridization of pure classical genres in which John Ford meets Jules Verne and H. G. Wells, the latter epitomizes a "new sincerity" that rejects any form of irony in its sanctimonious pursuit of lost purity. Despite their apparently antithetical perspectives, both types of genre films have emerged within the past decade as reactions to the same cultural milieu—namely, the media-saturated landscape of contemporary American culture. The goal of this article is to try to make sense of how these popular films make sense of our cultural existences and in so doing to explore the changing forms and functions of "genericity" in postmodern popular culture.

I use the term "genericity" here because I want to address not just specific genre films, but genre as a category of film production and film-viewing. Traditionally, Hollywood studios subdivided their annual production into specific genre films that, if nothing else, served as a useful way of striking a balance between product standardization and differentiation. Maintaining certain formulas that would stabilize audience expectations and, by extension, stabilize those audiences, was obviously in Hollywood's best interests. But how does the category of genre "work" today when popular entertainment is undergoing such a massive recategorization brought on by the ever-increasing number of entertainment options and the fragmentation of what was once thought to be a mass audience into a cluster of "target" audiences?

Genre films/genre theories: life on the new frontier

Just as generic texts have been a staple of the culture industries, genre theory has been all-pervasive within the criticism industries. Film scholars and social historians have tried to explain the cultural significance of the Western, the melodrama, and other popular genres since the 1940s, and they have employed a number of critical methodologies to explain the popularity of genres and what that popularity suggests about "mass consciousness." One of the most commonly used approaches once film study began to acquire a certain degree of rigor in the 1960s was myth study, i.e. reading popular narratives as the secularized myths of modern societies. This work depends on two interconnected assumptions: 1) films function as explanatory narratives told by multiple storytellers in multiple versions; and 2) out of this storytelling certain patterns emerge that reflect how the "mass consciousness" feels about any number of issues at a given time. The genre-as-myth approach most often incorporated the work of French anthropologist Claude Lévi-Strauss, whose analysis of myth in primitive cultures provided a theoretical framework for investigating just how popular stories could be interpreted as a symbolic working-out of a given culture's core values and its most pressing social problems. The most frequently borrowed principle of

Lévi-Strauss's methodology was his notion of "structuring antinomies," the binary oppositions around which the conflicts of any number of films were structured. This approach was used in reference to the musical and other genres (see Altman and Feuer), but it was most influential in the study of the Western. Jim Kitses, for example, in his introduction to *Horizons West* (1969), presents a table of antinomies that he believes are central to understanding the genre (Wilderness vs. Civilization, Individual vs. Community, Nature vs. Culture, etc.) and Will Wright (1975) traces the evolution of the Western by charting the changing configuration of the antinomies from the 1940s through the 1960s.

By the 1970s, however, this view that classical genres owe their success to their mythical dimensions came under closer scrutiny. John Cawelti, for example, argued that by the late 1960s–early 1970s, genre films ceased to function as pure, unalloyed myth, and that four types of what he calls "generic transformation" appeared: the burlesque, in which the conventions of the classical genre are pushed to absurd lengths and played for laughs, e.g. *Blazing Saddles* (1974); the nostalgia film, in which the glorious myths of Hollywood's Golden Age are revisited sentimentally, e.g. *True Grit* (1978); demythologization, in which the lessons of these classical genre films are revealed to be destructive and deluding, e.g. *Little Big Man* (1970); and affirmation of the myth for its own sake, in which the original myth is seen as antiquated, but nevertheless significant in its own way, e.g. *The Wild Bunch* (1979). The chief strength of Cawelti's overview is that it recognizes that Hollywood films could not be considered "pure myth" by the late 1960s, since all four forms of generic transformation frame the classical-genre-film-as-myth at one remove, from a self-conscious perspective in the present, clearly distanced from the imagined Golden Age. The chief limitation of Cawelti's argument is his explanation of why these transformations happened when they did. His contention that "generic exhaustion" occurred largely because a new generation of filmmakers and film-viewers (having grown up with television where older Hollywood films were ubiquitous) had acquired a degree of sophistication that made the old stories just that—old stories that failed to describe "the imaginative landscape of the latter half of the 20th century." Surely this increasing sophistication, the result of a fast-developing cinematic cultural literacy, was a major factor in shaping the changes in genre films by the late 1960s–early 1970s, but that explanation doesn't really address the interconnectedness of technological and demographic changes that accompanied those changes in cinematic literacy. The advent of television didn't increase just the average film-viewer's stock of stored narrative memories, it actually changed which genres were given highest priority by Hollywood, initially by triggering the industry's move to Cinemascope, Technicolor, and stereophonic sound that resulted in the greater prominence of the Western and historical epic. But by the late 1960s, television's impact on genre films was felt in another way. The ambiguity of television in American homes by the 1960s caused a profound shift in the nature of the film-going public. Families tended to stay home and watch television and would venture forth only rarely for special-event blockbusters. A new target audience emerged—namely, the youth audience, or more specifically a college-age audience—who by the late 1960s wanted a different form of entertainment, and to a certain extent received it in the form of "countercultural" films like *The Graduate* (1967), *Medium Cool* (1970), *Zabriske Point* (1970), *The Strawberry Statement* (1970), *Five Easy Pieces* (1970), which were marketed as a kind of genre unto themselves alongside the generic transformation films like *Bonnie and Clyde* (1967), *Little Big Man* (1970), etc. If genre-films-as-myth changed, it was due to the interconnectedness of social, technological, and demographic changes that gave rise to target myths for target audiences, a development that has serious ramifications for any claim that popular films reflect some sort of unitary, *mass* consciousness in some abstract sense.

If we are to understand the cultural context of genericity in the late 1980s–early 1990s, we need to examine the current set of pre-conditions formed by the interplay of cultural, technological, and demographic factors. Neither *Back to the Future III* nor *Dances With Wolves* fits any of Cawelti's categories particularly well—hardly surprising given the changes that have occurred in popular entertainment since the publication of his essay in 1978. The four types of generic transformation that were simultaneously at work in the 1960s and 1970s may have differed in regard to degree of respect shown a particular genre, but in each case the transformation is one that remains within the confines of a specific genre, whereas the eclectic, hybrid genre films of the eighties and nineties, like *Road Warrior* (1981), *Blade Runner* (1982), *Blue Velvet* (1986), *Near Dark* (1988), *Who Framed Roger Rabbit?* (1988), *Batman* (1989), *Thelma and Louise* (1991), all engage in specific transformation *across* genres. Just as these eclectic films were a new development in genericity in the 1980s, so too is the "new sincerity" of films like *Field of Dreams* (1989), *Dances With Wolves* (1990), and *Hook* (1991), all of which depend not on hybridization, but on an "ethnographic" rewriting of the classic genre film that serves as their inspiration, all attempting, using one strategy or another, to recover a lost "purity," which apparently pre-existed even the Golden Age of film genre.

Just as television changed the nature of popular entertainment in the 1950s and 1960s, a whole range of technological developments had a massive impact on the shape of genre films in the 1980s and 1990s. In his essay in this collection, Tom Schatz quotes the astounding increase in VCR ownership that developed in tandem with comparable developments in cable television, premium movie channels, and further refinements in both television monitors (specifically, simultaneous display of multiple channels and remote control) and playback options with the introduction of videodiscs and CD video. These interdependent developments cannot be reduced to any one overall effect. Some of the most significant ramifications of this new media technology have been: the exponential increase in the sheer volume of images that were transmitted to/playable in the average household, a comparable increase in software (titles available on videotape, disc, etc.), and parallel developments that allow for both the faster accessing and greater manipulability of that reservoir of images. The ever-expanding number of texts and technologies is both a reflection of and a significant contribution to the "array"—the perpetual circulation and recirculation of signs that forms the fabric of postmodern cultural life.

That a seemingly endless number of texts are subject to virtually immediate random access inevitably alters the relationship between classic and contemporary when both circulate alongside one another simultaneously. This simultaneity does not diminish the cultural "status" of the former so much as it changes its possible functions, which has far-reaching implications for how genre, and by extension popular culture, function in contemporary culture. The evolution of genre is traditionally conceived as a three-stage pattern of development: an initial period of consolidation in which specific narratives and visual conventions begin to coalesce into a recognizable configuration of features corresponding to a stable set of audience expectations. This period is followed by a "Golden Age," in which the interplay of by now thoroughly stabilized sets of stylistic features and audience expectations is subject to elaborate variations and permutations. The final phase is generally described in terms of all-purpose decline, in which the played-out conventions dissolve either into self-parody or self-reflexivity (end-of-the-West Westerns from *The Man Who Shot Liberty Valance* [1962] to *The Shootist* [1976]).

This three-stage model, however, doesn't adequately explain the re-emergence of the Western, primarily because that resurgence is in many ways unprecedented. Rather than conceiving of the return of the Western as some kind of "fourth stage," it is perhaps more profitable to see this "renaissance" phase in terms of technological and cultural changes that have produced a set of circumstances in which the central function of genericity is in the process of being redefined. The "recyclability" of texts from the past, the fact that once-forgotten popular texts can now be "accessed" almost at will changes the cultural function of genre films past *and* present. The omnipresence of what Umberto Eco has called the "already said," now represented and recirculated as the "still-being-said" is not just a matter of an ever-accumulating number of texts ready to be accessed, but also involves a transformation of the "cultural terrain" that contemporary genre films must somehow make sense of or map. If genre films of the 1930s and 1940s functioned as the myths of Depression-era and war-time American culture, how do they function when they come back around as "classics" or just campy old movies? How does the "cultural work" of these genre films change, especially when these mythologies of earlier periods now co-exist alongside the "new" genre films and the mythologies they activate?

This situation is described quite effectively by Lestat, the vampire narrator of Anne Rice's *The Vampire Lestat*. As the novel opens, Lestat explains that he came back from the dead because he was awakened by the "cacophony in the air"—the radio and television waves that penetrated even his coffin underground. Upon resurfacing, one of the things that he finds most surprising about life at the end of the 20th Century is that

> the old was not being routinely replaced by the new anymore . . . In the art and entertainment worlds all prior centuries were being "recycled" . . . In grand fluorescent-lighted emporiums, you could buy tapes of medieval madrigals and play them on your car stereo as you drove ninety miles an hour down the freeway. In the bookstores Renaissance poetry sold side by side with the novels of Dickens or Ernest Hemingway. Sex manuals lay on the same table with the Egyptian Book of the Dead. . . . Countless television programs poured their ceaseless flow of images into every air-cooled hotel room. But it was no series of hallucinations. This century had inherited the earth in every sense. (8–9)

The ever-expanding array to which this "inheritance" gives rise alters not just the circumstances of *representation*, but also, just as fundamentally, the *to-be-represented*, the "raw" experience of daily life, which now comes to us already framed in multiple ways, *always already* so highly mediated. The fact that the old is not replaced by the new anymore does not just change the historical development of specific genres, it also changes the function of genre films, which, if they can still be said to be engaged in symbolically "mapping" the cultural landscape, must do so now in reference to, and *through* the array that constitutes the landscape. Rice's vampire is a case in point. Lestat's monstrosity is inseparable from his media personality—we're allegedly reading his best-selling memoirs that he composes on his word-processor when he is not otherwise engaged in recording his best-selling albums or making his rock videos—all of which play globally. If the genre texts of the 1960s are distinguished by their increasing self-reflexivity about their antecedents in the Golden Age of Hollywood, the genre texts of the late 1980s–early 1990s demonstrate an even more sophisticated hyperconsciousness concerning not just narrative formulae, but the conditions of their own circulation and reception in the present, which has a massive impact on the nature of popular entertainment.

When the legend becomes hyperconscious, print the . . .

Two scenes from Robert Zemeckis's *Back to the Future III* are useful examples of this emergent type of genericity. In this film we follow the adventures of Marty and Doc on the Western frontier in the 1880s, but we are also encouraged to take simultaneous delight in the intertextual adventures that *Back to the Future* engages in as it negotiates the array, the endless proliferation of signs that constitutes the postmodern frontier. When the characters travel back in time to the Old West, their trip is actually a voyage into the Old Western, a point made most explicitly in the scene where Marty attempts to drive back to the 1880s to rescue Doe from certain death. His avenue to the past is the film screen, a metaphor literalized by his driving the time machine through a drive-in movie screen in order to reach the past. The screen, then, is a portal to a 19th Century that can exist only in the form of images, in the form of cinematic reconstructions, and their very materiality is overtly foregrounded by the text, a point made especially explicit by the fact that the drive-in happens to be located within Monument Valley. Once back in the Old Western, when the painted image of Indians gives way to the real Indians(!) who chase the DeLorean across the desert, Marty looks into his rearview mirror to check their location. This point of view shot is perhaps the most representative shot in the film because it synthesizes in a single image the relationship between past and present and between genre and postmodern culture. This image, a close-up of the mirror, taken from Marty's perspective, frames the approaching Indians perfectly—we see "history," but only as an image from the rearview mirror of the present. The literalizing of yet another metaphor concerning the visibility of the past from the present foregrounds once again, in comedic terms, one of the main themes of postmodern historiography—that history can exist for us now only in forms of representation, that we construct the significance of the past only as we frame it in the present. This, of course, has led to charges of trivialization of history (Sobchack), i.e., evil postmodern culture has "reduced" the world to images that it then cannibalizes, as if "History" were somehow accessible to us without the mediation of representation, and as such possesses some kind of "sanctity" that cannot be treated ironically through such juxtapositions. In this foregrounding of time-travel as a process inseparable from the production of images, *Back to the Future III*, resembles Julian Barnes *History of the World in 10½ Chapters*, in which the narrator states, "We cling to history as a series of salon pictures, conversation pieces whose participants we can easily reimagine back into life, when all the time it's more like a multi-media collage. . . . The history of the world? Just voices echoing in the dark; images that burn for a few centuries and then fade; stories, old stories that sometimes seem to overlap; strange links, impertinent connections" (240).

Within the Old West of *Back to the Future III*, we enter a narrative universe defined by impertinent connections, no longer containable by one set of generic conventions. We encounter, instead, different sets of generic conventions that intermingle, constituting a profoundly intertextual diegesis, nowhere more apparent than in the shot of the DeLorean time machine being pulled through the desert by a team of horses, the very co-presence of

John Ford and H. G. Wells demonstrating the film's ability to access both as simultaneous narrative options, each with a set of conventions that can be recombined at will. This simultaneity of options, each subject to a kind of random access, is epitomized by the scene in which Marty prepares for his final showdown with the villain. While practicing his draw in the mirror, dressed as Clint Eastwood in *A Fistful of Dollars* (1966), he calls up a few tough-guy lines, opting first for Eastwood's "Make my day" from his Dirty Harry/hard-boiled incarnation (*Dirty Harry*, 1971), then Travis Bickle's "Are you talkin' to me?" routine from *Taxi Driver* (1976). The simultaneous accessibility of the Spaghetti Westerner, the Hard-Boiled Cop, and the Urban Psychopath as potential heroic poses functions as a more sophisticated version of the print-outs that the Terminator sees before his eyes in Cameron's 1984 film, a menu of relevant lines that can be selected according to immediate need. The fact that the hero's choices are all cinematic quotations reflects not just the increasing sophistication of the cinematic literacy of *Back to the Future*'s audiences (and the profoundly intertextual nature of that literacy), but also the entertainment value that the ironic manipulation of that stored information now provides.

In contemporary popular culture, we see both the menu and its misuse; while the Terminator's options are all *appropriate* to a given situation, Marty's options are all *appropriated* from divergent contexts, all relevant insofar as they serve as macho poses, but inappropriate in that they purposely confuse time and genre. The Dirty Harry and Travis Bickle quotations are latter-day manifestations of the conventional gunfight, anachronisms in relation to the 1880s, but flashbacks in reference to the 1990s. Their co-presence in this scene reflects not the alleged "collapse of history," but a simultaneity that functions as a techno-palimpsest, in which earlier traces can be immediately called up, back to the surface to be replayed, or more precisely, recirculated. The act of appropriation problematizes distinctions between appropriate and inappropriate, as well as the stability of the categories of shared information that we might call cultural literacy. The categories are inappropriate only in reference to the topoi of the Old Western, but entirely appropriate to a culture in which those topoi are one of a series of push-button options. This foregrounded, hyperconscious intertextuality reflects changes in terms of audience competence and narrative technique, as well as a fundamental shift in what constitutes both entertainment and cultural literacy in the "Information Age."

Contemporary film criticism has been utterly unable to come to terms with these very profound changes in the nature of entertainment because this hyperconscious eclecticism is measured against 19th-Century notions of classical narrative and realist representation. The indictment drawn up by critics on the "left" and "right," who are always horrified by this unmanageable textuality that refuses to play by the old rules, always takes the same form—hyperconscious eclecticism is a sign of (choose one): a) the end of

"Narrative"; b) the end of "the Real," "History," etc.; c) the end of art and entertainment for anyone other than overstimulated promiscuous teenagers; d) a sign of all-purpose moral and intellectual decay. All of this has been caused by: a) the all-purpose postmodern malaise that is hell-bent on recycling the detrius of Western Civilization instead of presenting us with the "really Real," "History," etc.; b) the overwhelming desire for perpetual stimulation that makes reading "Great Books" or watching "fine films" passé; c) shorter attention spans caused by television, advertising, rock music, and permissive child-raising; d) unbridled greed in people who have read neither (choose one) Aristotle or Marx; e) technology in the hands of people described in d). What is also left out of these pronouncements is the possibility that the nature of entertainment, narrative, art, identification may be undergoing significant reformulation due to widespread changes in the nature of information distribution, access, and manipulability. That this simply doesn't exist as an option reveals the tenacity with which social critics from Allen Bloom to Jean-Louis Baudrillard still cling to notions of art, epistemology, and signification that were developed, at the very latest, in the 19th Century. The following quotations suggest the common concerns, as well as the hysterical tenor, of condemnations of the new *zeitgeist*.

> Picture a thirteen-year-old sitting in the living room of his family home, doing his math assignment while wearing his headphones and watching MTV. . . . A pubescent child whose body throbs with orgasmic rhythms, whose feelings are made articulate in hymns to the joys of onanism or the killing of parents. . . . In short, life is made into a nonstop, commercially prepackaged masturbatory fantasy. (Bloom, 74–75)
>
> Essentially a youthful crowd, this audience does not have very sophisticated tastes or expectations when it comes to narrative. Given that lack, they may never ask for strong, persuasive storytelling when they grow up. What we get . . . is not narrative as it has been traditionally defined, but a succession of undifferentiated sensations . . . there is in fact no *authentic* emotional build-up, consequently no catharsis at the movie's conclusion. . . . For in most movies today the traditional function has been inverted. Instead of the major dramatic incidents growing *naturally* out of the story, that is, out of the interaction of plausible characters with a recognizable moral and physical landscape, the opposite occurs. . . . [W]e are left without consoling coherences of old-fashioned movie narrative, left with anarchy, picking through the rubble it leaves in its wake, wondering what hit us. (Schickel, 3–4)
>
> We rarely see the kind of panoramic composition that once allowed a generous impression of quasi-global simultaneity . . . and that also,

> more subtly enriches the frame in most great movies, whose makers have offered *pictures*, composed of pleasurable "touches" and legible detail. These moving tableaux often, as André Bazin argued, gave their viewers more choice, and required some (often minimal) interpretive attention. Only now and then and in films that don't come out of Hollywood—Terry Gilliam's *Brazil*, Stanley Kubrick's *Full Metal Jacket*—do we perceive such exhilarating fullness. In contrast, today's American movies work without or against the potential depth and latitude of cinema, in favor of that systematic overemphasis deployed in advertising and all other propaganda. (Miller, 52)

The all-purpose complaint about overstimulation is framed by Richard Schickel in reference to its devastating impact on narrative, but what exactly is in crisis—narrative, or just traditional notions of narrative that depend on coherence, plausibility, *authentic* emotional build-up, *natural* outgrowths, and catharsis? This list of requirements grows out of conventions first developed in classical tragedy (and codified most obviously in Aristotle's *Poetics*) and then expanded in realist theater and literature of the 19th-Century. According to this definition, virtually all modernist and post-modernist stories are deficient narratives. The only acceptable film narratives would appear to be those that are simply cinematic versions of 19th-Century models. Cultural changes that have occurred in the 20th Century apparently should have no impact on the well-made narrative. But even if we bracket this problem and ignore the obvious condescension in the dismissal of viewers less "sophisticated" than Schickel, the most serious problem with his narrative complaint has to do with yet another stipulation—the "recognizable moral and physical landscape" that characters must inhabit. This definition simply dismisses another possibility—that the popular narratives of the 1980s and 1990s present a moral and physical landscape in a state of previously unfathomable change and that these stories just might be an attempt to make the chaotic, dissonant cultures of the later decades of the 20th Century somehow more manageable through their presentation of a new mediated landscape that can be successfully mapped out only by contemporary media, and not some antiquated notion of the well-made play. The alternatives that Schickel offers—classical narrative or anarchy—are uncannily similar to the binary, either/or, all-or-nothing opposition proposed by Matthew Arnold in *Culture and Anarchy*; culture can only be "Culture" if it imitates the culture of any time *other than* the present.

Mark Cripsin Miller's condemnation of contemporary film style is cast in the same nostalgic mode, but his presuppositions regarding what films supposedly "worked" in the good old days are even more problematic. Schickel's nostalgia is for old-fashioned storytelling that did indeed exist (and still does to a far greater extent than he is willing to allow), but Crispin Miller pines for an imaginary film-viewing state that never existed, based as it is on Bazin's now-discredited assumptions concerning the relationship among the camera, reality, and the spectator. Miller's thesis concerning the negative impact that advertising has had on filmmaking is a rhetorically powerful argument, but his grand alternative—how film used to work—is founded on a thoroughly outdated understanding of filmic representation. By invoking Bazin's idealist theory of representation, in which true cinematic geniuses allow the photographic plate to capture the "real" in an unmediated way, thereby allowing truth to leap directly onto the celluloid strip, Miller posits an authentic or genuine form of representation against which all other types of film practice will be automatically judged deficient. The problem here, of course, is the notion of film as unmediated reality, a "fullness" that spectators were able to contemplate, free to formulate their own interpretations out of the essential ambiguity of the filmic image. One of the main themes of film theory since the late 1960s has been the rejection of this sort of idealism, and a number of theorists have been investigating the various stylistic, institutional, and ideological apparatuses that intervene between camera and "reality," and then between image and spectator, all of which demonstrate that these relationships are never as unmediated as Bazin imagined them to be. Miller's sweeping rejection of Hollywood filmmaking depends on his appeal to a "classic" film style as imagined by an antiquated film theory developed in the 1950s to describe the masterpieces of the 1930s and 1940s. It is hardly surprising that such an approach would provide only a blindered view of recent filmmaking, unable to come to terms with the highly "mediated" nature of our contemporary cultural existences and the images needed to represent them. The "exhilarating fullness" of this world is due to the fact that the real now comes to us always already "imaged" in any number of ways, the "depth and latitude" of contemporary cinema depending on the negotiation of that thickness of representation, those sedimented layers of images that define the cultural significance of any subject matter.

In all such attacks on current popular films that decry their avoidance of traditional narrative and authentic representation, one finds the same assumption—that the increasing sophistication of the media produces a sensory overload in which individual viewers are overstimulated into numbness, reachable only through blunt appeals to animal appetites. But these technophobic denunciations of media "overload" never even begin to address the distinguishing features of recent popular narratives, namely the attempts to encounter directly that "overload," that semiotic excess, and turn it into a new form of narrative entertainment that necessarily involves altering the structure and function of narrative. Tim Burton's *Batman* is a useful example here, because it epitomizes these attempts to incorporate the array that now forms the "imaginative landscape" of contemporary cultural life, and the criticism devoted to this film by Schickel and Miller epitomizes just as explicitly the failure of the antiquated paradigms they use to evaluate it. Miller dismisses *Batman* as part of the "cartooning" of Hollywood, and

Schickel cites it as one more example of deficient narrative, of visual pyrotechnics instead of plot—"Its story—the conflict between its eponymous hero and the Joker for the soul of Gotham City—is all right, kind of fun. But that is not what the movie is primarily about. It is about—no kidding—urban design" (14). But Burton's film is about far more than urban design. It presents a decidedly "old-fashioned" plot, but it also situates the adventures of Batman and the Joker within the mediated culture of the present and makes their manipulation of the images that surround them a crucial part of the conflicts between them.

Batman is not just vaguely symptomatic of how popular narratives try to envision the array—its main characters actively engage in different strategies of image play. Throughout the film, we see the Joker in his headquarters, producing "cut-ups" from the photographs that surround him, and then in a later scene at the museum he defaces one painting after another either by painting over the original or writing his name over the surface. His "hijacking" of signs is more explicit in his seizure of the television signal when he interrupts scheduled programming with his own parodic advertisements. Batman's appropriation of images works according to a quite different dynamic. Like the Joker, Batman seems to spend a significant amount of time watching television, and like his adversary he is shown surrounded by images that he manipulates for his own purposes. Just as Joker is practically engulfed by the photographs he cuts up, the first sequence in the Batcave presents Batman in front of a bank of monitors, surrounded by footage of his guests that his hidden cameras have recorded, images that he "calls up" (rather than "cuts up") in order to summon a reality that escaped his purview the first time around. While the Joker's manipulations of images is a process of consistent deformation, Batman engages in a process of retrieval, drawing on a reservoir of images that constitutes the past. The tension between abduction and retrieval epitomizes the conflicting but complementary processes at work in the film—a text that alternately *hijacks* and *accesses* the traditional Batman topoi. German Expressionism, Gaudi's *Sagrada Familia* Cathedral, Hitchcock films, etc.

The foregrounding of disparate intertexts and the all-pervasive hyperconsciousness concerning the history of both "high art" and popular representation has become one of the most significant features of contemporary storytelling. Narrative action now operates at two levels simultaneously—in reference to character adventure and in reference to a text's adventures in the array of contemporary cultural production. That this self-referentiality should emerge as a response to that array is comparable to parallel developments in other disciplines. Mark Poster's recent essay on modes of information is a very productive attempt to specify the impact of new technologies on the nature of information, but it also reveals the necessity of dealing with the second half of the problem—the need to specify emerging forms of textuality used to negotiate the array. He argues:

> . . . the complex linguistic worlds of the media, the computer and the database it can access, the surveillance capabilities of the state and the corporation, and finally the discourse of science are each realms in which the representational function of language has been placed in question by different communicational patterns, each of which shift to forefront the self-referential aspect of language. In each case, the language in question is constituted as an intelligible field with a unique pattern of wrapping, whose power derives not so much from representing something else, but from its internal linguistic structure. While this feature of language is always present in its use—today, meaning increasingly sustained through mechanisms of self-referentiality and the non-linguistic thing, the referent, fades into obscurity, playing less and less of a role in the delicate process of sustaining cultural memory. (72)

While Poster wisely acknowledges that there is a plurality of discontinuous modes of information each with its own historical peculiarities, he still maintains that his self-referentiality necessarily means the loss of the "really Real" referent—a loss which has only devastating effects on communication and subjectivity; "instead of envisioning language as a tool of a rational autonomous subject intent on controlling a world of objects for the purpose of enhanced freedom, the new language structures refer back upon themselves, severing referentiality and thereby acting upon the subject and constituting it in new and disorienting ways" (75). But do these new structures sever referentiality or just redefine the nature of referentiality? The notion of the referent posited here presupposes that this self-referentiality necessarily replaces any other kind of referentiality, but this argument offers no compelling reason to assume that self-referentiality, *ipso facto*, cancels out other types of referentiality. The self-referentiality that is symptomatic of communication in techno-sophisticated cultures, is a recognition of the highly discursive, thoroughly institutionalized dimension of all signs. At this point these signs become doubly referential, referring to a "really real" world, but also to the reality of the array, which forms the fabric of day-to-day experience in those very cultures. It is the individual negotiations of the array that form the delicate process of not just maintaining but constantly rearticulating cultural memories.

This "double referentiality" is the basis of the strategies of *rearticulation* discussed in the essays by Ann Cvetkovich, Cathy Griggers, Sharon Willis, and Ava Preacher Collins in this volume. The individual voguers in *Paris is Burning* (1990), Callie Khouri's screenplay for *Thelma and Louise* (1991), and Jim Jarmusch's use of Elvis in *Mystery Train* (1989), all recognize the inseparability of these two levels of referentiality in regard to notions of gender and racial difference, the nature of sexual preference, and the determination of cultural value. All such distinctions are patterns of signs, conventionalized in such a way that they are now taken to be "real" and therefore must be exposed as such through strategies of rearticulation that change that real by foregrounding mechanisms of referentiality. *Thelma and Louise* addresses the reality of the subjugation of women through its concerted reworking of the reality of the buddy film and the Western, repeatedly emphasizing the interconnectedness of gender difference and cinematic representation. Willis states this very succinctly: "We women were raised on the same cinematic and televisual images and stories that men were, and we were identifying, perhaps with more resistance, or more intermittence, but identifying all the same, with the same male figures and masculine scenarios as our male contemporaries. This must be the framework in which images of women raiding those nearly worn-out stories, trying on those clichéd postures might have the effect of 'newness,' and might challenge our readings of those postures themselves, as it might challenge our analysis of process and the effects of identification in our histories as consumers of popular culture." Rather than disorientation, these strategies of rearticulation that reflect a hyperconsciousness about the impact of images on social categorization are a process of fundamental *reorientation* conducted on and through that double referentiality.

The divergent, often conflicting ways in which recent narratives rearticulate conventional structures of popular genres has become a distinguishing feature of contemporary textuality, but there is no uniform politics of rearticulation anymore than there is a single aesthetic of rearticulation. The ironic, hyperconscious reworking of the array varies, from the flatout comedic parody of *Back to the Future III* to the more unsettling, ambivalent parody of *Blue Velvet*, to the explicit hijacking of signs in a film like *Thelma and Louise*. While stakes and strategies may differ profoundly, they do have one thing in common—the recognition that the features of conventional genre films that are subjugated to such intensive rearticulation are not the mere detritus of exhausted cultures past: those icons, scenarios, visual conventions continue to carry with them some sort of cultural "charge" or resonance that must be reworked according to the exigencies of the present. The individual generic features then, are neither detritus nor reliquaries, but *artifacts* of another cultural moment that now circulate in different arenas, retaining vestiges of past significance reinscribed in the present.

In their frustration of the homogeneity and predictability considered the prerequisite for "genericity," these hybrid popular narratives present a paradoxical situation in which we encounter texts composed entirely of generic "artifacts" that contradict, as an assemblage, the function of genre as coordinator of narrative conventions and audience expectations. I use the term artifact here because the individual icon or semantic feature acquires a kind of different status, not really the same element as before, since it now comes back with a set of quotation marks that hover above it like an ironic halo. But neither is it really an exhausted piece of debris ready to be camped up. Finding an analogous sort of transformation is difficult because this transformation process is, to a great extent, unprecedented. One could point to the transformation/transportation that a tribal artifact undergoes when it is placed in the museum, when, for example, the ceremonial mask or doorlock becomes revalued as minimalist sculpture once it is solidly ensconced not just behind the glass, but with the institutional frameworks that guarantee its new value. Rather than the figural becoming merely functional, the poetic degraded to common prosaic speech, here the functional acquires a figural status, becoming marked as a special kind of expression that can no longer be taken literally. Generic artifacts, like tribal artifacts, acquire new discursive registers unforeseen in their initial contexts, but they differ in regard to stability of the rearticulation. Where the new value given to the mask is anchored within the discursive formation that is museum art, the generic artifact remains unanchored, subject to multiple transformations, multiple transportations while still retaining vestiges of the original semantic and syntactic relationships that once gave it a precise generic value.

When the legend becomes hyperconscious, print the array.

And the only words that came to mind were "the new sincerity"

Getting an adequate picture of contemporary genericity depends on our ability to recognize widespread changes in what constitutes narrative action and visual entertainment, but these ironic, eclectic texts are not the "whole story," or more appropriately, are not the *only* story. Another type of genre film has emerged since the late 1980s, which is also a response to the same media-sophisticated landscape. Rather than trying to master the array through ironic manipulation, these films attempt to reject it altogether, purposely evading the media-saturated terrain of the present in pursuit of an almost forgotten authenticity, attainable only through a sincerity that avoids any sort of irony or eclecticism. Films such as *Dances With Wolves, Hook*, and *Field of Dreams*, all fix this recoverable purity in an impossible past—impossible because it exists not just before the advent of media corruption, but because this past is, by definition, a never-never land of pure wish-fulfillment, in which the problems of the present are symbolically resolved in a past that not only did not, but could not exist.

In *Dances With Wolves*, that lost authenticity is situated in a West before the Western "got to it." In other words, the narrative of *Dances* focuses on the life of Native Americans before the arrival of the white man, a period traditionally ignored by the Western film. For most of the film, the only white man on the scene is John Dunbar, and he takes on the role of proto-ethnographer, rather than that of settler. His chief activity, observing and cataloguing the Sioux way of life, respects the purity of that tribe's existence. Dunbar's journal is all-important in this regard, since it serves as a guarantee of the authenticity of his position as ethnographer and as a symbol of his difference from other white men—a point made especially obvious when his journal is literally used as toilet paper by a pair of the most repulsive cavalrymen.

But *Dances With Wolves* makes this pre-history of the Western the site of another project—beyond an ostensible desire to depict the previously undepicted—in which the problems of White America of the 1990s are first diagnosed and then solved in the imaginary of that pre-history. The film repeatedly attempts to "demythologize" the classic Western, whether by inverting conventions or presenting what *really* happened. The manifest destiny ideology that floated implicitly or explicitly throughout virtually all classic Westerns concerned with the settling of the West is here rewritten as a ruthless imperialism. The traditional structuring antinomy, Civilization vs. Savagery, is mobilized here, but the polarities are reversed as the Sioux become the model civilization. This reversal is most apparent in the final scene in which the heroic Indian warriors recapture Dunbar, now one of their own, and kill off a few soldiers (now defined as savages) in the process. But at the same time, this rewriting of the history of the Western expansion from the perspective of Native Americans is far from an end in itself. The other major project of the narrative, John Dunbar's self-actualization, is thoroughly intertwined with that rewriting; the virtues of the Sioux of the 1860s are expressed in terms of another ideology generated by White America, specifically a "New Age" mentality that becomes increasingly prominent in the second half of the film, when Dunbar "finds himself." The Sioux language may be respected here in an unprecedented manner through the use of subtitles, but the content of their speech is remarkably similar to what my students called the "California speak" of the present.

The complicated, conflicted agenda of the New Sincerity genre becomes apparent in the "harmony scene" mentioned in the introduction to this essay. After Dunbar takes part in the buffalo hunt and the celebration afterward, he watches the tribe move on the next day. The scene begins with a long pan across a breathtaking sunset—a tableau shot in the tradition of the classic Western, in which the Sioux are exquisitely silhouetted as dark figures on the crest of the horizon against the purple sky. This extremely painterly composition, when combined with Dunbar's voice-over, accords the figures an almost divine status: "It seems everyday ends with a miracle here. And whatever God may be I thank God for this day. To stay any longer would have been useless. We had all the meat we could possibly carry. We had hunted for three days, losing half-a-dozen ponies, and only three men injured. I'd never known a people so eager to laugh, so devoted to family, so dedicated to each other, and the only word that came to mind was harmony." When we first see Dunbar, it is from the side, observing the tableau from the distance in a completely different light zone. But as the scene progresses, his point of view shots of this awe-inspiring, harmonious spectacle alternate with shots of

Dunbar, now framed by exactly the same majestic purple sunset. As he waves to his companions, he has been virtually united with them, set in harmony with them through the lighting and his Sioux chest-protector. Once this solidarity is established, there is a pause in the voice-over, and the last shot of the Sioux is followed by a low-angle close-up of Dunbar that monumentalizes him still further as he says, "Many times I'd felt alone, but until this afternoon I'd never felt completely lonely."

The progression here exemplifies the interdependency of the rewriting of history and the process of self-actualization in which the former repeatedly gives way to the latter. The voice-over praises the Sioux, but in the images they are framed as a decorative cluster of Noble Savages, with only the sympathetic White Man receiving the big close-up. Paradoxically, this scene, while it locates authenticity in the pre-history of the Golden Age of the Western, uses the Native American in a way that is remarkably similar to that employed by early 19th-Century European fiction such as Chateaubriand's *Atala, or the Love of Two Savages in the Desert* (1801), which virtually defied the Noble Savage. The ultimate "authenticity" here depends upon another exigency—whether the plight of the Noble Savage of the past can serve as a satisfactory site for the narcissistic projections of alienated Europeans in the present. This dimension of *Dances With Wolves* becomes particularly apparent later in the film, when Dunbar reflects on the battle with the Pawnee, a battle without a "dark political agenda." "I felt a pride I'd never felt before. I'd never really known who John Dunbar was. Perhaps the name itself had no meaning, but as I heard my Sioux name being called over and over, I knew for the first time who I really was." In *Back to the Future III*, the rearview mirror tableau of "Indians!" emphasized the artifice of any cinematic travels into history, that all Westerns are finally nothing more than highly conventionalized representations of an imaginary West. *Dances With Wolves* avoids any such ironic constructions in its attempt to locate the authentic vision of the past; nonetheless, the seemingly unmediated tableau becomes another kind of mirror, the idealized imaginary in which the troubled hero sees himself, a mirror in which he is magically healed, in harmony, although only in this unrecoverable past.

Dances With Wolves contains a number of distinguishing features of this New Sincerity genre film: the move back in time away from the corrupt sophistication of media culture toward a lost authenticity defined simultaneously as a yet-to-be-contaminated folk culture of elemental purity, and as the site of successful narcissistic projection, the hero's magic mirror; the foregrounding not only of the intertextual, but of the "Ur-textual," in which an originary genre text takes on a quasi-sacred function as the guarantee of authenticity; the fetishizing of "belief" rather than irony as the only way to resolve conflict; the introduction of a new generic imaginary that becomes the only site where unresolvable conflicts can be successfully resolved. While it is well beyond the scope of this essay to catalogue all the instances of this emergent configuration or to detail its various permutations, I hope a brief analysis of two representative films, *Hook* and *Field of Dreams*, will suggest how this configuration functions in other texts.

Spielberg's continuation of the Peter Pan story foregrounds all of these emergent conventions, and the differences between the Disney version and the Spielberg versions of J. M. Barrie's book throw the changing stakes of the New Sincerity genre film into sharp relief. While the former establishes the opposition between childhood and adulthood, the latter adds a level of hyper-self-awareness regarding the role film plays in constructing that difference, only to provide an imaginary transgression that takes the form of an ideal synthesis of the two. The indictment of media-saturated culture is omnipresent—the portable phone and camcorder are two major obstacles between Peter (now the lawyer as pirate) and his own children. The demonization of the camcorder involves one of the most interesting contradictions within the New Sincerity—that even though the search for lost purity and authenticity may depend on dazzling special effects and the blockbuster budgets they entail, there is nevertheless a free-floating technophobia. We know that Peter is a miserable failure as a father because he sends an assistant to videotape his son's baseball game, willfully foregoing the authentic, "unmediated" experience of watching his son's game "in person." The opposition between an authentic "liveness" seen as superior to an artificial technology is emphasized repeatedly in the opening scenes. The family goes to a school play to see one of the children perform as Wendy in a theatrical production of *Peter Pan*, which appears to charm everyone in the diegetic audience except Peter. When the family arrives at Wendy's London townhouse, she tells the children the story of Peter Pan, the tale-telling "primal scene" accentuated in much the same way as the reading of *Peter Pan* in a comparable scene in *E.T.* (1982). In the earlier Spielberg film, the transmission of the "Ur-story" is set up in a mis-en-abîme structure—while the mother reads the "clap your hands if you believe" passage to her daughter, the son and E.T. sit transfixed in the dark, listening unobserved in the closet just as the theater full of parents and children listen unobserved in the dark. The foregrounding of the Ur-text in *Hook* becomes most explicit when Wendy hands the adult Peter "the book"—apparently the first edition of Barrie's book, which, she tells Peter, was not fiction at all, but Barrie's transcription of the children's actual adventure, made possible by the fact that Barrie was their next door neighbor. Once back in the world of children's fantasy, Peter regains his lost purity by recovering his childish delight in the elemental among the Wild Boys—a folk culture par excellence—leading to a resolution that can be effected only in *the* never-never land. Peter succeeds as a father only by recovering the lost child within him, thereby fusing two contradictory desires in one impossible composite: the desire to become the consummate father and the desire to return to the bliss of childhood outside of any paternal control.

The determination to resolve the unresolvable in a never-never land that is available neither in the present nor the past, but in an imaginary prehistory or originary moment takes an even more fanciful form in *Field of Dreams*. The film begins with a brief family history of the main character, Ray Kinsella, accomplished through family photos and voice-over narration. The main point of this section is that Ray and his father, once close, especially in their love of baseball, broke irreconcilably during his teenage years. His father had "died" when his beloved White Sox threw the World Series in 1920 and later died an embittered shell of a man, old before his time. Once this troubled family history is established, the action in the present begins with Ray hearing voices in his cornfield. The field, like the Western landscape, is doubly fetishized as the yet to be corrupted preindustrial, agrarian paradise ("Is this heaven?" "No. It's Iowa."), and as the site of narcissistic projection, here taken to an even greater extreme as the land actually talks directly to Ray about his private psycho-drama. The Ur-text in this film is likewise taken to more elaborate lengths; the lost text becomes the lost team as the Black Sox magically reappear in the dream diamond in the midst of the cornfield. The purity of this "text" is emphasized through explicit comparison to the corrupt present. Shoeless Joe waxes rhapsodic about the elemental joys of the game, the "thrill of the grass," the fact that he would have played just for meal money (unlike the soulless mercenaries of contemporary major league baseball, of course). Within this eulogizing of the game, baseball as it was played by Shoeless Joe and company becomes a folk-cultural activity—an organic and, at the same time, mystical ritual. Grafted onto this nostalgia for baseball the way it used to be is a parallel nostalgia for the 1960s, and Ray believes he must "ease the pain" of Terence Mann, the famous counter-cultural writer who becomes a kind of proxy father-figure for Kinsella, first in the 1960s (after he reads Mann's *The Boat Rocker* he stops playing catch with his biological father), and then explicitly in the 1980s when they travel together in search of their dreams. The connection between the America of the late teens and the late 1960s is articulated by Terence Mann during his "People Will Come" speech near the film's conclusion—both periods are collapsed into mere passing moments alongside the eternal game that represents an eternal childhood.

> Ray, people will come, Ray. They'll come to Iowa for reasons they can't even fathom. They'll turn in to your driveway not knowing for sure why they're doing it. They'll arrive at your door, as innocent as children, longing for the past. . . . They'll find they have reserved seats somewhere along the baselines where they sat when they were children and cheered their heroes, and they'll watch the game and it'll be as if they dipped themselves in magic waters. The memories will be so thick they'll have to brush them away from their faces.

> People will come, Ray. The one constant through all the years, Ray, has been baseball. America has rolled by like an army of steamrollers. It's been erased like a blackboard, rebuilt and erased again. But baseball has marked the time. This field, this game, it's part of our past, Ray. It reminds us of all that once was good and could be again. Oh, people will come, Ray, people will definitely come.

Mann's oration perfectly describes the appeal of the New Sincerity. Like this mythical game, these films offer the recovery of lost purity, the attempt to recapture the elemental simplicity of childhood delight in a magical state that yields its perfect resolutions of the otherwise impossible conflict. Once Kinsella's proxy father departs with the players to document their stories and what is "out there," Ray finally reunites with his real father—but his father as a young man, a young baseball player years before he becomes a father. Generational tensions dissolve in this imaginary realm where boys can once again play catch with their fathers before their fathers became fathers, an impossible temporality that allows boys to reconcile with their lost fathers only when they're yet to be their fathers.

The two types of genre film that I have discussed here represent contradictory perspectives on "media culture," an ironic eclecticism that attempts to master the array through techno-sophistication, and a new sincerity that seeks to escape it through a fantasy technophobia. That both should appear as responses to media saturation is not surprising, nor is the simultaneity of these responses; the popular narratives of the late 1980s and early 1990s articulate a profound ambivalence that reflects the lack of any sort of unitary mass consciousness. Both types of these genre films involve a meta-mythological dimension, in which the cultural terrain that must be mapped is a world already sedimented with layers of popular mythologies, some old, some recent, but all co-present and subject to rearticulation according to different ideological agendas. These emergent forms of genericity do not mark the beginning of post-postmodernism or late postmodernism, especially since the latter might turn out to be as much of a misnomer as Late Capitalism. One could just as easily argue that what we have seen of postmodernism thus far is really a first phase, perhaps Early Postmodernism, the first tentative attempts at envisioning the impact of new technologies of mass communication and information processing on the structure of narrative. If, following Marshal Berman, we might say that Modernism was a period in which all that was solid melted into air, the current period is defined by a different dynamic, in which all that is aired eventually turns solid, the transitory coming back around as the monumental with a decidedly different cultural status and cultural resonance. Contemporary popular narratives mark the beginning of the next phase, when new forms of textuality emerge to absorb the impact of these changes, and in the process turn them into new forms of entertainment.

Works cited

Altman, Rick. *The American Film Musical*. Bloomington: Indiana University Press, 1987.

Aristotle. "The Poetics." *Aristotle's Theory of Poetry and Fine Art, with a Critical Text and Translation of the Poetics*. S. H. Butcher. New York: Dover, 1951.

Arnold, Matthew. *Culture and Anarchy*. Cambridge: Cambridge University Press, 1963.

Barnes, Julian. *History of the World in 10½ Chapters*. New York: Knopf, 1989.

Barrie, J. M. *Peter Pan in Kensington Gardens*. London: Hodder and Stroughton, 1906.

Baudrillard, Jean-Louis. "The Implosion of Meaning in the Media and the Information of the Social in the Masses." *Myths of Information: Technology and Postindustrial Culture*. Ed. Kathleen Woodward. Madison: Coda Press, 1980, pp. 137–148.

Bazin, André. *What Is Cinema?* Vols. I and II. Trans. Hugh Gray. Berkeley: University of California Press, 1971.

Berman, Marshall. *All That Is Solid Melts Into Air: The Experience of Modernity*. New York: Simon and Schuster, 1982.

Bloom, Allan. *The Closing of the American Mind: How Higher Education Has Failed Democracy and Impoverished the Souls of Today's Students*. New York: Simon and Schuster, 1987.

Cawelti, John. "*Chinatown* and Generic Transformation in Recent American Film." *Film Theory and Criticism*. Ed. Gerald Mast, Marshall Cohen. New York: Oxford University Press, 1978, pp. 498–511.

Chateaubriand, François René, Vicomte de. *Atala*. Paris: J. Corti, 1950, 1801.

Eco, Umberto. "Postmodernism, Irony and the Enjoyable." *Postscript to The Name of the Rose*. New York: Harcourt Brace Jovanovich, 1984, pp. 65–67.

Feuer, Jane. "The Self-Reflective Musical and the Myth of Entertainment." *Genre: The Musical*. Ed. Rick Altman. London: Routledge and Kegan Paul, 1981, pp. 208–215.

Kitses, Jim. *Horizons West: Anthony Mann, Budd Boetticher, Sam Peckinpah: Studies of Authorship within the Western*. Bloomington: Indiana University Press, 1969.

Lévi-Strauss, Claude. *Structured Anthropology*. Trans. Claire Jacobson, Brooke Grundfest Schoept. New York: Basic Books, 1963.

Miller, Mark Crispin. "Hollywood: The Ad." *Atlantic Monthly*. April, 1990, pp. 49–52.

Poster, Mark. "Words Without Thing: The Mode of Information." *October* 53. Summer, 1990, pp. 63–77.

Rice, Anne. *The Vampire Lestat*. New York: Ballantine, 1984.

Schickel, Richard. "The Crisis in Movie Narrative." *Gannett Center Journal*. Summer, 1989, pp. 1–15.

Sobchack, Vivian. *Screening Space: The American Science Fiction Film*. New York: Ungar, 1980.

Wright, Will. *Six Guns and Society: A Structural Study of the Western*. Berkeley: University of California Press, 1975.

39

ISSUES, CONCLUSIONS AND QUESTIONS

Steve Neale

Source: *Genre and Hollywood*, London: Routledge, 2000, pp. 251–255.

[. . .]

It is clear that in their descriptions of New Hollywood cinema, Gomery and Sartelle are using the terms 'genre' and 'generic' in different ways. For Sartelle they suggest the categories associated with Hollywood's output in the studio era and the extent to which the films themselves conformed to them. (New Hollywood 'is "post-generic", he writes (1996: 516), 'in the sense that, while films belonging to the traditional Hollywood genres were still being made, they coexisted with an explosion of emerging new categories'). For Gomery, they indicate films 'that could be most easily packaged, and sold on a mass scale to audiences around the world' (1996c: 480). If we add to these meanings some of the others discussed earlier on in this book, it becomes apparent once again that 'genre' and 'generic' are multifaceted concepts and terms: if genre can mean 'category', generic can mean 'constructed or marked for commercial consumption'; if genre can mean 'corpus', generic can mean 'conventionally comprehensible'; if genre can mean 'formula', generic can mean 'those aspects of representation that entail the generation of expectations'; and so on.

It is the multiple nature of these facets and meanings that have helped generate the variety of uses to which these concepts have been put. As we have seen, these uses have focused overwhelmingly on Hollywood and its films. They have varied from the provision of means by which to analyse the aesthetic workings and the industrial and mass-produced nature of Hollywood's films to the provision of means by which to theorize their socio-cultural significance. They have included the provision of aesthetic and ideological contexts for the discussion of individual films and auteurs (John Ford and the western, Douglas Sirk and melodrama, and so on). And they have included the provision of means by which to analyse the nature of Hollywood's output at specific points in time. Books and articles on genre have ranged from detailed studies of specific genres and generic traditions to studies which use these traditions as a way of discussing particular groups or collections of films. They have ranged as well from theoretical discussions of genre to discussions of its role in Hollywood's commercial and industrial practices and structures.

As I hope I have made apparent, much of this work is extremely valuable. However, as I hope I have also made apparent, some of its tenets, some of its practices and some of its presuppositions are open to question. Genre critics and theorists have repeatedly argued for the importance of genre as a means of conceptualizing the links between Hollywood's films and US society, between Hollywood's industry and Hollywood's art, between Hollywood's producers and Hollywood's consumers, and between Hollywood's present and Hollywood's past. However as Richard Maltby has argued (Maltby and Bowles 1994: 128–34; Maltby 1995: 107–43), most critics and theorists have in practice nearly always used the concept of genre as a way of avoiding detailed study of anything other than selective samples of Hollywood's art. As we have seen in the case of melodrama and *film noir*, 'Genre criticism has understood genre in Hollywood quite differently from the industry itself, ignoring most of the industry's own categories and introducing alternatives of its own' (1995: 116). As we have seen in Chapter 6, it has also constructed structural models and evolutionary schemas as a way of avoiding rather than conducting socio-cultural and historical analysis. Where structural models have substituted generically internal thematic antinomies for detailed contextual research, the 'imposition of an internal historical structure in which texts influence each other', a characteristic of all evolutionary schemas and most genre histories, has tended to 'eliminate the need to consider external questions of industry, economics and audience in favor of a search for recurrent textual structures' (ibid.). Finally, as we have repeatedly seen, rather than looking in full at the nature of Hollywood's output either in general or at any particular point in time, genre criticism has tended to concern itself with exemplary films and with canons of excellence (whether defined in terms of artistic merit, ideological subversiveness, or conformity to a particular theoretical model). In addition it has tended to assume throughout that Hollywood has always organized the production and distribution of its films in ways which dovetail not just with the genres it has identified but also with genre itself as a category. Genre criticism has thus not just constructed a series of misleading pictures of Hollywood's output, it has also, according to Maltby, constructed a misleading picture of 'the industry itself, which categorizes its product by production size and by the audience sector to whom it is primarily appealing, organizing its production schedules around cycles and sequels rather than genres as such' (1995: 130).

I myself would qualify this last point. While the evidence discussed in this chapter suggests that cycles and sequels were and are important as factors in the planning of productions, it also suggests that star-genre formulations, star-formula combinations, production trends, cyclic formulae, generic formulae, generic hybrids and traditionally defined genres were and are important as well. Thus while I endorse Maltby's insistence on the importance of industrial factors and of thorough historical and socio-cultural analysis, and while I share many of his views on the limitations of genre criticism and genre theory, I would myself maintain that the latter still have a role to play in understanding Hollywood, its history and its films. At least some of the definitions discussed in Chapter 3 make sense; and at least some of the terms and descriptions used by the industry coincide with those used by critics and theorists.

The limitations of existing genre criticism and theory need, nevertheless, to be acknowledged, and an agenda of the kind implicit in Maltby's comments needs to be set. In doing so, there are a number of examples to follow. Among them are Doherty's work on the 1950s teenpic (1988), Jacobs' work on the fallen woman films of the late 1920s, the 1930s and early 1940s (1991), Jenkins' work on early sound comedy (1992), Kapsis' work on the early 1980s horror film (1991), Klinger's work on 'local genres' (1994b), Leutrat's work on the 1920s western (1985), Maltby's work on the gangster films of the early 1930s (1993b), Riblet's work on Keystone comedy (1995), Singer's work of serial-queen melodrama (1990), Stanfield's work on the 1930s western (1999) and Tudor's work on the horror film (1989). In various ways and to varying degrees, this work is characterized by painstaking industrial, socio-cultural and historical research, by a thorough viewing of more than a handful of canonic films, and by willingness to question and abandon orthodox views. For the most part, however, it is confined to single well-recognized genres or to single intra-generic cycles. Studies are needed of unrecognized genres like racetrack pics, of semi-recognized genres like drama, of cross-generic cycles and production trends like overland bus and prestige films, and of hybrids and combinations of all kinds.[10]

In tandem with studies of well-recognized genres, studies like this are more likely to provide an accurate picture both of the industry and its output and of the socio-cultural significance and role of its films, particularly if focused on particular periods. As I hope I have shown, our picture of the 1980s and even of the 1930s is partial at best. The same is even more true of the 1910s, the 1920s and the 1990s. If we glance briefly at the 1950s, whose output and whose industrial and socio-cultural conditions and contexts are relatively well-explored, it soon becomes apparent that the role of circus films like *The Greatest Show on Earth*, *Trapeze* (1956) and *The Big Circus* (1959) in the move toward road shows, in the promotion of an upgraded version of the cinematic experience and in the promotion of a traditional image of old fashioned entertainment (a role it shares with show-business biopics in particular) has been all but ignored. It soon becomes apparent that the paranoid scenarios associated with 1950s science fiction, scenarios in which outsiders invade or infiltrate US communities, families and homes, are shared by crime films like *The Desperate Hours* (1955) and *Suddenly* (1954) and by westerns like *Day of the Outlaw* (1959), and are mirrored, doubled or reversed by heist films in western and gangster guise like *The Raid* and *Violent Saturday* (1955) and by numerous imperial adventure films, numerous cavalry westerns, numerous spy films, and numerous science fiction films about the exploration of outer space. And it soon becomes apparent that a preoccupation with race relations and ethnic identity can be found in virtually every area and in virtually every type of Hollywood production (Neale 1998). Studies of well-recognized genres in isolation are unlikely to shed further light on tendencies and trends such as these. A cross-generic and multi-cyclic approach, an approach which pays heed to 'local' and 'minor' genres and trends, and which in addition takes on board the factors involved in the 'production of culture perspective' adopted by Kapsis, is, to repeat, much more likely to produce reliable results.

Such an approach is also likely to dovetail with the more extensive conceptions of genre discussed towards the end of Chapter 1. For in addition to opening up other areas of the cinema to generic analysis, conceptions such as these permit a more inclusive and flexible approach to Hollywood's output, one which can encompass minor trends, local and non-canonic genres, cyclic contributions, star-formula combinations and hybrids. They also necessitate an attention to the industry, its relay and its audiences in ways which are likely to generate much more knowledge than we possess at the moment about the array of generic calculations at stake in film production, distribution and exhibition, about the construction of generic images in and through the industry's relay, and about the generic expectations and terms in circulation in the process of reception. To that extent they are likely, too, to support, to qualify and to promote debate around the statement which opens the chapter on genre in Maltby's book on Hollywood cinema and with which I would like to conclude. 'Hollywood', Maltby writes, 'is a generic cinema, which is not quite the same as saying that it is a cinema of genres' (1995: 107).

Note

10 For discussion of at least some minor, local or non-canonic genres, cycles and trends, see Cohan and Hark (1997); Doherty (1993b); Grindon (1996); Morey (1995); Rubin (1994) and Schaefer (1992).

References

(Most references to newspapers, magazines and trade journals are given in full in the text or the notes.)

Buscombe, E. and Pearson, R. (1998) *Back in the Saddle Again: New Essays on the Western*, London: British Film Institute.

Cohan, S. and Hark, I. R. (1993) *Screening the Male: Exploring Masculinities in Hollywood Cinema*, London: Routledge.

Doherty, T. (1988) *Teenagers and Teenpics: The Juvenilization of American Movies in the 1950s*, Boston: Unwin Hyman.

—— (1993b) 'The Age of Exploration: The Hollywood Travelogue Film', *Cineaste* 20, 2: 38–40.

Gomery D. (1996c) 'The New Hollywood', in Nowell-Smith 1996, 475–82.

Grindon, L. (1996) 'Body and Soul: The Structure of Meaning in the Boxing Film Genre', *Cinema Journal* 35, 4: 54–69.

Jacobs L. (1991) '*The Wages of Sin: Censorship and the Fallen Woman Cycle: 1928–1942*', Madison: University of Wisconsin Press.

Jenkins, H. (1992) *What Made Pistachio Nuts? Early Sound Comedy and the Vaudeville Aesthetic*, New York: Columbia Press.

Kapsis, R. E. (1991) 'Hollywood Genres and the Production of Culture Perspective', in B. A. Austin (ed.), *Current Research in Film: Audiences, Economics and the Law*, vol. 5, Norwood: Ablex, 68–85.

Karnick, K. B. and Jenkins, H. (1995a) *Classical Hollywood Comedy*, New York: Routledge.

Klinger B. (1994b) ' "Local" Genres: The Hollywood Adult Film in the 1950s', in J. Bratton, J. Cook and C. Gledhill (eds), *Melodrama: Stage Picture Screen*, London: British Film Institute, 134–46.

Leutrat, J.-L. (1985) *L'Alliance Brisée: Le Western des Années 1920*, Lyon: Presses Universitaires de Lyon.

Maltby, R. (1993b) ' "Grief in the Limelight": Al Capone, Howard Hughes, The Hays Code and the Politics of the Unstable Text', in J. Combs (ed.), *Movies and Politics: The Dynamic Relationship*, New York: Garland Publishing, 133–82.

—— (1995) *Hollywood Cinema: An Introduction*, Oxford: Blackwell.

Maltby, R. and Bowles, K. (1994) 'Hollywood: The Economics of Utopia', in J. Mitchell and R. Maidment (eds), *The United States in the Twentieth Century: Culture*, Sevenoaks: Hodder and Stoughton/Open University, 99–134.

Morey, A. (1995) ' "The Judge Called Me an Accessory": Women's Prison Films, 1950–1962', *Journal of Popular Film and Television* 23, 2: 80–7.

Neale, S. (1998) ' "Vanishing Americans": Racial and Ethnic Issues in the Interpretation and Context of Post-war "Pro-Indian" Westerns', in Buscombe and Pearson 1998, 8–28.

Nowell-Smith, G. (ed.) (1996) *The Oxford History of World Cinema*, Oxford: Oxford University Press.

Riblet, D. (1995) 'The Keystone Film Company and the Historiography of Early Slapstick', in Karnick and Jenkins 1995a, 168–89.

Rubin, M. (1994) 'MAKE LOVE MAKE WAR: Cultural Confusion and the Biker Film Cycle', *Film History* 6, 3: 355–81.

Sartelle, J. (1996) 'Dreams and Nightmares in the Hollywood Blockbuster', in Nowell-Smith 1996, 516–26.

Schaefer, E. (1992) 'Of Hygiene and Hollywood: Origins of the Exploitation Film', *The Velvet Light Trap* 30: 34–47.

Singer, B. (1990) 'Female Power in the Serial-Queen Melodrama: The Etiology of an Anomaly', *Camera Obscura* 22: 91–129.
Stanfield, P. (1999) 'Dixie Cowboys: Hollywood and the 1930s Western', unpublished Ph.D. thesis, Southampton Institute.
Tudor, A. (1989) *Monsters and Mad Scientists: A Cultural History of the Horror Movie*, Oxford: Blackwell.

Part 6

NARRATIVE AND NARRATION

40

S/Z AND *RULES OF THE GAME*

Julia Lesage

Source: *Jump Cut: A Review of Contemporary Cinema*, 12/13, Winter 1976/77, pp. 45–51.

My encounter with *S/Z*

It is not often that a film teacher comes upon any book that will entirely change her/his approach to teaching film. Before I read *S/Z* by Roland Barthes, my own method in teaching basic film or film and literature courses on the college level was the same method which I had learned—a combination of aesthetic history and analysis of the expressive uses of cinematic technique. However, my own interests as a Marxist and feminist critic led me to seek more precise ways to define and teach about the interface of society and art. The first wave of women's film festivals led me to consider in greater detail the role of women in the arts, but I soon faced the limitations of the concept of "the image of . . ." as an approach to teaching film courses, the content of which could be about any oppressed group.

Barthes' *S/Z* was a book I wanted to buy as soon as I had leafed through it in the French edition before it had been translated. It has a fine summary outline in the back and it has a lot of "gimmicks" and sections which engage the reader wherever she/he starts—in the beginning, middle, or end. I knew it would be useful for me even before I read it because Barthes seemed most interested in the interaction between artistic and social convention. Furthermore, he was clearly motivated to write the text for a radical reason: to give readers an understanding of those conventions which form the bulk of the presentation of bourgeois ideology in art. By raising unconscious mechanisms to a conscious level, the radical scholar teaches with a specific end in mind, that of giving people greater options for control over their own lives. Knowledge is power.

In my own work on Godard, I had come to accept as a given Godard's axiom that all films are fiction—documentaries, too. All those films which have a narrative framework subordinate their elements to a certain end. I was aware of the pitfalls of the so-called objectivity of cinema-verite, for all the viewer finally has of the original "pre-filmic" situation is a highly structured film. Barthes' treatment of literature in *S/Z* differs from most works of literary analysis in that he deemphasizes a purely internal analysis of a narrative art work and emphasizes the ways that elements from the writer's milieu have entered and are used on the microlevel of the text. In film, it would be as if he had done a lot of shot and single-frame analysis of the visual track. Because of his detailed look at precisely those types of things in literature that film critics look for in film study, I have tried to apply his approach to teaching and analyzing film, and it has proven useful in both classroom teaching and in feminist and Marxist film scholarship.

S/Z and its five codes

We can see that *S/Z* reveals a teacher's mind, for in this book Barthes gives us not only a way to apply semiotic, structuralist, psychoanalytic, linguistic, and poetic concepts to the analysis of a single literary work but also a concrete example of such an analysis. He traces out the conventions and cultural codes in a single work of short fiction, Balzac's *Sarrasine*. At the same time, he explains the theoretical basis of such an analysis so as to enable others to do the same critical work themselves. Throughout his career, much of Barthes' scholarly work has functioned implicitly as a polemic against and explicitly as a corrective to current critical practice. In this case, with *S/Z*, he rejects the deadly finality of an *explication de texte* or an Aristotelian or New Critical analysis of *Sarrasine*. Barthes uncovers no definitive "meaning" for the work, but rather he opens it up to multiple readings. Indeed he implies that the work of the critic/teacher is to teach not only how a tightly plotted work gives the illusion of cempleteness, but also the many ways in which that illusion of completeness is but one determinant, albeit a primary one, of the text.

Barthes' work as a whole is useful for those who want to understand how works of art mediate social assumptions and cultural patterns from the artist's and audience's milieu. Since cultural objects and patterns, such as dress, food, and drink, artifacts, traffic, architecture, etc., are the extra-cinematic material which forms the very stuff of narrative film, as do conventionally determined forms of verbal and gestural expression and human social interaction, film students can follow with interest Barthes theory, summarized in *Elements of Semiology* and drawn upon in *S/Z*, about how such artifacts and conventions of communication and interaction are organized into whole coded systems which follow laws first traced out in the field of linguistics.[1] *S/Z* itself suggests whole new ways to think of a film as an art object and an index of culture at the same time. To open up cinema to both a semiotic and rhetorical analysis in the way Barthes opens up literature in *S/Z* would lead to an increased understanding—in political, historical, anthropological, and cultural terms—of how the film narrative, image, and sound track both incorporate and also shape cultural conventions.

Barthes labels codes and conventions as they function in a work of art because, as he emphasizes in keeping with his larger purpose as a teacher of literature, naming these codes and conventions is a critical act by which we literally make sense out of a work and by which we gain control over previously unconscious ideological mechanisms in art, our psyches, and our milieu.[2] He emphasizes that rereading a work allows us to "multiply its signifiers," that is, to find new perspectives on it, new understandings about how the work itself is constituted. He wants readers to learn to name and define not only gross narrative and ideological structures but also to work "back along the threads of meaning," (p. 12)

> To read is to find meanings, and to find meanings is to name them; but these named meanings are swept toward other names; names call to each other, reassemble, and their grouping calls for further naming. (p. 11).

In *S/Z* and other works, Barthes presents a number of concepts which seem to have a direct applicability to film study. In *Writing Degree Zero* he first introduced his fruitful distinctions between "classic" and "modern" literature, i.e. between open and closed narrative works, distinctions which he maintains in *S/Z* where he chooses to analyze a closed narrative, a specifically "classic" text.[3] This analysis in *S/Z* can be extended to feature films since most commercial film narratives depend on a conventional story form: indeed, in the twentieth century with the sweep of Modernism in other arts, it is film itself that has given a new life to the tightly plotted, closed narrative form established in the nineteenth century.

In discussing the application of *S/Z* to film study, I shall concentrate on one film which has a complex narrative but which ties up all its narrative threads at the end—Barthes' criterion for a "classic" text. I chose Jean Renoir's THE RULES OF THE GAME as an exemplary text because it is readily accessible and reasonably well-known. Also, it seems to me, this film is one of the closest cinematic parallels we have to Balzac's work, since Renoir's themes about bourgeoise society come straight from the tradition of the realist bourgeois novel and bourgeois drama. However, just as Barthes analyzed one work in order to point out pervasive trends in the bourgeois narrative tradition which are still existent, largely unconscious, and "ideological," most other films with a closed narrative form could have been used as well.

Barthes uses the term *code* in a deliberately looser way than film semioticians such as Christian Metz or Raymond Bellour, who draw heavily on linguistic-oriented models of analysis.[4] Barthes' use of the word *code* is closely related to concepts of social and artistic convention and the rituals of everyday life. In this he is close to Umberto Eco, who presents a general theory of codes in *A Theory of Semiotics* (Eco seems heavily influenced by

Barthes).[5] According to Eco, conventions are limited and generally predictable within any given culture, for culture structures its members' lives and even their very perceptual capacities through various sets of pre-established (yet historically changing) intellectual and behavioral models. It is only because of these that people define what they perceive, assign meaning to that and respond significantly. Certain intellectual structures, such as language, are codes based on rigid rules. Others, such as visual or iconic codes, rhetorical ones, and—to a lesser degree—psychological ones are looser and vary to a greater degree across history and across cultures.

In daily life and in art, conventions establish what is probable, plausible or obvious. They provide whole clusters of seemingly natural details, and the fact that these details and the conventions behind them are *unremarkable* means that ordinarily we do not notice or discuss them, that they are lost until named. What Barthes wants most to analyze in *S/Z* are the social and artistic codifications shaping that phenomenon we call "realism." What this notion of realism usually tells us is that there is some denotation, some external reality, some conclusion to which the literary or cinematic text necessarily points. An example of this is Bazin's notion of cinema as "a window on the world." What Barthes teaches in *S/Z* is that the illusion of realism in a narrative is founded on the integrated functioning of five levels of codes, all of which work together to suggest what seems to be the Meaning (often signaled by the denouement) and all of which suggest other previously established cultural meanings beyond themselves.

Barthes distinguishes five main areas of cultural coding, or as he calls the codes, five "voices." He wants to trace the play of these codes within a single narrative work. He says that each of the codes forms a braid or lacework, one strand being picked up, worked into the major pattern and then left for a while, only to be returned to later; the interstices of the strands "are positions held and then left behind in the course of a gradual invasion of meaning," (p. 160). By themselves, the codes are merely expressive, but as they are intertwined artistically they are both manipulated and act upon each other to form that kind of meaning which results from a narrative work of art.

The five levels of coding that Barthes traces out in *Sarrasine* and which I shall discuss in detail in their applicability to film function as follows: 1) The Enigmatic Code structures the plot proper by implanting certain key questions or enigmas and then delaying the answers or giving false leads—thus giving us a story. 2) Action Codes establish what actions are conventionally, prescribed in certain situations and how much of each action is, must, or must not be shown. They let us know which actions are important or appropriate to present in a narrative. 3) Referential Codes enter the text through explicit references to the established knowledge of the time, such as science, medicine, history, literature, or the visual arts; on a more vulgar level, the artist may also refer to popular assumptions and common sense—

"what everyone knows." 4) The Semic Codes let us label persons and places in the narrative in an adjectival way. They "characterize" the character as a person with certain attributes and certain motives; these adjectival attributes (such as "undecided," "resolute," etc.) are the *semes*. 5) The Symbolic Code could also be called the psychoanalytic structuring of the text. Barthes draws primarily on Freud and Lévi-Strauss to describe the symbolic "economy" of a narrative and defines the major symbolic rhetorical device in literature as antithesis.

All five of these codes are bound by the heavy weight of convention and tradition—centuries of what Barthes calls the "what's already been written and done." The semic, symbolic and referential codes function more flexibly in the narrative than the enigmatic and action ones, the enigmatic being the most rigid and the symbolic, the most fluid of all. The codes determine specific moments in the text and suggestively reflect back to anterior moments or forward to ulterior moments in the narrative proper. They also relate to other texts and to the author's general ideological, historical and cultural milieu. All five levels are connotative and suggestive. Barthes described the relation between the way codes function sequentially in the text and the way they bear meaning that is "extra-textual" in the following way:

> Analytically, connotation is determined by two spaces: a sequential space, a series of orders, a space subject to the successivity of sentences, in which meaning proliferates by layering; and an agglomerative space, certain areas of the text correlating other meanings outside the material text and, with them, forming a "nebulae" of signifieds. (p. 8)

Connotations in film

Students of literature, sociology, art, and history study film as a way to study culture. One can trace out many large cultural myths and models in the film, such as assumptions about romantic love or the *parvenu*. Conventional ways of photographing women or of presenting the relations between social classes in film reveal as much about the cultural assumptions behind film as they contribute to the narrative. Yet if we are to understand how feature films mediate cultural structures, we must also understand how these cultural structures enter film. Older film studies, such as those of the auteur critics, could recognize, let us say, the feathers motif in the Von Sternberg films as a symbolic or metaphoric representation of femininity. More technically oriented studies such as those of the mise-en-scene critics discuss the connotative functions and cultural basis of halo lighting, deep focus, or Cinemascope. In a Barthesian analysis, analysis of theme or of expressive cinematographic techniques unique to a given director or film would be of only partial interest. Small gestures, architecture, fashion, furniture, time of day, assumptions about urban life, cars and traffic, food and drink customs, courtship customs, etc., bring important subcodes to and are the visual "stuff" of narrative film. Such subcodes function in the characterization and plot but also obviously derive their meaning from associations drawn from the society at large. Barthes' approach is superior to that of the auteur critics in that he does not reduce the text to, or only concentrate on, those signifiers which express the predelictions of a "creator." Rather he allows us to examine the ordinary ways that social coding enters into and is used by a work of art.

In an analysis of a single photographic image (in an essay which owes much in its methodology to Eco and Barthes) Stuart Hall notes how ideology—here, equal to the sum of a society's connotations—functions to provide a favored reading of a newsphotograph, an image socially reputed to be "factual" and "objective."

> Connotations add qualities and attributes to a denoted subject. Connotations refer subjects to social relations, social structure: to our routinized knowledge of social formation. Codes also refer objects to a structure of beliefs and valuations about the world.[6]

> In social life, these domains of meanings are both distinct enough to mobilize a whole set of associative meaning—yet overlapping enough so that an object may refer to more than one "associative field" . . . These criss-crossing sedimentations of meaning link the areas of social life. Together they constitute the "map of meanings" in a culture.[7]

In literature the denotative principle, the "one which seems to establish and to close the reading" (p. 9), is enacted by the Enigmatic Code, which Barthes also calls the "voice of truth." The Enigmatic Code establishes the sequence and the order by which we "find out things" in the narrative and limits and controls what we will attend to. I shall discuss this code at greater length later but here would also indicate that the same principle of a "nebulae" of connotations being limited by the sequential ordering of a little "drama" or even just a single sentence also determines the way we interpret or attend to the visual connotations in an advertisement, in photojournalism, in television, and in silent and sound film. For example, in an essay, "The Rhetoric of the Image," Barthes earlier analyzed the composition of a single photograph in which he found a synchronous play of connotative elements but also a preferred meaning suggested by the caption.[8] Similarly in any narrative film—silent or sound, fiction or documentary—the "story" of the film provides the anchor for the other connotative codes. The narrative limits the polyvalent image to a certain range of emotional and social interpretation.

In an implicit general attack on the abusive structuring of leisure in advanced capitalist societies, Barthes insists that we must create, not consume, aesthetic meaning. Both because of the commercial nature of film viewing and because of the chronologically determined, closed nature of narrative film structure with its beginning, middle, and end, most people want to see a feature film only once. Perhaps they sit through the beginning "to catch what they missed" if they came in late. In economic terms, they pay for a ticket and consume a show. In the structure of what they see, narrative tension determines the pacing of all the codes. People who see films only once anticipate primarily the end of the story. In Barthes terms they always repeat the same kind of chronological experience with the mind set that "this happens *before* or *after* that." Yet they and we stubbornly cling to the ideological belief that this first viewing is a "primary, naive, phenomenal reading which we will only, afterwards, have to 'explicate,' intellectualize." (p. 16). In a consumer society, the ideological function of such a belief is to valorize the craving for novelty, make everyone an authority on the "movies," and as a result make film studies as a discipline inherently suspect. Although some films seem more amenable to "instant" first reading, disposable like Kleenex and appealing completely to surface gratifications like pinball, and some films seem richer for multiple viewings, a Barthesian analysis opens up both kinds of texts to multiple readings, tracing out the ways in which the films use cultural significations and establish their own interconnected levels of meaning. It is *within* the context of such a reading that Barthes discusses the "richness" of a text like Balzac's *Sarrasine*, a richness which Barthes finds mainly on the level of symbolic interactions and reversals—which one could trace out only on rereading or re-viewing a work.

It takes a reeducation to make people want to see films twice or more. We tend to reread poems several times but experience novels and films only once. Barthes attributes that to the dominance of the narrative level, or plot. Knowing this, most film teachers instinctively discuss the role of convention and connotation in the acting, cinematic technique, decor, use of genre structures, etc., as they try to push students to attend to more than the plot. By tracing out how the various levels of coding interact in a single film seen several or many times, we can reread the film in a new way each time we see it. Analytically, re-viewing a film "multiplies it in its variety and plurality" (p. 16) as we learn to attend to other levels of signification beyond the linear experience imposed by the plot. The critical act teaches us to create our own aesthetic experience and saves us from a dulling consumption of art.

Although he borrows from Aristotle's *Poetics* and from sociology, in his own technique of analysis, Barthes is far from an Aristotelian who subordinates the parts to the whole, nor is he a sociologist who tabulates and analyzes cultural codes by means of literature. In *S/Z* he takes the novella *Sarrasine* and breaks it up into arbitrary convenient short sections which he calls *lexies*. After each section he notes the introduction of, passing, or working out of narrative enigmas, antitheses, cultural references, adjectivally describable connotations, and symbolic exchanges. Narrative enigmas are paced, never immediately answered; otherwise there would be no story. The other connotative and symbolic levels enter in as structured "noise" or counter communication against the enigmas, and this "noise" makes up the whole texture of the work. In the implantation of the codes, in the pacing and gaps of their "play," Barthes sees the uniqueness of any given narrative and an indication of the quality of the work of art.

To undertake a project like *S/Z* with a film would mean to have a class study perhaps just one film a semester. The film should be videotaped or shown on an editor-viewer, but in front of a large class one could just stop the projector. A good published film script would provide another important aid. To analyze any feature film short section by short section, one should minimally note down the following: the semic codes, which frequently can be worked out on the synchronous microlevel of still photography or a single frame; the action codes, seen chronologically on the level of the shot and in the editing of action sequences; the narrative codes, which, as Christian Metz has shown at some length, are worked out mainly on the level of the sequence; and the symbolic codes, which fluidly move between the composition of the frame, the filming of the shot, the editing within a sequence, and the combination of sequences to form the films as a whole. Indeed, to accomplish the equivalent of *S/Z* about a single film, one might best make an analytical videotape, or rather a series of tapes. These would alternate shots of the film (several taken together as a "lexie") with one's own analysis, which could then make use of clips from other films, photographs, diagrams, taped sounds and noises, and any other appropriate audio-visual support.

To describe in detail the five levels of coding and how they function in film, I have drawn all my examples from a single film, THE RULES OF THE GAME, yet obviously, without the film at hand for demonstration and in an essay of this length, I cannot give a total reading of the work. I have chosen my references here merely to show how each code can be traced in the work. Optimally, on videotape one could break the film up into small parts and note in each part where the various codes enter and how they are worked out across the length of the film. This is Barthes' method in *S/Z*, which is as multivalent and open to different emphases in interpretation as the critical attitude he wants audiences to achieve.

Narrative structure and the code of enigmas

When Barthes discusses the narrative construction of a novel, he does not talk about narrative as a formal *structure* at all. A plot depends on a code of multiple enigmas, which code is experienced by the ordinary film viewer as tension or suspense. Upon re-viewing a film we can see more clearly how the enigmatic code functions: the film centers in on the subject-to-be of an enigma; it poses, formulates, and develops the enigma; and it retards and finally provides an answer. The author must delay answering the principal enigmas about the protagonists to keep the story going. The way he/she delays narrative resolution (by partial and incomplete answers, double entendres, ambiguities, or lies) often defines the tone of the work.

The narrative points to but does not tell the whole truth about a character, especially a protagonist. Human figures distinguish themselves and become characters as the author develops their traits so as to develop and resolve enigmas. Because of the demands of the enigmas, the author both surpresses some character traits and develops others. One of the goals of a Barthesian analysis is to map how certain traits of characters are revealed at certain points; we arrive at a topology of the plot, in which of the space of the enigma corresponds to the space of the characterization, which is the semic space.

In the narrative, key structural elements (a gesture, a word, a locale) are first received as unimportant details. The gratuitousness of their introduction makes them seem natural. A narrative only progressively invests its key elements with their full meaning, but it uses what comes first—something we may not have understood fully when we first saw it—as evidence for what comes later. This is the narrative's defense against illogic. Circumstances are shown as compatible, and the characters' choices are seemingly made for a number of different, interconnecting reasons. Barthes calls these tactics "pseudo-logical liasons." In fact, meaning must be delayed or suspended and circumstances must be manipulated in order to tell a story at all.

The enigmatic code is a sequential one and reduces the plurality and reversibility of meanings within a given text. It is this characteristic sequentiality and closure of meaning in "classic" narrative against which modernist artists have reacted in both literature and film. As the enigmatic code functions in a traditional narrative like *Sarrasine*, it provides "the voice of truth" since it sweeps the reader along temporally in a rush of pseudological connections towards a promised final truth. In film, the syntactical form of the narrative is similarly shaped by this code, which imposes itself on the other codes in the editing, in the shot, or in the composition of the frame. The enigmatic code imposes a certain Irreversible order on the presentation of information and limits the multiple expressive possibilities of the medium at any given time. The more a film maintains interest or suspense, the more we read the elements within it in terms of the enigmatic code. By the time we reach the narrative climax, many tentative meanings that had suggested themselves earlier in the work are ultimately suppressed.

The enigmas of THE RULES OF THE GAME deal mainly with sexual relations and how they will be handled within a given society. The first enigma is planted when André Jurieu, a trans-Atlantic pilot, is greeted by a crowd on his triumphal return to La Bourget airport. He bitterly complains in a nationally broadcast radio interview that a certain woman, whom we find out in the next sequence is Christine de la Chesnaye, was not there to greet him. The enigma of André Jurieu's behavior and Christine de la Chesnaye's response occupy perhaps only the first third of the film, when Christine finally receives André at her husband's estate. Then, surrounded by the de la Chesnaye's whole circle of friends and house guests, she explains to all with pride that her *friendship* with André contributed to his success. This episode is—as Barthes calls any episode—both exemplum and signifier. The enigma of André Jurieu's love for Christine and what is to be done about it provides reasonable and sufficient cause for the final episode in which André is killed.

The other major enigma introduced early in the film is Robert de la Chesnaye's continued affair with the aristocrat Geneviève de Marrast in the face of his wife Christine's sincerity and love for him. Although this enigma seems quickly resolved (Robert phones Geneviève to arrange to tell her the affair is over), Christine sees him by accident in the woods kissing Geneviève goodbye. Here is a classic case of misunderstanding sustaining a major enigma, one necessary for moving the narrative to the climax. There must be a sexual rift between Robert and Christine although we must not doubt either one's sincerity. Furthermore, this mistake is introduced as something natural and accidental in the plot; it contributes to that confluence of circumstances which masks the artifice of the enigmatic code.

A costume party dominates the second half of the film. Numerous enigmas, involving the shifting sexual relations between more than half a dozen characters, are set and partially answered: lies and misunderstanding abound. It is at this point that the visual mise-en-scene of the film is crucial, for the audience's delight lies in the rapidity and simultaneity with which the multiple enigmatic situations flash before their eyes. For example, all these events happen almost simultaneously: Christine, thinking Robert loves Geneviève, has drunkenly gone off with a guest, Saint-Aubin, to the dining room. André, who loves Christine, attacks Saint-Aubin. The game keeper Schumacher knows his wife Lisette, Christine's maid, and Marceau, the poacher turned servant, are carrying on—in this scene he pursues Marceau with a pistol, firing, and being chased by Lisette and the other servants. Robert continues as master of ceremonies at the party, presiding at a stage show in front of guests. Geneviève and Jackie, a younger woman who is infatuated with André, faint and are carried off.

It is because Barthes does not try to present an Aristotelian analysis of plot but rather is concerned with analyzing the implantation, interaction, and resolution of multiple enigmas that his methodology is especially apt here. At this point in THE RULES OF THE GAME, the intrigue comes from the interweaving of all the love triangles. We ask, "What will Christine-Lisette-Geneviève-Jackie do?" and "What will André-Robert-Octave-Schumacher-Marceau do?" Certain enigmas predominate and move the plot further toward its conclusion. In particular, Christine's motives are ambiguously treated. At the masquerade party, all the action, which seemingly saturated the narrative with meaning, masked a major sub-question posed by the enigma, "What will Christine do." That is, now we must ask, "What are Christine's motives and whom does she love?" Indeed this enigma is answered ambiguously right up to the end of the film, for in the last third of the movie, Christine tells first André and then Octave, a tacky, good-humored family friend, that she loves each one. Both must believe in her love for the film to arrive at its narrative climax, in which André is sent by Octave, in an act of generosity on Octave's part, to run off with Christine. Finally, the concluding moments of the film are dominated by our questioning of Octave's relation to all the love triangles. He is the one most intimate with Christine as a friend, the real threat to her marriage, yet he has also flirted with Lisette, making the gamekeeper jealous and setting up the preconditions for the denouement. Like Christine's, Octave's own motives ambiguously fluctuate and it is hard to answer, "What will he do?"

A final series of coincidences are piled one on top of another, yet all are necessary for the "coincidence" and narrative climax of André's death. Christine wears Lisette's (Schumacher's wife's) cape. Schumacher no longer chases Marceau, since both had been fired after the party; when he and Marceau see Christine in Lisette's cape with Octave, they assume Lisette and Octave will now have an affair. When Octave sends his good friend André off to the rendezvous with Christine, he gives André his coat. Thus Schumacher shoots André, thinking it is Octave cuckolding him. All of these circumstances are "naturalized" by the fact that all the characters have participated in the exhausting chase scene during the party (as has the audience) and their nerves are frayed; they act hastily, without thinking, and each presumably also acts desperately from passion and/or love. Each of these coinciding circumstances was prepared for long in advance, "determined" in multiple ways. It is only the rate at which coincidence is presented which accelerates at the climax of the film.

This discussion of the implantation of major enigmas in THE RULES OF THE GAME lacks Barthes' subtlety, for in *S/Z* he does not just point out the enigmas but shows *how* they are centered, phrased, retarded, and developed. For example, by having André chide Christine in a public speech over national radio for not being at Le Bourget, Renoir establishes the enigma of what will happen to André's love with a good deal of wit, which is reinforced by images of the apparatus of microphones, wires and transmitters, and by the voice patterns of an excited woman interviewer and later of a standard interviewee, the flight engineer. The wit is developed further by the cut from the airport to Christine's bedroom; we see an extreme close up of the tubes of a radio apparatus, from which the same interview blares. Only when the camera moves up to frame Christine and Lisette in long shot do we realize that that was the back of an ordinary radio receiver and that we are in another place. Similarly when Christine enters her husband Robert's room, we hear the same radio program before we see Robert. When we realize that he is standing by his radio and listening to that program, we can imagine what he is thinking about his wife. All of this suggested and stated information is necessary for the development of the enigma, but the pacing of the visual and verbal details is especially witty in its use of an editing/sound technique which introduces sequences via the mechanism of the very radio program which gave rise to the original enigma. It is thus really only with the film at hand that one can best make the kind of demonstration that Barthes makes in *S/Z*.

Semic codes

As mentioned earlier, a photograph is particularly rich in connoted or semic information. In it we can usually find signified nationality, social class, erotic desirability, social situation, and threatening or non-threatening situation. These semic connotations are structured in an informal, "ideological" way. As Stuart Hall noted, in any given society, there is a lexicon of expressive features, which imposes on the polysemy or multiplicity of meaning inherent in any given situation not an invariable but a preferred meaning.

Barthes and Umberto Eco agree that we can label traits because of cultural stereotypes or "paradigms" of available images and sounds. Because of repetition through their constant usage in a culture, semic codes work through architectural, linguistic, fashion, culinary, etc. codes and subcodes. In a film semic connotation is borne not only by the visual image but also by stylistic subtleties in verbal language which connote class, emotion, irony, ignorance, etc.[9] There are also whole other emotional subcodes related to noise and music such as thriller sounds or romantic violins.[10]

Semes are adjectivally describable units of connotation. They are the labels we mentally attribute to character and locale. Because narrative film must utilize character to develop its enigmas and because there is a unique emphasis historically placed on the individual subject, semic connotation in cinema devolves mainly around the characters. We "read" the mise-en-scene to tell us something about them. Less frequently a sequence illustrates a theme not directly related to the actions of a character; such a sequence depends mainly on the connotated relation between images. Examples of this would be the sequence of neon lights in American cinema signifying "Broadway" or "going out on the town," or in THE RULES OF THE GAME, the death of the animals during the hunt.

More important, in film, both the content and the composition of the shots work to connote the social situation, motives, and emotions of the principal characters. In a single photograph; one can decide things about a person from body position, facial expression, gesture and especially from milieu. In the shot of a film, the character is also seen in movement; from speech and interaction with other characters we can make many more judgments about that person's social situation. There is a whole system at work of mutual and reciprocal expressions and recognition. Finally, as was noted earlier, narrative dominates and limits meaning so that we most frequently read a shot in terms of the story, which is what Barthes meant when he said that consumers (vs. creators) of texts end up receiving the same message.

We also read the semic codes historically because the way we label a character or situation is not only dependent on the sequential development of the text but also derives from our experience in the culture at large. Semic codes, similar to the action codes and codes of established cultural wisdom in the narrative, can be understood only in relation to previous mention in other texts. The units that we can label derive from "something that has been *already* seen, done, experienced; the code is the wake of that *already*." (p. 20) As Stuart Hall said in reference to newsphotographs, the sources of semic connotation are in the whole framework of social codes which are used in any discourse to convey second order meanings. Connotations thus "have the whole social order embedded or hidden within them: social practices and beliefs, the rank-order of power and interest, a structure of legitimations."[11]

Since ideological and cultural codes change with history, we can read the semes in any film or novel as a dated literature of signifiers. The artist's milieu always differs from ours, and we've often seen a film where the audience noticed as unusual or even silly semic connotations taken as natural within the artist's milieu. For example, the semes of beauty or erotic desirability, especially as connoted by fashion, vary from culture to culture. In THE RULES OF THE GAME, because of the way they are dressed and filmed and because of their role in the plot, we know that Lisette and Christine are desirable women, more so than Geneviève. However, the film does not signal so directly the male characters' desirability, and one wonders what the visual/verbal codes of erotic desirability in relation to the men were in Renoir's milieu or even now in France? How do we judge the sexual desirability of Robert, André, Octave, Marceau, or Saint-Aubin?

In any given shot we can see how a certain physical space is detached as seme-filled. In fiction and film a person is a collection of semes, the sum of which identify character. First of all, the filmmaker lets us know which character or object is important by keeping or putting that character in focus. Secondly, that character is seen more in the foreground and center frame. Lighting also expresses semes. Especially noticeable in THE RULES OF THE GAME is the halo of curls and fine whispy hairs around Christine's and Lisette's heads, which are made to shine by means of a strong spotlight just for that purpose—a light which then connotes "femininity." Close ups connote a special interest in the individual subject, in that person's thoughts and emotions; such a psychological interest characterizes traditional narrative fiction as well as feature film.

In a film, as in the theater, directors carefully control costuming so as to present a certain kind of person appropriate for a certain role. Both film and theater depend on fashion stereotypes or the semic code of dress. Christine is dressed in white silk, white fur, or an innocent Tyrolean folk costume. She usually has a soft white lace collar. Geneviève is dressed in black, a mannish hunting costume, an ornate oriental robe, or a harem costume. Lisette, like Christine, wears white ruffles around her neck. The respective semes which costuming connotes for these women are naturalness, sweetness and femininity for Christine and Lisette, and sophistication and brittleness for Geneviève.

In the same way, Christine's room, with its dressing table and white decor connotes the seme "femininity." Geneviève, on the other hand, lives in an apartment filled with bronze statues and hothouse flowers, and she entertains three men there with no women present. Her milieu connotes "worldliness," perhaps "ennui."

Barthes tabulates the semes in each *lexie* as they enter *Sarrasine*. A brief tabulation of some of the semes in THE RULES OF THE GAME would yield the following results: The *setting* frequently connotes worldliness, naturalness, mechanicity—especially in relation to Robert and his mechanical toys, artificiality, class, servitude, or richness. Some of these connotations Barthes also traced in *Sarrasine* and indicate a kind of subject matter and psychology dear to the bourgeoisie, i.e., the cost of being on top. The *dress code* connotes masculinity, femininity, eroticism, beauty, rigidity, informality, class, age, or sophistication. This code, combined with the gesture, voice, age, and movement codes, indicates how integral the capturing of, i.e. possessing, a beautiful young woman is as a function of bourgeois art. A beautiful women seems classless; she has this asset to trade for social gain—but the very concept of beauty in art and the semes which connote erotic desirability have been constructed by those in power who can buy beauty, men. The semes of beauty that men capture in art are their own fantasies. The *gesture code* in THE RULES OF THE GAME connotes roughness, sincerity, petulance, understanding, cynicism, obedience, power, gentility—sometimes excess gentility, awkwardness, world-weariness, dislike, hospitality or sadness, as well as erotic intent. Again, gestures are clearly codified according to class and sex. The *movement code* connotes age, adeptness or awkwardness, determination. Verbal characteristics such as *tone of voice and type of vocabulary* often connote emotions such as despair and humor, but they also convey important information about eroticism, power, and class.

The above still was taken from the scene immediately following the playlet at the masquerade party at La Colinére, where Christine saw Geneviève embrace Robert and then ran off with Saint-Aubin. After looking for Christine, Robert went into the dining room to change back into his evening jacket. Geneviève followed him and pressed him to go off with her. Octave, in a bear costume, had previously tried unsuccessfully to find someone to help him take it off. Here Geneviève's and Octave's costumes both connote their personalities—burly, awkward, unpolished, and maladroit Octave and jaded, sophisticated and brittle Geneviève (note the metallic jewels). Robert is meticulous, paying careful attention to his clothes, and his face has that expression of world-weariness characteristic of him throughout the film. He stands with his back to Geneviève. She is pressuring him. Octave is trying to pull her away.

This entire scene between Geneviève and Robert, where Robert refuses to commit himself to her, takes place in the center of a large open space in a large cold-looking room, the stag in the background being reminiscent of the slaughter at the hunt. Stuffed birds on the table add to the impression of artificiality and these birds will later be seen knocked on the floor when disorder and chaos invade the party. In addition, these birds refer us back to the hunt and forward to the death of André since both the animals and André are killed as an extension of property rights. The art work that Robert possesses at La Colinère, a representative sample seen in this picture, consists of statues and paintings of the hunt, stuffed animal trophies, and mechanical toys. In this scene where he tells Geneviève that he cannot leave with her, she realizes that his property and his obligations to his guests mean more to him than she does—the relation between propriety and property being one of the major themes in the film.

Barthes calls semic connotation that "noise" which both names and dissimulates the truth, and the richness of which often defines the artistic quality of the text. The density of semes, like the density of enigmas (connotation running parallel to enigma structure), varies within the text. It is the role of the critic to name the semes within the narrative and thus to define the personages. At times, a clustering of semes leads one to name larger *thematics* which define whole sequences within the work. In THE RULES OF THE GAME these semes expanded into thematics would be sincerity, naturalness, artifice and class; they are what Barthes calls meta-names.

The codes of cultural reference

> Resumes of common knowledge, the cultural codes provide the syllogisms of the narrative . . . with their major premise, based always on public opinion ("probable," as the old logic said). . . .

Barthes makes this observation as he discusses why the hapless lover dies in *Sarrasine*. Like André Jurieu in THE RULES OF THE GAME, Sarrasine is killed because he is ignorant of or perhaps willfully ignores the complexity of social mores. What triumphs for the other characters in both novella and film is the reality principle, which for them turns out to be composed of social reality and institutional codes. The cultural codes which "form the premises of the major syllogisms of the narrative" in THE RULES OF THE GAME relate to the title of the film. Renoir presents explicitly the rules governing marriage and adultery in high society, the rules of the hunt, the rules governing relations between masters and servants, and the rules governing peer relationships (courtesy, friendship, honor, jealousy, gossip) among masters and among servants. Renoir's major theme here is about the suffocating nature of received ideas; the "rules of the game" have an all-pervasive, determining influence over whatever might be natural so that the natural becomes lost. Thus the film as a whole, in its entire narrative structure, criticizes through art the received cultural codes shaping both society and its own art.

Most people read a film as they read a novel, not attending to the social and cultural conventions, the artifice, behind the actions and words presented. Thus, even though THE RULES OF THE GAME raises the theme of social convention vs. nature, it still presents the flow of its own discourse as natural, as "life."

> Although entirely derived from books, these codes, by a swivel characteristic of bourgeois ideology, which turns culture into nature, appears to establish reality, "Life." "Life" then, in the classic text, becomes a nauseating mixture of common opinions, a smothering layer of received ideas. (p. 206)

Within the flow of the narrative the codes of cultural reference inverse their bookish origin and are implanted in the words and actions of the characters as something natural or proverbial. For example, in this film the characters comment on how lovers should and do behave (the social lore of love and lust) as if these were ideas everyone shared; the audience is not led to challenge such assumptions. Explicitly described in the film is the way nature must submit to society, and the most smoothly coordinated *social* event is the hunt, which leads us directly to criticize aristocratic abuse of Nature, per se. Yet in the way things "happen," just as in any narrative film, the social events themselves flow along "naturally." We accept what happens among the characters as probable, likely, or natural, as "life."

In studying a film we should examine those cultural codes which the text explains (the rules of the game), which it assumes we know (masculinity/feminity, the psychology of persons of certain types, ages, nationalities, professions, etc.), or which the authors or characters just mention in passing ("We've all come here to hunt . . . not to write our memories:"[12]). Renoir carefully details the daily rituals and the codes of behavior between the de la Chesnayes, among the servants, and between the two groups. We expect a different pattern of behavior from Robert toward Christine than from Schumacher toward Lisette. The de la Chesnayes' marriage relies on codes of elegance, entertaining, courtesy, and hospitality. The servants' marriage is partially controlled by their work situation, Lisette preferring to be with her mistress Christine in Paris than with her husband at La Colinère: (Lisette being a conventional name for the maid-*confidante* in French comedy.)

When Schumacher gives Lisette a present of a warm cloak (code of practicality), she dismisses his gift as not pretty. When he chases her would-be lover Marceau with a gun (code of jealousy for lower class males), she pacifies him by saying she'll do anything he wants (psychology of the clever, dominated wife), even go back to his small town in Germany. This reflects the code of rural vs. urban mores, as Schumacher wants to get Lisette where she will not be able to flirt with other men, and also the code of ethnic psychology: rural Prussian vs. urban French.

In general, in narrative film, the audience calls upon its knowledge of a vulgar code of the psychology of human types. In THE RULES OF THE GAME the house guests at La Colinère quickly distinguish themselves as types. The General belongs to the ancien regime. The ingenue Jackie is a university student, which is supposed to account for her lack of sexual sophistication! Octave and an older woman factory owner are the jolly fat people, and the woman's conversation draws on codes of popular science and medicine, diets, and card games. A young homosexual male character enacts a highly coded role in the tradition that homosexuality in fiction is supposed to represent upper middle class decadence. Geneviève, presented in her own apartment earlier as the Paris sophisticate, is here forced into the stereotypical role of the cast-off lover. André Jurieu as well, even though the house guests receive him as a modern hero, enacts the role of a desperate lover.

Geneviève's whole character is sketched very quickly in an early sequence, which relies on our coded knowledge of the worldly woman. Whereas Christine wears white silk or ruffles, Geneviève is first seen wearing a black dress with a geometric lace design across her chest; she is smoking a cigarette held in a cigarette holder. She also entertains a group of men, serves mixed drinks (code of modernity), and cites a cynical line from Chamfort on the definition of love (code of "looseness"). When Robert comes to her apartment (geographical code—we see Trocadero from the window), she wears an ornate Chinese kimono and receives him in a room containing Oriental Buddhas, potted plants, and cut flowers (codes of excess, exoticism, chinoiserie, artifice, art, flowers). When Geneviève presents her guests mixed drinks, that is part of the code of modern hospitality. The codes of modern life must be contrasted with the codes of tradition if we are to grasp the full savor of the General's cliche (as a member of the *ancien regime*) which he repeats twice in reference to Robert: "That La Chesnaye doesn't lack for class, and that's becoming rare."

Actually the whole modern world enters the film only schematically. In the first scene we have rapidly presented a variety of codes intended to indicate "Modern Life." These are the codes of radio transmitters; those of Paris geography—Le Bourget; of crowd psychology; of cheers—"Bravo"; of newsworthy events; of the techniques, vocabulary and psychology of news reportage—both on the part of the interviewer and the interviewees; of contemporary history—the Lindbergh flight; and of the techniques of police control. Just as the airplanes flying over Paris in World War I provide that jarring image of modernity in Proust's *Remembrance of Things Past* to remind us that, in fact, aristocratic mores are a thing of the past, so too this first airport sequence, packed with assumptions about modern life, establishes the parameters of the game in THE RULES OF THE GAME, the film then ending with the General's words about the loss of aristocratic standards.

What Renoir refuses to do, and this is one of the virtues of the film, is to say that the modern (André) is better than the aristocrat (Robert) even though the film indicts aristocratic decadence. The contrast between aristocratic and modern, particularly as expressed by the General's cliche and by André's inability to understand Christine's position, functions to show that neither the aristocrats nor the "moderns" can understand each other except in terms of trite language and conceptual baggage. Indeed, the film presents this contrast between aristocrat and modern particularly ambiguously since Robert de la Chesnaye is a nouveau riche aristocrat, a Jew, and thus an outsider himself—which fact is harped on by some of the servants, who are more purist in such matters than their masters. To further complicate our attitude toward Robert, at the end he understands more than the other characters yet he will smoothly cover over André's murder as an accident.

In general, we read the semic codes, the level of adjectival amplification, on the level of the single frame or across small gestures. As soon as we see a setting or a personnage in film or in a photograph, we "label" it; that is, we rapidly interpret the semes insofar as they relate to characterization, mood, and the development of the plot. The codes of cultural reference work themselves out on a grosser scale, especially the dialogue. Often the two codes mesh. We can observe the art, architecture, gardens and statuary in La Colinère and derive the adjectival semes, "French aristocrat" or "dignity." But we can also examine in more detail how Renoir introduces and uses established cultural codes related to art and to the manor house or country estate.

Studying film with videotape would allow one to go back and notice the implantation of cultural codes which would otherwise pass quickly by as "natural." We can readily distinguish those codes which are repeated often enough to become stereotypes (André's excess of despair as a frustrated lover), but we often miss smaller ones that are not reinforced by an essential relation to the developing enigmas. Once we understand how much a film utilizes information and assumptions formulated anterior to the film, it becomes irrevocably clear that what cinema captures is social truth and institutionalized knowledge, not unmediated reality.

The action codes

Action codes tell us what is considered "normal" action in a culture and also how to present that action in a representation: certain details and the chronological ordering of these details seem necessary or appropriate in literary fiction and film. Action codes not only establish what actions are conventionally prescribed in certain situations (e.g., a kiss in a romantic scene) but also how much of each action must be or is shown. At the end of *S/Z* Barthes presents a list sequentially tabulating all the actions that were clearly definable in *Sarrasine*, and this list lets us see how conventional the range of actions in fiction is.

We know that very few complex actions—for example, surgery or cooking a meal—last as long on the screen as in real life. An exception is a filmed conversation when it is necessary for the audience to hear the whole thing. Even here, film technique rests on certain cultural assumptions. The conventional use of a series of close ups to film a conversation assumes that the audience's knowledge of the "rules" of how a conversation flows from one person to another will provide the continuity between shots of two individuals, each seen separately.

Two other common types of action sequences in narrative film are what Christian Metz calls "ordinary" and "episodic" sequences; in the former, bits of unnecessary action are eliminated; in the latter, representative stages in the development of an event or relationship are shown.[13] Obviously the decision about which actions to show in the various shots of a sequence depend on previous portrayals of action in film as well as audience expectations about what is "representative" or "unnecessary."

All film theorists from Eisenstein and Pudovkin to contemporary writers on film semiotics have seen a close relationship between editing codes and the representation of human actions. Such a relationship is most obvious in invisible editing or action cutting, but more recently scholars such as Laura Mulvey, Daniel Dayan and Raymond Bellour have demonstrated how the whole foundation of realist film editing—field and reverse cutting—is based on cultural assumptions about point of view which is based in film on the human glance.[14]

In THE RULES OF THE GAME many actions are presented schematically, particularly the moments of courtship. In only one larger action, the hunt, do we see many of the component parts detailed; here, too, each of the many participants—both aristocrats and servants are depicted doing only a few representative, clearly defined things. Of all the codes, the action codes are the hardest to analyze in detail on first viewing because they seem so ordinary and taken together, create such an illusion of continuity that they "form the main armature" (p. 255) of the "classic" text. Yet the presentation of cinematic action is never more than artifice. Whoever sees a film

> amasses certain data under some generic titles for action (*stroll, murder, rendezvous*), and this title embodies the sequence of actions; the sequence of actions exists when and because it can be given a name, it unfolds as this process of naming takes place, as a title is sought or confirmed. (p. 19)

The action codes, both in terms of the human actions presented within a shot and editing on the basis of action, often seem "natural." Because the narrative is "saturated" with mechanisms to create meaning, the audience fills in the causal chains, assuming continuity when really the filmic presentation is discontinuous. The seeming continuity in classical prose fiction and narrative feature films comes from the fact that the actions serve multiple functions: they have a purpose in the narrative and they have a connotative and symbolic value. Furthermore, these actions gain in sense and continuity as the traditional narrative makes them serve a double function: we see each action both as determined and as determining something else. In other words, actions, like the characters' choices, are overdetermined.[15]

Symbolic codes

A fifth level of narrative coding which Barthes discusses, in addition to enigmatic, semic, referential (to establish knowledge), and action codes is that of psychoanalytic or symbolic coding. Symbolic codes, or the *play* of symbols, as Barthes prefers to say, work themselves out in art in terms of motifs common to the culture as a whole. Thus psychoanalytic criticism of art or *auteur* analysis of film often seeks out themes, motifs, or archetypes. These symbolic structures are extremely fluid and do not reflect social rituals and expectations as obviously or as directly as the referential, semic, and action codes do.

Barthes uses Freud's language, but his analysis of the symbolic "economy" of the text comes directly from Lévi-Strauss. The latter, in his *Structural Anthropology*, asserted that we should study language, kinship, and economics in linguistic terms and interpret society as a whole in terms of a theory of communication. To cite Lévi-Strauss:

> This endeavor is possible on three levels, since the rules of kinship and marriage serve to insure the circulation of women between groups, just as economic rules serve to insure the circulation of goods and services, and linguistic rules the circulation of messages. These three forms of communication are also forms of exchange which are obviously interrelated (because marriage relations are associated with economic prestations, and language comes into play at all levels). It is therefore legitimate to seek homologies between them and define the formal characteristics of each type considered independently and of the transformations which make the transition possible from one to another.[16]

According to Barthes one can enter the symbolic field of the text on any of three levels: language, kinship or sex, and commercial economy. Language operates on the basis of an economy that is "usually protected by the separation of opposites" (p. 215), i.e., paradigms. The major rhetorical device which carries the symbolic motifs of the text is the antithesis, each term of which is exclusive and fully meaningful in its own right. Middle-ground figures transgress the antithesis, "pass through the wall of opposites" (p. 215), and abolish difference. Barthes also analyzes the symbolic field of the narrative by discussing the economy of genres and the economy of bodies, which Lévi-Strauss would call kinship codes; as Barthes says, their "parts cannot be interchanged." (p. 215)[17]

Barthes considers two ways that capitalist economic relations are symbolized in or rather form the "symbolic economy" of *Sarrasine* and his observations can also be applied to THE RULES OF THE GAME. The characters deal with each other personally by means of informal "contracts," and the narrative as a whole treats as nouveau riche, capitalist (vs. aristocratic, land-based) wealth. In both language and commerce, paradigmatic barriers let us understand the bases of equivalencies and exchange, which are the foundation of all meaning (under capitalism such exchange depends on private property). In the classical narrative, representation depends on an order of just equivalencies, by means of which we can regularly distinguish contraries, sexes, and possessions. Yet only when an excessive element enters which interrupts the normal circulation of the antitheses, sexes, property relations, or contracts that the narrative begins. It is the transgressor that impels the narrative, toward its climax or catastrophe. Symbolic and narrative requirements in a work of fiction finally merge, for narrative resolution not only means the final and irreversible "predicating" of the subject and the end of the story (for there is no more to say) but also the end of the symbolic search, what Barthes calls a symbolic closure or return to order.

In THE RULES OF THE GAME one can note a whole series of related symbolic antitheses which generally reinforce each other and which have a long tradition in the history of Western literature and art. Such antitheses include the following pairs: civilization vs. nature; sincerity/lies; ingenuousness/sophistication; simplicity/complexity; naive eros/eros socialized; organic life/artifacts; life/death; fecundity/emptiness; outdoors/indoors; lower/upper; servants/masters; the male camp/the female camp; richness/poverty; power/dependence; property/wildlife; childishness/maturity; the greenhouse/the manor house.

In addition, the characters are paired with doubles among the masters and the servants. The inflexible idealist Jurieu has his parallel on the servants' level in the inflexible Prussian gamekeeper Schumacher, who enacts his ritual bond with Jurieu by executing Jurieu. The poacher Marceau and Robert de la Chesnaye are specifically paired: Marceau shows Robert the art of poaching; Robert promotes Marceau to Marceau's long-dreamed-of role as a household servant; Marceau has dreams of elegance—in a uniform—and in the film Robert is the male who is most meticulously dressed. Both involved with mistresses and jealous rivals in one sequence, the two men share their views on women.

The servant Lisette is inseparable from Christine for she identifies with Christine completely. As the critic Philipe Esnault says, Lisette devours Christine with her eyes.[18] It is because Lisette loans Christine her cape when Christine goes off to the greenhouse with Octave that Schumacher thinks he is shooting his wife's lover. Also, Saint-Aubin is a double for Geneviève. After Christine discovers her husband's affair, she does not turn to André, as we might expect, but rather throws herself at one of the house guests, Saint-Aubin. He is otherwise an insignificant figure and one might wonder at his role as Christine's potential lover until his symbolic function as Geneviève's double is perceived: both are the accepted adulterous partners from the aristocrats' peer group—that is, for adultery within the "rules of the game." If she had had an affair with Saint-Aubin, Christine would not have left the group nor her social/marital obligations—as she had planned to do with either Octave or André. In the same way Robert had conducted an affair with Geneviève yet had felt fully responsible to both his marriage and his social ties. Thus the structure of doubles can be diagrammed as follows:

Upper Class Masters	André	Christine	St. Aubin/ Geneviève	Robert
Servants	Schumacher	Lisette		Marceau
	Purists Fools	Untamed Female Eros & Love	The Erotic Partners in Adultery Who Will Play by the Rules	Male Lovers Who Are Socially Adept

Not in this diagram is Octave, who at various points in the narrative acts as the *transgressor*.[19] In terms of class he is neither master nor servant, but a bohemian hanger-on in both the artistic and aristocratic worlds. (In Renoir's original outline for the film, Octave's economic dependence on the de la Chesnayes was made more explicit.) That Octave (the middle class intellectual!) might be in a position to love either a servant, Lisette, or an aristocrat, Christine, also leads to André's death, for Schumacher thinks he is killing Octave meeting Lisette.

At first glance, because of André's speech over the national airwaves denouncing the absent Christine, it might seem that André is the interloper, transgressing the marriage bonds between Christine and Robert. Yet this conflict is settled rapidly; Christine's sincerity leads Robert to break off his affair with Geneviève. Indeed the whole opening incident could have led to closer relations between Christine and Robert. But the film would have ended there! The transgressor who moves the narrative is Octave, who demands that Christine and Robert invite André to La Colinère. Once at La Colinère,

André is depressed at this friendly but formal reception by Christine and would leave except that he is encouraged by Octave to stay. Finally, Octave, who all along has been identified with Christine's father and who has offered her avuncular, asexual friendship and protection, succumbs to her declaration of love and her desire to flee her husband's milieu. Octave symbolically transgresses incest taboos. Lisette senses this and expresses her strong disapproval when Octave is about to elope with Christine, saying, "But imagine *those* two living together—I think that young people should live with the young and the old folks with the old." Reverting again to his role of offering Christine asexual love, Octave sends André off in his place and in his coat, causing not only André's death but also his own curse, his permanent exclusion from Christine and Robert's milieu.

Visually, Robert represents the ego, meticulously dressed for the right social occasion and showing on his face an extremely sensitive response to every social situation. Lisette and Christine—dressed in ruffles, filmed with halo lighting, shown smiling and in moments of sheer exuberance and joy—are pure feminine eros, a potential fecundating principle and the prizes sought after by men. In fact, they are dependent on both men and the social structure dominated by men. A principle that Lévi-Strauss states as an unquestioned given is that "in human society, it is the men who exchange the women and not vice versa."[20] THE RULES OF THE GAME partly deals with the two women's efforts to exert their emotional independence and to escape the limitations placed on that independence.

Geneviève in her dress and comportment represents eros socialized. She knows her place. Marceau and Schumacher competing for Lisette are the erotic id and the supergo in opposition. Octave and André are the two types of anal figures (as Norman O. Brown described the anality of the bourgeoisie in *Life Against Death*[21]). Octave, fat, unkempt, shaggy, is not only the avuncular protector of Christine but also a childlike figure, thus fit to be the friend of the petulant, idealistic, compulsive, and adolescent Jurieu.

Symbols are more diffuse than semes, which as we have seen are commonly accepted cultural indicators of qualities or adjectival "labels." As Barthes says in *Elements of Semiology*, a symbol is an inadequate representation; eg., a cross does not adequately express all of Christianity. A seme, on the other hand, conveys a fuller sense of its signified. Octave's *clumsiness* is conveyed rather fully by the way he moves, the de la Chesnaye's *richness* by the objects in their apartment, the architecture of their homes. On the other hand, Octave's pleas for someone to help him out of his bear's costume symbolize his sexuality and say something about his coming emergence from an avuncular role to that of Christine's potential lover. Geneviève, the sexually free woman, can finally be prevailed upon to help him out of the costume but she does so begrudgingly and in the process throws him to the floor.

To a large degree the semes can be read synchronically, on the level of the single image or on the level of the shot. The symbols, however, especially in the working out of the antitheses, mediations and transgressions, proceed diachronically. Substitutions, such as those of figures serving as doubles, are worked out on the syntagmatic level, and are frequently metonymic substitutions in which the whole is represented by a related part. The dying rabbit in the hunt scene stands for helplessness, animal life and fertility; the sacrificial death of André Jurieu; Christine's softness and love.

Barthes also finds implanted in the text other symbols such as a child-woman figure or queen-servant relationships. Obviously in THE RULES OF THE GAME the hunt and the masquerade are symbol-laden episodes that need almost no dialogue. Barthes insists that both the semes and the symbols are multivalent and reversible, so that the seme, "richness," or the antithesis, "nature/civilization," can be borne by any of the figures in the narrative in a multiplicity of ways. These reversals can be seen, for example, if we consider Christine's use of lipstick as "artifice" and Robert's rejecting Geneviève as his effort to act "sincerely" in his marriage—although Christine is otherwise often associated with naturalness and ingenuousness and Robert with sophistication.

Film and literature

Language is symbolic representation; cinema is primarily iconic. That is, the relation of word to object in writing or speaking is purely arbitrary, while cinema is built on photography, which gives a two-dimensional representation analagously similar to its object. In literature, the description of the human body depends on the fragmentation of a whole into its parts for the sake of metaphoric or connotative description in *words*; this necessary fragmentation influences the way the enigmatic, action, symbolic, and semic codes are worked out in literature; literary authors paraphrase other texts previously established in the same verbal (spoken and written) mode. A photograph offers us its iconic codes and its connotations all at once. In feature films, once the subject has been established by the enigmas, the setting or specific objects in that setting can fully connote a character even though that character is not on screen. Metonymy or the representation of the whole by one of its related parts is the major rhetorical device which carries symbolic and semic coding in feature films.

Christian Metz has demonstrated that the minimal syntagmatic unit in film is the shot; the discussion in this article of synchronous connotation on the level of the single frame is not intended to establish the frame as a complete signifying unit. Obviously much of Barthes' discussion of the relation between linguistic syntax and the literary narrative cannot be applied directly to film. Yet, because audiences receive the syntactic flow of shots and the editing in a film as "natural," one could also work out the ideological role of the shot in the way that Barthes describes the ideological role of the sentence.

The shot often masks our awareness of how a film uses cultural codes. It rigidifies denotation, and "it yields meaning with the security of an 'innocent' nature: that of syntax." (p. 264) Furthermore, since Metz demonstrates that all of narrative film's syntagmatic structures are dependent on intentionality or on the development of a "plot," one could well add a Barthesian analysis of film to Metz's analysis of film's major syntagmatic structures.[22] Just as a caption gives a preferred reading to a still photograph, so in feature films, as in classic literary narratives, the enigma "anchors" the connotations, actions, and symbols, and structures the cinematic sequence form itself.

Since Barthes is mostly concerned with language in its relation to narrative discourse and with the play of meaning across a number of semiotic codes of which verbal language is only one, his major methodological premises can well be applied to the study of film, which is still primarily a narrative art form. In addition his criteria for quality in traditional narrative art can help us evaluate popular culture, for Barthes does not build on some canon of great works but rather evaluates a closed narrative by its successful orchestration, integration, and manipulation of cultural and symbolic codes:

> . . . a "good" narrative fulfills both the plurality and the circularity of the codes: ceaselessly correcting the causality of the anecdote by the metonymy of the symbols and inversely, the simultaneity of the meanings by the operations which lead on and use up expectation to its end. (p. 77)

Notes

1 Roland Barthes, *S/Z*, trans. Richard Howard (New York: Farrar, Straus, and Giroux, 1974). Further citations from this edition are indicated by page numbers in the text. *Writing Degree Zero and Elements of Semiology*, trans. Annette Lavers and Colin Smith (Boston: Beacon, 1970).

2 The radical film/literary critic often seeks to raise unconscious ideological mechanisms to the level of consciousness so that we may "gain control" over them. Certainly those critics who combine a Marxist and a psychoanalytic approach, such as Christian Metz in his current work, have that intent. Such radical critical practice serves the function of both consciousness raising and theoretical investigation, but the notion of "gaining control" and ideological *change* must be dialectically related to a more general economic, social, and political movement for change in the society at large. "Where do correct ideas come from? . . ."

3 *Writing Degree Zero and Elements of Semiology, op. cit.*

4 Christian Metz, *Language and Cinema*, trans. Donna Jean Umiker-Sebeok (The Hague: Mouton, 1974). Raymond Bellour is concerned with "segmentals" and "supra-segmentals" in film, which are linguistic concepts. He presented a paper on the supra-segmentals in GIGI at the Milwaukee Film Conference in November 1975. See also his "The Obvious and the Code," *Screen*, 15, No. 4 (1974–75).

5 Umberto Eco, *A Theory of Semiotics*, trans. David Osmond-Smith (Bloomington: Indiana University Press, 1976).

6 Stuart Hall, "The Determinations of Newsphotographs," *Working Papers in Cultural Studies*, No. 3 (1972), p. 65.

7 *Ibid.*

8 Roland Barthes, "Rhetoric of the Image," *Working Papers in Cultural Studies*, No. 1 (1971).

9 In semantics, a seme is a unit of the signified. The seme is that quality which is signified by the connotation, eg., richness. Both Barthes and Eco conclude that in a semiotic sense the sum of all the connotations in a given society, the sum of all the "semes," define the society's ideological presuppositions.
10 Umberto Eco, "Towards a Semiotic Inquiry into the Television Message," *Working Papers in Cultural, Studies*, No. 3 (1972), p. 114.
11 Hall, p. 66.
12 *La Règle du jeu: L'Avant Scène du cinéma*, No. 52 (1965). Translation mine. All further citations of dialogue are cited and translated from here.
13 Christian Metz, *Film Language: A Semiotics of Cinema* (The Hague: Mouton, 1971).
14 Laura Mulvey, "Visual Pleasure and Narrative Cinema," *Screen*, 16, No. 3 (1975).
Daniel Dayan, "The Tutor Code of Classical Cinema," *Film Quarterly*, 28, No. 1 (1974).
Raymond Bellour, "THE BIRDS," trans. from *Cahiers du cinéma*, No. 216 (1969), available from the BFI Educational Advisory Service, 81 Dean Street, London W1.
15 Overdetermined is a Freudian concept, brought into current critical thought by Louis Althusser and frequently used by Barthes in *S/Z*. To paraphrase Althusser, one can apply his concept to the choices, motives and actions of the characters within a traditional closed narrative: the characters' choices, motives, and actions are inseparable from the total structure of the narrative in which they are found, inseparable from their formal conditions of existence and from the instances they govern. The characters' actions and choices are radically affected by these instances, determining and also determined in the one and the same movement, and determined by the various levels and instances of the narra- they animate. The narrative work as a whole is also overdetermined, reflecting and responding to the contradictions of the society in which it was engendered. See Althusser's *For Marx*, trans. Ben Brewster (New York: Vintage, 1970), p. 201. For a detailed analysis of the function and mechanisms of overdetermination in a single film, see Charles Eckert, "The Anatomy of a Proletarian Film: Warner's MARKED WOMAN," *Film Quarterly*, 17, No. 2 (1973–4).
16 Claude Lévi-Strauss, *Structural Anthropology* (New York: Anchor, 1967), p. 82.
17 Following Lévi-Strauss and Jacques Lacan, Barthes sees sexual differentiation and the exchange value of women as a structural determinant of the creation of both linguistic meaning and commercial or interpersonal "contracts" or relations. Such an analysis of the interrelation between psychic-linguistic-economic structures is deterministic in its premises, and feminists such as Juliet Mitchell who accept these premises do not demonstrate how these structures change across history or under socialism, or if they can be fundamentally altered at all. In this particular instance, I would only note in passing that proof of the inadequacy of Barthes' treatment of sexual symbolism is that he cannot deal with homosexuality and androgeny but must treat the story of a man's unwitting falling in love with a castrato only in terms of the antithesis between and "transgression" of an essential maleness and an essential femaleness.
18 Phillipe Esnault, "Le Jeu de la vérité." *L'Avant Scène du cinéma*, No. 52 (1965), p. 11.
19 See Lévi-Strauss, p. 221.
20 *Ibid*, p. 45.
21 Norman O. Brown, *Life Against Death: The Psychoanalytic Meaning of History* (Middletown, Conn.: Wesleyan University Press, 1959).
22 Metz, *Film Language: A Semiotics of Cinema*.

Publisher's Note:
It has not been possible to reprint Figures in THE RULES OF THE GAME discussed in this chapter article.

41

THE STRUCTURE OF MYTH [EXTRACT], MYTH AS A NARRATIVE OF SOCIAL ACTION [AND] INDIVIDUALS AND VALUES: THE CLASSICAL PLOT

Will Wright

Source: *Sixguns and Society: A Structural Study of the Western*, Berkeley, CA: University of California Press, 1977, pp. 16–28 (extract, pp. 25–28), 124–129 and 130–153.

The structure of myth

[. . .]

My method of narrative analysis will be to reduce the stories in a set of similar films to a single list of shared *functions*. These functions will be one-sentence statements that describe either a single action or a single attribute of a character. Thus, for example, the statement "The hero fights the villains" would be a function, while the statement "The hero fights and defeats the villains" would not be. Similarly, "The hero is unknown to the society" would be a function, but "The hero is unknown and a gunfighter" would not. The characters whose actions and attributes are described by these functions are generic, not specific—that is, the functions do not refer to particular heroes, such as Shane or the Ringo Kid, but to the role of the hero as a character in all the stories. Also, the character referred to by the functions need not be only one individual. The generalized character in a function can be, and often is, a group of characters in a film, all of whom share a single meaning in an opposition. Thus, a function will refer to "the villains" or "the society" as a single character with respect to structural action.

This method of narrative analysis is a liberalized version of a method originated by Vladimir Propp for the analysis of Russian folktales. His tales were much simpler than the Western, and he restricted his functions to descriptions of actions, whereas I have included attributes; moreover, his tales were folk, popularized and standardized by many retellings, whereas my tales are films—stories based on a social myth, but created by specific individuals for popular acceptance and never changed or standardized by public retelling. From a study of folk tales, Propp showed that the functions that characterize a set of stories occur in a rigid, unchangeable order; in each tale every function—that is, every action—must appear in exactly the same sequence. But this approach is unnecessarily restricting, for it is easy to recognize a set of essentially similar stories with slightly differing orders of events. The order of the functions that characterize a Western plot will not always correspond exactly to the order of events in a particular film; in fact, some functions, such as "The hero fights the villains," may occur more than once in some films. In a sense, Propp is right: the temporal order of actions in a narrative is of central importance for an understanding of the meaning of the narrative. But his solution to the problem of narrative order was too extreme, and in Chapter 4 I will show how a list of functions can be interpreted as ordered even if they do not always appear in exactly the same sequence in every story.

If the stories in a set of films are reduced to a single list of common functions, will not the unique characteristics of each film—the particular actors, scripts, settings—be lost? Not necessarily, since these characteristics provide realism and flavor to the stories. They embody the myth and are necessary for the communication of meaning; but they are extraneous to the analysis of that meaning. The list of functions that describes a narrative structure must not be so general that it applies indiscriminately to a wide range of different stories; it must be sufficiently detailed to clearly include a certain set of similar stories and to clearly exclude all others. The test, of course, is to read (or watch) some stories from a group that have been analyzed as having the same structure to see if the details that are lost significantly change the meaning of the stories from that suggested by structural analysis. In the case of this study of the Western, at least, I believe that such a test will not only verify the analysis presented but provide enjoyment.

It only remains to consider more exactly how these functions and oppositions interrelate. The oppositions reveal what the characters mean; the functions reveal what they do. As an example, suppose two characters, A and B, interact in Story 1 according to the following functions and coding (images representing concepts).

Story 1.
A loves B.
B ignores A.
A seduces B.
B leaves A.
A dies.

	upper class	middle class
male	B	
female		A

Now if A and B simply represented different sexes, this story would be a melodrama of love. But when A and B represent different classes, the story also becomes a drama of class differences and implies, perhaps, that it is proper to love and respect, but wrong to aspire to, the upper class. This is essentially the story, for example, of Lancelot and Elaine in Mallory's *Le Morte D'Arthur* (1469).

Now suppose Story 1 is replaced by Story 2.

Story 2.
A loves B.
B ignores A.
A seduces B.
B leaves A.
B dies.

	upper class	middle class
male		B
female	A	

Story 2 differs from Story 1 in only the last function, and it is concerned with exactly the same conceptual difference: upper class/middle class. But because of the narrative change and the change in coding, Story 2 tells of the attractiveness and independence of the middle class, the desire and impotence of the upper class, and the punishment of the middle class for its presumption. This story may indicate a changing social order as in Shakespeare's *Venus and Adonis* (1593).

Finally, consider Story 3 with the same coding as Story 2.

Story 3.
A hates B.
B rapes A.
B leaves A.
A dies.

	upper class	middle class
male	B	
female		A

This story tells of the nobility and purity of the middle class, and of its suffering at the hands of the evil upper class, a story that resembles, for example, Hardy's *Tess of the d'Urbervilles* (1891). In all three stories the conceptualization of social types is the same; but in each case the narrative structure changes to portray a different model of interaction between these types, and these changes can be seen to correspond to changes in social institutions and attitudes.

These examples, though overly simplified, illustrate the temporal as well as logical relationships between the functions and the oppositions to be found in the Western. The narrative structure varies in accordance with changing social actions and institutions. The oppositions, on the other hand, create images of social types that are fundamental in the consciousness of a society. These social types may change their mode of interaction, but as classifications of people the types themselves are much less likely to change. The concepts that define and differentiate people in a society are rooted in the beliefs and attitudes, and finally in the institutions, of that society; for them to change, the society itself must change to such a degree that it would essentially be a new society, which would consequently need a new myth. Thus, the concepts represented by the oppositions in the Western should remain the same throughout our forty-year study, while the characters that symbolize these concepts may change their interaction as American society changes its institutions. And this is what we will observe: a history of four narrative stages, in which each stage presents its model of social action in terms of the same types of people.

Myth as a narrative of social action

As a myth, the Western consists of paradigmatic and syntagmatic structures—conceptual oppositions and narrative functions. The oppositions create images of social types, which reflect basic social classifications of people. The narrative functions describe the interaction of these characters—both the actions and the situations of the narrative. I have argued that a myth provides a conceptual model of social action and that, therefore, the narrative action of the myth relates to the everyday social actions of individuals. The oppositions help create this model by making the characters significant. But the functions only describe actions and situations, and as such they are only statements, not symbols that help create conceptual order in human consciousness. That is, we have not as yet analyzed the narrative structure of myth, a grammar in the process of communication, as we did the binary structure.

We need an analysis of narrative structure that is not only descriptive but explanatory, that *explains* how individuals in a society interpret the narrative actions in their myths. Such an analysis would lead to an understanding of how actions of characters (social types) are interpreted as creating social situations (relations between characters) that are typical or desirable in everyday life. In particular, this analysis would again raise the problem of temporal order. How do the functions that characterize a myth or plot relate to one another in terms of cause and effect? Which actions can be interpreted as causing which situations? To resolve this problem and provide a basis for an analysis of narrative as communication, I will introduce the notion of *narrative sequence*. A narrative sequence is an ordered group of narrative functions that is typically smaller than the entire list of functions for a story but in which the sequence of the functions is unchangeable. Thus, the narrative structure of a myth or story consists of one or more narrative sequences, each of which is ordered internally but unordered with respect to the other sequences where there may be embedding and overlapping. This idea of narrative sequence provides an analytic connection between the functions as a description of a myth and the narrative structure as a model and communication of social action.

For an analysis of narrative sequence I will turn to the work of philosopher Arthur Danto, who argues in *The Analytical Philosophy of History* that narrative sequence is the basic form of historical explanation. In defending his argument, he provides an analysis of the structure and meaning of these sequences that will help us to clarify the symbolic structure of myth. Danto begins his discussion with a critique of the distinction between plain and significant narratives—narratives, that is, that only describe a series of events and narratives that also explain those events. This distinction is false, he argues, because all narratives both describe and explain. Narrative in itself is a *form* of explanation, a selection and an arrangement of events that make their successive occurrence understandable. "Narratives may be regarded as kinds of theories, capable of support, and introducing, by grouping them together in certain ways, a kind of order and structure into events" (Danto, p. 137). Any successful narrative description will necessarily include assumptions, made by the author or narrator, as to why particular events were chosen, why others were left out, and why the chosen events, arranged in this way, comprise a satisfactory description. These assumptions amount to an explanation of the events, in the sense that they provide reasons why the final events follow from, are the result of, the earlier events.

The key word is narrative. It is certainly possible to offer a description of an event—Bill sat in the chair—that provides no explanation; but it is not possible to offer a narrative description of this kind. Danto points out that this idea of narrative agrees with our ordinary behavior. If someone asks me why some event occurred, my response is to tell a story that incorporates this event into a sequence of prior events. If then narrative is a form of explanation, what kind of explanation is it and what is the structure of the explanation? One way to explain temporal or historical events—Danto argues that it is the only way—is to account for a *change*. If we are to explain a situation—say, why the car is dented—we must account for the change from when the car was not dented. "Simply to describe an automobile as *dented*, for example, is implicitly to refer to an earlier state of this same automobile in which it was not *dented*; and to demand an explanation of the change" (Danto, p. 233). Similarly, to explain the rise of European capitalism is to account for the change from feudalism to capitalism. This mode of explanation takes the form of initial and final descriptions of a situation with an intervening description of actions or occurrences that account for the change.

This form is exactly the form of narrative; in fact, having this form is a minimal requirement for a description of a sequence of events to be a narrative. For a story to be a story, it must include continuity of subject as well as a beginning, a middle, and an end—that is, an initial and closing situation and an account of the movement or change from one to the other. "A story is an account, I shall say an explanation, of how the change from beginning to end took place, and both the beginning *and* the end are part of the explanadum" (Danto, p. 234). From this idea of narrative—an explanation of a change within a given subject—we can derive the structure of the narrative sequence, the basic element of narrative. A narrative sequence reflects the general form of narrative in the restricted context of a specific situation and a specific action. Given a situation "x", the model offered by Danto is the following:

1. x is F at t-1
2. H happens to x at t-2
3. x is G at t-3, where t represents time

Each stage in the model consists of the description of a situation or an act on that situation. Since this is precisely the definition of a function, we can say that a narrative sequence is a set of three functions that account for a change in a specific situation, the initial and final descriptions of that situation being included in the sequence.

The complete narrative may consist of only one narrative sequence; usually it does not. Every narrative accounts for a change, but the change most stories seek to explain is too complex to be contained in one sequence. Most narratives are composed of many sequences that are embedded in and overlap one another; the entire story presents many changes that build to an account of the final situation. "Changes are nested within changes, and stories require increasingly complex middles to explain the outermost change. We might represent it graphically as follows:

()
(())
((()))
(((())))
. . . ((((())))) . . .

Obviously, this is too neat. For we have cases like the following:

(() () ())

which raise special questions of multiple causation and overdetermination, as well as cases like this

(() (()) ())

where we have overlaps" (Danto, p. 241).

This means, of course, that within one narrative sequence, the middle term, that explains the change, may not be a statement (function) but another sequence or even a series of sequences. For example, in Story 1 from Chapter 2, we had the five functions:

1. A loves B.
2. B ignores A.

3. A seduces B.
4. B leaves A.
5. A dies.

In this structure, one narrative sequence consists of the functions 2, 3, and 4—B ignores A, A seduces B, B leaves A. This sequence explains the change from B simply being unaware of A to B rejecting A. If we label this sequence a, then we can see that sequence a becomes the middle term in another narrative sequence, sequence b; that is, sequence a explains the change from A loves B to A dies:

$$
b\left\{\begin{array}{l}
a\left\{\begin{array}{l}
\text{1. A loves B.}\\
\quad\left\{\begin{array}{l}\text{2. B ignores A.}\\ \text{3. A seduces B.}\\ \text{4. B leaves A.}\end{array}\right.\\
\text{5. A dies.}
\end{array}\right.
\end{array}\right.
$$

Notice that sequence a is necessary for an explanation of the change in sequence b, since by itself neither function 2, 3, or 4 adequately accounts for the change from function 1 to function 5. This embedding structure, as we shall see, is one that often occurs in the Western.

As an explanation of change, a narrative sequence is also, in the context of a myth, an explanation of a relationship. This, of course, is the crucial point, since what I want to show is that narrative structure in a myth provides a model for establishing social relationships. With Danto's analysis of narrative, most of the work is done. A narrative sequence explains a change from a beginning situation to an ending situation. In a myth these situations are described in terms of relationships between characters—"The hero is unknown to society," "There is conflict between the villains and the society," and so on. Thus, in a myth, a narrative sequence explains a change in social relationships—the action of a character in the context of one social situation is seen to bring about a new situation, a new relationship of characters. But through the structure of oppositions, the characters represent social types; thus the narrative sequences explain the interaction and relationships of social types.

Only the exact sense of *explain* remains to be clarified. Remember that a narrative is not just possibly an explanation; it is inevitably an explanation. It explains how a certain situation came about from a prior situation. To explain this change, the story presents all of the information necessary to understand the change. The story offers a theory of the change, which cannot be challenged if the story is successful. This means two things: first, it means that the story accounts for what happens in it. If a story begins with a murder and ends with the capture of the murderer, the story must explain the capture, whether the explanation is police teamwork, technological sophistication, individual courage, or blind luck. No story could begin and end this way and not be, in some sense, "about" the capture. Second, and less obviously, if the story succeeds, we do not question its explanation. A story creates its own world, and in that world things happen and people act for the reasons given in the story. We may find the story uninteresting or even unbelievable, but we do not believe it happened another way. We do not, for example, finish *War and Peace* and feel that, even though Pierre is a fictional character, he probably did not do what the novel says he did. In its own context, the explanation given by a story is necessarily accepted. We may question its validity, but not its reliability.

This is because the situations that are explained by the story are also described by the story. As Danto puts it: "Phenomena *as such* are not explained. It is only phenomena *as covered by a description* which are capable of explanation, and then, when we speak of explaining them, it must be with reference to *that* description (Danto, p. 218). In a story, the descriptions of the situations are given in such a way that the important characteristics of these situations are exactly those treated by the explanation of the change. In this way the honesty of the story is assured. If, in our murder mystery, the murderer is caught because he plays the piano, then the fact that he plays the piano will be included in the description of his character. If we learn that he plays the piano, we can be sure that this fact will be important to our understanding of the story—the execution of the murder, the motivation, the capture, whatever. That is, everything in a story is important to the story. Unlike life, there is no extraneous information. If there were, the story would become boring (unsuccessful), so that later we would ask, "What was the point of that, or that?" As a child I used to wonder why, when people in movies coughed, I knew they would get sick and die, yet when members of my family coughed, I didn't worry. The reason was that one was a story.

Thus, we have three properties of narrative: they explain a change in situations, their explanations cannot be questioned in their own terms, and everything in the narrative contributes to the explanation. Returning to myths, then, we see that myths like other stories contain all the information necessary to understand its characters and events. The characters in a myth represent fundamental social types. The social types are located in a situation in which all the facts relevant to an understanding of their actions are known. Their actions, of course, create new relationships, and since these relationships are between images of significant kinds of people, the actions themselves become images of significant kinds of actions. Thus, a myth creates a conceptual model of important social types of people located in a complete social situation and taking significant social actions, actions that create social relationships. It is in this sense that a myth *explains* social interaction.

Individuals and values: the classical plot

To relate the various Western plots to their social context, I must provide an independent analysis of the social institutions of America and demonstrate the correlation between the structure of the Western and the structure of those institutions. Moreover, I must show that the structure of the institutions changes in accordance with changes in the structure of the Western and that this institutional change predates a little but approximately corresponds in time to the change in the structure of the myth. For this institutional analysis, I will turn to the work of several social analysts, none of whom is remotely interested in Western movies, analysts such as John Kenneth Galbraith, Jurgen Habermas, and C. B. MacPherson. Some of these men analyze the structure and ideology of the institutions of the market, while others are concerned with the shift in America from market capitalism to corporate capitalism and the effects of this shift on social institutions and public ideology. For my purposes, I will summarize their discussions briefly, perhaps too briefly, and then show how the basic components of market structure and ideology are faithfully portrayed in the classical Western, just as the basic components of corporate structure and ideology are faithfully portrayed in the professional Western. In this way, I can reveal a significant structural and temporal correspondence between social institutions and the Western without attempting to demonstrate a mechanism of direct influence. My purpose is not to show how institutions create a myth, nor to show how myths create institutions, but to show that the structure of any social myth, such as the Western, must symbolically reflect the structure of social actions as those actions are patterned and constrained by the central institutions of society.

The interaction of individuals is structured more or less directly by the institutions of society, such as the economy, family, and system of education. If these institutions are to function, the people of the society must act so as to maintain them. Thus, for example, in an industrial society workers must be motivated to continue to raise their standard of living and to accept the constraints and discipline of the factory or the office. Without such motivation, there is no way to insure they will work when they do not feel like working, a necessity of an industrial economy. On the other hand, the values and goals of a society are not so directly determined by its institutions, since these values are also derived from culture and traditions passed on from generation to generation. In a traditional society, where the institutions are often stable over long periods, there is usually a close fit between cultural values and institutional actions. But in a modern society, where institutions change rapidly, it can sometimes happen that the values and goals of the society are in conflict with institutional requirements. Sooner or later, through revolution or cultural change, the values and the institutions will become more compatible; but meanwhile, a conceptual dilemma exists for the people of the society, a dilemma which confronts traditional values with the attitudes inherent in institutional actions. It is this kind of dilemma and its solution in modern America that the Western symbolically addresses.

The most significant development in American institutions in the last forty years has been the change from a competitive, market society to a planned, corporate economy. According to John Kenneth Galbraith, this change began to take place around the end of World War II, or shortly thereafter. The self-regulating market with its process of supply and demand could no longer be depended upon to govern the forces of production, prices, and employment. As a result, in the fifties there was an increasing reliance on and commitment to economic regulation and planning by large corporations and especially by the federal government. Galbraith attributes this change to the economic necessities inherent in the massive industrial technology created after the war; but as Richard Barnet observes, it can also be understood as an increasing effort by the government to utilize its spending power to prevent the economic crises that the market had periodically created before the war. This is the policy of Keynesian economics, a policy which the Eisenhower Administration experimented with and the Kennedy Administration was committed to (Barnet, pp. 165–166).

The two major expressions of the Western myth, the classical and the professional plots, correspond in time and structure to these two periods of economic organization. In Chapter 7, I will discuss in greater depth the nature and causes of the shift to a corporate, regulated economy. In this chapter on the classical plot, my task is to examine the nature of the market economy and to demonstrate how the structure of the classical Western reflects the conflict between institutional constraints and the cultural values of a market society.

The market economy, which developed in Europe in the nineteenth century, was a unique event in history, since it demanded and enforced an institutional separation of society into economic and political spheres. According to Karl Polanyi, "a market economy is an economic system controlled, regulated, and directed by markets alone; order in the production and distribution of goods is entrusted to this self-regulating mechanism" (1956, p. 68). This implies that economic relations are no longer subject to control by social goals and values, the traditional realm of politics. The exchange of labor, land, and money is now determined by the needs of the autonomous market, not by the customs and traditions of cultural institutions. But labor is simply the everyday activity of humans, land is their natural environment, and money simply a symbol for goods and services, so that necessarily the market comes to regulate the ordinary social relationships of people in a market society. This economic regulation was historically new; in all previous societies, social relationships were governed by political and religious institutions, which responded to social values and directed the economy with respect to those values. "*Man's economy is, as a rule, submerged in his social relations*. The change from this to a society which was, on the contrary, submerged in the economic system was an entirely novel development" (Polanyi, 1965, p. 97). In particular this development meant that the individual was no longer seen as seeking social standing in accordance with values derived from social interaction, but was seen as an autonomous being whose primary motivations were individual and economic: satisfaction of hunger, desire for possessions, rampant self-interest. " 'Economic motives' reigned supreme in a world of their own, and the individual was made to act on them under pain of being trodden underfoot by the juggernaut market. Such a forced conversion to a utilitarian outlook fatefully warped Western man's understanding of himself" (Polanyi, 1965, p. 96).

Following an essay on technology and society by Jurgen Habermas, we can further clarify the conflict between the market and social goals by distinguishing the *institutional framework* of a society—the norms and values derived from social communication and interaction—from the *purposive-rational subsystems* which are embedded in the institutional framework and utilize instrumental or technical action for the accomplishment of social tasks. Thus religious or kinship structures would be based on moral rules of interaction and would be part of the institutional framework, while the economic system or the state apparatus would act to insure survival and order and would be based on rational and technical action. A "traditional society," then, is one in which the institutional framework successfully limits the growth of subsystems of purposive-rational action. Such subsystems exist in the traditional society, but their inherent "rationality" is never fully developed since they function within a mode of interaction that is legitimized by unquestioning acceptance of mythical, religious, or metaphysical interpretations of reality. When these traditional underpinnings of knowledge and action start to lose their authority and the instrumental subsystems are gradually freed from normative control, the society is beginning the process of modernization. Historically, this process has depended upon the development of capitalism, an economic system that follows its own internal rules.

> The capitalist mode of production can be comprehended as a mechanism that guarantees "permanent" expansion of subsystems of purposive-rational action and thereby overturns the traditionalist "superiority" of the institutional framework to the forces of production. Capitalism is the first mode of production in world history to institutionalize self-sustaining economic growth. (Habermas, p. 96)

With this change in the mode of production comes a crisis in the legitimizing of domination. The forces of production were previously subject to political, or traditional, authority; production and trade were organized to insure a traditional social order, and these activities took place in the context of ritual distinctions and obligations between gods, seasons, and classes.

Under capitalism, the rational, instrumental aspects of production for gain replace the ritual, political constraints on economic activity, and so the legitimacy of traditional authority is lost. In its place it is necessary to erect a new structure that authorizes and legitimizes the dominance of economic needs over political goals. Legitimation comes to be based on the exchange relations of the market itself, the notion of "just exchange." The market, through the working of supply and demand, determines production and thereby structures social relationships. These relationships are then legitimized and protected by the authority of the political order, which has become a caretaker for the market. As a result, political domination is no longer legitimated "from above" (through cultural tradition) but "from below" (through the relations of production and social labor).

> Only with the emergence of the capitalist mode of production can the legitimation of the institutional framework be linked immediately with the system of social labor. Only then can the property order change from a "political relation" to a "production relation," because it legitimates itself through the rationality of the market . . . and no longer through a legitimate power structure. It is now the political system which is justified in terms of the legitimate relations of production. (Habermas, p. 97)

Thus, the capitalist mode of production makes two contributions to the societies in which it arises: the effective release and permanent expansion of the subsystems of purposive-rational action, and the establishment of an economic legitimation that allows the political system to adapt to the new demands of rationality inherent in these subsystems.

Though capitalism destroyed the traditional legitimation of authority, it did not directly attack the institutional basis of social norms. Social goals and values were still established in an interaction context of public discussion. "Old style politics was forced, merely through its traditional form of legitimation, to define itself in relation to practical goals: the 'good life' was interpreted in a context of interaction relations. The same still held for the ideology of bourgeois society" (Habermas, p. 103). The values and goals of the "good life" changed, since they were no longer based on religion and myth but on the market principle of just exchange. However, "even this bourgeois ideology of justice, by adopting the category of reciprocity, still employs a relation of communicative action as the basis of legitimation" (Habermas, p. 97). The ideology of just exchange implied equality and opportunity and the possibility of achieving for everyone the "good life"—property, family, friends, peace, and freedom from domination. Of course, not all the values of bourgeois ideology were independent of the market and capitalist production; in fact, these values supported a pernicious form of economic domination, as Marx recognized. But in contrast to the ideology of technology, which we will discuss later, a large part of the public accepted the market and the economic legitimation of authority because they understood, and were committed to, the practical social goals of bourgeois ideology, which were to some extent traditional desires in human experience. The free market, as a subsystem of purposive-rational action, was seen as a means for creating a society based on consensual norms and communicative action, the "good society."

The institutions of capitalism, however, were not able to fulfill the goals of bourgeois ideology. "Capitalism's actual development manifestly contradicted the capitalist idea of a bourgeois society, emancipated from domination, in which power is neutralized" (Habermas, p. 101). The failure of the free market to satisfy its social promise can, in part, be attributed to the unique relation between the values and institutions of capitalism. In traditional society, with political legitimation "from above," the social values govern the institutions of society: to protect the institutions is to maintain the values. In capitalist society, with political legitimation "from below"—that is, from the relations of production—the economic institutions of society, based on the practice of the market, enter into a problematic relation with the values and goals of the society, based on the *principle* of just exchange. In this situation of contradiction between institutions and values, the society must make an ideological commitment to one or the other, as we shall see in our discussion of the professional Western plot.

For the present, however, we must notice the conceptual conflict between the values of bourgeois society and the institution of the market. Bourgeois values, though attached to the rationality of the market, are still founded on consensual norms that stress freedom, equality, peace, and the theoretical availability of meaningful human relationships—family, love, satisfying work—to everyone. The institutions of capitalism, however, structure actual human relationships according to the needs of the self-regulating market, which, of course, is not concerned with social values but with profit and production. The market "handed over the fate of man and nature to the play of an automaton running in its own grooves and governed by its own laws" (Polanyi, 1972, p. 96).

If men's social actions are structured by the market, then many of their social ideas and attitudes must also be structured by the market; for if men are to act, they must understand their actions as reasonable and significant. We have already seen how the notion of just exchange, derived from the market, becomes the basis for the values of bourgeois society. But what are the images of the individual and his role in society that the market, through its regulation of human activity, creates in the minds of its participants? Proper market behavior depends upon the idea of economic man, the self-interested individual; and it is this idea, grounded in institutional action, that is in conflict with the social goals and values based on the idea of interaction and just exchange. What are the dimensions of this image of economic man?

What is the view of the individual and society that has "fatefully warped Western man's understanding of himself"?

The distinguishing features of a market economy are (1) that the rewards for work are determined by the market, there is no authoritative social allocation of jobs or wages; and (2) that land and labor are commodities that can be bought and sold. Under these conditions, society does not guarantee the individual's ability to survive or to enjoy his life. Each individual's ability to produce and his access to the means of production depend upon his ability to make himself attractive to the market. In a market society, it is common for individuals to be separated from the means of production and required to sell their labor, if they can, in order to survive; each individual must strive to increase his wealth, his ability to control land and labor. In this effort, he must compete with all other individuals who must also strive to increase their wealth and thereby control his labor. In a market economy, the efforts of an individual to enjoy the benefits of his society are not directed at increasing those benefits for everyone, but are necessarily directed at preventing others from enjoying those benefits.

The individual must see himself as self-reliant and independent of the wills of others, except through the establishment of economic contracts. He must recognize his abilities and capacities as belonging to himself, not to the social group, and he must utilize these capacities in the most rational manner to increase his own wealth. This is the view of the individual inherent in the market, and it underlies the theory of possessive individualism, which provides a philosophical underpinning for the market. In his book *The Political Theory of Possessive Individualism*, from which this argument is taken, C. B. MacPherson lists the three assumptions about the individual and society which are basic to the idea of possessive individualism:

1. What makes a man human is freedom from dependence on the wills of others.
2. Freedom from dependence on others means freedom from any relations with others except those relations which the individual enters voluntarily with a view to his own interest.
3. The individual is essentially the proprietor of his own person and capacities, for which he owes nothing to society. (MacPherson, p. 263)

These assumptions, as MacPherson shows, are inherent in a market society and underlie the liberal theories of Hobbes, Locke, and other market philosophers. In more recent years, the existentialism of Sartre and the psychoanalysis of Freud have made similar assumptions about the individual and society. These philosophers, like ordinary men in a market economy, understand the nature of man to be essentially individualistic, since under the market this *is* his nature.

> The assumptions of possessive individualism are peculiarly appropriate to a possessive market society, for they state certain essential facts that are peculiar to that society. The individual in a possessive market society is human in his capacity as proprietor of his own person; . . . his society does consist of a series of market relations . . . However much he may wish it to be otherwise, his humanity does depend on his freedom from any but self interested contractural relations with others. (MacPherson, pp. 271–272, 275)

But a society that accepts this idea of the individual and the group is not one likely to create pleasant, satisfying social relationships. Philosophers as different as Karl Marx and John Stuart Mill have stressed the incompatibility of the attitudes of possessive individualism with the needs of a human society. Valuable human experience, it seems, depends on open, trusting communication based on shared social needs, goals, and interests; it is in this context that the natural rewards of family, love, work, community are enjoyed. But the market demands that members of society identify themselves as individuals who are directed by self-interest and characterized by independence and self-sufficiency. The values and goals of bourgeois society reflect the market principle of just exchange but are also grounded in the idea of the "good life," the achievement of equality, work, community, and mutual respect. The dilemma, then, is apparent: the values of human experience, the norms of the institutional framework of society, the moral order based on social interaction, are all in conflict with the values required by a self-regulating market.

This, of course, is not just a philosophical or intellectual conflict, but a conflict in experience, social concepts, and attitudes. As a myth, the Western addresses this conflict and provides a resolution. The Western does not pose the problem as the philosophers do—how can a human society result from a contractual combination of independent, calculating individuals? Rather, the myth asks a question that directly concerns us in our everyday actions—how do we, as autonomous, self-reliant individuals, relate to the society of others, a society of morality and love? In this formulation, both sides of the contradiction are retained, as they are in our society. The myth asks how we can maintain our independence and still be part of society, a problem faced by most of us almost constantly. Our analysis of the Western, then, should tell us how it establishes the context of this problem—what are the components of a society in which this problem is both significant and capable of solution? —and, of course, what is the solution.

In the classical plot the distinction between the individual and society is clear and rigorous. The hero is autonomous and unique, and the people of society are kind and decent. But the hero is not a part of society. He is unknown to the people of society, and the narrative tells of his efforts to be accepted by them. In this case, then, the myth takes the theoretical problem of the individual and society and turns it into a practical problem. The hero is not just an independent individual; he is a man who is also alone and outside. He is outside because of his independence, and the action of the story provides the means for him to remain independent and yet no longer be alone. Thus, the inside society/outside society opposition states one form of a basic conceptual and practical concern in our society. A distinction is made between different kinds of men—those who are outside and those who are inside—and the possibility of a relationship between them is created. This, I believe, corresponds to a distinction felt by most Americans, who in striving to become the autonomous individuals demanded by the market feel themselves to be outside of the group to which they want to belong.

The hero is also separated from society by the strong/weak opposition. His great strength is the source of his independence, just as the weakness of the people in society is an aspect of their dependence on one another and on the hero. The hero can take care of himself—he fears no one and needs no one—but society cannot take care of itself. This idea of strength is clearly contained in the three assumptions underlying the market concept of the individual. The hero is free from dependence on the will of others, and he is essentially the proprietor of his own person and capacities, for which he owes nothing to society. Society, of course, fulfills neither of these requisites. Thus the image of strength in the Western stresses the social concern with the individual in society; but we should not too closely identify the image with the concern. Virtually all myths and fairy tales involve a strong hero within a group of others who are weak. For an understanding of how the Western myth relates to American society, it is not the strength of the hero that is crucial but other characteristics. Most heroes fear no one; few other than the Western hero need no one.

Seen as a shorthand for independence versus dependence, the strong/weak opposition corresponds to an important distinction between kinds of people in our society—those who can take care of themselves and those who cannot. This distinction typically applies to the difference between men and women, and, to almost the same degree, between youth and old age. Significantly, in the Western, the image of society is usually that of women and older men. When there are young men who belong to society, they are likely to be small in stature, from the east, or blatant cowards. The heroine, being, it seems, naturally weak and dependent, must rely on the strong man who, by being strong, proves himself worthy of her trust and dependence. In this way women, the bearers of love and morality, are separated conceptually from men, particularly young men, by the strong/weak opposition. To some degree the same is true for older men, the bearers of law, business, and dignity. This conceptual difference between independence and dependence, which in the Western characterizes the difference between men and women, youth and old age, also exists in contemporary social attitudes towards these same groups; in both cases, the difference is felt to be between weakness and strength. Thus, the Western mirrors a distinction that is part of the daily experience of most Americans.

We have seen that the hero and the society are separated on the strong/weak axis as well as on the inside society/outside society axis. But the villains are also strong and opposed to society; they share this classification with the hero. Like the hero, their strength makes them independent; they do not need the people of society. They are typically the only men in the story who are of the same general age as the hero. Sometimes, as in *Shane*, one of the villains is an exceptionally tough older man, but this is rare among the most successful versions of the classical plot. Usually both the hero and the villains are young, strong, self-reliant men, while society consists of weak women and older men. This classification extends even to the women who are lovers or associates of the villains, such as Rhonda in *The Far Country* or Frenchy in *Destry Rides Again*. These women seem strong and villainous, but they prove themselves to be truly social, both through their love for the hero and their weakness. They seem to be able to take care of themselves, but they cannot and are killed. Thus, the strong (young men)/weak (women, older men) dichotomy is retained. Both the hero and the villains are strong and independent; and often, because of this, they share a special kind of mutual respect not extended to the members of society. But if the villains relate to the hero through strength, how do they relate to society? Where do they belong on the inside/outside axis?

Before addressing that question, let us turn to the third key opposition, between good and bad. This distinction separates the villains from the hero and society. In the classical plot, it is almost always coded in economic terms—the bad guys are much richer than the good guys. The villains are successful ranchers (*Shane*), saloon owners (*Dodge City, San Antonio, Destry Rides Again*), businessmen (*Union Pacific, Bend of the River*), officials (*Destry Rides Again, Far Country, Vera Cruz*), while the people of society are struggling settlers (*Bend of the River*), farmers (*Shane, Canyon Passage*), townspeople (*Dodge City, Cimarron*). Good and bad do not always correspond to rich and poor, however, since there are many films in which the good guys are also quite successful—*Cimarron, Duel in the Sun, The Far Country, Chisum*—just as there are films in which the villains are poor—*Bend of the River, Vera Cruz, Canyon Passage*. The good/bad distinction does not separate people by their success at making money but rather by their *motivations* for trying to make money. In the classical Western plot, conflict arises over land and the resources of land. While both the villains and society want to appropriate the land and its resources, they have different reasons—the good people want the land to build a society with families, churches, schools, law, and business, the villains want the land and its resources for personal gain. This theme is reiterated throughout the classical Western.

In *The Far Country*, for example, the people of society are as rich as the villains; they have all made huge gold strikes. But whereas the villains want to exploit the land and the people and take the gold away, the good people want to build a town with churches and schools in the middle of the Yukon wilderness. In *Vera Cruz*, this theme is taken to its logical conclusion—the villains are the aristocratic court of Maximillian, taking the exploited wealth of Mexico back to Europe, while the good people are the peasants of Mexico who want to take control of their own society. On a smaller scale, the two main characters of this film are hired gunfighters; one chooses to eschew personal profit in order to help the peasants, becoming the hero, while the other chooses to betray the peasants for his own interests, becoming the villain.

The good/bad opposition, then, separates the people who are concerned only with themselves from those who are concerned with others, and this distinction is clearly understood and commonly used in our society to classify kinds of people. Once again, it is a division that corresponds to a basic split between social experience and the theories of a market economy and possessive individualism. The market will work only if every person seeks his own interest and enters into relations with others only after rational calculation based on an expectation of personal gain. But, of course, social experience tells us that this model can neither explain nor provide satisfying relationships based on love and friendship. In the classical Western, the villains represent unbridled market self-interest. Not only their desires but their methods reflect this; out of supreme self-concern, they are capable of betraying trusts and attacking from ambush. On the other hand, the people of society represent social values—family, love, morality—and their code of honesty and fair play, even against evil, is derived from a basic respect and concern for others. But this social concern, both in the Western and in contemporary consciousness, is fundamentally associated with the market society as the ideal form of social relations. It is not a question of the market versus society but of a decent, social market versus an individual, exploitative market. In other words, the good/bad opposition does not reflect a conflict in social theory but in social experience. Both the villains and the settlers (or their equivalents) want to establish a market society. The villains represent the individualistic aspect of it, necessary but vicious and cruel, while the settlers represent the social aspect, decent and kind if helpless and unsuccessful. Both aspects are part of our daily social experience, and both are necessary for a market society to exist. Yet the conflict is deep, since it rests on the fundamental distinction between individual and society. Like the hero, the villains are individuals, the kind required by the theory and institutions of the market; they seek their own self-interest, they are free from dependence on the will of others, and they are proprietors of their own persons and capacities. They are strong and independent.

But unlike the hero, they are usually inside of society, or almost inside. Villains are typically involved in the institutions of society—saloons, business, ranches, and so forth—or at least they are somewhat identified with these institutions through their dress, interests, and background. There are exceptions, where a villain is as much or more outside of society than the hero—Cole in *Bend of the River*, Bragg in *Canyon Passage*, the gunman in *Hombre*. However, in each of these films there is another villain who is closely identified with society—Hendricks, the merchant; George, the gentleman and sophisticate; Favor, the Indian agent.

Though the villains are associated with social institutions, they are never completely in society, and here we must be clear as to what we mean by "society." We have been using the term in two different senses—social institutions and social interactions, market and morality. These two uses reflect the basic problem of the Western: how are they compatible? Society, properly speaking, consists of both market and morality as far as the classical Western is concerned. The villain, though he is both physically located and financially involved in society, is not fully a part of it since he does not share its morality. The hero, on the contrary, is usually a stranger to society, involved in neither its institutions nor its interaction. During the course of the narrative he often accepts both, but in the opening description he is truly outside of society, as in *Shane*. Logan in *Canyon Passage* is probably the most serious exception to this, yet even here, where the hero begins as a businessman engaged to be married, his difference from other heroes is only one of degree; he is involved in society, but in a very independent, almost scornful way, unlike everyone else in the village, and this point is stressed repeatedly throughout the film.

The primary function of the inside/outside society opposition is to separate the hero from society; this axis does not directly relate to the villains and therefore they have no fixed position on it. In the vengeance plot, many of the villains are outside of society, but in the classical Western the villains have a fairly well-entrenched position on this axis, more or less in the middle. In Lévi-Strauss' terms, they mediate between the hero and society, sharing properties of both, and are therefore neither completely in nor completely out of the social body. It is through the villains that the hero and society bridge the differences separating them. The picture that emerges is this: the hero and the villains are individuals who are strong, independent, and self-interested. The hero is outside of society, and his self-interest is an aspect of his being alone and self-reliant. The villains, however, are a part of society, and their self-interest is destructive of social needs and values. Since individualism and self-interest are required by market-centered institutions, villains are inherent in society and society is weak compared to their strength.

This situation is expressed in the classical Western through the three oppositions—good/bad, inside society/outside society, strong/weak—each of which provides a classification of differences between people based on the fundamental contradiction between individual and society in a market economy. The fourth opposition, civilization/wilderness, I will consider later in a more general context. Now let us turn to the narrative to see how the classical Western structures interaction between the different kinds of people defined by the three oppositions above.

First, for convenience, I will list again the functions of the classical plot.

1. The hero enters a social group.
2. The hero is unknown to the society.
3. The hero is revealed to have an exceptional ability.
4. The society recognizes a difference between themselves and the hero; the hero is given a special status.
5. The society does not completely accept the hero.
6. There is a conflict of interests between the villains and the society.
7. The villains are stronger than the society; the society is weak.
8. There is a strong friendship or respect between the hero and a villain.
9. The villains threaten the society.
10. The hero avoids involvement in the conflict.
11. The villains endanger a friend of the hero's.
12. The hero fights the villains.
13. The hero defeats the villains.
14. The society is safe.
15. The society accepts the hero.
16. The hero loses or gives up his special status.

These sixteen functions outline the narrative, though not all of them appear in every story. The meaning of the narrative is not contained in the list but in the structure of the functions, the series of narrative sequences that move the action from beginning to end and explain the changes in the relations between characters. It is this structure that we must exhibit if we are to understand the Western as a model for action. To do so, we must identify the narrative sequences within the list of functions.

This is not a particularly difficult task. Functions 2, 3 and 4 form a sequence I shall call the "Status" sequence. The hero demonstrates his strength, revealing himself to be a gunfighter, and he is given a special status by the people of society—the status of a gunfighter. The change from being unknown to being known with a specific status is caused by the hero's ability with a gun. As a gunfighter, the hero is regarded as a man to fear and respect, but he is not accepted by society—his special status prevents it.

Functions 1 and 5 comprise the beginning and end of another sequence, the sequence "Outside." The hero enters society but is not accepted by it. The reason for this change, the cause of society's rejection, is that the hero is not a member of society and his strength gives him a special position outside of it. The middle term, or the action of the "Outside" sequence, is the sequence formed by functions 2, 3, and 4, the "Status" sequence. The "Outside" sequence, then, explains the change from the hero's entering society to his not being accepted by it. He is rejected not because he is unknown, not because he is strong, and not because he has special status, but because of the conjunction of all three. This is a case in which one sequence is embedded in another.

Outside {
1. The hero enters a social group.

   Status {
   2. The hero is unknown to the society.
   3. The hero is revealed to have an exceptional ability.
   4. The hero is given a special status. }

5. The society does not completely accept the hero. }

These sequences are essentially descriptive; they state two of the oppositions and set the stage for further action. In the "Outside" sequence the hero reveals his strength—his individuality and independence—and is set apart from society, a clear reiteration of the strong/weak dichotomy. Both functions 1 and 2 state that the hero is outside of society, and the sequence reinforces and extends this classification. According to the sequence, the hero is not only circumstantially outside but characteristically outside. The sequences "Status" and "Outside" restate and explain these two oppositions without developing them. If the strong/weak and inside/outside distinctions are clearly made without it, the sequences are not really necessary. In *Union Pacific* and *San Antonio* the heroes are not unknown, though they are strong and outside of society. Logan, in *Canyon Passage*, is a member of society who is well known; and for this reason the dialogue is used to stress his difference.

"Weakness," another sequence, is formed by functions 6, 7 and 9 and shows how the villains, because of their strength and society's weakness, threaten the survival of society. There is a natural conflict based, at one level, on the good/bad opposition and, at a deeper level, on the contradiction between institutions and human values in a market society. A rancher tries to drive away farmers (*Shane*), a judge tries to rob miners of their claims (*The Far Country*), a criminal tries to start an Indian war by running guns (*Northwest Mounted Police*). In each case, if the villains succeed, the people of society will either be killed or forced to abandon their homes—society will be destroyed. But society is weak and helpless before the strength of the villains. Torrey is easily killed by Wilson in *Shane*; Dusty the miner is killed and Rube the sheriff is humiliated by the villains in *The Far Country*; Matt Cole is ambushed and killed in *Dodge City*. After these defeats, the survival of society is doubtful—the farmers and the miners begin to leave in *Shane* and *The Far Country*; the town will die in *Dodge City*; the fort will be destroyed in *Northwest Mounted Police*. The classical plot is the only version of the Western myth in which the villains' desire for personal gain inevitably threatens the very existence of society; and this threat, as the "Weakness" sequence tells us, derives from the conflict between strong villains and a weak society.

This is not a startling revelation; nevertheless, if our structural analysis is successful, it will help to clarify the interrelationships between our conceptual classifications and familiar concrete images. The "Weakness" sequence advances the story from being a simple conflict between society and the villains, good and bad, by showing how the villains threaten the very survival of society. This is important, because it shows that society is incomplete and insufficient as well as weak. Villains are inherent in society and, if opposed only by society, will inevitably destroy its morality and human values. The Western myth concerns the hero, and "Weakness" refines the situation in which he will act. He is outside and strong, the villains are inside and strong, and society is weak and threatened.

Two other sequences, which do not always appear, further develop and refine the situation. In the first the hero is unknown; he and the villain demonstrate their strength; they share a mutual respect and often friendship. In this sequence, "Friendship," the beginning and end are functions 2 and 8, and the middle term, or action, is a combination of functions 3 and 7. The sequence shows that, because of their unusual strength, the hero and the villain are quite similar and have a special kind of relationship—they are natural brothers, so to speak. The hero changes from being unknown to being respected, and he respects the villain, who is the only other strong character in the story. This sequence appears in most of the films I have studied—*Cimarron*, *Union Pacific*, *Duel in the Sun*, *Yellow Sky*, *Whispering Smith*, *Shane* (to a degree), *Bend of the River*, *The Far Country*, *Vera Cruz*. The hero is not always unknown to the villain; in *Cimarron*, *Union Pacific* and *Whispering Smith*, they are old friends.

This "Friendship" sequence underscores the mutual strength of the hero and villain and their difference from society. It stresses that these two men are individuals and, as such, understand one another. Their independence makes them capable of a special relationship of respect and/or friendship. And with only one or two exceptions, in the classical plot only these two men seem to be able to have such a relationship. The villains cannot trust each other, and the people of society are weak and undependable. While there is love between the hero and a woman, real friendship or respect apart from love exists almost exclusively between the hero and the villain. It is as though only independent and strong individuals can truly share respect and become friends. In the classical plot, this notion is used mainly to distinguish the hero and the villain and to set up their eventual conflict. But in the professional plot, as we shall see, this view of friendship is developed into a major conceptual resource of the Western.

The second sequence that refines the situation consists of functions 10, 11 and 12, in which the hero attempts to remain aloof from the conflict between the villain and society. He is outside and independent, it is not his fight. But he has made a friend—Wash in *Destry Rides Again*, young Harry Cole in *Dodge City*, Starret in *Shane*, Ben in *The Far Country*, Jesse in *Duel in the*

Sun—who is killed, harmed, or threatened by the villains. After this, the hero abandons his neutrality and fights. The sequence, "Commitment," stresses more than any other the independence and self-interest of the hero. He is not particularly concerned with the decency and morality of society or with their destruction; he only decides to fight for society when he becomes personally involved through an attack made on a friend who is already a part of society. At this point, his own self-interest becomes a factor. Strictly speaking, of course, it doesn't. If he were truly independent, he could ignore his friend; but in the classical Western, having a friend associates the hero with society, as the "Commitment" sequence shows. The hero is not an absolute individual, capable of remaining completely outside; total independence cannot be maintained. He has need of the social values of friendship and loyalty, and these values require that he become involved with society. It is necessary if he is to become fully human. The "Commitment" sequence informs us that the individual needs society, just as in another sequence we will see that society needs the individual.

Some films do not contain the "Commitment" sequence—*Cimarron*, *Union Pacific*, *San Antonio*, *Bend of the River*—but perhaps it is fair to say that the best classical Westerns (such as *Shane*, *Dodge City*, *Destry Rides Again*, *Duel in the Sun*, *Yellow Sky*, *The Far Country*, *Vera Cruz*, *Canyon Passage*, and *Hombre*) generally include it. Without this sequence the hero's commitment to the values of society would have to be present from the start. When the hero has already accepted social values, even though society has not accepted him—as in *Bend of the River*—the oppositions are weakened and the force of the narrative is weakened. When this sequence appears, it establishes the first strong connection between the hero and society and motivates the action that climaxes the narrative. Without it, both the connection and the motivation are assumed but not demonstrated, Thus, the "Commitment" sequence sharpens the oppositions and crystallizes the penultimate relationship between hero and society. It need not appear; the information it contains is not completely necessary, since the decisive action concerning that relationship takes place elsewhere. But its presence makes the film stronger, and in the professional plot the ideas of friendship and loyalty underlying both the "Commitment" and "Friendship" sequences are developed into a central aspect of the narrative.

The discussion of these sequences may seemingly contain contradictions. I have noted that the hero has a friend in society, while showing that the only real occurrence of respect and sometimes friendship is between the hero and the villain. But these statements do not conflict, since the hero's friend in society is a friend almost in the sense of a pet dog who is pleasant but ineffectual. Usually this friend is categorically different from the hero—in *Destry Rides Again* and *The Far Country* he is old, in *Dodge City* he is a child, and in *Vera Cruz* he is black. These friends are close to the hero but dependent on him. Except perhaps for Starret in *Shane*, only the villain is portrayed as a possible equal to the hero; therefore, mutual respect or friendship based on such respect is only possible between these two men.

Functions 12, 3 and 13 comprise an obvious but important sequence. The fight is the climax of the narrative and plays a critical role in the structure. The entire sequence, "Fight," is also an action that causes other changes—that is, the sequence itself is embedded in other sequences. Probably the most interesting thing about the sequence is that the hero fights and defeats the villains alone. He has only his strength to rely on, and it is sufficient. Usually, the hero is all alone—*Shane*, *The Far Country*, *Yellow Sky*—and wins through remarkable ability. Sometimes he has help, but it is always his strength that makes the difference. After the fight and the victory, society is safe. This change is explained by the sequence "Safe"—function 9, "Fight," function 14.

"Safe"
- 9. The villains threaten the society.
- "Fight"
  - 12. The hero fights the villains.
  - 3. The hero is revealed to have an exceptional ability.
  - 13. The hero defeats the villains.
- 14. The society is safe.

The "Fight" sequence causes the change from function 9 to function 14—the hero's fight and victory explains the saving of society. The important point is that the hero is alone. The sequence shows how the hero saves society by his own ability, independently of others. The villains threaten society, and only the hero's strength prevents them from destroying it. This sequence, then, demonstrates the critical importance of the individual to society. We have seen that society inevitably produces individuals within it, but that they are villains. Society is powerless against these villains and can only be helped by another individual who is outside society. Without the hero, society cannot survive, yet it cannot produce him; it can only produce villains. The hero must be separate from society. While he is separate, he needs the social values of friendship and love; but if he were part of society, he would be weak and dependent. His strength comes from relying only on himself, not on others or on social institutions; and, of course, it is this strength that is necessary to society. The sequence "Safe," together with the sequence "Commitment," outlines the basic relationship between the individual and society as it appears in the classical Western. The hero's characteristics of strength, independence, and self-reliance are not truly social values and do not exist in society per se; but without access to these abilities, society cannot exist. On the other hand, the social values of love, law, friendship, and family are not truly individual values, but without them the individual cannot be fulfilled. Thus, the existence of society and the happiness of the individual depend upon a negotiation between the two positions or sets of values; and this negotiation centers on the threat of the villains, for it is this threat that disturbs the separation and makes the interaction both possible and necessary.

The sequence "Safe" indicates through its action that a weaker group can only be successfully helped by independence and self-reliance. If society is to be saved—or, in more general terms, if others are to be aided—the individual must act for them, not with them. Efforts to work with a group through mutual support are doomed to failure, just as society fails to defend itself from the villains. If an individual—in the generic sense—is to help others, he must be an individual in the market sense; that is, he must depend only on himself and act as he knows best. Reliance and trust in a group will only weaken him. He must act independently and do what is best for the people he wants to help, even if, as in *Shane*, they themselves oppose it. His strength and thus his ability to succeed depends upon his autonomy and self-reliance. Successful acts are individual acts; only the weak and unsuccessful, albeit decent and kind, work with and depend upon a group.

The narrative of the classical Western, particularly the sequence "Safe," explains how the fight successfully helps a group. The image of this specific act involves violence; and thus, of course, it is possible that the violence itself should be part of the action model. But while the violence adds excitement to the story, it is not, I believe, usually included in the meaning of the fight. This meaning involves independence and self-sufficiency, and the fight is usually interpreted in this way. Violence makes the meaning very clear, and is useful as a plot device; yet the same point can be made by other actions, as, for example, the hero's not fighting in *The Big Country*. Violence is sometimes taken literally and applied as such, but it is no more part of the meaning of the Western than it is part of the meaning of Shakespeare, except insofar as violence is a central and inevitable aspect of the conflict between individual and society in a market economy. Violence is a central and inevitable aspect of our society, and thus the Western is not encouraging it but honestly expressing it. In another sense, the Western is probably less about violence than Shakespeare, for in a myth the characters primarily represent concepts or principles and appear only secondarily, if at all, as real people; but in dramatic or narrative literature, the characters primarily represent real psychological beings and express principles to a smaller degree. Violence in a myth is generally concerned with opposing or reconciling principles, while in literature violence truly exists between people and is consequently more convincing and more deeply felt.

"Acceptance," the next sequence, further expands the consequences of the fight. Now the sequence "Safe" appears as the cause of the change.

- "Accept-tance"
  - 5. The society does not completely accept the hero.
  - "Safe"
    - 9. The villains threaten the society.
    - "Fight"
      - 12. The hero fights the villains.
      - 3. The hero is revealed to have an exceptional ability.
      - 11. The hero defeats the villains.
    - 14. The society is safe.
  - 15. The society accepts the hero.

His saving of society explains the hero's final acceptance. The threat of the villains, the fight, and the victory are now seen as means by which the hero can overcome his initial rejection by society and be accepted. He is originally outside of society, a gunfighter who is respected but not approved of. The use of his strength demonstrates to the people of society that they do need his ability and he is therefore accepted by them.

As a model for action, the sequence "Acceptance" refines and completes the sequence "Safe." The inside/outside opposition reflects a distinction felt in our society between those who are accepted by a group and those who are not. This distinction is most meaningful when it separates the individual from the group that he either wants to be accepted into or more respected by, since it reflects a basic conceptual and practical problem created by our market-oriented society. The classical Western raises this problem, and the sequence "Acceptance" presents a solution to it. The individual is outside, not accepted, because he is different, particularly because of his independence. He can become accepted by helping the group and proving to them that they need him; he accomplishes this not by joining the group and helping them to work together but by becoming even more independent, working alone, relying only on himself, while attempting to aid and succor the group. In this way he is more likely to succeed; he will gain more respect, and the group will realize that they do need him and will accept him with a special appreciation.

The myth attempts to resolve the problem of the individual and society by stressing individuality. This is curious, since nonacceptance results from individuality, and the problem is for the individual to become accepted by the group. But it is understandable, because the myth is not a theoretical effort to analyze an institutional contradiction but a conceptual and unconscious effort to live with the contradiction by providing a model of action which can utilize and overcome it. To this end, the Western creates a situation in which extreme individuality is the reasonable and inevitable solution to the problem of the individual and the group—the problem of acceptance. This is one reason why the settling of the American West provides such a successful context for a myth concerned with this issue. In a scientific, skeptical society, myths cannot depend upon magic and supernatural events and must have a more realistic base for the narrative action.

The West and its characters really did exist, and in this setting extreme individualism as a successful resource is convincing and acceptable, even if it is inaccurate because of its mythical dimension. This context allows for a clear and acceptable image of society in a weakened and threatened situation. In a myth concerned with a social contradiction—in this case, the individual and society—neither pole of the contradiction can be abandoned or rejected. Rather, they must be made compatible. The classical Western attempts to make them compatible by stressing individualism in a situation where it is necessary and finally accepted gladly by society.

"Equality," the final sequence, is concerned with the hero's change in status. This change is explained by the sequence "Acceptance" and all the action embedded in it.

"Equality"
- 4. The hero is given a special status.
- "Acceptance"
  - 5. The society does not completely accept the hero.
  - "Safe"
    - 9. The villains threaten the society.
    - "Fight"
      - 12. The hero fights the villains.
      - 3. The hero is revealed to have an exceptional ability.
      - 13. The hero defeats the villains.
    - 14. The society is safe.
  - 15. The society accepts the hero.
- 16. The hero loses or gives up his special status.

After he has used his strength to save society and been accepted, the hero gives up the special status that was awarded him because of his ability as a gunfighter. He is still respected and admired as a special person, but he no longer maintains the role that made him different and gave him unique status. He marries, settles down, and gives up his guns (*The Far Country*, *Bend of the River*, *Yellow Sky*, *San Antonio*); he marries, becomes a businessman, and gives up his guns (*Union Pacific*); he leaves the society (*Cimarron*, *Dodge City*, *Shane*, *Canyon Passage*); or he dies (*Duel in the Sun*, *Hombre*, *The Plainsman*). The "Equality" sequence serves as a frame to the core of the narrative action and may be the most typically American aspect of the myth. Function 4, the hero's status—together with the reliance on and acceptance of the hero—indicates willingness to create and depend on an elite or aristocracy of strength in times of trouble. Although he is not a part of the group, the hero is respected and feared as a protector and defender with special rights and privileges. Fear and respect is also given to the villain with whom the hero must contend, in a realm of action inaccessible to ordinary men. This aristocratic tendency is clearly compatible with the individual/society distinction—for if "the individual is essentially the proprietor of his own person and capacities, for which he owes nothing to society," then all accomplishments are essentially individual and it is natural to depend on strong individuals to resolve problems concerning everyone.

Of course, most myths involve special men performing tasks that exceed the capacities of ordinary men. What is particularly interesting about the Western is where these men come from and how they are treated. In many myths, such as the Greek or the Icelandic sagas, the hero is an aristocrat by birth; in others, particularly fairy tales, he rises through his exploits from the common people to the nobility. But the Western heroes are not initially a part of society, as are the heroes of most myths, and their social stratum is if anything below that of the people for whom they fight. They are typically saddle tramps, outlaws, or hired gunfighters. In the Western the hero belongs nowhere, he is fighting just to enter a society. In doing so, he too rises from a common origin to an aristocratic position; but after he has won his entry and defended the social group, he does something that few if any other mythical heroes do: he gives up his aristocratic status and chooses to become just another member of society. He remains a special person, a leader in the eyes of the people, yet he abandons all the ceremony and institutional trappings that might insure a unique, powerful position for him.

Thus, in the classical Western we have an aristocratic tendency with a democratic bias. Under threatening circumstances, it is reasonable and proper to rely on a strong and elite group of men; but when the danger has passed, they must become equal with everyone else, a requirement, in fact, they have been fighting to insure. As a model for action that relates to the separation between strong and weak, this sequence indicates that the strong must protect and defend the weak but that they have no special rights or powers over them. The weak must be protected from duties and responsibilities beyond their capacities and from attacks on their persons or properties; but otherwise, they are the equal of those who are strong and must therefore be respected and deferred to. Now if in this description we substitute "women" and "men" for "weak" and "strong," we will have a fairly accurate account of the relations between men and women in American society, at least until the mid-fifties, when the classical Western began to disappear. Although foreign visitors have frequently remarked on the unusual degree of respect and power given to American women in personal relationships with men, especially in the family, women's liberation has correctly pointed out the prevalence of attitudes that systematically deny women access to institutional positions of real power and responsibility. These attitudes assume that women are neither interested in nor strong enough for such positions; as women, they are not capable of the tough-minded, rationality required for holding power and must, for their own sakes, be protected from it.

More than anything else, the sequence "Equality" describes the kind of society validated by the classical Western. We have discussed this society before, but it will be helpful to reiterate its properties here. It is a society that stresses the value of the family, seeks the rule of law, and trusts in the legal structure of American democracy. Its members believe in the institutions of the market economy; they respect hard work and business, even though they recognize that business is often corrupt. They respect religious beliefs, without giving them great stress; they recognize that violence is sometimes necessary, but do not accept it as a way of life, and desire a peaceful community where violence is the exception. Above all, it is an egalitarian society where no one, except a villain, sets himself apart from others. All are legally and morally equal, and though abilities differ everyone is assumed to be decent and kind. This is the society the hero chooses to join by surrendering his unique position of status and power; and this renunciation is necessary—if the hero did not give up his status, society would be different. If he maintained his position, the hero would change its egalitarian nature and create a powerful and undemocratic elite. This would be unacceptable to society and to the hero.

The social values are clear. While they may involve difficult contradictions, such as that between individual and society, they are nevertheless firm and respected as ideal foundations for a good community. This is the bourgeois ideal of a society based on interaction and communication as well as the concepts and actions of market individualism. Later, in the professional plot, this image of society virtually disappears, having undergone the transformations expressed in the vengeance variation and the transition theme. In terms of the classical plot, however, we must recognize that the change described by the sequence "Equality"—the natural claim to status and power followed by the voluntary relinquishing of it—constitutes a remarkable narrative tribute to the strength of this bourgeois view of the "good society."

Selective bibliography

Barnet, Richard J. 1972 *Roots of War*. Atheneum, New York.

Bazin, André 1971 *What is Cinema*? University of California Press, Berkeley.

Burke, Kenneth 1969 *A Rhetoric of Motives*. University of California Press, Los Angeles.

Cawelti, John G. 1971 *The Six-Gun Mystique*. Bowling Green Popular Press, Bowling Green, Ohio.

Commoner, Barry 1971 *The Closing Circle*. Alfred A. Knopf, New York.

Danto, Arthur C. 1968 *Analytical Philosophy of History*. Cambridge University Press, London.

Drucker, Peter F. 1970 *Technology, Management, and Society*. Harper and Row, New York and Evanston.

Emery, P. E. 1959 "Psychological Effects of the Western Film: A Study in Television Viewing," *Human Relations*, Vol. 12, No. 3.

Galbraith, John Kenneth 1968 *The New Industrial State*. The New American Library, New York.

Georges, Robert A. 1968 *Studies on Mythology*. The Dorsey Press, Homewood, Illinois.

Habermas, Jurgen 1970 *Toward a Rational Society*. Beacon Press, Boston.

Jakobson, R. (with M. Halle) 1956 *Fundamentals of Language*. Mouton and Co., The Hague.

Kitses, Jim 1969 *Horizons West*. Thames and Hudson, Ltd., London.

Lévi-Strauss, Claude 1966 *The Savage Mind*. University of Chicago Press, Chicago, Illinois.

—— 1967a *Structural Anthropology*. Anchor Books, Doubleday, Garden City, New York.

—— 1967b "The Story of Asdiwal," in *The Structural Study of Myth and Totemism*. Edmund Leach, (editor). Tavistock Publications, London.

—— 1969 *The Raw and the Cooked*. Harper and Row, New York.

MacPherson, C. B. 1962 *The Political Theory of Possessive Individualism*. Oxford University Press, London.

Munden, Kenneth J., M.D. 1958 "A Contribution to the Psychological Understanding of the Cowboy and His Myth," *American Imago*, Vol. 15, No. 2.

Propp, Vladimir 1968 *Morphology of the Folktale*. University of Texas Press, Austin.

Polanyi, Karl 1965 *The Great Transformation*. Beacon Press, Boston.

Saussure, F. de. 1960 *Course in General Linguistics*. Philosophical Library, New York.

Smith, Henry Nash 1950 *The Virgin Land*. Vintage Books, Random House, New York.

U.S. Congress, Senate, Select Committee on Presidential Campaign Activities. 1973 *Watergate and Related Activities. Phase 1: Watergate Investigation*. 73rd Congress, 1st Session.

Warshow, Robert 1964 *The Immediate Experience*. Anchor Books, Doubleday, Garden City, New York.

42

PRINCIPLES OF NARRATION

David Bordwell

Source: *Narration in the Fiction Film*, Madison, WI: University of Wisconsin Press, 1985, pp. 48–62.

My account of *Rear Window* does not constitute a critical interpretation. I have not labeled Jeff a voyeur, judged his peeping nice or naughty, or sought to establish him as a "castrated" adventurer fantasizing the dismembering of a woman's body. Indeed, my sketch is not even an analysis of the film, since specifying the spectator's activity cannot itself provide that. For the viewer, constructing the story takes precedence; the effects of the text are registered, but its causes go unremarked. This is not to say that these activities are, strictly speaking, unconscious; most work of narrative comprehension seems to occur in what Freud called the *pre*conscious, the realm of elements "capable of entering consciousness."[1] The spectator simply has no concepts or terms for the textual elements and systems that shape responses. It is the job of theory to construct them, the job of analysis to show them at work. A full theory of narration must be able to specify the objective devices and forms that elicit the spectator's activity. That is the task of this and the next three chapters. Theory must also go beyond the perceiver's relation to the text by situating the text within contexts of which the perceiver is seldom explicitly aware. These contexts are historical ones, and I shall consider those most pertinent to narration in Part 3. What an account of the spectator's work has taught us is that theory and analysis must explain not only localized effects but whole films, treating them as eliciting the spectator's ongoing construction of the story. Eisenstein's advice to his students holds good for the study of narration as textual form: "Think in stages of a process."[2]

From this chapter forward, my focus is on how film form and style function in relation to narrational strategies and ends. As an alternative, we could undertake empirical investigations of how actual spectators construe particular films. While worthwhile, this enterprise would not necessarily lead to insights into how films encourage, sustain, block, or undercut specific viewing operations. As I have said throughout, formal systems both *cue* and *constrain* the viewer's construction of a story. The theory I propose cannot predict any actual response; it can only construct distinctions and historical contexts which suggest the most logically coherent range of conventionally permissible responses.

We have seen theories of narration founder upon superficial analogies between film and other media—literature or theater (the mimetic approach); literature, speech, or writing (the diegetic approach). The theory I propose sees narration as a formal activity, a notion comparable to Eisenstein's rhetoric of form. In keeping with a perceptual-cognitive approach to the spectator's work, this theory treats narration as a process which is not in its basic aims specific to any medium. As a dynamic process, narration deploys the materials and procedures of each medium for its ends. Thinking of narration in this way yields considerable scope for investigation while still allowing us to build in the specific possibilities of the film medium. In addition, a form-centered approach sets itself the task of explaining how narration functions in the totality of the film. Narrational patterning is a major part of the process by which we grasp films as more or less coherent wholes.

Fabula, syuzhet, and style

In previous chapters I have assumed a difference between the story that is represented and the actual representation of it, the form in which the perceiver actually encounters it. This crucial distinction may go back to Aristotle,[3] but it was most fully theorized by the Russian Formalists, and it is indispensable to a theory of narration.

Presented with two narrative events, we look for causal or spatial or temporal links. The imaginary construct we create, progressively and retroactively, was termed by Formalists the *fabula* (sometimes translated as "story"). More specifically, the fabula embodies the action as a chronological, cause-and-effect chain of events occurring within a given duration and a spatial field. In *Rear Window*, as in most detective tales, there is an overt process of fabula construction, since the investigation of the crime involves establishing certain connections among events. Putting the fabula together requires us to construct the story of the ongoing inquiry while at the same time framing and testing hypotheses about past events. That is, the story of the investigation is a search for the concealed story of a crime. By the end of the typical detective tale, all story events can be fitted into a single pattern of time, space, and causality.

The fabula is thus a pattern which perceivers of narratives create through assumptions and inferences. It is the developing result of picking up narrative cues, applying schemata, framing and testing hypotheses. Ideally, the fabula can be embodied in a verbal synopsis, as general or as detailed as circumstances require. Yet the fabula, however imaginary, is not a whimsical or arbitrary construct. The viewer builds the fabula on the basis of prototype schemata (identifiable types of persons, actions, locales, etc.), template schemata (principally the "canonic" story), and procedural schemata (a search for appropriate motivations and relations of causality, time, and space). To the extent that these processes are intersubjective, so is the fabula that is created. In principle, viewers of a film will agree about either what the story is or what factors obscure or render ambiguous the adequate construction of the story.

It would be an error to take the fabula, or story, as the profilmic event. A film's fabula is never materially present on the screen or soundtrack. When we see a shot of Jeff looking out his window, his action is a representation which signals us to infer a story event (Jeff looks out his window). The same piece of information might have been conveyed many other ways, many of them requiring no sight or sound of Jeff at all. The staging of the action, as Eisenstein showed, is itself a representational act. This theoretical move lets us avoid that a priori favoring of certain film techniques characteristic of mimetic theories.

The fabula, writes Tynianov, "can only be guessed at, but it is not a given."[4] What is given? What sorts of phenomenally present materials and forms do we encounter? We can analyze the film as consisting of two systems and a remaining body of material, diagramed in figure 1. The *syuzhet* (usually translated as "plot") is the actual arrangement and presentation of the fabula in the film. It is not the text in toto.[5] It is a more abstract construct, the patterning of the story as a blow-by-blow recounting of the film could render it. The syuzhet is a system because it arranges components—the story events and states of affairs—according to specific principles. As Boris Tomashevsky puts it: "The fabula is opposed to the syuzhet, which is built out of the same events, but the syuzhet respects their order in the work and the series of information processes which designate them."[6] "Syuzhet" names the architectonics of the film's presentation of the fabula; hence the rightward arrow in the diagram.[7] Logically, syuzhet patterning is independent of the medium; the same syuzhet patterns could be embodied in a novel, a play, or a film.

Style also constitutes a system in that it too mobilizes components—particular instantiations of film techniques—according to principles of organization. There are other uses of the term "style" (e.g., to designate

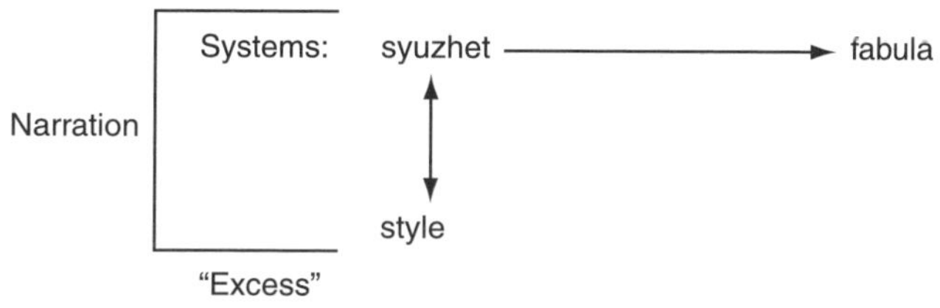

Figure 1 Film as Phenomenal Process.

recurrent features of structure or texture in a body of films, such as "neo-realist style"), but in this context, "style" simply names the film's systematic use of cinematic devices. Style is thus wholly ingredient to the medium. Style interacts with syuzhet in various ways; hence the two-way arrow in the diagram.

An example may illustrate how syuzhet and style differ. In *Rear Window*, the syuzhet consists of the particular pattern of events (actions, scenes, turning points, plot twists) depicting the tale of Mrs. Thorwald's murder and its investigation and the tale of Lisa and Jeff's romance. When in the preceding chapter I described formal patterns of withheld knowledge or abrupt revelation, I was referring principally to the construction of the syuzhet. The same film, however, can be described as a steady flow of applications of cinematic techniques—mise-en-scène, cinematography, editing, and sound. In one scene, Jeff and Stella are spotted by Thorwald. They step quickly back into Jeff's room (figure movement, setting); they whisper (sound) and douse the lamp (lighting); the camera tracks quickly back to a long shot (cinematography); and all of this occurs after the crucial shot of Thorwald turning to look out his window (editing).

Note that in a narrative film these two systems coexist. They can do this because syuzhet and style each treat different aspects of the phenomenal process. The syuzhet embodies the film as a "dramaturgical" process; style embodies it as a "technical" one. While it would often be arbitrary to separate the two systems in the process of perception, the distinction has precedent in much narrative theory.[8] Indeed, we shall discover one mode of narration that requires us to keep syuzhet and style conceptually separate. Assuming that the distinction is warranted, I want now to spell out the relations between syuzhet and fabula, and syuzhet and style.

In discussing the spectator's activity, I stressed the role of narrative schemata.[9] The theoretical concept of the syuzhet offers a way of analyzing the aspects of a film that the spectator organizes into an ongoing story. It should be clear, though, that the syuzhet is not identical with what Chapter 3 called the canonic story format. The latter, we can now see, comprises schematic assumptions about both the fabula and the syuzhet. The viewer's tendency to assume that characters have goals pertains to causality in the fabula; it does not imply anything about syuzhet organization. But the assumption that the spectator will encounter an exposition or an ending pertains to the organization of the syuzhet. The "canonic story" nonetheless offers an example of how assumptions about syuzhet and fabula factors play a considerable role in narrative comprehension.

As a distinction, the fabula/syuzhet pair cuts across media. At a gross level, the same fabula could be inferred from a novel, a film, a painting, or a play. Thus one difficulty of enunciative theories—the forced analogy between linguistic categories and nonverbal phenomena—vanishes. As Meir Sternberg puts it, any narrative medium utilizes "a largely extraverbal logic" that includes "the twofold development of the action, as it objectively and straightforwardly progresses in the fictive world from beginning to end (within the fabula) and as it is deformed and patterned into progressing in our mind during the reading-process (within the syuzhet)."[10] The conception of syuzhet avoids surface-phenomena distinctions (such as person, tense, metalanguage) and relies upon more supple principles basic to all narrative representation. Consequently, and contrary to what some writers believe, the fabula/syuzhet distinction does not replicate the *histoire/discours* distinction held by enunciation theories.[11] The fabula is not an unmarked enunciative act; it is not a speech act at all but a set of inferences.

I asserted that the syuzhet composes story situations and events according to specifiable principles. Chapter 3 showed that when we perceive and comprehend a narrative text, we tend to construct certain patterns among events. We can now see how the film's syuzhet provides a basis for this activity. Three sorts of principles relate the syuzhet to the fabula.

1. *Narrative "logic."* In constructing a fabula, the perceiver defines some phenomena as events while constructing relations among them. These relations are primarily causal ones. An event will be assumed to be a consequence of another event, of a character trait, or of some general law. The syuzhet can facilitate this process by systematically encouraging us to make linear causal inferences. But the syuzhet can also arrange events so as to block or complicate the construction of causal relations. This happens with the false clues in *Rear Window*. Narrative logic also includes a more abstract principle of similarity and difference which I call *parallelism*. Thorwald's murder of his wife has no significant effect on most of his neighbors; one function of the courtyard vignettes is to parallel the romantic relations of Jeff and Lisa with other male/female relations. What counts as an event, a cause, an effect, a similarity, or a difference—all will be determined within the context of the individual film.

2. *Time*. Narrative time has several aspects, well analyzed by Gérard Genette. The syuzhet can cue us to construct fabula events in any sequence (a matter of *order*). The syuzhet can suggest fabula events as occurring in virtually any time span (*duration*). And the syuzhet can signal fabula events as taking place any number of times (*frequency*). These aspects can all assist or block the viewer's construction of fabula time. Again, temporal representation will vary with historical convention and the context of the individual film.

3. *Space*. Fabula events must be represented as occurring in a spatial frame of reference, however vague or abstract. The syuzhet can facilitate construction of fabula space by informing us of the relevant surroundings and the positions and paths assumed by the story's agents. The confinement to Jeff's courtyard in *Rear Window* is an instance of the use of syuzhet devices to advance our construction of fabula space. But the film could also

impede our comprehension by suspending, muddling, or undercutting our construction of space.

Depending on how the syuzhet presents the fabula, there will be particular spectatorial effects. Armed with the notion of different narrative principles and the concept of the syuzhet's distortion of fabula information, we can begin to account for the concrete narrational work of any film. It is obvious, for instance, that *Rear Window* depends upon withholding certain fabula information; we can now see that our schematizing and hypothesizing activities are guided by the syuzhet's cues about causality, time, and space. The basic-training aspect of the film's early portions—its tendency to give visual cues, let us draw inferences, and then confirm or disconfirm them by verbal statement—arises from manipulation of causal information. To take a specific scene: while Jeff is asleep, we see a woman leave with Thorwald and wonder if she is his wife; the syuzhet has generated this suspicion that Mrs. Thorwald is still alive by not showing us this woman (who is not Mrs. Thorwald) entering the apartment. The syuzhet of *Rear Window* also blocks our knowledge by limiting space; we can use only narrowly restricted views of the courtyard to construct the fabula. And *Rear Window* is not exceptional in its limitations, concealments, and revelations. For theoretical purposes it may sometimes be convenient to take as an ideal baseline an instance in which the syuzhet is constructed so as to permit maximum access to the fabula. But every syuzhet uses retardation to postpone complete construction of the fabula. At the very least, the end of the story, or the means whereby we arrive there, will be withheld. Thus the syuzhet aims not to let us construct the fabula in some logically pristine state but rather to guide us to construct the fabula in a specific way, by arousing in us particular expectations at this or that point, eliciting our curiosity or suspense, and pulling surprises along the way.

In some cases, the syuzhet will include masses of material that block our construction of the fabula. Such material may encourage us to treat the syuzhet as interpreting or commenting on the fabula. In *October*, both Kerensky and General Kornilov appeal to the slogan "For God and Country." Suddenly we cut to a series of statues of gods from many cultures. These shots do not help us to construct the spatial, temporal, or logical connections among story events; in fabula terms they are a digression. Nonetheless, the sequence constitutes syuzhet manipulation. As a little dissertation on the very idea of God, the passage emphasizes the cultural variability of religion and suggests that an appeal to the holy often veils political opportunism. The inserted material insists in its patterned development that we motivate it transtextually, as a species of rhetorical argument. A novelist's commentary, however digressive, forms an integral part of the syuzhet, and so do Eisenstein's essayistic interpolations.

The syuzhet, then, is the dramaturgy of the fiction film, the organized set of cues prompting us to infer and assemble story information. As the diagram on p. [247] suggests, the film's style can interact with the syuzhet in various ways. Film technique is customarily used to perform syuzhet tasks—providing information, cueing hypotheses, and so forth. In the "normal" film, that is, the syuzhet system controls the stylistic system—in Formalist terms, the syuzhet is the "dominant." For example, patterns in the syuzhet's presentation of story information will be matched by stylistic patterns, as when at the close of *Rear Window* a camera movement homologous to that in the opening underlines the changes in the lives of the courtyard's inhabitants.

Still, this is not to say that the systematic employment of film techniques—that is, the film's style—is wholly a vehicle for the syuzhet. When alternative techniques exist for a given syuzhet purpose, it may make a difference which technique is chosen. For instance, the syuzhet may require that two story events be cued as occurring simultaneously. The simultaneity may be denoted by crosscutting from one event to the other, by staging the two actions in depth, by use of split-screen techniques, or by the inclusion of particular objects in the setting (such as a television set broadcasting a "live" event). Whatever stylistic choice is made may have different effects on the spectator's perceptual and cognitive activity. Style is thus a notable factor in its own right, even when it is "only" supporting the syuzhet.

Film style can also take shapes not justified by the syuzhet's manipulation of story information. If in *Rear Window* Hitchcock systematically cut from Jeff's gaze to closeups of misleading or irrelevant objects which he could not see, then the stylistic procedure itself could vie for prominence with the syuzhet's task of presenting the story. True, we might take this stylistic flourish as a syuzhet maneuver to baffle us about causality or space; but if the device were repeated systematically across the film with no clear link to the developing syuzhet and fabula, then the more economical explanation would be that style has come forward to claim our attention independent of syuzhet/fabula relations. Chapter 12 will show how this happens in a variety of films. For analytical purposes, then, we must grant a potential disparity between the stylistic system and the syuzhet system, even if such a tendency is rare.

It is evident that both syuzhet and style invite the spectator to apply the motivational rationales discussed in Chapter 3. At the syuzhet level, when Jeff and Stella recoil from Thorwald's look, the audience justifies this event as psychologically plausible and compositionally necessary for what follows. At the stylistic level, when Jeff scans the apartment block and the next shot is of Thorwald's windows, we assume the shot to be compositionally relevant, grant it a certain realism (Jeff's point of view), and acquiesce to a generic convention (this could be a suspenseful buildup). In the hypothetical example of patterned cutaways to irrelevant objects, we would try to motivate them compositionally, realistically, or transtextually; but if all were unequal to the task set by the style, we would have a case of "artistic motivation," whereby the materials and forms of the medium constitute the chief object of interest.

It is time for a formal definition. In the fiction film, narration is *the process whereby the film's syuzhet and style interact in the course of cueing and channeling the spectator's construction of the fabula.* Thus it is not only when the syuzhet arranges fabula information that the film narrates. Narration also includes stylistic processes. It would of course be possible to treat narration solely as a matter of syuzhet/fabula relations, but this would leave out the ways in which the filmic texture affects the spectator's activity. We have already seen that the spectator possesses stylistic schemata as well as others, and these invariably affect the overall process of narrative representation. Moreover, by including style within narration, we can analyze stylistic departures from the syuzhet's project. In an earlier example, a cut from Jeff's gaze to irrelevant objects would be a narrational act as much as would a cut to relevant ones. Narration is the dynamic interaction between the syuzhet's transmission of story information and what Tynianov called "the movement, the rise and fall of the stylistic masses."[12]

Is there anything in a narrative film that is not narrational? Any image or sound can contribute to narration, but we can also attend to an element for its sheer perceptual salience. Roland Barthes has spoken of a film's "third meaning," one lying beyond denotation and connotation: the realm in which casual lines, colors, expressions, and textures become "fellow travelers" of the story.[13] Kristin Thompson has identified these elements as "excess," materials which may stand out perceptually but which do not fit either narrative or stylistic patterns.[14] (See fig. 1.) As we have seen, the spectator's categories push her or him to construct objects and denotative meaning from the outset. The canonic story in particular favors the dominance of story-world factors. From this standpoint, it is as if nothing but narration matters. But in the first shot of *Rear Window*, we can choose not to construct a story world and instead savor random colors, gestures, and sounds. These "excessive" elements are utterly unjustified, even by aesthetic motivation. Now, this attitude is actually quite difficult to maintain over a long period, since it offers little perceptual and cognitive payoff. The *trouvailles* will never add up. Nonetheless, there may be aspects of a film that we cannot attribute to narration. In some cases, as Thompson shows with *Ivan the Terrible*, "excess" may offer a useful way into the film's overall formal work. "A perception of a film that includes its excess implies an awareness of the structures (including conventions) at work in the film, since excess is precisely those elements that escape unifying impulses. Such an approach to viewing films can allow us to look further into a film, renewing its ability to intrigue us by its strangeness."[15]

Whatever its suggestiveness as a critical concept, excess lies outside my concern here. The rest of this book is devoted to the process of narration. In the rest of this chapter and in all of the next, I will concentrate on basic principles of syuzhet patterning. We need to examine how a syuzhet may organize story material, how it may limit or expand our access to fabula information. We also need to understand overall narrational strategies, the broad aims that syuzhet tactics and film style may fulfill. Subsequent chapters will concentrate on how narration may render fabula time and space, and there we will take up specific stylistic procedures.

Tactics of syuzhet construction

The analysis of narration can begin with the syuzhet's tactics for presenting fabula information. We must grasp how the syuzhet manages its basic task—the presentation of story logic, time, and space—always recalling that in practice we never get ideally maximum access to the fabula. In general, the syuzhet shapes our perception of the fabula by controlling (1) the quantity of fabula information to which we have access; (2) the degree of pertinence we can attribute to the presented information; and (3) the formal correspondences between syuzhet presentation and fabula data.

Assume that an ideal syuzhet supplies information in the "correct" amount to permit coherent and steady construction of the fabula. Given this hypostatized reference point, we can distinguish a syuzhet which supplies too little information about the story and a syuzhet which supplies too much: in other words, a "rarefied" syuzhet versus an "overloaded" one.

Now at any given point an ordinary narrative may give us more or less information than the hypostatized ideal. A detective tale might bamboozle us with a plethora of clues and a paucity of motives. Our normal syuzhet, then, reduces to a demand for enough information for the construction of a fabula according to conventions of genre or mode. *Rear Window* holds back some data and sometimes gives us "too much" to assimilate at the moment, but eventually the quantity proves "just right" for generic needs. The momentarily overloaded or rarified approach of the mystery film is in fact normal for syuzhet construction in its genre. But our detective story would leap out of its genre if it were radically to pursue either strategy in its recounting of the detective's investigation or in its construction of the solution. For example, Antonioni's *Blow-Up* fails as a detective story: it presents too few pieces of information to enable the protagonist, or us, to solve the crime (or even to determine what the crime involves). Two conclusions follow. At local points, "ordinary" films can indulge in either overload or rarefaction tactics; and extraordinary films can indulge in either, or both, consistently and throughout.

Again, assume an ideal syuzhet which supplies information which is relevant to the coherent and steady construction of the fabula. Opposed to this, we can situate any syuzhet which indulges in information not relevant to such construction. Godard's films, for instance, are often peppered with citations, skewed allusions, and interruptions which cannot be clearly related to the story. We tend to take these as digressions. It is of course often difficult to judge the pertinence of a piece of information at the moment it emerges. Something which seems out of place may eventually slot itself neatly into the total fabula. (Here we touch on the problem of gaps, to be taken up shortly.) In any case, in judging the pertinence of information as in judging its quantity, the analyst will need to specify generic and other transtextual constraints. The criteria of relevance in a drama will not be appropriate to a farce. And some films, such as *L'année dernière á Marienbad* or *Not Reconciled*, make it hard to determine a main fabula path from which we could measure deviations—exactly a point which characterizes these films' formal operations.

The most analytically important variable is the set of formal correspondences between fabula and syuzhet. That is, to what extent does the unfolding syuzhet correspond to the logical, temporal, and spatial nature of the fabula we construct? Are there disparities, incompatibilities, lacks of synchronization? Any syuzhet selects what fabula events to present and combines them in particular ways. Selection creates gaps; combination creates composition.

No syuzhet explicitly presents all of the fabula events that we presume took place. A princess is born; in the next scene she is eighteen years old. In leaving a gap in the syuzhet, the narration implies that nothing extraordinary took place in those intervening years. We will assume that the princess had an infancy, a childhood, and an adolescence. (Knowing the conventions of fairy tales, we might also expect that she will soon meet a prince.) Temporal gaps are the most common sort, but any mystery or riddle narrative may also contain causal gaps. (Why is Mrs. Thorwald missing?) The syuzhet can present us with spatial gaps too, as when it withholds knowledge about a character's whereabouts or neglects to define the action's locales. Gaps are among the clearest cues for the viewer to act upon, since they evoke the entire process of schema formation and hypothesis testing.

Sternberg points out that gaps can be *temporary* or *permanent*.[16] That is, the informational hole in the fabula can be plugged (quickly or eventually) or never plugged. In our fairy tale, the gap is fleeting: we leave the princess's cradle and then see her as a young woman; we very rapidly fill in the gap. In a detective story, the crucial causal gap—e.g., what became of Mrs. Thorwald—is maintained much longer, but it too is eventually plugged. In some narratives, however, a gap remains open to the end; Iago's motive is the classic example. We can characterize syuzhet processes as working to open, prolong, or close gaps in fabula events.

We can also describe a gap as relatively *diffuse* or *focused*. How the princess passed those eighteen years is unspecified; we can fill the gap only with general and typical assumptions. But "Did Thorwald kill his wife?" is a clear-cut question demanding a precise answer. Sometimes a syuzhet will conjure up a diffuse gap only to bring it into focus later. For instance, a flashback might jump back to an otherwise unremarked interval and sharpen our sense of what information might fill the gap.

The syuzhet can also *flaunt* or *suppress* gaps in the fabula. A gap is flaunted when we know that there is something we need to know. Our fairy tale calls the temporal gap to our attention, demanding that we fill the eighteen years of the princess's life with the help of our conventional assumptions. A detective story also typically calls attention to its gaps, making us fret over our lack of certain data. Other syuzhets do not call attention to their gaps. That *Rear Window* does not show Thorwald's mistress enter his apartment is a striking case of a suppressed gap. At the time we see her leave, we do not know that her entry has been omitted.

It should be evident that selections of fabula events shape the constructive activities of the spectator. Temporary gaps point us forward and build up surprise; a permanent gap invites us to apply a "scanning" strategy, sorting back through single episodes looking for information we might have missed. A focused gap obviously tends to solicit exclusive and homogeneous hypotheses, while a diffuse gap yields room for more open-ended inferential work. A flaunted gap may warn us to pay attention: either the omitted fabula information will become important later, or the narration is misleading us by stressing something that will prove insignificant. If a gap is suppressed, however, surprise is the likely result, especially if the omitted information ranks low on a scale of probabilities. These are only general indications, but they suggest the range of effects that "gapping" tactics can achieve. In each case, it must be remembered, the viewer will strive to justify the very presence of the gap by appeal to principles of compositional, realistic, transtextual, and artistic motivation.

Gaps are created by choosing to present certain pieces of fabula information and to hold back others. The pieces of information selected can be combined in a great variety of ways. In cinema, the narration can arrange fabula information temporally or spatially, as we shall see in Chapters 6 and 7. For now we can look at two general principles that govern syuzhet composition in any medium: retardation and redundancy. Both offer clear-cut instances of how textual form both triggers and constrains spectator activity.

We have already noted the overall importance of retardation in cueing the spectator's comprehension. Only by delaying the revelation of some information can the syuzhet arouse anticipation, curiosity, suspense, and surprise. For example, *Rear Window* lays out its fabula information so that (a) the crucial murder evidence emerges piecemeal and the case is not solved too quickly, and (b) the murder investigation suspends and (possibly) resolves Jeff and Lisa's romantic problems. The "God and Country" sequence of *October* breaks off from presenting the fabula and interpolates material that not only retards the outcome of the story action (how will the battle between Kornilov and Kerensky turn out?) but also has its own miniature retardatory curve: the point could have been made by an intertitle rather than dozens of shots which form, to say the least, a fairly difficult passage.

The very centrality of retardation as a principle demands that we make some distinctions. Meir Sternberg has shown that retardatory material can be considered from many angles: the nature of the material (action, description, commentary, etc.), the magnitude of it, its location (how annoying is it here?), its relation to what it retards, how it is motivated, how it functions, its relation to transtextual norms, and its relation to basic properties of the medium.[17] We could then characterize *Rear Window's* red herrings—the false leads of Thorwald's trunk and the zinnia garden—as retardatory material which is action centered, large-scale (each false lead takes several scenes to work out), positioned to maximize suspense, motivated compositionally and generically, and, because manifested in props and setting, conforming to a conception of the film medium as one suitable for revealing dramatic situations through significant objects (Hitchcock's well-known adherence to Pudovkin's dictum about "plastic material"). The "God and Country" sequence, on the other hand, represents commentary and not fabula action; though it is of relatively short duration, its nondiegetic motivation subscribes to different conventions of genre and mode (the Soviet montage film); it is more annoying in its placement and even more so in its cryptic working out; and its rebus-like syntax links it to a quite different conception of film (Eisenstein's "intellectual cinema"). In any given case, we can apply these distinctions to characterize how the syuzhet impedes the viewer's acquisition of fabula information.

Retardation may occur when the syuzhet postpones revealing certain items of fabula information. Because this postponement stands out most sharply in expositional passages, Sternberg has studied them most closely, and his efforts show how overall patterns of retardation have perceptual and cognitive consequences.

Exposition is measured with respect to what theorists of drama call the "point of attack," that juncture in the fabula that forms the initial "discriminated occasion" in the syuzhet. But the receiver of the narrative must be informed of the fabula events previous to this initial scene. The transmission of this information is the task of the exposition, and several choices present themselves. At some point in the syuzhet we might be given the prior fabula information in a lump, a practice Sternberg calls *concentrated* exposition. Or the narration might scatter the information through the syuzhet, interweaving it with ongoing present action. This is *distributed* exposition. *Rear Window* utilizes concentrated exposition in its first two scenes. We are provided, visually in the first sequence and both visually and sonically in the second, with the pertinent background to Jeff's situation. The exposition can also be put at any syuzhet point: in the beginning (*preliminary* exposition, as in *Rear Window*) or later (*delayed* exposition). We have then three general expositional possibilities. The classic fairy tale employs preliminary and concentrated exposition: "Once upon a time" usually signals it. Popular fiction and film typically weave all the exposition into the first scene or two, thus employing preliminary and fairly concentrated exposition. The crime plot in the detective tale is usually revealed through delayed and concentrated exposition, a long scene near the end of the syuzhet recounting the events leading up to the crime. And Ibsen's practice of "continuous exposition" constitutes an adherence to both delayed and distributed principles: prior fabula events come to light gradually throughout the entire play.

As Sternberg shows, each of these options triggers different inferential activities on the part of the spectator. Concentrated and preliminary exposition supplies a strong primacy effect, solid grounds for confident hypothesis formation. Distributed and delayed exposition encourages curiosity about prior events and can lead to a suspension of strong or absolute hypotheses. There is also that exposition peppered with warning signals, which Sternberg calls a "rhetoric of anticipatory caution."[18] In a limit case, our primacy effect might be completely undermined by the suppression of key fabula information; we would then be forced to revise our assumptions and hypotheses when the data come to light. Sternberg calls this "the rise and fall of first impressions."[19]

The syuzhet also repeats. In cinema, an intertitle may describe an action, and then we see that action; or scenes will be presented that allude, visually or sonically, to events already completed. Such repetitions reinforce assumptions, inferences, and hypotheses about story information. Let us call this sort of functional, significant repetition "redundancy."

The possibilities of redundancy in any narration have been exhaustively surveyed by Susan R. Suleiman; I abbreviate and modify her categories.

1. At the level of the fabula, any given event, character, quality, story function, environment, or character commentary may be redundant with respect to any other. For example, A may declare B to be a rake; that statement can be redundant in view of B's overt behavior (he tries to seduce women), or his story function (he is put there to seduce the heroine), or his name, or his surroundings, or other characters' judgments, or all of these.

2. At the level of the syuzhet, the narration can achieve redundancy by reiterating its relation to the perceiver; by repeating its own commentary about an event or character; or by adhering to a consistent point of view. In *October*, the mock-heroic comparison of Kerensky to historic figures achieves redundancy by all these means: reiteration of direct address; constant comparison between him and the statuary, architecture, and bric-a-brac of the Winter Palace; and adherence to a satiric omniscience throughout.

3. At the level of the relations between syuzhet and fabula, redundancy can be achieved by representing an event more than once (as Todorov puts it, "Each event is narrated at least twice"[20]), or by making any fabula event, character, quality, story function, environment, or character commentary redundant with respect to narrational commentary. At the start of *Rear*

Window, the furnishings of Jeff's apartment tell us that he is adventurous; in the second scene, Jeff tells his editor (and us) the same thing.

In most narrative texts, redundancy operates so completely on all these levels that we scarcely notice it—until we encounter a text that is not so redundant, or not redundant in ways that we are used to. Suleiman's scheme lets us spell out exactly how a film can reinforce important information and thus guide our grasp of the syuzhet.

To sum up: In any narrative text in any medium, the syuzhet controls the amount and the degree of pertinence of the information we receive. The syuzhet creates various sorts of gaps in our construction of the fabula; it also combines information according to principles of retardation and redundancy. All of these procedures function to cue and guide the spectator's narrative activity.

Knowledge, self-consciousness, and communicativeness

Choosing what to include in the syuzhet and what to leave tacit, deciding how to retard the syuzhet and where redundancy is needed—such particular syuzhet tactics depend on broad narrational strategies. How can we characterize these strategies? Meir Sternberg has suggested three categories that will prove helpful. Although his terms are ones usually reserved for conscious agents, they can be applied to narrative processes with the same legitimacy with which we call a picture "graceful." I should add that these characteristics are properly narrational in that they not only shape syuzhet processes but often involve stylistic options too.

A film's narration can be called more or less *knowledgeable* about the fabula it represents. Every film will employ norms of relevant knowledge for our construction of the fabula. In a mystery film, circumstantial information divulged about past events can have more structural centrality than information about a character's current state of mind. In a musical or melodrama, however, information about immediate states of mind might take priority. We know these norms through acquaintance with genre conventions and through qualitative and quantitative factors in the given film (placement of information in a highlighting context, repetition of information across the film). But knowledgeability has other aspects as well.

First, what *range* of knowledge does the narration have at its disposal? The narration can be more or less *restricted. Rear Window*, for instance, confines itself almost wholly to what Jeff knows (with a few significant exceptions). In *The Birth of a Nation*, on the other hand, the narration presents more information about the overall story action than any character has.

Unlike prose fiction, the fictional film seldom confines its narration to what only a single character knows. Most commonly, portions of the syuzhet will be organized around one character's knowledge and other portions will confine themselves to the knowledge held by another character. Such restrictions and divisions will inevitably create gaps in the fabula. We tend to motivate restricted narration realistically ("After all, we know as much as she plausibly could") but to motivate more unrestricted narration transtextually ("In films of this sort, you always know more . . ."). Both sorts of narration are, of course, fundamentally motivated by compositional requirements.

We can ask a second question. How profound is the knowledge available to the narration? This is a matter of *depth*, of degrees of subjectivity and objectivity. A narration may present the whole of a character's mental life, either conscious or unconscious; it may confine itself to the character's optical or auditory experience; it may eschew any but behavioral indications of psychological states; it may even minimize those. For example, although the narration of *The Birth of a Nation* is relatively unrestricted in range, it penetrates the characters' minds less deeply than does the narration of, say, *Secrets of a Soul*, which represents the protagonist's dreams. *The Maltese Falcon*, which contains one shot cued as being through Spade's eyes, is less subjective than *Rear Window*, with its many optical point-of-view shots. Again, depth of knowledge can be justified on compositional, realistic, and/or transtextual grounds.

Range and depth of information can be related in various ways. Restricted narration does not guarantee greater depth, nor does depth at any point guarantee that the narration will stay constantly limited. Hitchcock's films alternate between sequences of great subjectivity and sequences that flaunt the narration's unrestricted knowledge. In general, narrative films are constantly modulating the range and depth of the narration's knowledge. Such shifts provide strong cues for hypothesis formation.

Narration also relates "rhetorically" to the perceiver, and this opens up other areas of inquiry. To what extent does the narration display a recognition that it is addressing an audience? We can call this the degree of *self-consciousness*. For example, Eisenstein's films often intensify an emotional climax by having characters look at or gesture to the audience. Similarly, a retrospective voice-over commentary can push the narration toward a greater self-consciousness, especially if the addressee is not another fictional character. We can see many tactics of redundancy, such as repetition of fabula information by the syuzhet, as evidencing a degree of self-consciousness (e.g., Eisenstein's repeated intercutting of Kerensky with statues). At the beginning of *Rear Window*, the camera movement presents aspects of courtyard life for purposes of quick exposition. In contrast, the artificial but relatively inoffensive frontality of figure position we observed in figure 1 earlier is less self-conscious than these cases. When we speak of being "aware of manipulation" in a Lang film and "unaware" of such manipulation in a Hawks film, we are usually referring to the narration's greater or lesser acknowledgement that a tale is being presented for a perceiver.

The concept of self-consciousness offers distinct advantages over "enunciative" accounts of speaker-listener relations, such as the applications of Benveniste's grammatical theory. For one thing, self-consciousness is a matter of degree, not of absolutes (as, say, "first person" and "third person" are). All filmic narrations are self-conscious, but some are more so than others. Furthermore, "self-consciousness" varies in degree and function within different genres and modes of film practice. Groucho Marx's asides to the audience are more self-conscious than Popeye's muttered imprecations, but the patriotic voice-over of Capra's *Why We Fight* is more self-conscious than either. The staging of most Hollywood shots reveals a moderate self-consciousness by grouping characters for our best view. In a musical, characters may sing directly to us—a moment of stronger narrational self-consciousness codified by the genre. By contrast, Antonioni will stage scenes with characters turned away from us, and the overt suppression of their expressions and reactions becomes in context a token of the narration's awareness of the viewer. In the celebrated filling station sequence of *Deux ou trois choses que je sais d'elle*, Godard's voice-over commentator is so acutely aware of the audience that he is at a loss to decide what to show us next. As a critical category, self-consciousness helps us consider to what extent and with what effects the film lets a recognition of the audience's presence shape the syuzhet.

At one point in Hitchcock's *Shadow of a Doubt* (1943), the sinister Uncle Charlie settles down to read the evening paper. Earlier in the film our knowledge has occasionally been restricted to his knowledge (as in the first scene, when he learned that two men were shadowing him). There has even been some depth of subjectivity, with certain shots being framed from his optical point of view. Now, while he reads, he is filmed from a low angle, the outspread newspaper blocking his face. There is silence. A puff of cigar smoke. Slowly the paper is lowered, and Charlie is now frowning thoughtfully. He looks off right. Cut to his optical point of view of the opposite end of the room: no one notices him. Cut back to Uncle Charlie, who calls his niece Ann to him. He proceeds to make a toy house out of newspaper and, in tearing out a portion, folds it up and slips it into his pocket.

This short passage shows how a narration shifts its depth of knowledge (objective to more subjective) and how it can gain a degree of self-consciousness (the pause in telling us Uncle Charlie's reaction). The scene also illustrates another aspect of narration—what Sternberg calls its *communicativeness*. Although a narration has a particular range of knowledge available, the narration may or may not communicate all that information. In literature, for example, a diarist-narrator will have a very restricted ken, but she or he can be completely communicative about what she or he knows. In *Shadow of a Doubt*, the narration has established itself as restrictive (frequently limited to Charlie's knowledge) and potentially subjective (e.g., previous optical point-of-view shots). Now, however, the low-angle shot of Charlie reading does not reveal the newspaper article that he sees. It is not just that the narration flaunts this curiosity gap, though it certainly does. The narration holds back exactly the sort of information to which it has earlier claimed complete access. The suppressiveness of the newspaper shot is emphasized all the more when, after Charlie lowers the paper, the narration immediately switches to his optical point of view. If we had been permitted to share his vision an instant sooner, we would have seen the offending article. As it is, the film will make us wait some time to find out.

The degree of communicativeness can be judged by considering how willingly the narration shares the information to which its degree of knowledge entitles it. The unrestricted narration of *The Birth of a Nation* is highly communicative; the only information withheld is of a "suspense" variety (i.e., what will happen next). The sharply restricted narration of *Rear Window* is likewise generally communicative in that (on the whole) it tells us all that Jeff knows at any given moment. If *The Birth of a Nation* were suddenly to conceal the fact that the Little Colonel founds the Ku Klux Klan, or if *Rear Window* were to withhold some crucial action of Jeff's, the narration would tend toward a lesser degree of communicativeness. That a highly "omniscient" narration and a highly restricted narration may both be considered communicative shows the importance of context.

As with self-consciousness, every film is uncommunicative to at least a slight degree; there may be a fluctuating relation between the film's overall informational norm and the extent of concealment at various moments. In one sense, any deviation from a film's internal norm of communicativeness becomes a mark of suppressiveness. The narration could tell more, but it doesn't. Transtextual motivation, however, can make the suppression less overt. When Jeff is asleep, we see Thorwald leave his apartment with the woman in black. This violates the narration's restriction to Jeff's knowledge, and it might be seen as unmasking what the film suppresses all along (that is, what Thorwald is up to). But now generic norms take over. It is a convention of mystery and detective tales that the narration can inject hints, clues, and false leads which the detective does not recognize at the moment, as long as the detective eventually learns or infers the information and as long as the solution to the mystery is not given away prematurely. In *Rear Window*, both conditions are satisfied. To put it more technically, the detective tale tones down its occasional suppressive operations by realistic motivation (restricting the bulk of the narration to what the detective could plausibly know) and by generic convention. A different norm of communicativeness can be found in the melodrama, where more omniscient narration tends to emphasize communicativeness so as to play up ironic and pathetic twists of which the characters are unaware. In general, we must distinguish between generically codified shifts in the range or depth of knowledge and more or less overt indications of suppressiveness.

The best critical solution to the problem of communicativeness is to weigh transtextual norms against intrinsic structural demands. Withholding key pieces of information is a convention of the mystery film, so to some extent

Shadow of a Doubt obeys generic rules in the scene we have considered. But the flagrancy with which the narration indicates its suppressiveness must be seen as playing a role within the film's overall form. The film begins by being restricted to Uncle Charlie's knowledge but soon starts to undermine that when he escapes from the police by means not shown to us. In the course of the film Little Charlie gradually replaces Uncle Charlie as the principal agent of knowledge; it is she who solves the mystery surrounding her uncle. The scene we have considered is pivotal here, marking another stage in the "weaning away" of the audience from Uncle Charlie's range of knowledge. Thereafter, the film will modulate quite carefully from restricted to unrestricted states, and from overt communicativeness to momentary but overt suppressiveness and back again. At certain moments our knowledge is greater than that of the characters, and the narration may call attention to the fact; at other moments (e.g., the newspaper scene), we know less than the character, and the narration points that out too. The final effect of these manipulations is double: to make the spectator play with simultaneous hypotheses about Uncle Charlie's past and motives; and to create in the viewer the shadow of a doubt about the narration's own trustworthiness. In at least some cases, then, overt marks of communicativeness or suppressiveness can also convey a degree of self-consciousness.

The categories of knowledgeability, self-consciousness, and communicativeness can be used to clarify two common but imprecise critical concepts. In cinema, the concept of "point of view" has usually been loosely employed, especially within the mimetic tradition. When critics speak of a character's point of view, they are usually referring to the range and/or depth of knowledge which the narration supplies. With respect to range, *Rear Window* comes close to Jeff's "point of view." With respect to depth, a film like *La guerre est finie*, which plunges us into the protagonist's inner life, may be considered to give us Diego's subjective "point of view." More broadly, when critics discuss narrational "point of view" (or the narrator's point of view), they are usually referring to any or all of the properties I have picked out—knowledgeability, self-consciousness, and communicativeness. Speaking of Hitchcock's "point of view" as intruding on a scene usually implies a great range of knowledge, a high degree of self-consciousness, and perhaps some overt manipulations of communicativeness. To avoid blurring these distinctions, I will use the term "point of view" only to refer to the optical or auditory vantage point of a character; thus "point-of-view shot" is synonymous with "optically subjective shot."

Similarly, these concepts can specify the term "unreliability" a little more. If "reliable" means "forthcoming," the more communicative the narration, the more reliable it is. In the *Shadow of a Doubt* scene, the suppression of Charlie's view of the newspaper article causes us to mistrust the narration to some degree; henceforth we must be on our guard for what it might withhold. "Reliability" can also imply objective accuracy, in which case the range and depth of knowledge can become factors. A narration which confined itself to a character's mental states might be highly communicative but it would not necessarily inspire confidence in its veracity. The framed story of *The Cabinet of Dr. Caligari* is a case in point. We also spot "unreliable" narration as it is occurring or recognize it only after the fact. In *Rashomon*, the flashbacks are motivated as representations of various character's court testimony; since we are warned at the outset (through an "anticipatory caution" in the exposition) that the accounts are incompatible, we view each flashback as at best an overall hypothesis and at worst a fabrication. The characters must take the responsibility for the "unreliability" of their narration. But in *Stage Fright*, probably the canonic case of unreliable narration in classical cinema, we are given a flashback putatively both trustworthy and accurate but which turns out to have been the visual and auditory representation of a lie. It is not just the character's yarn that is unreliable. The film's narration shows itself to be duplicitous by neglecting to suggest any inadequacies in Johnnie's account and by appearing to be highly communicative—not just reporting what the liar said but showing it as if it were indeed objectively true.

As categories of information transmission, knowledgeability, self-consciousness, and communicativeness all bear on how film style and syuzhet construction manipulate time, space, and narrative logic to enable the spectator to construct a particular unfolding fabula. I should add, however, that other, less central narrational factors may be present. These are *judgmental* factors, often called "tone" by literary critics. When we say that a film takes pity on its characters or has contempt for its audience, we are talking, however loosely, about ways in which a film's narration can strike an attitude with respect either to the fabula or to the perceiver. The "God and Country" sequence of *October* would exemplify a strikingly judgmental syuzhet passage. We cannot list such attitudes exhaustively, and many acts of narration probably do not possess them, but for our survey to be complete we should mention some clear cases.

We are most familiar with narrational judgment as a function of particular stylistic devices. In a silent film, an expository intertitle may make no bones about the narration's attitude. A title in *The Birth of a Nation* identifies an old man as "the kindly master of Cameron Hall." Music can indicate narrational attitude in a similarly direct way: sympathetic (the "Diane" tune in *Seventh Heaven*), ironic ("We'll Meet Again" at the close of *Dr. Strangelove*), or comic (Irish folk tunes in *The Quiet Man*). It is a cliché of some films that a distant high angle at the end connotes a compassionate, detached attitude. Within given styles and conventions, many devices can imply judgments on the story action.

It is generally more fruitful, though, to look for attitudes as emergent qualities of the systems at work within entire films. For instance, the narrational attitude toward Uncle Charlie in *Shadow of a Doubt* is less a matter of camera angle or figure placement at any one moment than a function of an overall narrational strategy that presents certain aspects of his conduct as both fascinating and inexplicable. In *The Birth of a Nation*, the narration's attitude toward the Cameron household is governed by its role in the film's total narrative economy: the family is the causal, spatial, and temporal center of the film. Similarly, any narration's "attitude" toward the perceiver usually emerges from the general properties of narration. A highly suppressive narration, as in Lang or Hitchcock, might be considered to look down on the audience. A more communicative narration, such as is found in Ford or Capra, makes more straightforward and "sincere" appeals. While our critical vocabulary for narrational judgment remains weak, we can usually ground our intuitions in the formal properties of narration I have indicated.

Narrator, author

Throughout my discussion, one particular question may have nagged the reader. I have not referred to the narrator of a film. In what senses can we speak of a narrator as the source of narration?

If a character is presented as recounting story actions in some fashion (telling, recollecting, etc.), as Marlowe does during most of *Murder My Sweet*, the film possesses a character-narrator. Or a person not part of the story world may be identified as the source of parts of the narration. In *Jules and Jim*, a voice-over commentary points up the diegetic world; in *La ronde*, a *meneur de jeu* appears in flesh and blood to address the audience. Such films contain explicit, noncharacter narrators. But, as Edward Branigan has demonstrated, such personified narrators are invariably swallowed up in the overall narrational process of the film, which they do *not* produce.[21] So the interesting theoretical problem involves an implicit, nonpersonified narrator. Even if no voice or body gets identified as a locus of narration, can we still speak of a narrator as being present in a film? In other words, must we go beyond the process of narration to locate an entity which is its source?

Some theorists believe so. Diegetic theories often identify the narrator as the enunciator, the film's "speaker," but we have already seen that the analogy to speech fails because of the weak correspondences between verbal deixis and the techniques of cinema. Other theorists suggest that the source of narration is akin to Wayne Booth's "implied author." The implied author is the invisible puppeteer, not a speaker or visible presence but the omnipotent artistic figure behind the work.[22] In film, Albert Laffay speaks of *le grand imagier*, the master of images: a fictional and invisible personage who chooses and organizes what we shall perceive.[23] On Laffay's account, at the center of a narrative film stands a ghostly master of ceremonies, invisible twin of the *meneur de jeu* of *La ronde*.

Since any utterance can be construed with respect to a putative source, literary theory may be justified in looking for a speaking voice or narrator.[24]

But in watching films, we are seldom aware of being told something by an entity resembling a human being. Even with the dissective attention of criticism, we cannot construct a narrator for Vidor's film *War and Peace* with the exactitude with which we can assign attributes to the narrator of Tolstoy's original novel. As for the implied author, this construct adds nothing to our understanding of filmic narration. No trait we could assign to an implied author of a film could not more simply be ascribed to the narration itself: it sometimes suppresses information, it often restricts our knowledge, it generates curiosity, it creates a tone, and so on. To give every film a narrator or implied author is to indulge in an anthropomorphic fiction.

There is a fairly important theoretical choice involved here. Literary theories of the implied-author, such as Seymour Chatman's, take the process of narration to be grounded in the classic communication diagram: a message is passed from sender to receiver.[25] This has committed theorists to seeking out noncharacter narrators and implied authors, not to mention "narratees" and "implied readers." These entities, especially the latter two, are sometimes very hard to find in a narrative text. I suggest, however, that narration is better understood as the organization of a set of cues for the construction of a story. This presupposes a perceiver, but not any sender, of a message. This scheme allows for the possibility that the *narrational process may sometimes mimic the communication situation more or less fully*. A text's narration may emit cues that suggest a narrator, or a "narratee," or it may not. This explains the range of examples, and the asymmetrical structures, that we often find: some texts do not signal a narrator, or a narratee; others signal one, but not the other. For instance, Robert Bresson's film *Pickpocket* starts with a prologue asserting that the "author" is presenting images and sounds to explain the story. As we shall see in Chapter 12, this is a way of marking stylistic factors as having an overt, dynamic relation to the syuzhet. Most films, however, do not provide anything like such a definable narrator, and there is no reason to expect they will. On the principle that we ought not to proliferate theoretical entities without need, there is no point in positing communication as the fundamental process of all narration, only to grant that most films "efface" or "conceal" this process. Far better, I think, to give the narrational process the power to signal under certain circumstances that the spectator should construct a narrator. When this occurs, we must recall that this narrator is the product of specific organizational principles, historical factors, and viewers' mental sets. Contrary to what the communication model implies, this sort of narrator does not create the narration; the narration, appealing to historical norms of viewing, creates the narrator. In Part 3, we will consider how this might work. For now, I need only signal that we need not build the narrator in on the ground floor of our theory. No purpose is served by assigning every film to a *deus absconditis*.

Notes

1 Sigmund Freud, "The Unconscious" (1915), in *Collected Papers*, Vol. 4, ed. James Strachey (London: Hogarth Press, 1956), 106. On this point, see also Noël Carroll, "Address to the Heathen," *October* no. 23 (Winter 1982): 130–134.

2 Vladimir Nizhny, *Lessons with Eisenstein*, trans. and ed. Ivor Montagu and Jay Leyda (New York: Hill and Wang, 1962), 110.

3 See Aristotle, *Poetics*, commentary by D. W. Lucas (Oxford: Clarendon Press, 1968), 53–54, 100.

4 Yuri Tynianov, "Plot and Story-Line in the Cinema," *Russian Poetics in Translation* 5 (1978): 20.

5 Since writing Chapters 1–7 of David Bordwell, Janet Staiger, and Kristin Thompson, *The Classical Hollywood Cinema: Film Style and Mode of Production to 1960* (New York: Columbia University Press, 1985), I have reconsidered the plot/story distinction. There Chapter 2 asserted that plot (syuzhet) consists of "the totality of formal and stylistic materials in the film," and Chapter 3 called narration that aspect of plot which transmits story information. This formulation now seems to me inadequate, both as a reading of the Formalists and as an account of film form. For the reasons presented in the present chapter, I take narration to be the all-inclusive process which uses both *syuzhet* and style to cue spectators to construct a *fabula*, or story. This revision of theoretical terms does not seem to me to affect the analytical and descriptive claims I make in *The Classical Hollywood Cinema*, but it does offer greater theoretical precision.

6 Boris Tomashevsky, "Thematics," in Lee T. Lemon and Marion J. Reis, eds., *Russian Formalist Criticism: Four Essays*, (Lincoln: University of Nebraska Press, 1965), 66–67.

7 My emphasis upon the fabula as an emergent spectatorial construct is characteristic of "late" Russian Formalist poetics; the early writings of Shklovsky in particular tend to treat the fabula as a preexistent raw material for artistic elaboration. Nonetheless, at times we must use the language of carpentry or sculpture in describing the syuzhet's operations. For the narrative artist does in some sense work "on" the fabula *as he may assume that the perceiver will construct it*. In the previous chapter, I claimed that the narrative film is so made as to encourage the spectator to execute story-constructing activities. These activities can in turn be presupposed by the filmmaker. For the artist, presenting a story "out of" chronological order is just that: a transformation of that arrangement which a spectator would presumably make when presented with more "linear" cues. (Here a theoretical approach emphasizing narrative as a *structure* overlaps with that treating narration as a temporal *activity*.) The perceiver, given a narrative text, is invited to recognize a syuzhet and infer a fabula from it, whereas the artist constructs a syuzhet according to assumptions about how the spectator could infer a fabula from it. And these assumptions will form part of the artist's material.

8 Most Russian Formalist narrative theory assumes a distinction between syuzhet and style, as witnessed in the title of Viktor Shklovsky's 1919 essay, "On the Connection Between Devices of Syuzhet Construction and General Stylistic Devices" (*Twentieth-Century Studies* nos. 7/8 [December 1972]: 48–72). Although Shklovsky believed that syuzhet construction and stylistic elements often parallel each other, he presupposed them to occupy distinct domains. Boris Tomashevsky and Boris Eichenbaum also held this view. More recently, both Meir Sternberg and Seymour Chatman exclude style from the realm of the syuzhet. See Sternberg, *Expositional Modes and Temporal Ordering in Fiction* (Baltimore: Johns Hopkins University Press, 1978), 34; and Chatman, *Story and Discourse: Narrative*

Structure in Fiction and Film (Ithaca: Cornell University Press, 1978), 10–11, 24. Yuri Tynianov speaks of the syuzhet as "the story's dynamics, composed of the interactions of all the linkages of material (including the story as a linkage of actions)—stylistic linkage, story linkage, etc." ("On the Foundations of Cinema," in Herbert Eagle, ed., *Russian Formalist Film Theory* [Ann Arbor: University of Michigan Slavic Publications, 1981], 96). The passage is cryptic, but it suggests that the syuzhet includes both "story linkage" and style, in which case Tynianov's conception would be structurally congruent with mine: what I and others call "syuzhet," he calls "story linkage," and what he calls "syuzhet" I call narration.

9 See p. 31, above.

10 Sternberg, *Expositional Modes and Temporal Ordering in Fiction*, 34.

11 Cf. Chatman, *Story and Discourse*, 19–20; Gérard Genette, *Figures II* (Paris: Seuil, 1969), 66.

12 Tynianov, "Plot and Story-Line in the Cinema": 20.

13 Roland Barthes, "The Third Meaning," *Image Music Text*, trans. and ed. Stephen Heath (New York: Hill and Wang, 1977), 64.

14 Kristin Thompson, *Ivan the Terrible: A Neoformalist Analysis* (Princeton: Princeton University Press, 1981), 287–295.

15 Ibid., 302.

16 Sternberg's term "gap" does not coincide with the usage of phenomenological theorists of narrative like Wolfgang Iser. For Iser, a gap is any "indeterminate" portion of a text which calls forth "a free play of interpretation" ("Indeterminacy and the Reader's Response," in J. Hillis Miller, ed., *Aspects of Narrative* [New York: Columbia University Press, 1971], 11). He finds gaps between action segments, between character thought and deed, between different points of view. For Sternberg, however, gaps arise only from the relation of syuzhet to fabula. I shall suggest that they are usually quite determinate, especially given the canonic schemata of story construction.

17 Sternberg, *Expositional Modes and Temporal Ordering in Fiction*, 161–162.

18 Ibid., 129.

19 Ibid., 98–99.

20 Tzvetan Todorov, "La lecture comme construction," *Les genres du discours* (Paris: Seuil, 1978), 89.

21 Edward Branigan, *Point of View in the Cinema: A Theory of Narration and Subjectivity in Classical Film* (New York: Mouton, 1984), 40–49.

22 Wayne Booth, *The Rhetoric of Fiction* (Chicago: University of Chicago Press, 1961), 71–75.

23 Albert Laffay, *Logique du cinéma: Création et spectacle* (Paris: Masson, 1964), 81.

24 But not necessarily. The works of S. Y. Kuroda, Ann Banfield, and others suggest that literary narration may be defined by its inability to be taken as proceeding from a speaker. See Ann Banfield, *Unspeakable Sentences: Narration and Representation in the Language of Fiction* (London: Routledge and Kegan Paul, 1982).

25 Chatman, *Story and Discourse*, 147–151.

43

FORM WARS: THE POLITICAL UNCONSCIOUS OF FORMALIST THEORY

Bill Nichols

Source: *South Atlantic Quarterly*, 88, 2, Spring 1989, pp. 487–515.

Narrative's not the thing it used to be. More than standing as one form of artistic expression to be worried over by those attending to the nature of art, narrative has become a central preoccupation in its own right, pushing matters of art and levels of culture to the side. What is a narrative? From that structuralist question issued an agenda distinct from ones that emerge from questions about artistic expression, literary creation, or the relationship of art and society. An object distinct from literary questions of aesthetic value came into being. And for a while it appeared that this object might become the raw material of a science. From Northrop Frye's *Anatomy of Criticism* to the Christian Metz of *Language and Cinema*, the stage was set for the science, or poetics, of narrative.

This was always, however, a science with a difference. The object was not an aspect of nature, as in the natural sciences, nor of directly manifested human behavior, as in the social sciences, but a verbal, written or semiotic structure, a representation distinguishable from other semiotic structures less on the basis of aesthetic values than of discursive features. How does narrative differ from other discursive structures that might be called, collectively, non-narrative? What social functions does narrative play that other structures do not? And what qualities do representations possess that narrative inflects in systematic ways?

These questions take science into unfamiliar terrain, and other issues compound the difficulty. The study of the individual work, even when filtered through scientisms like "textual system," invites an attention to specificity that belies the general principles upon which a science need rest. (In fact, many of the structural and post-structural theories that raised a scientific banner seem in retrospect quite formulaic and reductive.) Matters of ideology, central to so much discussion of narrative systems from Roland Barthes's *Mythologies* to Fredric Jameson's *The Political Unconscious*, also confound any notion of an objective narrative structure readily detached from its historical, social context. But perhaps most forcefully of all, psychoanalysis and feminism knocked the idea of a narrative science for a large, political loop. Narrative, once it was linked irrevocably to Oedipus, lost its innocence. Stories place us within their webs of meaning in ways inseparable from questions of the politics of gender. They do so in ways that are intimately related to narrative structure and the psychic processes by which we engage with a story, and that extend far beyond matters of content. These are issues that call for qualification, critique, rereading, rewriting, and contestation more than for taxonomies, anatomies, and dispassionate science. And in the pursuit of these issues the original impetus and yearning for a science or poetics of narrative has been largely turned aside, ignored, or rejected.

A capsule summary of what several writers have said about narrative suggests some of the ways in which questions of ideology and gender have provided the political ground against which the figure of narrative comes into view:

HAYDEN WHITE: [Historiographic] narrative masks its status as discourse to imply that historical reality has the appearance of narrative and, with it, an inherent moral order. Narratives address issues of order, desire, and law, authority and its legitimation or subversion. "The historical narrative . . . reveals to us a world that is putatively 'finished,' done with, over, and yet not dissolved, not falling apart. In this world, reality wears the mask of a meaning, the completeness and fullness of which we can only *imagine*. . . . The demand for closure in the historical story is a demand, I suggest, for moral meaning, a demand that sequences of real events be assessed as to their significance as elements of a *moral* drama."

COLIN MACCABE: [Realist, Hollywood] narrative cannot represent contradiction because there is a hierarchy in which the final level [of authorial omniscience] functions to embody truth or certainty. Such narrative is inadequate to a radical politics of any kind because the form recuperates any type of radical content, placing it within the grip of Truth. It is the form itself that must be rejected. Moments of subversion must give way to strategies of subversion.

RAYMOND BELLOUR: [Classic, Hollywood] narrative form embodies the oedipal trajectory (masculine maturation through "tests" of ability and through the discovery of a suitable mate—a trajectory usually subsumed under the categories of sex and violence in popular criticism). Narrative is the enactment of desire. Narrative posits woman as different in order to reassure men that they are the same as those other men who produce the narrative, define its moral order, and shape the destiny of characters accordingly.

LAURA MULVEY: [Hollywood, dominant] narrative constructs men's pleasure at women's expense. Men identify with active male characters and adopt either sadistic or fetishistic/voyeuristic relations to women characters. These narratives take an ambivalent view of women because the view given is from within the imaginary where women do not have the phallus and symbolize its loss or lack and are therefore a threat as well as an attraction. Male pleasure at the expense of women must be rejected and a new aesthetics created.

ROLAND BARTHES: [Classic, readerly] narrative is the result of weaving five major codes together to give the sense of the real even though this is entirely a textual effect. These codes can be dissected into their smallest units (units which the analyst constructs) to show how they achieve the effect of a lifelike narrative dependent on the naturalizing agency of the sentence. Narratives work "on the page" to lift the reader "off the page." Psychological character attributes like volition, pensiveness, and the sense of an unsaid wealth of mystery and complexity are all the result of specific textual strategies that give the effect of a world without its substance and a logic without its proofs.

FREDRIC JAMESON: [Classic, novelistic] narrative must always be historically located on three levels: in terms of (1) the experiential embodiment of social contradictions, constituting a felt reality that, in fact, may never have had so strong and compelling a presence prior to its embodiment; (2) the textual and often dialogical manifestation and working out of central aspects of class conflict and discourse such as *ressentiment* in nineteenth-century novels; and (3) the history and ideology of form where the novel at any given moment carries within it traces of sign systems from distinct modes of production (patriarchal or oedipal modes, for example, as well as capitalist ones). Poised between ideology and utopia, narratives require a double hermeneutic that is in turn both suspicious and revelatory, teasing out the links between history, the unconscious of hegemony and ideology on the one hand and history, the political unconscious and utopia on the other.

DAVID BORDWELL: "We can, in short, study narrative as a *process*, the activity of selecting, arranging, and rendering story material in order to achieve specific time-bound effects on a perceiver. I shall call this process *narration*, and it is the central concern of this book. . . . I argue that filmic narration involves two principal formal systems, syuzhet [plot] and style, which cue the spectator to frame hypotheses and draw inferences. [The spectator] is a hypothetical entity executing the operations relevant to constructing a story out of the film's representations. . . . [Metaphors like the "position" or "place" of the subject] lead us to conceive of the perceiver as backed into a corner by conventions of perspective, editing, narrative point of view, and psychic unity. A film, I suggest, does not 'position' anybody. A film cues the spectator to execute a definable variety of *operations*."

This last summation, culled from the first twenty-nine pages of Bordwell's *Narration in the Fiction Film*, sounds a different note.[1] The quest for scientific knowledge, with all its ostensible brackets of the social, ideological, and political, is with us once again, now in the form of a continuation of the work of the Russian formalists and the resurrection of the project of a narrative poetics.

Like the champions of this project in the 1970s, who promoted their cause in *Screen* and elsewhere, Bordwell is intolerant of impressionistic criticism, thematic readings that lack a solid formal basis, and analyses that neglect underlying structures and processes in favor of meaning or explication. But Bordwell is also intolerant of theories that try to cram filmic narration into the confined categories of linguistics (especially the *histoire/discours* distinction). He does not choose to base his poetics on the terra infirma of structuralist linguistics but instead turns to formalism and cognitive theory. With this move, Bordwell overcomes one of the major limitations of the earlier quest for a science of narrative—the disregard of the viewer in favor of textual structures—although not the far greater one of disregard for the *subjectivity* of the viewer as historical being.

The achievement, though, is not trivial. Whereas the earlier science of semiotics painted itself into a corner full of arid taxonomies that floated in an ahistorical ether, Bordwell points the way to a science, or poetics, centered on how a viewer might process narrational information. In other words, he demonstrates what a true science of narration might be by defining an object of study both suitable to a science and yet not totally devoid of intersubjective relations. He also demonstrates the limitations that continue to plague any poetics of narrative: the price we pay for the science we get is quite a steep one.

Why formalism? Why a poetics? I suggest some answers to these questions in another article that concentrates on the ways in which politically motivated criticism, broadly conceived, has, in recent years, become lumped into the monolithic category of "ideological criticism" the better to dismiss it as single-minded and insensitive.[2] My assertion there, and here, is that this monolith is an imaginary construct that could only be posited from an antithetical position since it flattens significant differences. The converse point seems far more apt: that "ideological criticism" readily fractures into a plurality of approaches (gay, lesbian, black, third world, feminist, psychoanalytic, Marxist, sociological, poststructuralist, and so on) which are often inimicable in specific ways and share a fairly diffuse affinity. What ideological criticisms in fact lack is a master code or narrative, a fixed agenda (such as Marxism is wont to provide) that would unify them. Unity itself has fallen into question and a politics of affinity replaces it. This very diversity—a turning away from "master narratives" and masters, from grand theory and the self-legitimated, authorizing agency at its center—necessarily welcomes the pluralism that terms like "ideological criticism" belie. The value of this designation lies less in its descriptive accuracy than in its rhetorical agency: it helps make room for a presumably open-ended, nonmonolithic, nonideological theory and criticism that will restore those qualities of nuance and detail, complexity and contingency, that ideological preoccupations neglect.

Neo-formalism is one such alternative to "ideological criticism" and its most active proselytizer is David Bordwell.[3] This approach values the strict delimitation of the object of study, rigorous attentiveness to textual specificity, and an emphasis on pattern or order as a form of organization in contradistinction to thematic meaning or ideological effect. Neo-formalism may not simply contest the meanings that a feminism, say, might find, but contest the very grounds on which meaning rests. Thus in a debate with the editor of *Enclitic*, Bordwell compares a Lacanian analysis of the look, specifically the glance of a character in a fiction film and how this constructs a voyeuristic dynamics, with his own approach to the look and the construction of narrative space: ". . . the analysis of the articulation of space in a sequence seems to me no less semantic in revealing how a denotative space is (or is not) constructed—this construction yielding meanings and effects."[4] Which meanings and effects, however, becomes an issue deferred, perhaps interminably.

At best, the formal analysis of denotative dimensions of film narrative may offer the solid, scientific base upon which more ideological criticisms can rest. In the "conclusion" to *Narration in the Fiction Film*, Bordwell admits that his work does not answer questions of sexuality and fantasy, nor cultural, economic, and ideological questions, but it may set out the terrain upon which such matters can be analyzed more clearly. "Studies of ideology in cinema can usefully recognize that through schemata a society's ideological constructs are taken up by its members; and that narrational modes are central mediations between ideology and its manifestations in artworks." He ends his point with an injunction: "If ideological analysis is to avoid vacuous overgeneralization, it must reckon in the concrete ways that narrational processes function in filmic representation."[5] But can a neo-formalism provide the scientific knowledge that might become the ground for ideological analysis? Factual knowledge seems less at issue than the concepts and categories used to generate facts. As Bordwell himself argues, in a prolix rebuttal to an equally prolix critique of "the Wisconsin project" (works by Bordwell, Kristin Thompson, and Janet Staiger) in *Screen* magazine, ". . . the materialist researcher should hold that the theorist's conceptual frame of reference at least filters what concepts and data are selected and perhaps even governs what concepts and data are recognizable."[6]

Whether Bordwell himself subscribes to this position is left unclear, but Fredric Jameson offers no such uncertainty. In his dramatic critique and use of the work of Greimas, Jameson argues that Marxism subsumes other interpretive modes and retains some of their findings through a "radical historicizing of their mental operations." Jameson goes on to say that Greimas's semiotic rectangle can not only be a tool of Marxist analysis but that by analyzing the tool itself, it can be shown to map "the limits of a specific ideological consciousness and [mark] the conceptual points beyond which that consciousness cannot go, and between which it is condemned to oscillate."[7]

Bordwell's analysis of narrational process has many strengths, not least among them its supple blend of theory, criticism, and, to a more limited extent, history. In fact, much of the instructiveness of his work lies in the close readings he provides of diverse films, precisely those parts of the book most quickly set aside in reviews, where his theory of cognitive processing is more easily summarized and debated. These readings are all the more distinctive for not focusing on moments of subversion or crisis, on gaps or fissures, on the hidden apparatus that achieves "suture," continuity, or closure, and for not making broad claims on the basis of cursory and selective reference to texts of dubious representativeness. Bordwell's readings tend to focus on what often seem the most pedestrian moments of sometimes pedestrian films as well as the seemingly unremarkable moments of extraordinary ones. His discussion of a dinner scene from *Miss Lulu Bett*, for example, identifies how narration constructs a scenographic space of volume, consistency, and axes of action relative to the camera to orient us in relation to characters and their conduct. His discussion of time in *The Spider's Stratagem* demonstrates how the film embeds inconsistent cues about temporal relationships and subjectivity (the alignment of the camera with the character's point of view) in very concrete and minute ways in order to render space and time fundamentally ambiguous.[8] The readings exemplify processes at work in classical and art-cinema narration, but do so by showing how such processes are embedded in the most local levels of the text where cognitive activity is continuously at play.

These critical readings lend his theoretical account considerable weight by insisting that the theory accounts for films in their entirety rather than, as much poststructural criticism has, suggesting that the bulk of a film is devoted to a repetitive process of containing excess, positioning the viewer, and assuring ideological effects—processes that leave little to specify or puzzle at a local level unless crisis is in the air. These poststructural accounts seek out telling moments when ruptures or reflexivity appear, flaws or barings of the device occur, in order to expose the overall ideological operation.

A prime example of this more sporadic reading strategy is Stephen Heath's "Narrative Space," an essay that gives excellent articulation to the poststructural critique of narrative but that also allows a general theory to govern narrative process so consistently that the routine operations of a text become unproblematic. In this context specific scenes and instances are cited that expose what is usually lost from view. An example is Heath's astute selection of a single moment in Hitchcock's *Suspicion*—when a detective becomes inexplicably and improperly distracted by a portrait—as a moment of risk. The detective's roving eye threatens to derail the narrative. It momentarily threatens to expose the constant process of containment that holds the narrative on track and prevents its slippage toward "somewhere else again, another scene, another story, another space."[9]

Bordwell's attempt to account for every moment as part of a continuous process, never inactive and never mechanical, holds great appeal in a time of symptomatic readings. He never fails to attend to the entire body of the text rather than rush to identify symptoms. This is quite vividly demonstrated in his reading of what he somewhat oddly calls the "parametric" mode of narration: films that give priority to style rather than plot (or syuzhet). He dwells on works of stylistic sparseness, such as those by Dreyer and Bresson where there is a great temptation to seize on the few laconic moments that seem to bear the full weight of the emotional and thematic import, or on the specific, recurring strategies that seem to support the work's characteristic themes. Bordwell takes issue with both of these approaches and shows no small measure of disdain for (unidentified) thematic critics who squeeze meaning from works not designed to yield it: "The sense of an order whose finest grain we can glimpse but not grasp helps produce the connotative effects of which thematic criticism records the trace. These effects arise from a formal manipulation that is, in a strong sense, *nonsignifying*—closer to music than to the novel."[10] Bordwell likens parametric, sparse styles to serial music and, through a close analysis of passages of *Pickpocket* and other films, shows how minute variations in stylistic parameters like shot/reverse-shot or camera tracking movements generate a sense of order and aesthetic pleasure that may also be mistaken for ineffable or religious meaning.

In large measure, Bordwell argues that the effects of narrative process present us with a coherence which bears meaning because it is organized to do so; it is therefore possible to describe this process and its coherence without attending to the meanings that derive from it. Further, to attend to meanings without first establishing a narrative poetics typically results in positing anthropomorphisms (like the "ideal spectator," "implied author," and omniscient or "invisible observer") where none exist or where they exist as secondary consequences, not initiating agencies. He argues that narration may mimic everyday encounters between senders and receivers of messages and cue us to posit a narrator or authorial presence but that this is not at all necessary. When it does occur, Bordwell argues, "we must recall that this narrator is the product of specific, organizational principles, historical factors, and viewers' mental sets. . . . [T]his sort of narrator does not create the narration; the narration, appealing to historical norms of viewing, creates the narrator."[11]

Narration may therefore be read as emanating from an anthropomorphic source, but this is a procedural effect much like the impression that a computer playing chess is "intelligent," and thus human. Bordwell prefers to focus on the process itself, not its effects or meanings. He also prefers to eschew any phenomenological impulse to ponder the trace of an intersubjective address that such locutions as "implied author" invoke. For him, narrational process involves continuous, active engagement by the viewer instead of the passive "positioning" described by poststructural theory. Though active, it requires primarily problem-solving intelligence rather than socially grounded evaluative or interpretive skill.

Cognitive activity begins with our predisposition to sort sensory information into patterns that lead to inferences about the world that then guide subsequent information processing. Bordwell calls the patterns that emerge "schemata." Once schemata form, comprehension precedes by top-down and bottom-up processes of inference-making and hypothesis-formation. We make assumptions and hold to expectations, subjecting the process to constant review and revision. Knowledge becomes a model we use to answer questions about the world. The model we form in relation to fictional worlds is the fabula: "the imaginary construct we create, progressively and retroactively, was termed by Formalists the *fabula*," or story. "The fabula is thus a pattern which perceivers of narrative create through assumptions and inferences."[12] The fabula is an expanded version of those end-of-film recountings by crime investigators of what-really-happened-and-why-it-was-important that take place in certain detective films.

Interestingly, this definition aligns the fabula with those artificial intelligence models of knowledge where problem-solving occurs without reference to human subjectivity. A mental model is some kind of machinery or set of operants that "[provide] us with a simple explanation of what we mean by knowledge: *Jack's knowledge about* **A** *is simply whichever mental models, processes, or agencies Jack's other agencies can use to answer questions about* **A**."[13] The process of fabula-formation demonstrates our knowledge of narrative at the level of comprehension. Narrative poetics studies this process in a scientific spirit, in the sense that, according to Benjamin Hrushovski, the term science "delimits conveniently the purposes of such a systematic field of knowledge, which has as its primary aim the understanding of a field of reality and the construction of theoretical models for that purpose, and is clearly distinct from subjective, impressionistic or didactic criticism."[14]

Narrative comprehension becomes an exact science. The viewer, the "hypothetical entity," executes operations based on inferences and assumptions to generate the fabula from the syuzhet, which provides cues as to the order, frequency, and duration of events. The viewer performs tasks that can be readily scored against a master answer key since messy questions of connotation and interpretation have been deferred. This allows a poetics or science of narrative to identify its object as narrational process, something which yields repeatable and verifiable results (the fabula). Impressionism and subjectivity are avoided; objectivity and scientific knowledge prevail.

Yet the process of comprehension must contend with the nonmaterial presence of the fabula. In fiction, the fabula is our creation, the story we construct from the material cues given to us by the plot and style. What's more, the narrational process has a variety of tactics available to organize its presentation of fabula information: it can convey different degrees of knowledgeableness about important data from highly restricted—limited to a single character's knowledge—to completely unrestricted. It can signal different degrees of "subjectivity" or alignment with the thoughts and perceptions of characters. Narratives vary in their degree of self-consciousness: from a strong sense of narrative overtness, where the viewer is made aware that "a tale is being presented for a perceiver," to the invisibility usually attributed to "classic" or readerly narrative. A narrative may also exhibit varying degrees of communicativeness: what the narrative's degree of knowledge entitles it to know may or may not be relayed to the viewer in a direct and timely fashion. Information may be suppressed only to be revealed later, as in many detective films, or suppressed never to be revealed, as in many "art-cinema" films where ambiguity becomes a prized effect. Finally, there is tone, that array of "judgmental factors," in Bordwell's scheme, that suggests the attitude of the narrative toward its own characters, or viewers, a quality that receives minimal attention in the remainder of the study.[15]

Bordwell's model is one of "hollow forms," operational processes devoid of any necessary meaning, that then cluster themselves to establish norms (or paradigms). These norms arise in history but, accepting the license offered by Hrushovski's description of a historical poetics, Bordwell proposes to study them synchronically, as stable systems existing in history, persisting across time, but relatively independent of the messinesses of historical determinations. (Bordwell calls his approach "diachronic" as opposed to a synchronic taxonomy of procedural schemata. I prefer to see his approach as the distillation of a synchronic system from its historical surrounding.) Extrinsic norms are the most pertinent historically: "the canonized style, the mainstream practice—and deviations from that." Historical study, for Bordwell, is the effort to determine how extrinsic norms combine into patterns less variable than genre and more fundamental than schools, movements, and "entire national cinemas."[16] History is the realm from which the synchronic order of a mode of narration can be extracted by the scholar who then describes the formal order of the object he has defined. Showing that a mode of narration actually existed, out of all the possible modes of narration that might have existed, confers the title "historical" on Bordwell's enterprise. Questions of how the rest of existence, or history, receives representation, how history impinges on, or how narration invokes the viewer's subjectivity or compels paradox and contradiction in relation to a given mode, lie outside Bordwell's restricted conception of historical placement.

Two of Bordwell's modes—classical and art-cinema—are quite extensive in historical scope, but the other two—Soviet historical-materialist and "parametric" narration—are surprisingly limited in their historical occurrence. How these modes impinge on one another, and, in particular, to what extent the dominant, classical mode of narration conditions or inflects the historical form of the other modes, which can be seen as revolts against it, remains unexamined. Each mode occupies a separate piece of historical turf. Each mode simply invites the viewer to take a different tack. Classical narration asks the viewer to "construe the syuzhet and the stylistic system in a single way: construct a denotative, univocal, integral fabula." The "art-cinema" mode of narration charges the viewer with the task, "Interpret this film, and interpret it so as to maximize ambiguity." The "historical-materialist" mode of narration, exemplified by the Soviet cinema of the twenties, asks the viewer to regard the syuzhet as a rhetorical argument of conceptual simplicity accompanied by stylistic complexity; "this is done by calling on procedural schemata that urge: when in doubt, construct a fabula event as perceptually forceful and politically significant."[17]

Bordwell's concept of history and historical placement then leads him to argue that the spirit of historical-materialist narration lives on in an interrogative cinema deriving from Brecht and posing more open-ended questions of political efficacy for a contemporary scene where "no fixed doctrine serves as a point of departure."[18] Although this demonstrates a certain measure of historical endurance for the mode, within Bordwell's self-imposed confines of the feature fiction film (mainly before 1970), it overlooks at least two more intriguing questions: the degree to which historical-materialist narration exists in ideological tension with the classical mode that has co-opted it as "Hollywood montage" (those succinct summaries of duration or process in which conflict disappears in favor of evocation), and the extent to which historical-materialist narration informed a great deal of documentary filmmaking practice only to reemerge in yet another sanitized narrational mode as the television commercial.

Ads repeatedly display the characteristics Bordwell attributes to historical-materialist narration: argument by example, forceful perceptual engagement, and significant political effect, albeit a politics measured in terms of consumption and an inoculation against any more direct political involvement. What Bordwell says of Soviet cinema applies uncannily well to advertisements: ". . . the fabula world stands for a set of abstract propositions whose validity the film at once presupposes and reasserts. The film's argument works by appeal to example; the narrative cause and effect demonstrate the necessity [for a given proposition]. . . . Narrative causality is construed as supraindividual . . . [C]haracters thus get defined chiefly through their class position, job, social actions, and political views. . . . [T]hey become prototypes of whole classes, milieux, or historical epochs."[19]

None of these parallels and transformations receive consideration, however, leaving the "history" of this mode strangely pristine, as if a relatively obscure interrogative cinema had quietly gone its own way alongside the other modes and the cinema had remained thematically, formally, and institutionally immune to television and commerce. He disregards the massive struggle to channel meaning and control effect that the broad social history of montage, rhetoric, style, and historical-materialist narration might examine. By letting each mode exist in its own temporal cocoon, Bordwell avoids the urgent questions of how "revolts" against reigning norms arise, contend, undergo repression or distortion, and do so in relation to formal properties as well as thematic issues. Instead, his approach tends to dramatize how formal systems take on a life of their own, drawing on historical referents to vitalize their own dynamic, but remaining impressively immune to any materialist history.

Bordwell's priorities lie with the formal system that a poetics provides for study. This leads him to pose a relation between history and form that is diametrically opposite that of an ideological or Marxist analysis, even though he tells us elsewhere that "narrational modes are central mediations between ideology and its manifestations in artworks." In summarizing the achievements of Resnais's *La guerre est finie*, for example, Bordwell describes how "political material" comes to be "appropriated and transformed by formal conventions: . . . By focusing on the individual psyche and maintaining a shifting narrational game with the spectator, *La guerre est finie* transmutes political material into a unique treatment of the conventions of a particular narrational mode."[20] Might we not also say that the film transmutes a particular narrational mode into a unique treatment of political material? Or that formal conventions become appropriated and transformed by the force of political material? These inversions are the basis for Jameson's argument for a political subtext: "The literary or aesthetic act . . . cannot simply allow 'reality' to persevere inertly in its own being. . . . [T]he literary work or cultural object, *as though for the first time*, brings into being that very situation to which it is also, at one and the same time, a reaction."[21] In Jameson's dialectical view, the "reality" of the political material does not truly precede its textual realization: the text gives us our most vivid apprehension of a historical world whose significance eludes us until caught within the webs of textual form. Such a perspective, however, cannot be simply appended to Bordwell's scheme; it requires opening up the formalist circle to which poetics attends.

But history for Bordwell is merely the temporal ground against which the full range of formal options associated with a mode of narration congregate into more restricted, specific paradigms. These specific norms persist across time, with variations on the basic paradigm continually occurring (new stories, or fabula, in classic narration; new *auteurs*, or personal styles, in art-cinema; a tradition of interrogative cinema for historical-materialist film and so on). Throughout Bordwell's text, history exists as a relatively inert ground for the dynamics of cognitive, narrational process. Why a given mode might appear at a specific moment, or how that mode's characteristics, its extrinsic norms, might bear the trace of historical-material determinations over time, remains outside the bounds of the study. Bordwell's view seems to be that he has laid out the streets and waterlines for his theoretical subdevelopment; all that others need to do is hook them up to the historical/ideological power grid of their choice.

An aura of quaintness presides over Bordwell's project. His references are almost entirely to a cinema that has never seen or heard of television, to a sample of texts that takes into account nothing of Latin American, Asian, African, Australian, or Canadian production, to a perspective in which the last twenty years or so of production are of only passing importance, and to a vision of history so severely restricted to the cinema that the massive, formal similarities and social parallels between film and other arts go almost entirely unnoticed.[22] Bordwell cheerfully deflects criticisms of these gaps by reminding critics that he has stated his goals openly and has frankly admitted to what he is not doing as well as to what he is.[23] In true formalist spirit, seeking answers to questions provides its own justification and the nature or use-value of the questions, or answers, the purposes and intentions that might surround them, can be comfortably bracketed in the service of science and the avoidance of subjectivity.

This quaintness gains in magnification when it is compared to the feminist critique of narrative. Bordwell's adroit demolition of mimetic and diegetic theories of narration centers on the work of writers like Münsterberg, Arnheim, Kuleshov, Bazin, and Eisenstein for mimetic theory and, for diegetic theory, Barthes, Metz, Bellour, Heath, and MacCabe, who is credited with "the most influential instance of a structuralist approach to filmic narration," astonishing news to the film studies community, I suspect. Conveniently, it seems, there have not been any women nor any feminist theories based on mimetic and diegetic assumptions that need to be cleared away as well, no "vague and atomistic analogies among representational systems" lodged within the feminist perspective, no privileging of certain (film) techniques at the expense of others, nor any efforts lacking in the broad and supple principles Bordwell wishes to introduce.[24]

Feminist film theory, which I would argue has been the most influential form of narrative critique in the past two decades, can be ignored presumably because its structuralist underpinning has been knocked away or because Bordwell has provided a more satisfactory foundation on which it can readily rebuild. Feminist theory is an intriguing "gap" or omission in a text that often goes to some pains to announce what it is excluding from consideration. By making mimetic and diegetic theory into "bad" science performed by other males, Bordwell presents himself as a friendly helper to the befuddled among us who are still casting about for a scientific way to make sense of the narrational process. Feminism, with its own distinctly subjective agenda, simply doesn't enter into the picture. Bordwell proposes a poetics, or science, that comfortably excludes feminist theory and regards the viewer as a sexless, genderless, classless, stateless "hypothetical entity." He also biases viewer activity to favor information processing over parallel acts of engagment (empathy, identification, scopophilia, etc.) and interpretation. These are significant clues to the cost of a narrative science.

His choice of categories and of hierarchies among them determines his results in numerous ways, as does his attempt to found an "objective" level of syuzhet presentation, distinguishable from "subjective" and rhetorical levels. Objectivity, or the denotative level of narrative, which Bordwell identifies as the direct presentation of the fabula when it is not relayed through a character's subjectivity and when the narrational process does not call particular attention to itself, serves as the cornerstone of the syuzhet/fabula relationship. Every film contains a mix of "objective diegetic reality, characters' mental states, and inserted narrational commentary," and by first knowing what is objective or denotative, the viewer can then go on to determine what is subjective or argumentative.[25]

Objectivity is central to the project of describing the fabula as singular and empirically accessible, and constructing the fabula is the viewer's primary task. Even this fundamental tenet, though, is open to question. The case for the centrality of fabula construction is made most strongly for classical cinema, at the level of narrative comprehension, but its centrality becomes increasingly dubious as we take up art-cinema, historical-materialist, and parametric modes of narration where unraveling a "story" becomes less and less essential. For the viewer's task with historical-materialist cinema—to construct a "fabula *event* as perceptually forceful and politically significant"—requires closer attention to the locus of represented events, the syuzhet, than to the "never materially present," "imaginary," "verbal synopsis" that we construct.[26] The force and significance of *events* derive from their material, stylistic embodiment in the syuzhet, not our reconstitution of them into something more summary-like.

And if the all-absorbing task of fabula construction is much less absorbing than Bordwell claims (such that the comprehension of style and syuzhet relations comes to the fore, for instance), then objectivity may be less clearly decidable than Bordwell wishes. An early casuality of Bordwell's clean-cut objective/subjective/narrational commentary declension is the link proposed by Barthes and others among connotation, myth, and ideology. (Barthes's later rejection of denotation's claim to ontological status—"denotation is not the first meaning, but pretends to be so; under this illusion, it is ultimately no more than the *last* of the connotations . . . the superior myth by which the text pretends to return to the nature of language, to language as nature"—receives no consideration at all.)[27] Bordwell regards all third-person representation as the objective denotation of a fictional space. Connotation or subjective representation becomes confined to a character's subjectivity, as evidenced by devices like point of view shots, rather than linked to a culture's ideology. If this relay of an objective diegetic world or of character subjectivity is interrupted, this must then be the work of the narrative calling attention to itself, rhetorically signaling its awareness of its own viewer.

Bordwell invokes style (unusual camera angles or movements, odd editing patterns, disjunctive sounds) as the narrative's mechanism for calling attention to itself. This schema very neatly isolates the narrational process from reference to anything beyond itself: subjectivity and commentary fold back into the narrational process rather than inflect the fabula world with meaning or significance such that the narrative becomes about something other than itself. For a narrative to be "about" something beyond itself would require a theory of comprehension that includes rather than brackets interpretation; it would require an understanding of the fabula as the construction of an imaginary world rather than as the computer-like deciphering of a story's intelligibility. It would throw into doubt whether a clear-cut, objective fabula world exists apart from the stylistic inflections that inform it, not only in order to call attention to the narrational process, but even more to establish the nature of the imaginary world the narrational process constructs.

The difference can be illustrated by Bordwell's analysis of melodrama. He characterizes melodrama as a highly communicative narration, with few "focused" gaps (specific pieces of missing information), unrestricted range (not tied to what characters know), a strong primacy effect (where what happens at the outset colors everything that follows), an effect that prompts minimal curiosity about the past, and a strong feeling of suspense about the future. Melodrama also cues us to expect an emphasis on how characters will react to new revelations and depends on retardation (delaying the introduction of important fabula information in the syuzhet) and coincidence to intensify our engagement.

It is somewhat difficult to recognize this as the same object that has occupied a great deal of feminist attention. The central place of female characters and subjectivity, the relation of this subjectivity to sexist ideology, the importance of beginnings not in terms of a nonexplanatory tautology ("primacy effect") but in terms of narrative structure and psychoanalytic theory (disturbance and closure, condensation and displacement),[28] the debates on the function of style in relation to a return of repressed, character-based symptoms where oddities of style are not commentary but a crucial dimension to the imaginary world itself, the representation of male power and female desire, and the political effect of melodrama on viewers, especially women—none of this is anywhere to be seen in Bordwell's analysis. Were his "hypothetical entity" (that information-processing unit also known as a viewer who produces intelligibility from syuzhet/style systems) to become a human subject—embodied, gendered, and situated in history, the moves from comprehension to interpretation, from information to meaning, from imaginary fabulas to imaginary worlds would immediately take on enough urgency to break through Bordwell's perpetual oscillation between the encapsulated, formal poles of syuzhet signifiers and fabula signifieds.

Science craves objectivity—a somewhat unscientific way of speaking of its procedures and protocols. The extent of this craving can be seen in

Bordwell's dry, matter-of-fact treatment of retardation, the ways in which a narrative's beginning initiates a journey which the middle of the narrative must delay and retard, not once but frequently, through a range of techniques. For Bordwell, this is just another process, requiring procedural schemata to cope with it. Bordwell describes how a melodrama will use gaps in the relay of information to retard the narrative and cue the viewer in the formation of hypotheses: "The syuzhet also manipulates interest through unfocused temporal gaps. The melodrama's syuzhet will inform us of initiation of a chain of action and then skip over some time or move to another line of action; we will then wonder what happened in the interval. . . . In general, the practice of parallel plotting retards the revelation of fabula information, compelling us to suspend questions about the progress of one line of action while another occupies our attention."[29]

Compare this to Roland Barthes's treatment of the hermeneutic code and the management of enigmas. Barthes brushes aside immediately any sense of an objective, information-based process.[30] Enigmas conform to a strategy for the organization of desire and meaning. Enigmas sustain a paradoxically static dynamics, prolonging the original uncertainty in the face of the narrative's ineluctable march forward. This hermeneutic code distinguishes narrative from exposition by giving truth a structural, nonobjective definition: truth "is what is *at the end* of expectation," what comes last, with the closure of narrative teleology. Retardation is not merely an aspect of a formal process but part of a code inflected by the historical world in which it functions: "the hermeneutic narrative, in which truth predicates an incomplete subject, based on expectations and desire for its imminent closure, is dated, linked to the kerygmatic civilization of meaning and truth, appeal and fulfillment."[31] Retardation, by this account, is never only formal, never strictly or simply a matter of cues and hypotheses, information and comprehension, but instead part of a socially symbolic act *always* laden with meaning.

But Bordwell assumes that objectivity is self-evident. If we do not enter a character's subjectivity, if the narration does not offer commentary, and if style does not depart unexpectedly from norms we have begun to apply, then we are left with the denotative relation between syuzhet and fabula. The only fly in the ointment is "denotative." Virtually all cybernetic theory and semiotics allow for some slippage between signifier and signified, between signal and information, between information and meaning. Bordwell does not want slippage but certainty. The notion of a "ground" that provides a context for a sign and renders some attributes of it more pertinent than others, not only adds the complicating likelihood that different viewers will construct different fabula en route to different interpretations and meanings, but also suggests that empty or "hollow" forms are not entirely so free-floating. They remain anchored to a ground—the term is Charles Peirce's—through the purposefulness of communication and perception.[32]

Bordwell locates himself off any such ground. Fabula construction and narrative comprehension are processes of model building, of constituting a model of narration that we can use to answer questions about narration (to paraphrase Marvin Minsky). This is a project in which the simulation or model becomes the real or, better, displaces the real as a ground in favor of an implosion of meaning into "hollow forms." (Mental models bear uncanny resemblance to those industrial models which Baudrillard identifies as "third-order simulacra," from which new forms arise by means of the modulation of difference more than from copying or serial reproduction.[33]

For humans, information processing is linked to purpose on more than one level and more than locally. Aspects of a sign, or of the syuzhet, are brought into pertinence, foregrounded, purposefully. The qualities made pertinent by the ground, by the context marked out by the constraints of a discursive formation and the history of the subject, have to do with rhetoric, ideology, contradiction, and struggle. In science and in culture, the interpretant and its ground (the signifier and its context, the syuzhet and style) do not anchor denotative truths so much as existential meanings. An excellent example of this point occurs in Teresa de Lauretis's *Alice Doesn't* when de Lauretis examines Virginia Woolf's account of her realization of her status as a woman in terms of how the ground, in this case a ground of sexist ideology, foregrounds one possible interpretation of a passing male's comment so that cognitive activity, interpretation, meaning, and history all coalesce into what de Lauretis aptly calls "experience." Experience becomes the ground on which *nachträglichkeit* operates, that second order process of learning to learn that confounds any simple or linear concept of cognition and knowledge.

Bordwell's concept of empty or "hollow forms" deserves some attention of its own. This hollowness is necessitated by the absence of meaning and interpretation, by the restriction of subjectivity to the optical point of view of characters, by the isolation of gaps, retardation, and suspense from a hermeneutics à la Barthes, or a psychodynamics à la Laura Mulvey's case for sexist pathologies, or Gay Studlar's case for a masochistic aesthetic.[34] The viewer does not engage with the text subjectively in Bordwell's model, but cognitively, as an information processor, a level of engagement, that if it can be isolated at all, can only be turned into an end in itself by slicing through its densely reticulated associations. What this implies is that empty or hollow forms are only so while they are being constituted for the first time, while hypotheses and inferences are being made that lead to the emergence of form, or pattern, from noise. But once constituted these forms are also, simultaneously, grounded. They become part of our experience, or history, and to the extent that they are materialized in texts or social practices, they become part of our collective history as well. The context in which they arise informs them. The meanings they have accrued, whether in the course of a single film or across a large expanse of social history, accompany them. We do not first process and comprehend texts; we are simultaneously moved and subjectively engaged by them. We do not simply recognize a sign, form, or syuzhet pattern and automatically process a narrative in a particular way. Instead, according to Peirce's system, we attach overlapping interpretants to a given sign so that it is no longer and never again empty. These interpretants, which allow us to establish purposeful, affective relations to the world, narrative or real, are:

1. The emotional interpretant that associates connotative richness, feelings, and affect with a sign.
2. The "energetic" or active interpretant that generates physical or intellectual effort; generally this would be the kind of cognitive processing discussed by Bordwell as well as physical actions and those purposive responses from which narrative normally excuses us.
3. The "logical" interpretant whereby the subject's tendencies toward action or comprehension become modified as a result of the experience of applying these emotional and active interpretants to particular tasks or situations. This may also be called the existential interpretant since it places us in an enduring but alterable relation to a sign or set of signs. This interpretant engenders habit and the potential for a change of habit (or "schemata"). Action or comprehension, then, occurs not only in relation to immediate contingency but also in relation to sets of expectations and assumptions, predispositions, tendencies, and habits. Such activity does not "fall from the sky"; it is concretely, materially grounded in the referential, ideological nature of communication and discourse.[35]

This activity is of a different order and kind from that proposed by Bordwell, who limits himself to the cognitive processing of empty narrative forms. Though he refrains from a direct critique of alternative approaches, such as psychoanalysis, he goes on to add, ". . . I see no reason to claim for the unconscious any activities which can be explained on other grounds." And within this formal separatism, it is cognitive activity that Bordwell sets out to rescue and explain: explain in terms of a constructivist psychology and rescue because in his view ideological criticism has deprived the viewer of his or her activity. The vocabulary of positioning and constituting subjects, of ideological effect and the work of the apparatus, of *histoire* and *discours* all serve to deprive the subject of initiative. Cognitive processing becomes a way to restore activity to the subject: "The spectator performs cognitive operations which are no less active for being habitual and familiar."[36]

Habit, though, is not simply pre- or unconscious repetition. It is, precisely through being unconscious, where cognition and ideology meet, where existential interpretants join us to social webs of signification, where, in another vocabulary, qualification takes place.[37] I am not aware of any poststructural theory that claims the viewer or reader is inert, passive, and inactive at the level of cognitive processing. On the contrary, this level is taken for granted (too cavalierly no doubt) in order to argue that the viewer's activity still leaves him or her positioned or placed within a larger ideological structure that remains unquestioned, that persists through habit, that constitutes a ground upon which subjectivities form. Most poststructural analysis stresses moments of risk and strategies of containment that are always jeopardized by the return of what these strategies sought to repress, deny, or displace. Even if the process of containment were mostly successful, the potential for action remains (at least through poststructural criticism itself). The viewer's passivity, or more properly, his or her constitution within subjectivities like the masculinist scopophilia analyzed by Laura Mulvey, remains at risk; the potential for active contestation is always there.

Contestation has the ring of socially significant action, of existential interpretants recast against a ground of raised consciousness. That is, post-structuralism has never rejected the level of cognitive activity "redeemed" by Bordwell; instead, it has associated that activity with the social ends it served. The postmodern "positioned" viewer does not cease to function mentally; cognition, however, serves to sustain a limited range of subjectivity. Schemata do not treat empty forms but highly loaded ones. Priority goes to determining the existential, unconscious anchors that hold mental processing to certain paths more than others, not to the denial of such activity in its entirety. By showing in detail how the viewer is cognitively active during the story telling process, Bordwell gives us a more complete picture of narrative, but since such activity was never denied by other theorists, only contextualized, he can hardly be said to have rescued the viewer from theories that deprived us of a set of mental activities, despite his frequent claims to the contrary.[38]

Given his linear, one-dimensional model, Bordwell must neglect the subjective and socially constrained processes of interpretation. Likewise, he gives little attention to retroactive reading (and none to the central formalist tenet of *ostranie*). His analysis suggests that all viewers form the same fabula after one viewing where the recall and revision of previous syuzhet or stylistic material during the course of the narrative plays a secondary role. The greater the degree of retroactive reading and repunctuating according to logical type (classes and classes of classes, commentary and metacommentary, etc.), the greater the degree to which the fabula is subject to variation and dispute. It becomes increasingly less "in" the narrative process, waiting for us to reconstitute it, and more in the act of reading itself, subject, therefore, to all the personal, historical, and ideological inflections that reading is heir to. What's more, retroactive reading and the effect of *ostranie* are themselves of a different logical type. Whether in the course of viewing a film for the first time or during a process of critical analysis, retrospection is dialectical. It is part and parcel of our cognitive activity but of a different order from the mere reception of data or the comprehension of information; retrospection places information in the context of other information.

Retroactive reading (Freud's *nachträglichkeit*) involves comprehending "the diversity of contexts to put the information in (learning how to learn)."[39] Part of this contextual diversity would surely be the way in which the fabula constitutes a world, populated by values and bearing significance, rather than simply being a plot made intelligible. But to propose a dialectical cognitive process also opens out onto worlds and readings where loaded forms are placed into diverse contexts not by "hypothetical entities" programmed for narrative comprehension, but by gendered, historically situated subjects who may not only read but simultaneously reread, not only view but review, not only comprehend but also, and at the same time, resist, challenge, qualify, and contend, who view works not only in accord with a comprehension program but also negotiate, revise, or resist that very process.

This alternative would require unbinding style and rhetoric from the constraints Bordwell places on them. Style might do more than "simply [name] the film's systematic use of cinematic devices." Rhetoric might be more than "argument" where "the fabula world stands for a set of abstract propositions whose validity the film at once presupposes and reasserts."[40] Style might become a qualitative dimension that guides us in the effort to differentiate levels, assess tone, assign value, and establish identificatory or subjective relations simultaneously with cognitive ones. Since style doesn't create or determine the syuzhet's unfolding, it is secondary to Bordwell, but if it creates and determines the *world* of the narrative, it becomes a primary means of establishing a domain and the nature of its plausibility. Rhetoric might become an omnipresent element of persuasion, linked inevitably to address, intentionality, and meaning, as it is in Soviet cinema and in advertising but as it also is in classical and art-cinema. It would involve not only moments of obvious argument or assertion but the more diffuse, omnipresent process of persuading us of the moral or ideological pertinence of the world we encounter.

Logic has its limits and narrative constantly exceeds them. Narrative depends on paradox and contradiction to activate cognitive processes, if we choose to call them that, which require exercises in logical typing and the "Aha!" discovery of new contexts, new interpretive grounds for making sense of things. Taxonomies of syuzhet/fabula temporal relations that discuss the four possible combinations of simultaneity and successiveness between the two (successive syuzhet occurrences representing simultaneous fabula occurrences, for example), which Bordwell discusses in detail, involve nothing dialectical. Such categories are valuable to an analytic logic only; they provide no assistance in the task of explaining insight, discovery, or reinterpretation. His questions circle around the task of constructing the fabula: where does this occurrence fit in the story, is this commentary or description, how are space and time configured, what schemata will render this narrative comprehensible? Bordwell readily concedes that other questions can be asked, but the question of whether the ones he poses exist in such isolation from human subjectivity, desire, and power haunts the entire project.

So though formally correct, Bordwell may be wrong in a more fundamental sense. Localized knowledge has its value and logic is one of its most indispensable tools. Global knowledge—to which concepts like *nachträglichkeit*, *aufhebung*, *ostranie*, insight, paradox, discovery, intuition, synthesis, and totalization apply—also has its value and logic, and those reasoning procedures that rely on clear-cut rules to reach verifiable conclusions can be one of its most treacherous allies. How are we to regard the individual who takes up a delimited challenge resourcefully and produces results, perhaps brilliantly, if those results run contrary to some more global need? Within a local frame, the individual deserves acknowledgment and reward; within a global frame, such a response may be extremely dubious.

We must set aside the temptation to create a false, binary polarization by ignoring logical types and elevating the local to the status of the global so that achievement within a restricted or specified domain becomes the sole criterion with "larger questions" ruled irrelevant or a challenge only to the user, not the producer of the result. A more appropriate criterion involves recognizing that the pursuit of local knowledge has its virtues: it is quicker and allows for many, simultaneous but discrete forms of inquiry; it excuses errors or failure that follow from accepting the established rules governing that particular domain without introducing complicating issues of larger effect or competing claims. In this context, assessment of use-value might come more appropriately from asking how that dimension of ourselves whose task it is to learn *how* to learn (how to learn which strategies and assumptions serve us best in given circumstances) may benefit from the methods, tactics, and results we employ.

By this criterion, the use-value of Bordwell's effort must be said to be sharply limited, particularly in its lack of a human dimension from which we may learn. *Narration in the Fiction Film* could be regarded as a prolegomenon to the production of a computer program or expert system designed to construct the fabula from a given syuzhet and style. But the work allows for no history, no subjectivity. Bordwell conceives of history as the dimension in which specifiable modes of narration coalesce rather than as the ground (in Peirce's sense) of human experience. And he conceives of subjectivity as optical alignment with a character's point of view rather than as the fulcrum point of power and desire, those determinative structures which "pursue aims in indifference to perceptual reality, creating the imagised, eroticised concept of the world that forms the perception of the subject and makes a mockery of empirical objectivity."[41]

Bordwell's is a poetics that, at a local level, succeeds according to his own criteria: it is comprehensive, discriminates effectively, possesses coherence, matches the domain of data, and is fecund. At a more global level these claims become doubtful: this is a poetics that excludes more cinema and modes of visual representation than it includes, that neglects differences that make a difference, that achieves coherence by excluding history and subjectivity, that treats narrative as data or information for genderless, classless, stateless "processors," and whose fecundity is that of any system that has the wherewithal to perpetuate itself. As such it is of value wherever narrative is processed by "hypothetical" entities or "organisms"—better called, perhaps, cyborgs. For gendered, historically situated subjects whose very being is at stake within the arena of history, Bordwell's poetics must seem a terribly diminishing thing.

Notes

1 David Bordwell, *Narration in the Fiction Film* (Madison, 1985).
2 Bill Nichols, "Ideological and Marxist Criticism: Towards a Metahermeneutics," *Studies in the Literary Imagination* 19.1 (1986): 83–107.
3 Of primary concern here is Bordwell's *Narration in the Fiction Film.* Also exemplary of a neo-formalist approach and of a proselytizing posture is David Bordwell and Kristin Thompson, *Film Art: An Introduction* (New York, 1985), which is one of the most widely used introductory texts in the country. Other neo-formalist works include David Bordwell, Kristin Thompson, and Janet Staiger, *The Classical Hollywood Cinema: Film Style and Mode of Production to 1960* (New York, 1985); Kristin Thompson, *Eisenstein's Ivan the Terrible: A Neoformalist Analysis* (Princeton, 1981); and Edward Brannigan, *Point of View in the Cinema: A Theory of Narration and Subjectivity in Classical Film* (Berlin, 1984). In a somewhat more empirically centered vein is Barry Salt, *Film Style and Technology: History and Analysis* (London, 1983). One of the few books applying cognitive psychology (and generative linguistics) to filmic narration prior to Bordwell's is John M. Carroll, *Toward a Structural Psychology of Cinema* (The Hague, 1980).
4 David Bordwell, "Textual Analysis Revisited," *Enclitic 7.1* (1983): 93.
5 Bordwell, *Narration*, 335–36.
6 David Bordwell, "Adventures in the Highlands of Theory," *Screen* 29.1 (1988): 84 (a reply to Barry King's two-part critique, "The Classical Hollywood Cinema," *Screen* 27.6 [1986]: 74–88, and "The Story Continues . . .," *Screen* 28.3 [1987]: 56–82).
7 Fredric Jameson, *The Political Unconscious: Narrative as a Socially Symbolic Act* (Ithaca, 1981), 47.
8 Bordwell, *Narration*, 169–77, 88–98.
9 Stephen Heath, "Narrative Space," in *Questions of Cinema* (Bloomington, 1981), 24.
10 Bordwell, *Narration*, 306.
11 Ibid., 62.
12 Ibid., 49.
13 Marvin Minsky, *The Society of Mind* (New York, 1985), 303.
14 Benjamin Hrushovski, "Poetics, Criticism, Science," *PTL: Poetics and Theory of Literature* 1 (January 1976): vi.
15 Bordwell, *Narration*, 58, 61.
16 Ibid., 150.
17 Ibid., 165, 212, 243.

18 Ibid., 272.
19 Ibid., 243, 235.
20 Ibid., 335, 228.
21 Jameson, *Political Unconscious*, 81–82; emphasis mine.
22 See, for example, Michael Schudsen, *Advertising, the Uneasy Persuasion: Its Dubious Impact on American Society* (New York, 1984), especially "Advertising as Capitalist Realism," 209–33.
23 Bordwell, "Adventures in the Highlands," 82–84.
24 Bordwell, *Narration*, 18, 26.
25 Ibid., 162.
26 Ibid., 243, 49; emphasis mine.
27 Roland Barthes, *S/Z*, trans. Richard Miller (New York, 1974), 9.
28 In *Steps to an Ecology of Mind* (New York, 1972), Gregory Bateson speaks of the use of such principles in science under the rubric of the "dormative effect," the "explanation" originally given to the question of why certain derivatives of the poppy plant produced a depressive reaction in humans: something that cannot be explained is identified by the result it produces so that the naming of this result gives the appearance of having explained the cause. What has actually happened is that a pseudo-explanation has arisen to mark the limits of knowledge within a given theory or of the theory itself. Bateson sees this procedure as indicative of the muddle in the social sciences generally: "The state of mind or habit which goes from data to dormative hypothesis and back to data is self-reinforcing. [It leads to] a mass of quasi-theoretical speculation unconnected to any core of fundamental knowledge" (xx).
29 Bordwell, *Narration*, 71.
30 Barthes, *S/Z*, 75–77.
31 Bordwell, *Narration*, 76.
32 Charles Peirce, *Collected Papers*, ed. Charles Hartshorne and Paul Weiss (Cambridge, Mass., 1931–58), 1: 291–98.
33 Jean Baudrillard, *Simulations*, trans. Paul Foss et al. (New York, 1983). Bordwell's disavowal of any such postmodern regress in favor of certainty and science is ironically underlined by the strange, apparently nonsignifying juxtaposition of two essays on the general topic of "cybernetics, ownership, ontology," in *Screen* 29.1 (1988): 4–46 (John Frow, "Repetition and Limitation: Computer Software and Copyright Law," and Bill Nichols, "The Work of Culture in the Age of Cybernetic Systems") and a lengthy debate among Janet Staiger, Kristin Thompson, David Bordwell, and their reviewer, Barry King (Barry King, "A Reply to Bordwell, Staiger and Thompson," *Screen* 29.1 [1988]: 98–118; see also King, "Classical Hollywood Cinema" and "The Story Continues . . .").
34 Laura Mulvey, "Visual Pleasure and Narrative Cinema." and Gay Studlar, "Masochism and the Perverse Pleasures of the Cinema," in *Movies and Methods*, ed. Bill Nichols, 2 vols. (Berkeley, 1985).
35 Peirce, *Collected Papers*, 5: 326–27.
36 Bordwell, *Narration*, 30, 164.
37 See Göran Therborn, *The Ideology of Power and the Power of Ideology* (London, 1980), for a full discussion of qualification as an alternative concept to Althusser's subject subjected to a Subject. Qualification carries the double meaning of becoming qualified for social tasks and also of becoming capable of challenging or qualifying these tasks and their accompanying subjectivities.
38 Bordwell, *Narration*, xiii, 29–47, 53, 164.
39 Anthony Wilden, *The Rules Are No Game* (New York, 1987), 249. Wilden argues that all "Aha!" style experience "marks a new level of organization or patterning that produces a reinterpretation of the past, a rereading, in a new context, of the

logical typing and other relationships of past events, and thus a re-evaluation of the future" (250).

40 Bordwell, *Narration*, 50, 235.

41 Mulvey, "Visual Pleasure," in Nichols, ed., *Movies and Methods*, 2: 308.

44

THEORY AND HISTORY: NARRATIVE DISCOURSE AND THE NARRATOR SYSTEM

Tom Gunning

Source: *D. W. Griffith and the Origins of American Narrative Film: The Early Years at Biograph*, Urbana, IL: University of Illinois Press, 1991, pp. 10–30.

Can film theory and film history interact in a treatment of a specific historical series of films? Because my intention is to deal with Griffith's Biograph films as both esthetic works and industrial products, esthetic forms as well as modes of production, distribution and exhibition are essential to this work. But I am trying to do more than apply two different approaches to these films, critical on the one hand and industrial economic and social on the other. Because I maintain that the change in narrative form that one can trace through the early Biograph films can in part be understood as a response to changes within the film industry and its role in American society, I also want these different approaches to intersect. To demonstrate a change in narrative form, I must define with theoretical precision the way narrative operates in film. To show the relation of this interior change to the broader horizons of the film industry and social discourse about film, I must have a model of how that industry was structured and a concept of how these interior and exterior structures effect each other.

Can a structural approach to the narrative discourse of films intersect with a treatment of the industrial and social context of their production, or do they cancel each other out with different methods and conceptions of what a film is? There is a potential tension between my textual analysis of films and my consideration of their larger context. My basic conceptions of textual analysis are drawn from the tradition of literary structualism (Todorov and Genette, in particular). This tradition, particularly in its founding phase, tended to approach literary texts as closed systems. The founding concept of structural linguistics, Fernand de Saussure's understanding of the linguistic sign, short-circuits the reference that language bears to an extra-linguistic reality. For Saussure, the linguistic sign "unites not a thing and a name, but a concept and a sound image."[1] Labeled respectively the *signified* and the *signifier*, these elements form a closed system in which the signified is not identical to the "thing out there," to which it refers, but is an entirely linguistic entity.[2] Application of this principle to literature (or film) would seem to define it as a similarly closed system in which social forces outside the text could not be invoked to explain the operation of the system. Insulated from social forces through its constitution as a closed system, a structuralist view of a film text seems utterly at odds with a historical approach.

But even structuralists have begun to question the principle that their analysis must exclude any consideration of social phenomena. The concept of the closed text has been broadly questioned without sacrificing the idea of a text as a coherent system. Tzvetan Todorov, for example, has found that any treatment of texts must move through a sea of discourses that surrounds and penetrates them. Instead of a nontextual exterior reality, the social context provides yet another form of discourse. "Life" declares Todorov, "is a bio-graphy, the world a socio-graph, and we never reach an 'extra-symbolic' or 'prelinguistic' state." A full understanding of a text involves opening it to a series of other discourses as we move, as Todorov puts it, "from one discourse to another, from the text to the text."[3] An understanding of film in relation to social and ideological history can be seen as a movement from the filmic discourse of an individual text to the economic or ideological discourse that penetrates it. Opening up a filmic text to a broader context does not necessarily move from representation to reality or from cause to effect. Rather, it traces relations between, as Raymond Williams puts it, different signifying systems of a culture.[4] Furthermore, if we are dealing with language as discourse rather than a lexical system of signs, we are already moving beyond closed systems (without, however, ignoring signifying practices). In the linguist Emile Benveniste's consideration of the enunciation of the *enoncé* (the actual instance of discourse, such as the act of speaking), language opens up once more to the function of production and reference. As Paul Ricoeur has said, "In the phenomenon of the sentence, language passes outside of itself."[5] A historical approach to works of art requires a dual focus which acknowledges their esthetic identity but is also attuned to their function as social discourse.

Rigorous textual analysis is vital to the social history of film. Likewise, understanding film's relation to a culture's signifying systems is necessary for insightful textual analysis. This interrelation is delicate, however, and must be made with caution. Mechanistic ideas of causality are to be avoided. It should not be claimed that, for example, the Motion Picture Patents Company issued a particular directive and, presto, Griffith's *A Drunkard's Reformation* (1909) appeared. Many aspects of Griffith's filmic discourse are immanent to the filmic system. The most sophisticated attempts to place art works within a social context have emphasized the subtle mediations that relate such works to their social and ideological backgrounds and have drawn upon semiotic or formalist understanding of the discourse of art. Raymond Williams avoids describing the influence of economic forces on cultural production as a complete determinism, seeing it rather as "setting limits and exerting pressures."[6] M. M. Bakhtin and P. M. Medvedev's pioneering attempt at a sociological poetics likewise maintained that a social approach to art should never lose sight of the unique qualities of the work as art, and warned against drawing simplistic relations between base and superstructure, such as declaring "a poem's rhymes and stanzas are fitted together according to economic causality."[7]

In recent years, at least in film study, it is more often art's function as social action that has been overlooked. All too often art's unique discourse has been approached as if it were a private language. Considering film divorced from not only its social context but also from the context of its industrial production has severely limited the historical usefulness of textual analysis. Williams points out that such textual analysis privileges the consuming of a text over a consideration of its production: "The real social conditions of production were in any case neglected because they were believed to be at best secondary. The true relation was seen always as between the taste, the sensibility or the training of the reader and this isolated work, this object 'as in itself it really is,' as most people came to put it."[8] While the reception of a film, both by contemporary film analysts and contemporaneous audiences, must always claim the attention of film historians, this reception is not an atemporal isolated individual delectation, but a historical process open to the processes of social discourse.

Christian Metz's concept of the "cinematic institution" makes a clear interrelation between the "exterior" film industry and the "interior" structures such as narrative form. For Metz, the film industry rests upon a definition of the spectator contained within the film text. He states that "the cinematic institution is not just the cinema industry . . . it is also the mental machinery—another industry—which spectators accustomed to the cinema have internalized historically and which has adapted them to the consumption of films."[9] The outer aspect of the "cinematic institution," which Metz defines as "the financial investment in cinematic undertakings, the material manufacture of films, their distribution, their hire to cinemas,"[10] is founded upon an inner aspect, targeting a particular type of spectator. The film text's address to its spectator meshes with the industrial processes of production, distribution, and exhibition. Both rest upon a definition of the film experience and together define that experience. Analysis of films reveals their address to the spectator, while an exploration of the industrial context shows how that address was defined and exploited technologically and economically.

The historical context of films extends beyond texts to two spheres. First, individual films relate to the film industry which produced, distributed, and exhibited them. Second, these specific cinematic modes of production relate to the larger forces of social history. This work attempts a thorough consideration of only the first sphere. However, the relations I draw between films and their industrial context provide an opening to broader social horizons. Such issues as film censorship or the use of populist rhetoric and temperance themes in Biograph films indicate the routes further studies might take.

The transformation of the film industry in 1908–9 provided a new definition of the film commodity, a new image for film. This new understanding of the film commodity had impact (without absolutely determining) on the changes in filmic discourse which Griffith exemplifies. How a film was produced, how it was sold, who its audience was, and how it was distributed and exhibited all underwent radical change. And these changes provoke responses, interior transformations, in film form. Returning to Todorov's comments about moving from one discourse to another, the broader context for Griffith's films that I trace in this work could be described as the new discourse about film that appeared in 1908–9.

This new discourse took several forms, the first of which was primarily economic. A struggle for domination of the film industry took place that ended in the formation of the Motion Picture Patents Company (MPPC), the first American film trust. The company that employed Griffith, the American Mutoscope and Biograph Company, was at the center of the struggle, first as an excluded party, then as a full partner. New policies in production, distribution, and exhibition instituted by the MPPC provide a detailed ideological discourse about the nature of film. The discussions of film contained in the emerging trade journals also provide an important discourse redefining the image of film. The statements of public officials on such issues as film censorship reveal the extent to which this image was accepted or rejected by the legal representatives of society. Changes in modes of exhibition—the types of theaters where films were shown and the sorts of programs in which they were included—indicate how audiences were expected to receive films through a reorientation of the film-viewing experience. But the films themselves take center stage in my work. Through a close analysis of a number of Griffith's films from the beginning of his career I will both open these films to their historical context and pay full attention to the intricacies of their esthetic structures. Rather than cancelling out, these two processes complete each other.

A close examination of the first films D. W. Griffith made for the Biograph Company reveals a transformation in the narrative form of film. This transformation was part of a wide-ranging change in the way films were made, shown, and the social role they assumed. In no way is it simply the result of a single visionary filmmaker "inventing" a new cinematic language. Griffith's films both responded to and affected a broad transformation of film in American culture.

But to truly understand and be able to describe this transformation we must tackle a series of definitions. If these films display a transformation in narrative form, the nature of narrative in general and narrative in film needs definition. Therefore this historical work needs to linger over concerns that are more frequently thought of as theoretical. Perhaps this theoretical labor will provide a path through a thicket of subtle distinctions rather than create an intellectual jungle of its own.

In investigating narrative, we are hardly faced with a chartless wilderness. The nature of narrative has been a theoretical topic since theoretical investigations began and has been particularly scrutinized in recent decades. But we can begin with basic observations. The structure of the word *storytelling* provides a starting point for definition—its essentially double nature involving both a story to be told and the telling of that story.

The work of the literary critic Gérard Genette has focused precisely on narrative discourse, the *telling* of storytelling, and will form my recurrent reference. Genette distinguishes three different meanings for the term *narrative* (*recit* in French). First, narrative can refer to the actual language of a text that tells a story, as Seymour Chatman puts it, "the means by which the [narrative] content is communicated."[11] The second meaning of narrative refers to the content communicated by the discourse, "the succession of events, real or fictitious, that are the subject of this discourse" and which could be studied "without regard to the medium, linguistic or other" in which they are expressed. The third meaning refers to the event of "someone recounting something, the act of narrating in itself."[12] Genette analyzes narrative from these three perspectives: the means of expression, the events conveyed by these means, and the act of enunciation that expresses them.

Genette proposes the term *story* for the content conveyed by a narrative. The term *narrative* he reserves for the first meaning of the term, "the signifier, statement, discourse or narrative text itself" which communicates the story. The act of telling a story, producing a narrative, Genette terms *narrating*.[13] I shall use Genette's terms with a slight modification. To avoid the equivocal term *narrative*, I shall call the means of expression of a story *narrative discourse*, a term Genette often uses for the same concept. Genette's description of narrative discourse in literature provides a model for my treatment of Griffith, although my discussion is tailored to the demands of film rather than literature and to the requirements of a specific body of work.

My work on Griffith will not focus primarily on the analysis of story, but on narrative discourse. However, as Genette points out, the analysis of narrative discourse "implies a study of relationships," and to describe any one of the three aspects of narrative necessarily involves the others.[14] The logic of story can shape narrative discourse, making how it begins, develops, and ends. Therefore some attention to the basic structure or logic of story is called for. Todorov, revising the Aristotelean beginning, middle, and end, offers the following useful definition of story structure (or in his terms *plot*): "The minimal complete plot consists in the passage from one equilibrium to another. An 'ideal' narrative begins with a stable situation which is disturbed by some power of force. There results a state of disequilibrium: by the action of a force directed in the opposite direction, the equilibrium is re-established; the second equilibrium is similar to the first, but the two are never identical."[15] As David Bordwell has pointed out, this equilibrium model corresponds to the "canonical story format," the story pattern most easily recognized and comprehended within our culture.[16] It also corresponds to the stories found in the majority of Griffith's Biograph films.

Narrative discourse is precisely the text itself—the actual arrangement of signifiers that communicate the story—words in literature, moving images and written titles in silent films. It is only through this means of expression that we come in contact with either story or the act of narrating. The story is an imaginary construction that the spectator or reader creates while reading the narrative discourse of the actual text. Likewise, access to the act of narrating (in written literature and in film, at least) is dependent on the traces of telling that exist in the text. The text itself, words, images, or both, is all that we have, and discussions of the other aspects of narrative must begin from the text and refer back to it.[17]

Within narrative discourse Genette defines three functions that relate to either story or the act of narration. The first two relate narrative discourse to story. The first of these is tense, which deals with the temporal relations between narrative discourse and story.[18] Narrative discourse can manipulate the temporal order and form of story events. This temporal patterning shapes and arranges the story, involving the reader or spectator in an often-complex activity of reconstruction. Within tense, Genette describes three principle manipulations of story events. The first, dealing with the succession of events in a narrative, is order. The second, duration, deals with the compression or extension of events within a narrative, while the third, frequency, describes the possibility of multiple retellings of a single event.

The second function of narrative discourse defined by Genette, mood, also relates the discourse to the story it tells. Controlling the reader's access to the events of the story, mood corresponds in many ways to what Anglo-American criticism has called point of view, the narration's perspective of the story told. Genette feels that "one can tell *more* or tell *less* what one tells, and can tell it *according to one point of view or another*." Mood indicates the way the narrative discourse operates as a sort of screen between reader or spectator and the story as it unfolds: "the narrative can furnish the reader with more or fewer details, and in a more or less direct way, and can thus seem (to adopt a common and convenient spatial metaphor, which is not to be taken literally) to keep at a greater or lesser *distance* from what it tells."[19] This perspective on the action may correspond to the viewpoint of a particular character within the story, in which case we say the narrative adopts the character's point of view.

The last of Genette's categories, voice, deals with the relation between narrative discourse and the act of narrating—the traces of telling left in the text through which we sense a storyteller addressing an implied or real audience.[20] In literature this aspect would not only include such determinations as the person of the narrator (the familiar; first-, or third-person narrator), but also a wider range of means to reflect the act of narrating in the text, for example, the temporal relation between the story and the act of telling it, and a variety of ways in which the narrator asserts its presence.

My use of Genette comes from an appreciation of his precision and systematic analysis, rather than a belief that all film theory must be founded in linguistic or literary concepts. But are Genette's concepts applicable to film analysis, and if so, what sort of transformations must they undergo? More fundamentally, should the terms *narrative* and *narration* be restricted to literature and verbal language? We speak quite commonly of narrative film, and even narrative dance, painting, and pantomime. What allows this concept to cross between diverse media?

The answer lies in the double nature of storytelling, its division into the story constructed by the reader or viewer and the specific discourse that tells the story. I strongly endorse André Gaudreault's statement, "Any message by means of which any story whatsoever is communicated can rightfully be considered as a narrative."[21] Any communication of a story will be composed of Genette's triad of story, narrative discourse, and act of narrating. Because his narrative functions of tense, mood, and voice describe the interrelations between these universal aspects of narrative, I believe they apply to any narrative media.[22] But the task remains of describing film's specific narrative discourse. Genette clearly states that although story can be studied "without regard to the medium, linguistic or otherwise . . .,"[23] narrative discourse (because it exists in actual text) cannot be divorced from its specific medium.

Fundamental differences between literature and film rush to meet us. These differences derive from the noncommensurable nature of the types of signs each medium employs. Whereas literature is never directly iconic, film, as a series of photographic representational signs, is. This aspect of the filmic sign gives it a unique narrative status. While in language, as Genette points out (using the vocabulary of the Anglo-American tradition of Lubbock and Booth), "Showing can only be a *way of telling*,"[24] film in contrast can show more immediately than it can tell.

But across the chasm between showing and telling the two narrative discourses seem to signal each other. Certain literary narratives have sought to give the impressions of "showing" in spite of their lack of film's direct access to the visual. In literature the impression (or as Genette would put it, the illusion) of showing is the result of a narrator's consciously chosen and carefully devised strategy. Genette notes that a narrator may seem to abdicate the role of choosing only the most significant elements and instead gather a number of "useless and contingent" details in order to give the impression of showing.[25]

In film, this excess of mimesis over meaning appears automatically with the photographic image. Although a filmmaker can make images relatively abstract, they will still contain a plethora of information compared to a verbal description. For example, the first films that the Lumière brothers shot in the open air seem much more detailed and realistic than those the Edison Company shot against the dark background of the "Black Maria." But even Edison's films are crowded with the excess of photographic reality. Automatically present are details of posture, costuming, and gesture whose verbal description would overwhelm a written text (e.g., in Edison's kinetoscope film of Annie Oakley, her expression, the way she swings her rifle, the fringe on her costume, the puffs of smoke that seem to issue from the glass balls she shoots, etc.). Film *shows* automatically, recording a world of contingent events and unimportant details.

This dominance of showing over telling is the concealed reef over which the concept of the filmic narrator sails in peril. Does a film "tell" a story? Filmic discourse has an ability to appear nearly neutral. A single shot can seem to show a great deal while telling very little about it. If we approach film as a narrative form which presents stories to an audience, it nonetheless would be foolish to ignore a unique quality of its narrative discourse—its inherent photographic tendency toward mimesis, toward the representation of a world from which the filmic narrator can seem to be absent.

However, this aspect of film does not destroy the concept of the filmic narrator; rather it defines its role. The primary task of the filmic narrator must be to overcome the initial resistance of the photographic material to telling by creating a hierarchy of narratively important elements within a mass of contingent details. Through filmic discourse, these images of the world become addressed to the spectator, moving from natural phenomenon to cultural products, meanings arranged for a spectator. The filmic narrator shapes and defines visual meanings.

This is partly accomplished by a fourth aspect of narrative discourse that I will add to Genette's triad of story, discourse, and the act of narrating—narrativization. This is less an aspect separate from the other three than a term for the bond among them, and one that takes on particular importance in film. Defined by Stephen Heath, narrativization is precisely what holds Genette's three aspects of narrative together.[26] The process of narrativization binds narrative discourse to story and rules the narrator's address to the spectator. It organizes discourse to tell a story, binding its elements into this single process. In this process the energies of a film are channeled toward the explication of a story, and through this channeling create and define a situation for the spectator.[27]

The concept of narrativization focuses the transformation of showing into telling, film's bending of its excessive realism to narrative purposes. Narrativization, which would be something of a tautology in a literary text where the signs are naturally predisposed to telling, regulates the balance between mimetic and narrative functions in the filmic sign. According to Heath, narrativization "seek[s] to maintain a tight balance between the photographic image as a reproduction of reality and the narrative as the sense, the intelligibility, of that reality." The narrative discourse of a film "picks up—indicating by framing, shot angle, lighting, dialogue mention, musical underscoring, and so on—the notable elements . . .,"[28] thus carving a story out of a photographed reality.

Film's innate tendency toward mimesis becomes a sign of narrative realism, naturalizing the process of storytelling as the inclusion of apparently useless detail does in verbal narrative. Simultaneously the process of narrativization delivers a sense to this realism, through filmic discourse which "picks up" and selects precisely those meanings necessary for the story to be told. In this way the filmic image, without losing (indeed, using) its capacity for showing, defines its unique way of telling.

The narrative discourse of film involves a unique transaction between showing and telling. The photographic image clearly possesses a unique ability to show. But how do films pick up and indicate the significant elements within this detailed and contingent reality and endow them with a narrative meaning? What is it that tells the story in a narrative film? What are the marks within the film (or to use David Bordwell's more psychological and dynamic term, the cues)[29] by which the film conveys its story to the viewer?

Describing the narrative discourse of film must involve cutting up the filmic text so that its dynamic forces are exposed. Of course a narrative text functions as a whole, and analysis only untangles the synthesis that makes it work. I believe film's narrative discourse can best be described as the interrelation of three different levels that interrelate and express narrative information: the pro-filmic, the enframed image, and the process of editing.[30] I do not claim that they function in isolation, nor do I construct a hierarchy of importance, although I will show that some levels perform some tasks more economically than others. Although I will primarily deal with these levels as they are perceived by viewers, it is not irrelevant that they roughly correspond to the essential stages of film production as well: the periods of before, during, and after shooting.

The pro-filmic refers to everything placed in front of the camera to be filmed. It includes such things as the actors (and therefore casting decisions and performance style), lighting, set design, selection of locations, and selection of props. Strictly speaking, pro-filmic elements do not appear on the screen except through the next level of discourse, their capture on film as enframed images. However film viewers see the images on the screen as images of things, and the selection of the things that make up the image plays an extremely important role in conveying narrative information. Every film makes a selection of elements based on a preexisting set of possibilities (this actor and performance style rather than that one; that sort of set design rather than another). Therefore, as narrative discourse the pro-filmic embodies a series of choices and reveals a narrative intention behind the choices. The viewer receives the results of these choices and makes inferences based on them.

Gaudreault, who in his book *Du Litteraire au filmique* (1988) has largely adopted my schema of filmic discourse, describes the manipulation by the narrator of the pro-filmic as "mise-en-scene," referring particularly to the theatrical sense of this term.[31] Too often ignored in narrative theories, the pro-filmic plays an important role in narrative discourse.[32] Many of Griffith's innovations in filmic discourse lay in this area (e.g., the "restraint in expression" in acting style mentioned in his New York *Dramatic Mirror* advertisement).

The second level of filmic discourse is what I call the *enframed image*. At this level of filmic discourse the pro-filmic is transformed from preexistent events and objects into images on celluloid. The process is far from neutral. Placing an image within a frame entails arranging composition and spatial relations. The act of filming transforms the pro-filmic into a two-dimensional image, filmed from a particular point of view, framed within the camera aperture that geometrically defines the borders of the image. The whole host of formal devices that derive from the effects of perspective, selection of camera distance and angle, framing for composition, and the effects of movement within a frame determine specific choices available within this level of discourse. Whether on a conscious or preconscious level the viewer recognizes this construction of the image as a powerful narrative cue. Gaudreault borrows a term from Eisenstein, *mise-en-cadre*, the placement within the frame, to describe the activity responsible for this level of discourse.[33] New approaches in this level of filmic discourse, such as the role of composition in revealing character's moods, are also seen in Griffith's Biograph work.

The enframed image can also involve a number of other procedures including setting exposure, control of focus, selection of lenses or film stocks with different properties, manipulations of camera speed, and placing devices in front of the lens (such as Bitzer's vignette-masking diaphragms). Camera movement also falls into this category. Putting the frame itself into motion, camera movement can be a powerful device, creating a strong sense of an intervening narrator and strongly marked narrative cues. I also include in this category the processes of filming that involve re-photography and are carried out after the principle photography, such as split screens, superimpositions, and matting processes.

The third level of filmic discourse consists of editing. In most production practices this occurs after the act of filming and involves the cutting and selection of shots as well as their assembly into syntagmas. This process of combination is stressed by Gaudreault's terminology for the activity of editing, the neologism *mise-en-chain*.[34] In Genette's enumeration of the functions of narrative discourse, one seems particularly suited to this level of discourse—that of tense. Tense deals with the differences that can arise between the temporality of events as presented in narrative discourse and their time relations within the story being told. The single unedited shot, outside of an edited sequence, allows few differentiations between the time of narrative discourse and that of story.[35] This is evident in temporal order, because it is only through editing that a flashback or flashforward can be clearly signified. There have been attempts to create temporal disjunctions within a single shot, as in *A Love in Germany* (Wadja, 1984) or the opening of *Him and Me* (Benning, 1982), but these remain rarities and involve imitations of editing processes through camera movement. Likewise, the temporal relations between narrative discourse and story that Genette groups under duration, such as summary, elipsis, or narrative pauses all have clear equivalents in editing processes, with only awkward semi-equivalents within the single shot.[36] Finally to the extent that the temporal relations that Genette groups under frequency can appear in film (e.g., the repetitive account of a single event, as in the multiple presentations of the rape in *Rashomon*), they seem strongly dependent on editing.

The particular suppleness of editing comes from the discontinuity between shots that allows articulation between them, including the temporal differentiations mentioned previously. But spatial articulations are equally important in the process of editing, such as the synthetic space created by continuity editing or the disjunctions of space that occur in other editing styles. Spatial articulations are less defined in literature than in film. They represent an element of the filmic narrator that has no direct equivalent in Genette's treatment of literary narrative discourse. However spatial figures in film tend to be closely interrelated with temporal articulations, and I will generally deal with them together.

In the history of film theory, discussions of the "essential nature" of film have often focused on editing. These have ranged from the proclamation of the supremacy of editing by the early Soviet theorists, through its deemphasis in the work of Bazin, to the reevaluation by theorists such as Marie Ropars-Wuilleurnier and Gaudreault.[37] While editing represents a particularly supple level of filmic discourse, I maintain that all three levels must be considered in describing film's narrative discourse. As Bordwell has written, "all film techniques, even those involving the 'profilmic event,' function narrationally, constructing the story world for specific effects."[38]

The emphasis on editing in my analysis of Griffith therefore derives from Griffith's individual and historical situation rather than theoretical privileging. Production during this period favored editing over, for example, an elaborate system of camera movement such as appears in some film production after the 1930s. However, historical and technical determinants are not the sole factor. During the same period as Griffith's Biograph career, Louis Feuillade, as well as other directors at Gaumont, such as Léonce Perret and Georges Monca, created a narrative style less dependent on editing, favoring elements such as composition and lighting. The emphatic role of editing in Griffith's filmmaking must partly derive from his own choices. The importance of editing in this work therefore derives from the films I am discussing.

Each of these levels integrates the one before, transforming it as it does so. Their effect on a spectator is generally due to their interrelation, and I separate them for analysis. These three aspects of filmic discourse—the pro-filmic, the enframed image, and editing—almost always work in concert and represent the mediation between story and spectator in film. They are how films "tell" stories. Taken together, they constitute the filmic narrator.

Because film's narrative discourse represents the actual text of a film—its existence as a series of filmic images—no narrative film can exist except through its narrative discourse. It logically follows that every narrative film has a filmic narrator embodied by this discourse. The three levels of filmic discourse are not optional ornaments of style. They form the very mode of existence for any narrative film. But within a specific film, the particular stance and tone of its filmic narrator is determined by choices made within the levels of filmic discourse. Therefore the filmic narrator appears in a wide range of forms determined by specific choices within and among the three levels of filmic discourse (e.g., expressionist set design, high angle of camera, and match cutting). Relating these choices to the functions of narrative discourse that Genette lays out allows us to distinguish different types of filmic narrators. However, even if a certain type of narrator has a tendency to give the impression that "events seem to narrate themselves" without the intervention of a narrator (what the linguist Emile Benveniste calls *histoire*),[39] the narrator can never disappear entirely but can only be concealed. As Todorov writes, "Events never 'tell themselves'; the act of verbalization is irreducible."[40]

I would assert that the same is true in film. Although what has been termed "classical film narrative" labors to present the illusion of a direct presentation of events, this is always a labor of concealment, the construction of an illusion. As Paul Ricoeur has said of the ideology of literary transparency from which the classical style of film arises, "the rhetoric of dissimulation, the summit of the rhetoric of fiction, must not fool the critic, even if it may fool the reader."[41] As we shall see, Griffith plays an ambiguous role in the establishment of this classical style.

If the marks of enunciation in filmic discourse (which reveal the hand of the narrator) can only be camouflaged and not eradicated, we can establish a range of filmic narrators stretching from the apparent "invisibility" of the classical Hollywood film to the heavily rhetorical montage of, for example,

Eisenstein—and it is significant that Griffith is often cited as a seminal influence on both extremes. Arranged synchronically, different degrees of assertiveness in the narrative discourse of films could distinguish among the narrative styles of different filmmakers, different cultures, or simply different films. Arranged diachronically, such differences could provide a historical view of the development of film narrative.

While narrative discourse embodies the telling of a story by a filmic narrator, the process of narration involves an interrelation between a narrator and what semioticians call a "narratee."[42] The dynamic aspect of this interaction should be stressed. Although implied by Genette, the role of the narratee has been discussed more explicitly by American film theorists whose concern with the activity of the viewer gives Genette's model a more dynamic twist.[43]

Edward Branigan, in *Point of View in the Cinema*, defines narration as an *activity*. This activity involves more than Genette's act of narrating because it involves the reader or viewer as well as the narrator. As Branigan puts it, narration is "a dialectical process between narrator and reader *through which* is realized a narrative."[44] We have already caught sight of this activity in the simple fact that the reader or viewer constructs (or reconstructs) the story from the narrative discourse of the text. Bordwell's attempt to describe film narration through the concepts of Constructivist psychology similarly foregrounds the spectator's activity. According to Bordwell the spectator uses cues within the narrative texts "to make assumptions, draw inferences about current story events, and frame and test hypothesies about prior and upcoming events."[45]

Although my approach differs from Bordwell and Branigan's, I fully agree with their vision of an active spectator who contributes to the construction of the narrative. Their focus on the dynamic interaction between narrative discourse and reader or viewer allows me to specify that film's narrative discourse does not overpower a passive spectator but provides patterns within films that provoke active mental responses and set in motion the range of cognitive processes Bordwell describes. A particular narrative discourse addresses a spectator in a particular way, eliciting specific sorts of activities. The change Griffith brings to the way films are narrated is at the same time a change in the way films are viewed. Along with a new sort of filmic narrator, Griffith's transformation of filmic discourse constructs a new sort of spectator for film. Or to put it in a way that gives the spectator due, the spectator constructs a new sort of film experience as cued by Griffith's narrative discourse.

Both Branigan and Bordwell stress the role of the spectator at the expense of the narrator. In fact, they reject this term, preferring impersonal rubics, Branigan opting for "activity of narration"[46] and Bordwell for "narration." Their discomfort with the term *narrator* is in part understandable and methodologically useful and in part disturbing. Both authors stress the impersonal, text-immanent nature of narrative discourse and describe the narrator as an "anthropomorphic fiction."[47] It is theoretically important to avoid identifying a narrator with a biological person such as the author. Narrative discourse is made up of words and images, not flesh and blood. Such theoretical precisions are necessary to maintain the integrity of the esthetic text. I will occasionally use the term *narrative discourse* rather than *narrator* in order to stress that I am dealing with images and their construction rather than a person.

However, the depersonalization of narrative discourse brings its own theoretical blindspot that distorts the way films are received by spectators, and the way they function within history and society. Bordwell particularly seems to set aside the fact that in our perception of films we are aware of them as products, as entities manufactured by human beings with evident purposes and designs upon us. In spite of his emphasis on the spectator's role he distorts the address that films level at audiences. The alert and active spectator proposed by Bordwell's psychological description must realize that these images come from *somewhere*. When Bordwell declares that his theory of narration "presupposes a perceiver, but not a sender, of a message,"[48] one wonders what sort of message this is—and in what universe a receiver can respond to a message without wondering about a sender.

The limits of this depersonalization become particularly clear when Bordwell sets his model of narration in motion. What he has excluded in theory re-emerges in his practice. For Bordwell, narration can be "self conscious," can "voluntarily restrict itself," "refuse to mark," or can "flaunt its ability"[49]—to take only a few examples which indicate that he cannot avoid speaking of this impersonal function as volitional and endowed with something very much like human consciousness. Bordwell grounds some of his objection to the concept of the narrator in the transparency of the classical style, claiming that classical films are not endowed with a perceptible narrator, although certain modernist films do signal that the "spectator should construct a narrator." Only certain exceptional films therefore possess narrators, and even this sort of narrator "does not create the narration" but is constructed by the spectator.[50]

Bordwell's theory is not irrational; the narrative discourse of film with its tendency toward showing does possess a transparent quality that verbal discourse lacks. And certainly the narrator as the embodiment of narrative discourse does not stand outside the text. The narrator communicates to the spectator only through the spectator's engagement with the narrative discourse, so in a sense the spectator does construct the narrator, just as he or she does the story, from the narrative discourse. But storytelling implies a storyteller as surely as it does a story. We must be careful in describing the nature of this teller, this narrator.

In films and literature, the narrator is not a flesh-and-blood entity. The narrator, in my understanding of the term, is a theoretical entity, as divorced from an actual person as Bordwell's spectator is from a particular viewer. But preserving the more personal term *narrator* not only avoids academic abstraction but also responds to the experience a reader or spectator has of being addressed by a story. This address can be described by the volitional activities that slip back in Bordwell's window of praxis after being barred at his theoretical door. We receive a text as though it were saying something to us, as though, in the words of my colleague Robert Stein, it has designs on us. We experience it as an intentional object, designed to have certain effects on us.[51] More than a random set of cues, the narrator embodies the design organizing narrative discourse, the intentions which unify its effects. It corresponds to that force in narrative that Peter Brooks calls plot or plotting, "the design and intention of narrative, what shapes a story and gives it a certain direction or intent of meaning."[52] These designs do not exist outside the text but are evident in the rhetorical arrangement of its devices. The more active term *narrator* stresses that this discourse, to paraphrase Brooks, involves force as well as form. It is not only constructed by the reader or spectator, but also addresses and affects him or her through specific devices. Thus in describing film's narrative discourse I have described each level as activities which arrange and organize material in order to address a spectator. No narrative film exists, even the "transparent" films of the classical style, without making such an address.

Another reason for maintaining the term *narrator* is that although it is theoretically separate from the author and processes of production that created the work, it does provide, in the words of Ricoeur, the image of the author within the text. As a series of intentions it recalls the narrative's nature as a unified manufactured object, the product of human labor. As Ricoeur asserts, "the reader does not ascribe this unification to the rules of composition alone but extends it to the choices and to the norms that make the text, precisely, the work of some speaker, hence a work produced by someone and not by nature."[53] Bordwell's theory tends to occult the spectator's perception of a film as something produced. It belongs to the tendency Raymond Williams attacked of dealing with art works solely from the point of view of consumption, ignoring the process of production.[54] Griffith's films address us through their narrative discourse, which creates the sense of an intervening figure who has arranged the images on the screen in a particular manner with specific social consequences. The concept of the filmic narrator helps us relate filmic form to broader contexts.

How does one relate this series of theoretical definitions to my historical task of describing the narrative form of Griffith's first Biograph films and their place in the larger history of narrative form in film as a whole? The chapters that follow show that this theoretical discussion, far from being removed from the tasks of history, allows me to describe Griffith's place in film history with a new precision. I have called the approach to storytelling that Griffith develops in his first films the *narrator system*, the system of filmic devices through which Griffith centers on the task of narration.

What sort of entity is the narrator system? It is an abstraction from the films that Griffith directed in his first years at Biograph which describes Griffith's systematic approach to narrative form. It is not the only approach to narrative form found in his first films. As the chapters that deal with specific films will show, Griffith developed the narrator system gradually, and for awhile it jockeyed for prominence with other approaches. Further, the narrator system, although specific to Griffith, appeared within an international change in narrative form which occurred during the years 1908–13.

The narrator system is one particular synthesis of filmic discourse occurring in the general move to a cinema of narrative integration. During this period filmmakers began to center their work on the task of storytelling. This constitutes the chief intention of the narrator system as well, but it remains the narrative form of a particular filmmaker and production company. Much of what I will say about the narrator system applies as well to the cinema of narrative integration, but not everything. The extreme importance of parallel editing in the narrator system, for instance, was influential on other filmmakers of the period but is by no means universal. However the particularity of the narrator system comes less from its deviations from the norms of cinema of narrative integration than from its extreme expression of them. With Griffith, the emphasis on the tasks of storytelling is brought to a particular intensity.

Genette's analysis of narrative discourse provides a specific outline of the way the narrator system performs its narrative tasks. However, my use of Genette's categories in analyzing Griffith's Biograph films involves an immense simplification. Genette's basic categories offer a comprehensive narrative analysis. However, the application of the categories is extremely limited in comparison to Genette's own work. By no means all the aspects which Genette discusses in his analysis of Proust will find their equivalent in my description of the narrator system. Tense, mood, and voice as found in Griffith are far from the complicated and subtle examples Genette draws from *The Remembrance of Things Past*.

The narrator system takes on a series of tasks in the realm of tense. As I stated earlier, the issues involved in tense in the cinema are expressed most easily through editing. Assembling several shots allows temporal relations that are elusive in the single unedited shot. Tense in film involves the temporal marking of shots in relation to each other. This is not restricted to such situations as flashbacks or elipses between shots. Even the creation of a continuity of time over two shots involves temporal marking because continuity of time in an edited sequence is a synthetic product not at all identical to the time in which events are actually filmed. The temporal marking of the relation between any two shots forms the basis of tense in film.

Before Griffith, temporal relations between shots were often extremely ambiguous. During the period of Griffith's filmmaking at Biograph this temporal ambiguity nearly disappeared, and the rules of temporal continuity over shots were established. Griffith's parallel editing also marked temporal and spatial relations quite specifically in contrast to the ambiguous temporality of earlier cinema. The narrator system, therefore, establishes temporal marking unambiguously, conveying continuity and simultaneity within a variety of spatial relations.

I will primarily deal with the aspect of mood in the narrator system through Griffith's approach to characterization. Although Genette does not privilege this aspect over others in mood, its key role in differentiating Griffith from earlier filmmakers makes it central to the narrator system. The access that Griffith allows us to characters' emotions and motivations for their actions define his particular development of an authorial point of view.

Although it is tempting to see the films of Porter, Méliès, and other early filmmakers as bereft of character psychology, they contain some signs of characterization. However, these are primarily restricted to pro-filmic elements such as performance, costuming, and make-up. The narrator system conveys characterization by the other levels of filmic discourse as well, such as composition and editing. In addition, Griffith transformed the pro-filmic signs of characterization. Performance, make-up, and casting changed enormously under Griffith while other pro-filmic elements such as the selection of props and settings took on new psychological significance.

Griffith's narrative discourse expressed a range of moral judgments on his characters, an intervening narratorial function that belongs to Genette's category of voice. These moral judgments take a more blatant form than the examples of authorial presence Genette analyzes in the work of Proust. If primitive, they nonetheless assert the narrator's presence through commenting on the story. Although there are tendencies toward asserting a judgment in compositional schemes in Griffith's Biograph films, editing predominantly plays this role in the narrator system. A contrast established through juxtaposing shots expresses most of Griffith's moral judgments.

Each of these aspects of the narrator system can be further specified in terms of their narrativization, their direct expression of story. These devices played important roles in the film industry's desire to fashion films on the model of the respectable forms of the novel and drama. The temporal marking of shots exemplified by parallel editing finds its fusing with story—its narrativization—in the technique of suspense. As the original "master of suspense" in film narrative, Griffith demonstrated the hold of his narrative discourse on both story and spectator with his famous last-minute rescues.

The approach to characterization in the narrator system asserts its hold on story through an expression of psychology, the portrayal of mental acts such as memories or emotional reactions, which then provide motivations for characters' actions and decisions. A number of figures of the narrator system convey characters' memories, concerns, or fears. These mental or emotional states play crucial narrative roles in Griffith's filmmaking in contrast to earlier filmmakers. Although performances in early cinema represent a variety of emotional states, characterization rarely played a determinate role in the story. In Griffith's early Biograph films, the psychology of characters—their motivations and decisions—frequently determined the turning point of a story and were emphasized through filmic discourse.

Of course we are dealing with psychology of a rather elementary sort. The narrator system does not provide the analysis of character psychology found in the nineteenth-century novel, even in its more popular versions. And the ways in which Griffith conveyed the subjectivity of characters, while presaging the point-of-view shot and memory flashback of later cinema, still stop short of these later figures. Nonetheless the narrator system centers filmic discourse and narrative development much more strongly on the psychological motivation of characters than earlier cinema.

As I already indicated, the voice of the filmic narrator in Griffith's films asserts its relation to story primarily through an expression of moral judgment. Voice is narrativized and ideologized as the voice of morality. The role of morality in Griffith's narrativization is pervasive and determines the construction of story as well, so that narrative resolution frequently involves a fablelike moral. But morality in Griffith's Biograph films is not restricted to the triumph of virtue over vice in the story (which certainly appears in films before him), but rather in a filmic discourse which expresses judgments on proper and improper behavior.

Suspense, psychology, and morality: although they do not exhaust all aspects of the narrator system these concepts do plot its cardinal points. But where does D. W. Griffith figure into the scheme?

Notes

1 John Lyons, *Introduction to Theoretical Linguistics* (Cambridge: Cambridge University Press, 1971), p. 66. See also Ferdinand de Saussure, *Course in General Linguistics*, ed. Charles Bally and Albert Sechehaye in collaboration with Albert Riedlinger, trans. Wade Baskin (New York: McGraw-Hill, 1966), pp. 77–100.

2 See Paul Ricoeur, *Interpretation Theory: Discourse and the Surplus of Meaning* (Fort Worth: Texas Christian University Press, 1976), pp. 5–6.

3 Tvtezan Todorov, *Introduction to Poetics*, trans. Richard Howard (Minneapolis: University of Minnesota Press, 1981), pp. 60–61.

4 Raymond Williams, *The Sociology of Culture* (New York: Schocken Books, 1982), particularly pp. 12–13.

5 Paul Ricoeur, *The Rule of Metaphor: Multi-disciplinary Studies of the Creation of Meaning in Language*, trans. Robert Czerny, Kathleen McLaughlin, and John Costello (Toronto: University of Toronto Press, 1977), p. 74.

6 Raymond Williams, "Base and Superstructure in Marxist Cultural Theory," in *Problems in Materialism and Culture: Selected Essays* (London: NLB, Verso Editions, 1980), p. 32.

7 M. M. Bakhtin and P. M. Medvedev, *The Formal Method in Literary Scholarship: A Critical Introduction to Sociological Poetics*, trans. Wlad Godzich (Cambridge: Harvard University Press, 1985), pp. 27, 15.

8 Williams, "Base and Superstructure," p. 46.

9 Christian Metz, *The Imaginary Signifier: Psychoanalysis and the Cinema*, trans. Celia Britton et al. (Bloomington: Indiana University Press, 1982), p. 7.
10 Metz, *The Imaginary Signifier*, p. 8.
11 Seymour Chatman, *Story and Discourse: Narrative Structure in Fiction and Film* (Ithaca: Cornell University Press, 1978), p. 19.
12 Gérard Genette, *Narrative Discourse: An Essay in Method*, trans. Jane E. Lewin (Ithaca: Cornell University Press, 1980), pp. 25–27.
13 Genette, *Narrative Discourse*, p. 27.
14 Ibid., pp. 27, 29.
15 Todorov, *Introduction to Poetics*, p. 38.
16 David Bordwell, *Narration in the Fiction Film* (Madison: University of Wisconsin Press, 1985), p. 35.
17 Genette, *Narrative Discourse*, pp. 28–29.
18 Ibid., p. 31.
19 Ibid., pp. 161–62.
20 Ibid., p. 31.
21 André Gaudreault, *Du Litteraire au filmique: System du récit* (Paris: Meridiens Klincksieck, 1988), p. 84 (my translation).
22 See letter from Genette quoted in Gaudreault, *Du Litteraire*, p. 29 (footnote), which states in part: "Personally, I favor more and more a narrow definition of narrative, *haplé diégésis*, a statement of actions by a narrator who expresses the actions by verbal means (oral or written) and in this sense a theatrical or filmic narrative does not exist for me" (my translation). I am indebted to Gaudreault's work, including his dissertation, which he was kind enough to make available. Although some of my conclusions differ from his, I am constantly in debt to his thoroughness and clarity in approaching the issue.
23 Genette, *Narrative Discourse*, p. 25.
24 Ibid., p. 166.
25 Ibid.
26 See, Stephen Heath, *Questions of Cinema* (Bloomington: Indiana University Press, 1981), pp. 107–8 and passim.
27 Heath, *Questions of Cinema*, p. 109.
28 Ibid., p. 122. Heath's understanding of narrativization is dependent on the Lacanian theory of the constitution of the subject and the Althusserian theory of ideology. If I am bypassing a complete discussion of these issues in relation to Griffith's work, it is because I find the constant circulating of various film texts through this system to be a time-consuming process often undertaken at the expense of other essential issues. For those who would claim that no historical treatment of this material is valid without such an approach, I can only say that I am aware of these methods of analysis, and have certainly, but not exclusively, been influenced by them.
29 Bordwell, *Narration*, pp. 31–33.
30 This schema does not deal with the important issue of sound in film, which is not relevant to the films I examine herein, and would have to be approached as a fourth level, itself in need of subdividing.
31 Gaudreault, *Du Litteraire*, p. 199.
32 However both David Bordwell and George M. Wilson accord the pro-filmic considerable attention in their respective works, *Narration in the Fiction Film*, and *Narration in Light: Studies in Cinematic Point of View* (Baltimore: Johns Hopkins University Press, 1986).
33 Gaudreault, *Du Littaire*, p. 199.
34 Ibid.

35 See Genette, *Narrative Discourse*, p. 35. There are exceptions to this, however, that do not relate to Griffith's Biograph films but should be included theoretically. Within the level of the enframed image, which corresponds to the production stage of shooting and re-photography, there is the possibility of slow or fast motion, created by shooting or printing, which sets up a differentiation between story time and discourse time. Likewise, the soundtrack can set up a host of temporal relations, most obviously through voice-over, which are not described herein. This seems another indication that sound would operate as a fourth level of filmic discourse, with strong roles in all three of Genette's aspects of narrative discourse.
36 Ibid., pp. 86–112.
37 See, Gaudreault, *Du Littaire*, pp. 105–15, and Marie-Claire Ropars-Wuilleumier, "Function du montage dans la constitution du récit au cinema," *Revue des sciences humanies* 36 (Jan.–March 1971): 51–52.
38 Bordwell, *Narration*, p. 12.
39 Emil Benveniste, *Problems in General Linguistics* (Coral Gables: University of Miami Press, 1970), p. 208.
40 Todorov, *Introduction*, p. 39.
41 Paul Ricoeur, *Time and Narrative*, trans. Kathleen Blamey and David Pellauer (Chicago: University of Chicago Press, 1988), vol. 3, p. 161.
42 Todorov, *Introduction*, p. 40.
43 And in spite of his own apparent confusion on this matter, (see, for example, *Narration*, p. 63), the narratee corresponds precisely to Bordwell's conception of the spectator, "a hypothetical entity executing the operations relevant to constructing a story out of the film's representations," ibid., p. 30.
44 Edward R. Branigan, *Point of View in the Cinema: A Theory of Narration and Subjectivity in Classical Film* (Amsterdam: Mouton Publishers, 1984), p. 39.
45 Bordwell, *Narration*, p. 39.
46 Branigan, *Point of View*, p. 40.
47 Ibid.; Bordwell, *Narration*, p. 62.
48 Bordwell, *Narration*, p. 62.
49 Ibid., pp. 58, 65, 89, 146.
50 Ibid., p. 62.
51 I use the term *intentional* in its phenomenological meaning indicating a product of human consciousness, rather than its psychological meaning. I am not claiming that a particular definable intention lies behind every narrative, or that criticism should reconstruct this intention. This would lead of course to the intentional fallacy. The intention behind a narrative as an intentional object may remain unspecified, its very vagueness drawing a response from the reader or spectator.
52 Peter Brooks, *Reading for the Plot: Design and Intention in Narrative* (New York: Random House, 1984), p. xi.
53 Ricoeur, *Time and Narrative*, vol. 3, p. 162.
54 Bordwell's own historical work pioneered a new serious consideration of the process of production. However I find a contradiction between his theoretical apparatus and his important scholarly work on production modes. Likewise, the brilliance of his analysis of the narrative discourse of films in *Narration in the Fiction Film* seems unencumbered by what I consider his theoretical weak spot, because intentionality actually reemerges in his specific analyses.

45

LEVELS OF NARRATION

Edward Branigan

Source: *Narrative Comprehension and Film*, London: Routledge, 1992, pp. 86–124.

Eight levels

Perception must occur within boundaries and limits: perception *of* what *under* which conditions? It is not enough to simply locate film comprehension under the general conditions imposed by the projection of a strip of celluloid containing photographic transparencies and recorded sound. More and finer distinctions about perceptual "contexts" will be required in order to understand how our understanding of narrative proceeds. The basic organization of events into a narrative pattern is directed by a narrative schema. However, as the focus of inquiry shifts from "what happens" to the "how and when" of our knowing what happens, a deeper narrational schema will be found setting the conditions for, and directing, the operation of a narrative schema. These conditions may change from moment to moment. Colin MacCabe's "hierarchy of discourses," Ben Brewster's "hierarchies of relative knowledge," and Alan Williams's "four films" can all be interpreted as attempts to define suitable contexts, or *levels*, within which specific mental operations will be successful in organizing aural and visual data into a narrative pattern of events. Levels of a text are postulated in order to explain how data is systematically recast by the spectator from one perceptual context to another. What is remembered and what is forgotten by a spectator is systematic, not accidental. Generally the spectator engages the text in multiple ways, assuming a variety of roles for different contexts at different times. In order to delineate the various roles that specify how information may be acquired and shaped into a narrative pattern, we will need a new vocabulary.

Susan Lanser, drawing on the work of many theorists, has proposed a hierarchy of roles, or levels, which describe typical ways that a reader participates in a literary text. An actual text may be described according to how it shifts among these levels to build a hierarchy (or other configuration) of relative knowledge. In figure 1, I have expanded Lanser's basic levels from six

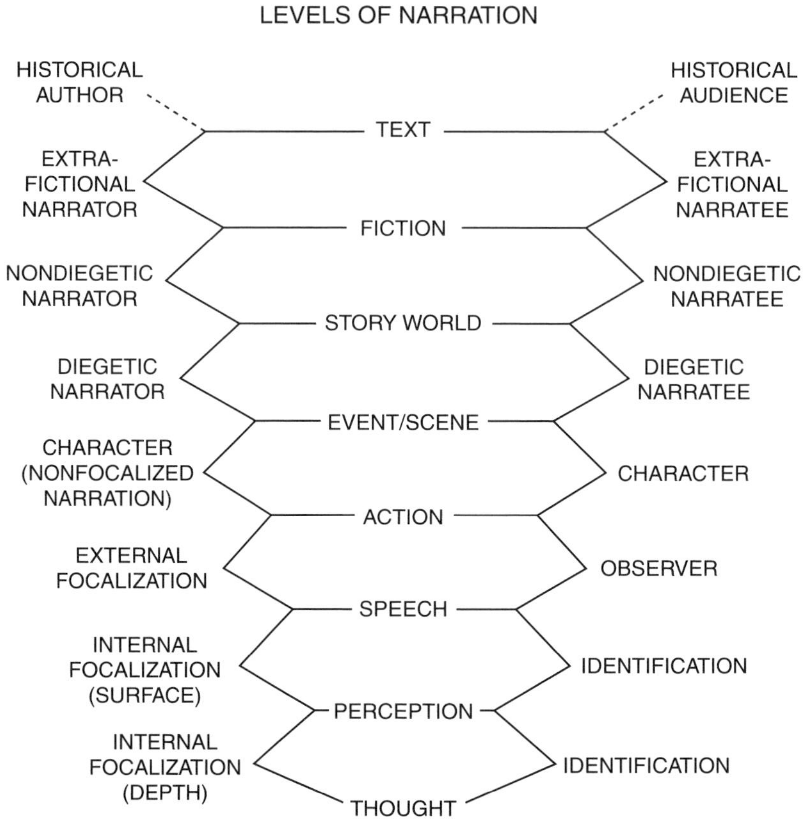

Figure 1 Eight levels of narration
A text is composed of a hierarchical series of levels of narration, each defining an epistemological context within which to describe data. A particular text may define any number of levels to any degree of precision along a continuum from the internal dynamics of a character to a representation of the historical conditions governing the manufacture of the artifact itself.

to eight and represented them as positions on a continuum rather than as sharply exclusive alternatives.[1] I will now examine these levels in relation to film comprehension.

I will define a "text" as a certain *collection of descriptions of an artifact* where the artifact must be one that materializes a symbol system, and the descriptions that are offered of it must be sanctioned by a society.[2] Thus a "text" is more than the material of an artifact and more than the symbols materialized; a text is always subject to change according to a social consensus about the nature of the symbols that have been materialized.

The concept of a "historical author" of a text has a similar complexity: part psychological, part social. As for the psychological, Roland Barthes observes, "The one *who speaks* (in the narrative) is not the one *who writes* (in real life) and the one *who writes* is not the one *who is*."[3] An author, however, exists not only as a biographical person, or persons, who has created a text, but also as a cultural *legend* created by texts (i.e., under one or more descriptions).[4] Being an author is performing for/in a social group. For example, Alfred Hitchcock as an individual is defined by the events of his life, traits of his personality, the labor he expended in making films, his view of himself, and the shaping influences of his time. He is one of the text's first critics. With respect to the "historical audience," however, he is also a character, or legend of the time. The audience knows Hitchcock on the basis of popular beliefs about him and by virtue of sharing with him certain kinds of knowledge about society. Hitchcock's public persona (which he alertly helped to author) is composed of his famous profile, a bit of theme music, television monologues, interviews, publicity, cameo appearances in his films, and so on. As a result his name has become a *brand name* guaranteeing a certain kind of experience: "Alfred Hitchcock's" *Vertigo* promises suspense, obsession, deceit, ambivalence, mordant wit, violence, and sexual malaise. We bring this "Hitchcock" with us to the theater because we are members of his community and use his name in describing certain artifacts. In this sense, "Hitchcock" is not only the one "who writes" for an audience, but also the one "who is written by" his audience.

A text emerges, then, from a historical situation that presupposes a social consensus about artifacts and biographical authors. All texts have such a *non*fictional dimension: films are made with materials and labor, marketed, and have measurable social and psychological effects; costs are incurred. However, films may also exist as interpreted fictionally, and may even explicitly address the problem of interpreting a world fictionally. Thus there must exist a transitional level that mediates between nonfiction and fiction. In order to avoid contradiction and paradox, then, statements *about* an embedded fiction cannot be made from within the fiction itself, but rather must emerge from a context more abstract than that to which they refer.[5] Hence an *extra*-fictional level in the text is required in order to talk about objects *as* fictional on a "lower" level of the text. Fiction arises out of nonfiction. The truth or falsity of a fictional reference is, of course, another matter. The reason that nonfictional descriptions are "prior" to fictional descriptions in this way is that fictional descriptions do not yet refer, or refer only partially, and one must begin interpreting somewhere; that is, one must begin with at least a reference to the possibility of referring fictionally. (Chapter 7 will consider in more detail the distinction between nonfiction and fiction.)

Consider the extra-fictional narrator in the precredit sequence of *The Wrong Man* (1956). A distant figure is strongly backlit, casting a gigantic shadow into the foreground of what appears to be a vast empty soundstage. The person's features cannot be distinguished. We hear:

> This is Alfred Hitchcock speaking. In the past, I have given you many kinds of suspense pictures. But this time I would like you to see a different one. The difference lies in the fact that this is a true story, every word of it. And yet, it contains elements that are stranger than all the fiction that has gone into many of the thrillers that I've made before.

The third sentence with its ambiguous use of "different one" (a new kind of suspense picture, or a new kind of picture?) together with the last sentence[6] manage to intimate that truth is only another kind of "suspense" and will be fully as entertaining as the fiction films the audience has come to expect from Hitchcock's work. And indeed the explicit pronouncements about a simple truth do not prevent what follows from incorporating both fictional and narrative patterns.[7] But this is not to say that the precredit speech is merely a deception; rather, its function is to begin to put into place an *ordered* sequence of perspectives within which to interpret the "truth" of the story. After all, the audience is well aware that "every word" of the story can*not* be *equally* true as claimed; that is, true to the same degree and in the same way. The film has clearly been made after the fact, with actors and dialogue; it includes picture and music as well as word; events are witnessed without the witness being seen, and so forth. The film depends on us accepting these sorts of stipulations; it does not attempt to hide them, but merely to organize them. Because of the necessity of imposing an organization on our interpretive activities, "Hitchcock" – although existing in the film considered as a text – must stand "outside" the film considered as a fiction in talking about what is to follow; that is, Hitchcock's voice and image here are extra-fictional.[8] Thus at least two films are working on us at this moment: a historical artifact of a man who talked on a soundstage, and a (purported) nonfictional discourse in which a man is talking about what will later be talked about and shown. These "two films" are the first two levels of figure 1: the historical and the extra-fictional.

The extra-fictional voice need not be as "personalized" and explicit as the dim figure who speaks in the precredit sequence of *The Wrong Man*. Either the actual speaker may become more prominent and intrusive, and be given psychological traits, or else he or she may become less identifiable,[9] even (as we will shortly discover) invisible and inaudible. Both the location and time of the speaking act may also be made relatively explicit or implicit. What defines the extra-fictional is its relationship to the other levels: how we imagine visual and/or aural data to be functioning with respect to other conceivable groupings of visual and/or aural data. Thus within each of the levels of narration displayed in figure 1, there exist many fine gradations which may be exploited by a given text in presenting a variety of contexts for its information.

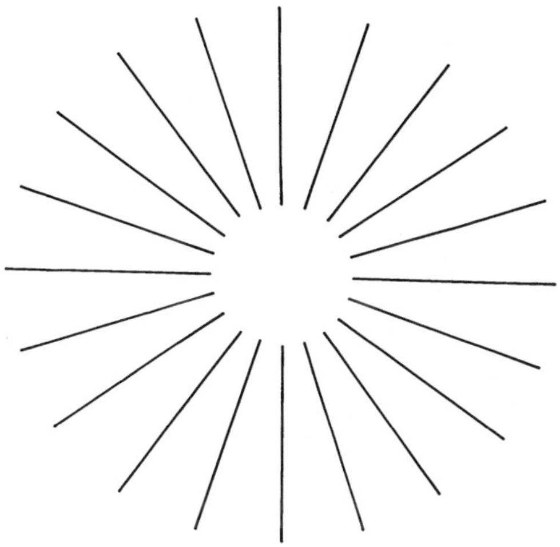

Figure 2 An implicit circle
An implicit circle composed of what is missing from a series of straight lines. Narration, too, may be implicit, composed of what is missing from a pattern of explicit narrations.

It is essential to realize that a narration may be *implicit* in a text. I will risk a visual analogy in order to clarify the important concept of implicitness. In figure 2, a series of straight lines have been used to create an implicit, or virtual circle.[10] The circumference of the circle is nonphysically existent. The circle emerges as a pattern of what has been omitted, or is missing, in the actual configuration of lines. One can imagine, of course, a more complex series of lines, perhaps criss-crossing, that would render the implicit circle less certain or open to other interpretations. My claim is that narration may be implicit in a similar way. In order to recognize such a narration, one will need to be sensitive to the explicit narrations, especially to what has been omitted, or is missing, in the direct regulation of knowledge in a text.[11]

I would like to analyze a particular implicit narration by focusing on one that is quite powerful and the topic of much general study by narrative theorists – an implicit extra-fictional narration that theorists often personify as "the implied author." The opening scene of *The Wrong Man* ends by following a character, Manny Balestrero (Henry Fonda), as he leaves a nightclub. We first see two policemen who happen to be walking by the front of the club (fig. 3; shot 1). Then each of the next two shots, because of a meticulous blocking of the action combined with exact compositions and cutting, *make it appear visually* that Manny (entering frame left through a door) is overtaken by the police and is walking with a policeman on each side (figs 4–6; shots 2A, 2B, 3). We know that this is only a visual illusion – that is, an effect produced by the timing and unique angles of view – for we can also

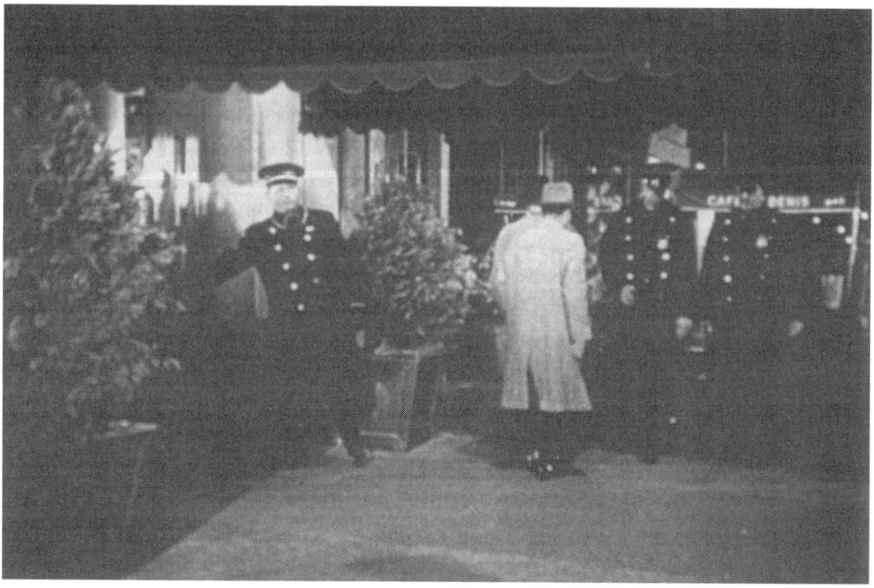

Figure 3 The Wrong Man (shot 1)

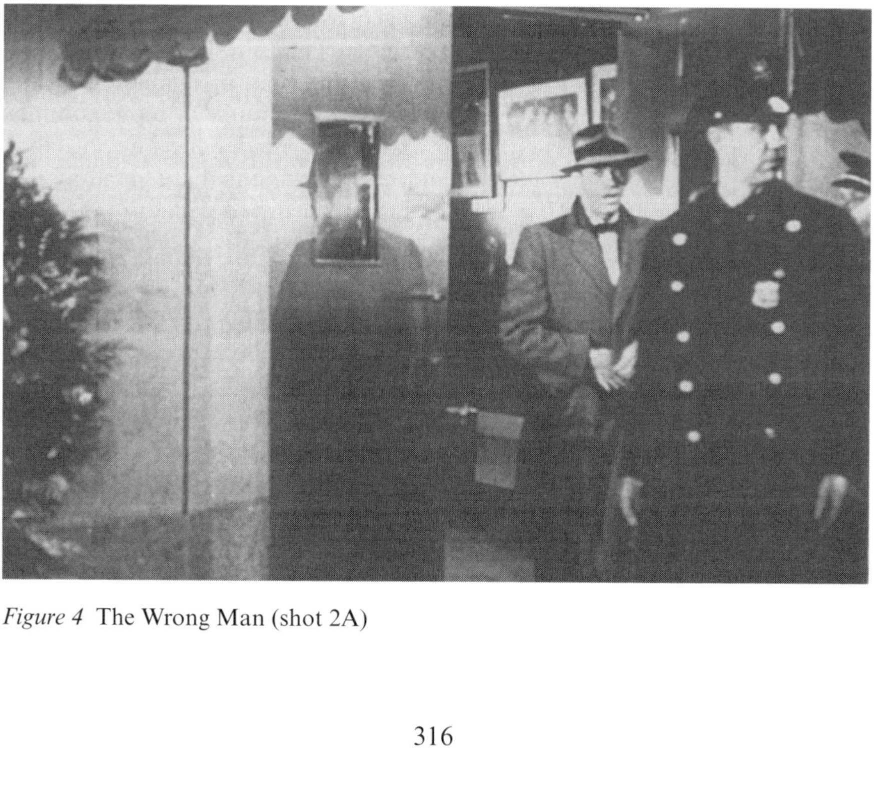

Figure 4 The Wrong Man (shot 2A)

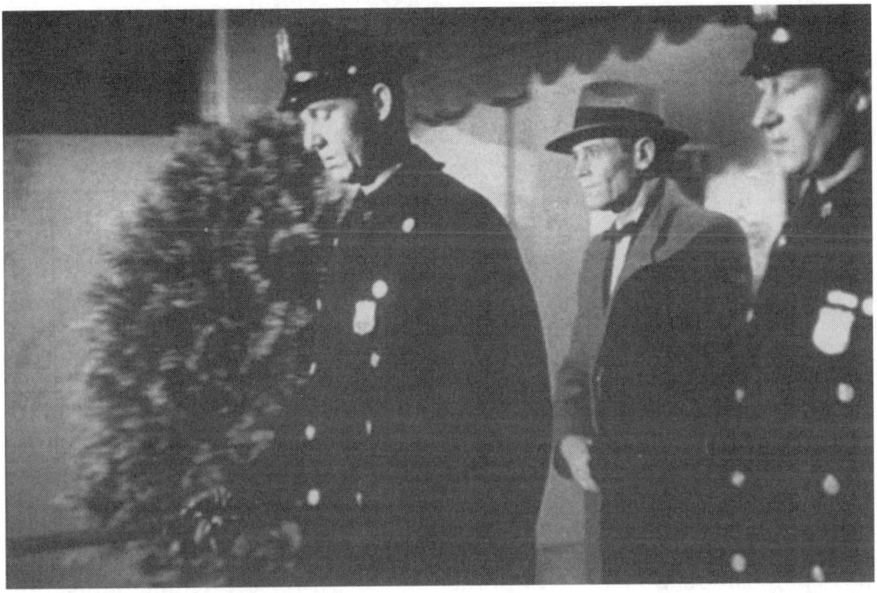

Figure 5 The Wrong Man (shot 2B)

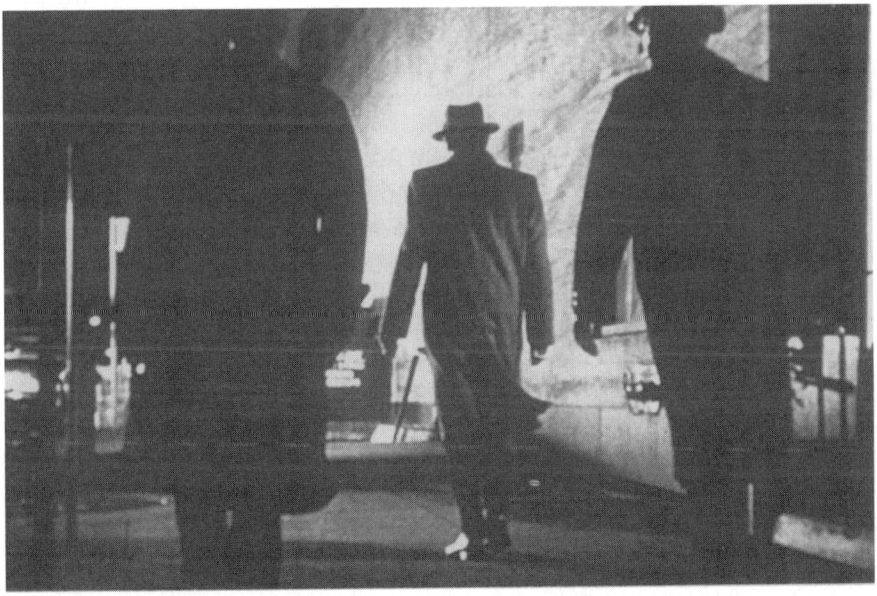

Figure 6 The Wrong Man (shot 3)

clearly see that both of the policemen walk past Manny on his left and not on both sides of him. Nevertheless, in both shots it does appear as though Manny is wedged between the policemen and has been trapped. There is an unmistakable sense in which Manny, who has committed no crime, has been seized by the police as their man. We neither see nor hear any obvious narrator describe the significance of this event. We have, however, literally seen how circumstances may create a false impression; how Manny may become a wrong man. Fortunately, the mistaken impression is seemingly ours alone and has caused no harm. This "perception of a misperception" (if we have even noticed it!) exists *only under a particular description* of the text; that is, only within a certain inscribed context can we recognize the event in this way. (We must, for example, be especially sensitive to the space and time created on the screen by cinematic devices and to relationships with the space and time of the story world.[12]) I will refer to this particular context as an implicit extra-fictional narration, or as the "voice" of an "implied author." A very powerful narration is at work here; one which virtually defines the limits of what can be seen and heard by us in the film but without defining the conditions of its own existence; one, moreover, which is able to predict events and anticipate the moral of the story prior to the epilogue. Indeed variations on this composition which places Manny between two threatening figures will appear throughout the film. Furthermore, the implied authorial narration *reminds* us about the police in the next scene when we hear distant sirens while Manny reads a newspaper. The sirens mean nothing to Manny and there is no indication that he notices them at all. The spectator, however, is already being positioned to know more than Manny and to fear for him. Just as "Manny" himself may be interpreted from an abstract, non-character context, so the explicit "Hitchcock" that we saw and heard in the precredit sequence may be *reinterpreted* as merely a kind of character playing a role in a still more abstract film, framed by yet another "Hitchcock" who is *not* seen and heard, namely, the implied author of *The Wrong Man*. The implied author, in turn, is framed by – but not reducible to – the historical "Hitchcock" who, unlike the other two Hitchcocks (one implied by an extra-fictional context, and one explicit in an extra-fictional role), expressed general distaste for the film, except for its aesthetic juxtaposition of fear and irony.[13]

An implied author and a chameleon text

We have already encounted the subtle but powerful effects of an implied author in analyzing films other than *The Wrong Man*: In chapter 2 we found an implicit (extra-fictional) pattern of impossible causation in *The Lady from Shanghai*, virtual space in *Dr Mabuse, the Gambler*, and an integration of graphic and story patterns in *The 39 Steps*. I will not attempt to adjudicate among the various definitions and types of "implied author" that have been proposed by theorists.[14] It will be useful, however, to examine one formulation of the concept. My purpose will be to illustrate that concepts in narrative theories are closely aligned with more general theories directed at the ontology and epistemology of film.

Christian Metz describes the implied author in the following way:

> The impression that *someone is speaking* [in a narrative] is bound not to the empirical presence of a definite, known, or knowable speaker but to the listener's spontaneous perception of the linguistic nature of the object . . . The spectator [of a narrative film] perceives images which have obviously been selected (they could have been other images) and arranged (their order could have been different). In a sense, he is leafing through an album of predetermined pictures, and it is not he who is turning the pages but some "master of ceremonies," some "grand image-maker" who (before being recognized as the author, if it is an *auteur* film, or, if not, in the absence of an author) is first and foremost *the film itself as a linguistic object* . . . or more precisely a sort of "potential linguistic focus" situated somewhere behind the film, and representing the basis that makes the film possible.[15]

Metz is striving to isolate an aspect of our narrative comprehension which is not reducible to what a biographical author says he or she intended to accomplish with a film. For Metz, the implied author is merely an anthropomorphic and shorthand way of designating a rather diffuse but fundamental set of operations which we sense as underlying what *we* do in making sense and in making patterns. Metz believes that these operations are amenable to linguistic analyses in accordance with his view of the nature of film as a kind of linguistic (and social) object. He mentions two fundamental operations – selection and arrangement – though others may be imagined, such as duration (the amount of time that something consumes), exclusion, and emphasis. These are subtle effects because if they were made *explicit* in the film, one would simply be forced to analyze another process of *implicit* selection and arrangement to account for the creation of a context in which something *else* could be made explicit. No matter how "objective" and final the narration seems, it could be the result of any one of many implicit narrations that might be imagined one level higher. Hence there will always be a measure of *uncertainty* about what is being depicted.[16] Although a film may explicitly dramatize what goes on "behind" the scenes – such as the setting up of the lights and camera – such a drama itself is really only another scene, and the dramatizing or construction of *that* scene is *not* shown explicitly. Clearly, with the concept of implied authorial narration one is at the very boundary of the text, at the very limit of what might still be justified as being *in* the text as opposed to being in a world, or in an intertext, which frames the text.

The point I wish to make is that for Metz, one must analyze the implicit selection and arrangement of film narration by using linguistic concepts, such as paradigm and syntagm, because linguistics is conceived as the master epistemological framework for describing human knowledge. One may reject some or all of Metz's linguistic assumptions and still hold on to the concept of an implied author, but only by creating a new set of terms and concepts which themselves imply a view of the fundamental nature of film and how it may be known.

I wish to return to the two shots in *The Wrong Man* which seem to show Manny walking between two policemen (figs 3–6). Although I have described these shots as being part of an implied authorial narration, they may be described in a very different way as follows: Manny emerges from the nightclub, saying 'Goodnight John' to the doorman, and walks toward the subway while two policemen stroll by the front of the club and cars are heard passing in the street. One could imagine this sort of description being offered by a casual bystander who happened to be near the club when Manny emerged. It is just as accurate as the first description, but its context, or epistemological boundary, is different: it is justified by the diegesis, by the world of the characters as we understand *that* world by apparently being *in* it as a bystander might be in it. That is to say, the accuracy of this new description is being judged against a new epistemological background. I will refer jointly to the new description and its background as an implicit diegetic narration, or implied "diegetic narrator." (I will discuss *non*diegetic narration later.) How can a narrator be both "implied" and "diegetic"; that is, be invisible and yet within the story world? This situation is the pictorial equivalent of a subjunctive conditional: "If a bystander *had been* present, he or she *would have seen* Manny emerge from the club . . . and *would have heard* . . ." Though a bystander was not present, we presume such a person could have been (and might have been dramatized by the text), and if so, would have been subject to the same physical laws and conditions which govern Manny. There is nothing illegitimate about posing a hypothesis or making a stipulation about the "facts" so long as the frame of reference for arranging the data (here, the diegesis) is not confused with the data itself; this is why it is important to keep in mind the assumptions under which data is being interpreted – assumptions which I have referred to as different "levels" of the narration. The same two shots of Manny and the policemen can be differently described, and function differently in our comprehension, because in the case of implied authorial narration our frame of reference is the entire (nonfictional) text while in the case of implied diegetic narration our frame of reference is the (fictional) story world.

The differing descriptions of these two shots of *The Wrong Man* ascribed to an implied author and to an implied diegetic narrator illustrate a crucial principle of narration:

> In general, several levels of narration will be operating simultaneously with varying degrees of explicitness and compatibility; that is, the spectator may describe the text in several different ways, all of which may be accurate, each within a particular context and for a particular purpose.

Thus one may say that the opening of *The Wrong Man* is a product of the implied author, but in doing so, one is merely offering a specific kind of generalization which has specific limits. The implied author is at work, but not exclusively, for at a finer grain (another segmentation or analytical breakdown) other boundaries on our knowledge are temporarily in effect. In analyzing narration, one must ask what degree of precision will be necessary in order to answer a given question about a spectator's state of knowledge.

The simultaneity of narrations can also explain how the music heard by the spectator in the first scene of *The Wrong Man* may be interpreted in three very different ways without necessarily producing confusion or contradiction.[17] The scene opens with an exterior shot of the nightclub and then moves inside. However the music heard from outside the club is just as loud as what we hear inside. The lack of "sound perspective" strongly suggests that the music is initially extra-fictional. The music accompanies the credit sequence whose titles are superimposed over the interior of the nightclub. The credits are extrafictional: "Warner Bros. Pictures Presents . . . Henry Fonda . . . Vera Miles . . . in Aflred Hitchcock's . . . 'THE WRONG MAN' . . ." By being associated with the credits, the music becomes extra-fictional. While the credits are being shown, however, we see a series of dissolves within the nightclub which indicate that we are also seeing *excerpts* from an *entire evening* of dancing at the club. That is, the music that we hear is also being presented as *typical* of an evening of dancing at the club. Such music is *non*diegetic because it can only be heard by us; patrons of the club are hearing specific music at specific times, not a sample of the music that was played during the evening. By keeping the dissolves of the title superimpositions separate from the dissolves which condense story time within the club, two levels of narration are defined – the extra-fictional and the nondiegetic allowing the music to shift from one to the other, or be in both places at once. However, as the evening wears on and the density of people in the club decreases, the orchestration of the music decreases and a band in the background becomes visible. When the credits finish we continue to hear the "same" musical number but now it is revealed that it is *diegetic* music being played by the band, one of whose members is Manny. When the band stops playing, the music ceases. Evidently the single musical number which we have heard could not have been played for an entire evening; instead, approximately 1¾ minutes of screen music is used to present the (extra-fictional) credits, represent typical (nondiegetic) music for an evening at the club, and be the actual, final (diegetic) song played by the band that evening. The "same" music functions very differently depending upon the context, precisely because several distinct contexts are made to fit. Thus the music may sound the "same" to us throughout and yet be heard in three different ways. Our (bottom-up) perception of the musical sounds emanating from the screen has been smoothly integrated with our (top-down) hypotheses about the (changing) relationships of music to a story world.[18]

The integration of screen data with events from a particular story through the use of music is also manifested through our natural use of the preposition "in" when describing these musical events. The music is "in" the club in many ways. It accompanies the credits which are seen "in" the club, but equally we may imagine that it is: typical music for the club, typical music for a jazz band of 1953, typical music for this band, music heard by a typical patron or someone in particular, as well as the last song played that night of January 14. The text is open and receptive to a number of interpretations; yet, at the same time, the verbal description we apply is seemingly quite definite about what it means to be "in" the club at the beginning of the film. The "camera," too, appears to be both in the club with the patrons and yet not quite in the club when showing the title credits. In fact, we are forced to conclude that the preposition "in" is flexible and adaptable and, like "implicit" narration, may be found to have many uses. This illustrates how a number of interpretations by different spectators may be accommodated by this preposition *without* suggesting that there is necessarily more than one interpretation or that a spectator must search for another one. I believe that this use of the music, and this use of the preposition describing the music, is in miniature form what is meant by the "excessive obviousness" of classical film narrative: the text sustains a reading which is generally compatible with whatever we *first* believe and does not usually demand a unique or counter-intuitive explication. Normally, the classical narrative does not give the appearance of ambiguity, nor does it encourage multiple interpretations, but rather, like the chameleon, it is adaptable, resilient and accommodating.[19] It will try to be what the spectator believes it to be.

There are limits, of course, to the amount of textual material that can be absorbed into a chameleon effect. For example, the relationships among the resolution, epilogue, and the other elements of a narrative schema need not be peaceful, and may be dramatized to a greater or lesser degree. David Bordwell observes that in *The Wrong Man* an *uncaused* resolution (based on a prayer and a "miracle") is joined with *two* epilogues (the first unhappy but caused; the second happy but uncaused). According to Bordwell, these aberrations leave the spectator "not only dispirited but dissatisfied."[20] This is true, however, only within the context of the large-scale structure of the film, for the ending of the film need not greatly affect our understanding of particular episodes and causal sequences, or the implications of those sequences. Moreover, the beginning of the film, which stages the presence of Hitchcock and his declarations about a factual film, predicts that there will be friction among the levels of narration. Endings are not supposed to be "neat" in the genre of the documentary. Furthermore, the implied authorial narration, which in the opening scene dramatized the perception of a misperception (Manny apparently being "arrested" by two policemen), prepares the spectator for unsettling, and uncaused, effects. Two apparently arbitrary camera views were allowed to affect our beliefs about Manny's world, even though at that time our beliefs were unwarranted. The implication was that a misperception could arise in quite an arbitrary and unpredictable way. Thus a kind of fatalism mixed with punishment might be at work in the text and detected in Hitchcock's other films. (For example, in typical fashion the psychological trauma is ultimately focused on a woman – in this case Manny's wife.) By "remembering" the documentary genre and Hitchcock's other films, we open a gap in the text of *The Wrong Man*: descriptions of the power that is apparently applied in the telling (through authorial narration) now conflict with descriptions that make the story cohere in the fashion of a narrative schema. That is, a fatalistic attitude appears in spite of (or perhaps, because of) opposition from other aspects of the story-telling that strive for "consistency" among the narrations. Here, "consistency" is earned through the temporal presuppositions of a narrative schema that encapsulates our belief that certain kinds of causality rule our world, and may be found in the basic unity of initiating event, resolution, and epilogue. The ending of Hitchcock's film can be of little comfort when our happiness is shown to be as arbitrarily obtained as our unhappiness.

I want to mention a final type of narration that appears in the opening of *The Wrong Man* and that bears upon our judgments of consistency and inconsistency in the film. While we listen to the music "in" the club, but before the credits begin, a title appears on the screen that represents a new sort of narration:

> The early morning hours of January the fourteenth, nineteen hundred and fifty-three, a day in the life of Christopher Emanuel Balestrero that he will never forget . . .

In terms of a narrative *schema*, this title combined with the picture we see functions to *orient* us with respect to the present state of affairs in the story world. The title is *about* the story world and hence derives from what I will call an unmarked *non*diegetic narration, or implied "nondiegetic narrator." The narrative could have oriented us by presenting the same information in another way; for example, by allowing us to overhear a conversation at one of the tables in the club. The information would be the same, but its method of presentation (as diegetic narration) would be different. A character's knowledge is limited in a way in which the words of the title are not and hence we could not ascribe the same authority and reliability to the words of a character as we can to the superimposed title. When the title assures us that something decisive will happen to Manny, we must pay serious attention to whatever may happen.[21] In a sense, we might say that the narration is not "implied" at all because the title card itself is explicitly present, even though we do not know the precise identity of the person "speaking." Implicit and explicit are a matter of degree and judgment, but that does not mean they are vague or indistinct since one may be as precise in describing the narration as the occasion demands; the important task is to measure differences from one narration to the next.[22]

One may choose to believe that this explanatory title ("a day . . . he will never forget") is actually a continuation of the same voice we heard earlier ("This is Alfred Hitchcock speaking"); that is, we may believe that the title speaks *about* the fiction from a nonfictional standpoint, not just *about* the story world from within the fiction. If so, one must at least concede that the "voice" is less personalized when rendered in a written, third-person form, and that both a fade and a dissolve have intervened between the two "voices" making the place and time of the second utterance less definite: is "Hitchcock" still standing on the empty soundstage? Does he speak, write, or silently think these words of the explanatory title? (As we shall see in chapter 7, a lack of specificity is a mark of the fictional.) There is no answer to these questions in the film; more importantly, any answer we may give is uninformative beyond the fact that there are differences (i.e., if it is still "Hitchcock," he has at least become more distant as the story world gains in prominence). Our uncertainty about the "voice" of the title is confined to a relatively narrow range and has no important effect on our global interpretation of the film. We may believe whatever we wish about the speaker of this title card so long as our beliefs take their place in a hierarchy with respect to the other narrations. Narration, too, may exhibit a chameleon effect. (However, as we shall see in chapters 6 and 7, a film may exploit uncertainties of narration and fuzzy boundaries to create startling and far-reaching effects.) A text is under no obligation to make use of a level of narration, much less make good use of it. Establishing exact categories for the narrations is usually less important than recognizing pertinent relationships and gradations among the narrations. By continuing to experiment and to search for possible configurations for the various levels, a spectator becomes sensitive to the changing boundaries of sense data which the text wishes to impose. Ultimately it is the spectator's task to judge when there is enough difference to make a difference in the role he or she must play in making sense of the text.

Focalization

The first four levels in the hierarchy of narrations that we have discussed make use of narrators. The last four levels recognize that characters also provide us information about the story world, but in ways quite different from narrators. A character who acts, speaks, observes, or has thoughts is not strictly telling or presenting anything to us for the reason that spectators, or readers, are not characters in that world. Characters may "tell" the story to us in a broad sense, but only through "living in" their world and speaking to other characters. Indeed, one might almost say that these conditions, or restrictions, define what we mean by the concept of a "character."

There are, however, several different ways in which characters may "live in" their world. One way we learn about characters is through their actions and speech in much the same way that characters learn from each other. In this special context, our knowledge is limited to what is explicitly enacted by the characters, what they do and say. In this limited context, a character is essentially an *agent* who is defined by actions.[23] For example, a plot synopsis of *The Wrong Man* – explaining who the story is about and *what* happens – is a way of thinking about character agency in this way: "Frightening account of what happens to a man and his wife when he is wrongly accused of being the man who has performed a series of hold-ups."[24] In chapter 1, I argued that narrative may be conceived as "a series of episodes collected as a *focused* causal chain." In this definition the notion of a focus, "continuing center," or protagonist, is inextricably bound up with the very notion of cause and effect: character and action define, as well as limit, each other's logical development. The spectator has an intrinsic interest in characters as agents since comprehending a narrative event requires at least recognizing how agents interact with one another in a *causal* framework, rather than, for instance, interacting as storytellers or dreamers. Characters, of course, may become storytellers or dreamers by recounting events to someone. These events may even be dramatized visually for the spectator as in a character flashback or dream sequence. In both these cases, however, the character has a new and *different* function in the text at another level, no longer as an actor who defines, and is defined by, a causal chain, but as a diegetic narrator (i.e., a narrator limited by the laws of the story world) who is now recounting a story within the story: he or she as an actor in a past event becomes the *object* of his or her narration in the present. Levels may multiply but there still exists a primary character-agent defined by actions and events. I will refer to this primary level of actions as a neutral, or nonfocalized, narration (or depiction) of character. Introducing the narratological concept of *focalization* is meant to remind us that a character's role in a narrative may change from being an actual, or potential, *focus* of a causal chain to being the *source* of our knowledge of a causal chain: the character may become either a (higher level) narrator or a (lower level) focalizer. How does a "focalizer" differ from a "narrator"?

Identifying a character as an agent within a causal scheme is already to implicitly raise the issue of that character's *awareness* of events in his or her world. An agent is a subject with a presumed, but as yet unspecified, set of personality traits, or subjectivity. A narrative text, however, is under no obligation to provide information about an agent's awareness beyond the tentative inferences we may draw from causal events. To the degree that specific information is provided, however, one may speak of focalization through (by) a character, either internally or externally. For Henry James, such a character was a "reflector." The term is apt since it replaces the notion of "communication" with the notion of "private thought" – a reflection *on* something – that nevertheless manages to sum up and clarify a surrounding situation and so also become a reflection *of* something. Focalization (reflection) involves a character neither speaking (narrating, reporting, communicating) nor acting (focusing, focused by), but rather actually *experiencing* something through seeing or hearing it.[25] Focalization also extends to more complex experiencing of objects: thinking, remembering, interpreting, wondering, fearing, believing, desiring, understanding, feeling guilt. Such verbs of consciousness are marked in language by the fact that an indirect object is not appropriate: we can say "Manny sees the police," but not "Manny sees the police to John." By contrast, verbs of communication (e.g., say, claim, shout, advise, reply, promise, ask, read, sing, confess) may take indirect objects designating a recipient of the communication: "Manny said goodnight *to* John." When consciousness is represented in pictures rather than in words, the indirect object which is inappropriate becomes the observer who is ineffective: a diegetic observer at the scene would be limited to external cues and could not know the character's experience. For example, if John sees that Manny looks toward the police, he may *infer* that Manny sees the police; nevertheless this inference may be false or incomplete (Manny looks but sees something else; or he sees the police but does not take special notice of them; or sees them and thinks about mowing his lawn, etc.). In general, inferences that John might make about Manny's thoughts are only speculative.

The auditory equivalent of the distinction between "looking" and "seeing" is "listening" and "hearing." The first term of each of these pairs has an *inter*subjective quality to it (i.e., a person's behavior may suggest when he or she is looking or listening), and hence is appropriate in a communicative context (where such a fact could be reported by a narrator), or for nonfocalized description, while the second term of each pair is more closely aligned to a private (internally or externally focalized) experience or thought which is not open to inspection in the same way (and hence can be reported only by a focalizer).[26] In the case of complex experiences of character consciousness, a diegetic observer, or narrator, would be wholly inadequate to the task. For example, if Manny's memories were to motivate a flashback sequence in the film, a diegetic observer would see only that Manny was staring vacantly into space. The spectator of the film, however, might well see and hear Manny's conscious memories (initiated perhaps by a dissolve), but only by identifying them uniquely as Manny's, that is, as inaccessible to a diegetic observer – experienced by Manny but not narrated literally by him to us or to a bystander. In *internal* focalization, story world and screen are meant to collapse into each other, forming a perfect identity in the name of a character.

"Here is exactly what Manny sees: these shapes and colors are in his head," or "Here are his thoughts." The spectator's task is to identify the story world with the mental understanding of a specific character. (Hence in figure 1 the spectator's role in internal focalization is one of "identification."[27]) Of course, in the broadest sense Manny and his memories are created for us by higher-level narrations (e.g., the extra-fictional narrator); but even so, one cannot simply equate focalization with narration since incomplete or inaccurate character perception is attributed first to the character, not to a narrator. Focalization displays character perception as a consequence of the events of the character's world even if other (nondiegetic) worlds are also affected. That is, focalization represents the *fact* of character perception, even if we may discover later that the character misperceived and even if our misperception about the character turns out to have other consequences in our ongoing experience of the story. Although the levels of narration are arranged as a series of dependencies, like the folds of an accordion, that does not mean that each level, within its prescribed context, does not have a unique function to perform in representing a complex epistemological field.

Private experiences of a character may be rendered externally or internally. External focalization represents a measure of character awareness but from outside the character. It is semi-subjective in the manner of an eyeline match: we see *what* Manny looks at, *when* he looks, but *not from* his unique spatial position; we must *infer* that we have seen what he has seen and how he has seen it. An eyeline match, however, is only one device which acts to externally focalize narrative through character. Three of the first five shots following the credit sequence of *The Wrong Man* as well as the next twenty-seven shots isolate Manny and his activities through a variety of techniques. For example, the camera moves to follow Manny's movements and also to anticipate his movements. The camera *waits* on a subway platform as a train stops and Manny gets off; later the image is black as the camera waits in a darkened bedroom for him to arrive and turn on the lights. The camera also follows his attention as he looks at four separate pages of a newspaper with varying expressions on his face. We see each of the pages and are invited to imagine Manny's thoughts: what significance do these specific pages have for him and what are the connections among them? (The connections will become clearer as the narrative progresses.) The scene ends on a close-up of him. The first thirty-two shots of the film clearly establish Manny as a center of attention, and we learn much about him even though he has said nothing about himself and there is virtually no dialogue ("Hi ya Manny. How's the family?"). Overall the narrative of these shots has been externally focalized through Manny.[28]

Internal focalization is more fully private and subjective than external focalization. No character can witness these experiences in another character. Internal focalization ranges from simple perception (e.g., the point-of-view shot), to impressions (e.g., the out-of-focus point-of-view shot depicting a character who is drunk, dizzy, or drugged), to "deeper thoughts" (e.g., dreams, hallucinations, and memories).[29] One of many examples of internal focalization in *The Wrong Man* occurs when Manny is placed alone in a prison cell. We see twenty-one shots of Manny looking at objects and walking nervously about the cell (external focalization). These shots are interrupted by another scene so we do not know exactly how long Manny's intense feelings build up within him; or rather, we are invited to imagine whatever amount of time we believe necessary for such feelings to become excruciating. Finally, we see Manny, horrified and ashamed, clench his hands, lean against a wall, and *close* his eyes. The camera then begins a sequence of jerky, swaying movements that increase in speed and spiral around Manny's head and the wall but without moving closer to him. The shot ends with a crescendo of discordant music and a long fade-out. The bizarre camera framings are meant to represent Manny's deep (nonverbal?) internalization of his circumstances.

Focalization through a character depends upon other, higher levels of narration that, for example, define and ground the character who is to have an experience.[30] These other narrations are always superimposed in a film; occasionally several may be relatively explicit, and may even be in conflict with one another. This situation may produce unusual representations of character subjectivity. For example, in Ingmar Bergman's *Wild Strawberries* (1957) a character holds up a mirror to reflect the face of another character. This shot, however, is actually the result of at least six different levels of narration operating simultaneously, but not always in harmony.[31] We understand this particular mirror shot in relation to a historical author, "Ingmar Bergman," who is (1) presenting a story in which a character in the story, Isak Borg, becomes a diegetic narrator who is (2) recounting in voice-over a story he has written about an automobile trip he took one day. We hear Borg narrating the story about himself but we never see him speaking. Instead we see Borg (3) riding in the automobile and conversing with various people he meets during the fateful automobile trip; that is, another Borg is now acting, and being acted upon, in the diegesis as simply a (nonfocalized and externally focalized) character. While riding in the car, however, we also see him fall asleep and hear the "previous" Borg explain in voice-over: "I dozed off, but was haunted by vivid and humiliating dreams." The sleeping Borg (4) imagines seeing himself at his present age of 78 in a new locale. This "new" 78-year-old Borg then (5) witnesses various events of his boyhood (many of which he could not actually have seen when he was a boy). We see him as a witness within his own dream and we also see the past events he watches/remembers/infers; that is, we see two degrees of internal focalization. The people he sees within his dream are shown at the age they were when Borg was a boy. One of these persons, a 20-year-old woman named Sara, however, suddenly confronts the 78-year-old Borg within his dream as he is observing past events. In confronting him, she has assumed a new role since the Sara that Borg remembers as a 20-year-old could not, of course, have had a conversation with the person Borg would become fifty-eight years later. In fact, in an earlier dream/memory he had tried to speak with her but had discovered that he was apparently invisible and inaudible. Nevertheless, in this particular dream/memory of Borg she suddenly speaks to him and holds up a mirror that (6) reflects his face as a 78-year-old man taking an automobile trip: "Have you looked in the mirror, Isak? Then I'll show you what you look like." We see the reflection of Borg in the mirror, first over his shoulder, and then later, the reflection alone. It seems to be an external focalization of Borg produced by Sara. Isak Borg has become an object for himself, but which "Isak Borg" is being thus framed and reflected, for what purpose, and who is really presenting it? Sara's "impossible" words may be understood figuratively: by allowing him to view himself simultaneously from multiple "distances," Borg is being prodded to consider the kind of person he has become.

The narrational structure of the shot may be represented as a sequence of six frames within frames as follows:

[[[[[[. . . mirror reflection . . .]]]]]]

The power of the shot derives in part from its sudden knotting together of distinct narrations to create contradiction and paradox. The distinct time frames in which Isak Borg functions as a voice-over narrator, actor, and focalizer are collapsed by the mirror reflection into a paradoxical time in which the notion of "Isak Borg" has an unexpected complexity. One might even include "Ingmar Bergman" within the tangle of narrations by noticing that his initials are the same as those of "Isak Borg" and that his surname can nearly be shortened to "Borg." The subtle intricacy of this moment depends upon the creation of various levels within the narration that are posited as logically distinct, followed by a transgression of the boundaries.[32]

Levels of the narration may be structured to create unusual effects because they mark differing epistemological domains which may be complementary or opposed. Moreover, there are three distinct types of narration. In a strict sense, a narrator offers statements *about*; an actor/agent acts *on* or is acted upon; and a focalizer has an experience *of*. More precisely, narration, action, and focalization are three alternative modes of describing how knowledge may be stated, or obtained. Since all three modes may be used to describe the same character or object, what distinguishes them is the differing presuppositions imposed on the spectator, or reader, as a condition of acquiring knowledge. Further, there is evidence that this tripartite division is connected to universal features of human language.[33] At the very least, these three types of "agency" are convenient fictions which serve to mark how a field of knowledge is being divided at a particular time (see fig. 7).[34] Note that, in general, since several narrations may be operating simultaneously, a shot in a film may be subject to different interpretations with respect to each of these

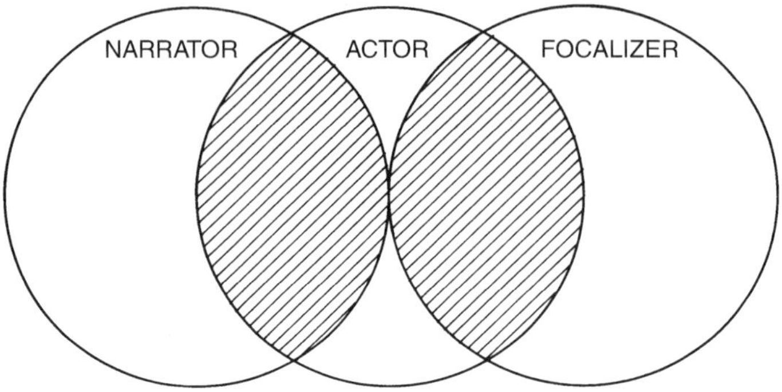

Figure 7 The three types of agency
Narration in general is the overall regulation and distribution of knowledge which determines when and how a reader acquires knowledge from a text. It is composed of three related activities associated with three nominal agents: the narrator, actor, and focalizer. These agents are convenient fictions which serve to mark how the field of knowledge is being divided at a particular time. Some theorists would add a fourth overlapping circle to the left of "narrator" to create, in effect, two types of narrator: on the far left, a "pure showing" by an unobtrusive "presenter" which intersects with a circle which would be confined to "verbal recounting." The new contrast would be between narrators who show (present) and those who tell (speak and write); or perhaps the contrast would be between narrators who use pictures and those who use words.

three possibilities for perception. Also, the terminology will shift depending upon the selection of a reference point. For example, if a character in a film is watching a television show, all the music from the television will be diegetic with respect to that character even if some of the music is nondiegetic with respect to characters who exist only on the show. Therefore, in interpreting narration it will be crucial for the analyst to specify the arrangement of levels and the (top-down) course of reading that is in effect.

Although there is a firm distinction among narration, (nonfocalized) action, and (external and internal) focalization, it is often convenient in analyzing narrative to use the terms "narration" and "narrator" in a general sense to refer to all three types of agency in order to concentrate on the overall regulation and distribution of knowledge throughout a text that determines how and when a reader acquires knowledge. I will usually use "narration" and "narrator" in a broad way, relying upon context to indicate when they are to be understood in a narrow way (i.e., as opposed to both acting and focalizing).

Focalization is an attempt to represent "consciousness of."[35] In treating it as part of the above tripartite division of activities, I have defined focalization (in figs 1 and 7) in a way significantly different from other writers.[36] For instance, Mieke Bal allows unidentified and undramatized *narrators* as well as characters to focalize events.[37] However, allowing experiences to appear without a definition of an "experiencer" – that is, experiences not attributed to a particular individual but rendered in the "third person" – risks dissipating the distinction between narration and focalization. How are we to know the difference among narrators who remember, imagine, or directly experience a scene? And how would these situations differ from an invisible narrator who merely presented a scene by "setting the stage" and arranging the action for us to witness? Or who merely reported a scene without mentioning any of the experiences which led to the report? Moreover, what is to be gained by allowing impersonal, "personal" experiences in the text? Of course, if a narrator is given a body and a personality, then he or she may focalize events, but only because he or she has thereby become a "character" of sorts. Seymour Chatman argues that a narrator cannot focalize at all because a narrator is outside the story, in a different time and place, and thus can only report, not see and hear events unfold.[38] The very act of reporting implies that the narrator already knows more than a reader, or knows it sooner, and hence is on a different level of the hierarchies of relative knowledge. (However, Chatman goes even further and concludes that focalization is not a distinct or viable category with which to analyze narration.)

I have also defined "nonfocalization" in a new way. Gérard Genette, for instance, treats it as a global aspect of narration related to the "omniscience" of a narrator. He argues that a narrator's power to know more than any character or reader may be demonstrated by entering many characters' minds resulting in a net zero focalization, or nonfocalization, for the text as a whole.[39] Nonfocalization in Genette's sense might better be called "multi-focalization." Even so, it is not a necessary component of omniscience nor is it useful in examining local effects of character action and awareness.

Communication

Susan Lanser incorporates three additional concepts in her version of figure 1 which I have not used: status, contact, and stance. The reason is that Lanser interprets the levels of narration as a *communication* between a "sender" (on the left side of the illustration) and a "receiver of a message" (on the right). Her three concepts describe the sender's relationships, respectively, to his or her "speech act," to the receiver, and to the message. The goal of the entire system is "maximal authority" and "maximal reception."[40] I have avoided these three concepts in an attempt to remain neutral between a communication theory and various other theories which seek to explicate in quite different ways the goals and processes which drive narration. I do not wish to debate here the merits and demerits of a communication approach to an analysis of the comprehension of narrative texts. I do believe, however, that communication theories have substantial limitations. The following are typical statements in support of a communication model:

> Just as there is, within the narrative, a large exchange function (enacted by giver and recipient), similarly, in homological fashion, the narrative, viewed as object, is the basis of a communication: there is a giver of narrative and a recipient of narrative. In linguistic communication, *I* and *you* are presupposed by each other; similarly, a narrative cannot take place without a narrator and a listener (or reader).[41]
>
> (Roland Barthes, 1966)

> Every narrative . . . is a *mélange* of four basic components: speaker, speech event, agents, and narrated event. As such it is structurally equivalent to instances of daily discourse in which someone reports something.[42]
>
> (Dudley Andrew, 1984)

> A narrative is a communication; hence, it presupposes two parties, a sender and a receiver.[43]
>
> (Seymour Chatman, 1978)

Barthes begins with the fact that characters communicate with each other and then decides that narrative must be the most general communication of all. Chatman begins with narrative as a communication and then discovers perceivers who must be in communication. Both arguments seem to reduce the processes, effects, and uses of narrative to a single purpose so that perceiving has a single goal; as Barthes suggests, "listening" becomes the same as "reading." James Kinneavy flatly states that "all uses" of language depend upon an encoder, a signal, a decoder, and the reality to which the message refers. This four-part structure, he asserts, is so basic that it simply "speaks for itself"![44] Apparently, everything that solicits meaning is to be imagined as a speech, a hypothetical speech, or a message transmitted from somewhere.

Other theorists have been much more skeptical about communication models:

> Writing is not the communication of a message which starts from the author and proceeds to the reader; it is specifically the voice of reading itself: *in the text, only the reader speaks*.[45]
>
> (Roland Barthes, 1970)

> [W]e have come to take for granted that we explain textual details by adducing narrators and explain narrators by adducing qualities of real people. . . . [However, much of] literature is interesting and compelling precisely because it does something other than illustrate the personality of a narrator. For the moment I want to suggest that this strategy of naturalization and anthropomorphism should be

recognized not as an analytical perspective on fiction, but as part of the fiction-making process. That is to say, making narrators is not an analytical operation that lies outside the domain of fiction but very much a continuation of fiction-making: dealing with details by imagining a narrator; telling a story about a narrator and his/her response so as to make sense of them.[46]

(Jonathan Culler, 1984)

No trait we could assign to an implied author of a film could not more simply be ascribed to the narration itself: it sometimes suppresses information, it often restricts our knowledge, it generates curiosity, it creates a tone, and so on. To give every film a narrator or implied author is to indulge in an anthropomorphic fiction. . . . I suggest . . . that narration is better understood as the organization of a set of cues for the construction of a story. This presupposes a perceiver, but not any sender, of a message. This scheme allows for the possibility that the *narrational process may sometimes mimic the communication situation more or less fully*. A text's narration may emit cues that suggest a narrator, or a "narratee," or it may not. . . . [T]here is no point in positing communication as the fundamental process of all narration, only to grant that most films "efface" or "conceal" this process. Far better, I think, to give the narrational process the power to signal under certain circumstances that the spectator should construct a narrator. When this occurs, we must recall that this narrator is the product of specific organizational principles, historical factors, and viewers' mental sets. Contrary to what the communication model implies, this sort of narrator does not create the narration; the narration, appealing to historical norms of viewing, creates the narrator. . . . [W]e need not build the narrator in on the ground floor of our theory. No purpose is served by assigning every film to a *deus absconditis*.[47]

(David Bordwell, 1985)

It is not merely in the contexts of literature and film that communication models seem inadequate; they have also been attacked on general linguistic and philosophical grounds.[48] Nevertheless, escaping the "anthropomorphic fiction" embodied in the word "narrator" is not easy. Bordwell still speaks of narration in vaguely animate terms as an "organization" that has the power to "suppress," "restrict," "generate," "emit cues," "signal," "mimic," and "create." It may well be that "narrator" is a metaphor, but if so, one that permeates our thinking about the world, and is in need of explanation on that basis. "Narrator" and related terms are well-established in critical practice as well as in ordinary language. Are such metaphors an accident of speaking, a mere convenience, a delusion we should learn to live without, or something more fundamental dealing with our embodiment in a world? How do these ways of speaking address our intuitive sense of the appropriateness of speaking in this way? Perhaps these metaphors are evidence of a displacement of the human ego onto the world, or else of an overriding faith in *ordinary causality* and in our presumed roles as *actors* able to make order in the world.[49] Personifying narration would seem to have a real function in our lives even if narration is not a personality made real nor a communication made public.[50]

According to Wallace Martin, most theorists of narrative attempt to find a position somewhere between accepting or rejecting the communication model.[51] He suggests three intermediate positions, which I interpret as follows:

1 Narrative texts contain special and private spaces for a reader's personal involvement with the story beyond what may be communicated.
2 Narrative is a cooperative enterprise whereby both reader and writer contribute [equally?] by virtue of being members of particular historical communitities that share cultural values and literary conventions. Although the reader and writer share the responsibility for producing sense, they may perform different functions.
3 Narrative is the product not of readers, writers, and conventions, but of an act of reading. Readers and writers possess identical skills of comprehension. A writer is merely the first reader. The central problem therefore is to describe consciousness and investigate the various skills of comprehension: what conditions make a reading possible?

It would seem that these intermediate positions might overlap with one another and even be compatible with certain communication theories.[52] This reminds us that there are many functions for perceivers to perform in using and exchanging narrative, and many ways for perception to relate to purpose. If a text is sometimes a "communication," it is almost certainly operating in other ways as well.

Text under a description

In Wallace Martin's third option above, the act of reading is seen as an act of problem-solving by the reader. According to Robert de Beaugrande, problem-solving means that:

> The elements of knowledge are considered already present in the mind, and the task is to decide how to connect them together to suit a plan and a topic. . . . The task of communicating is then not to *fill* other people's minds with content, but to instruct them *how* to *limit* and *select among* the content they already have in their minds.[53]

When the narrative object is narrowed to the acts of comprehension by which it is known, then I believe it is possible to conceive of an "author" as merely another reader with no *a priori* message to deliver. Narration becomes the labor through which a reader generates any warranted description of sensory data – any admissible way of segmenting which yields perceptual boundaries, the collection of which becomes "the text." "Narrator," "actor," and "focalizer" are then merely convenient labels which allow the reader to fashion his or her own redescription, or transformation, of one perception of the "here-and-now" context into a new perception of it. All three types of agent are *in* the text according to a differential hierarchy. The complexity of the preposition "in" and its relationship to embedding and being embedded (recall our discussion of the credit music being heard "in" the club) points to a dynamic and basic quality of narration: the transformation of one epistemological context into another, a movement from (embedded) level to (embedding) level. As an illustration of this way of avoiding a communication model, and as a summary of the levels of narration discussed above in connection with *The Wrong Man*, consider the following verbal (re)descriptions of the film:

1 *Historical author*: "But I did fancy the opening of the picture because of my own fear of the police."[54]
2 *Implied author*: "Manny is overtaken by two policemen who seem to walk on either side of him *as if* to take him into custody, but in fact they do not walk on either side of him and do not (yet) take him into custody."
3 *Extra-fictional narrator*: "This is Alfred Hitchcock speaking."
4 *Nondiegetic narrator*: Title card: "The early morning hours of January the fourteenth, nineteen hundred and fifty-three, a day in the life of Christopher Emanuel Balestrero that he will never forget . . ."
5 (*Implied*) *diegetic narrator*: "If a bystander *had been* present, he or she *would have seen* Manny emerge from the club . . . and *would have heard* . . ."
6 *Nonfocalized narration (character as agent)*: "Frightening account of what happens to a man and his wife when he is wrongly accused of being the man who has performed a series of hold-ups."[55]
7 *External focalization*: Eyeline match: "Manny *looks at* x."
8 *Internal focalization (surface)*: Point-of-view shot: "I [Manny] [now] *see* x [there] [from where I stand]."
9 *Internal focalization (depth)*: "I [Manny] remember . . . wish . . . fear . . . x."

My claim is that "narration" exists whenever we *transform* data from one to another of the above forms.[56] Whether we are an "author" or a "reader" is no longer pertinent: the central activity of narration is the redescription of data under epistemological constraint. The subtle ways in which we apply and use prepositions are often a clue to the constraints in effect for a given description.[57] For example, an interpretive statement may be justified by saying that we are looking "over," "at," "with," "through," or "into" a character (according to whether we adopt a nondiegetic, diegetic, nonfocalized, externally focalized or internally focalized frame of reference). The use of these sorts of preposition does not signify an attitude toward the character, but merely declares the set of assumptions by which we imagine a given relationship to the character and to his or her world, and by which we justify an interpretive statement. One may also imagine degrees by which we see "into" a character (how far? how deeply?), degrees by which we see "through" a character (how completely? how clearly?), and degrees of involvement associated with the other prepositions.

By conceiving narration as a type of verbal (and imagistic?) description offered by a spectator, one is, in effect, analyzing *interpretive* statements. One is mapping a course of thought, the use of language, rather than discovering the absolute properties of an object or discovering "cues" that are "in" an object – the text objectified. Interpretation thus construed exhibits something of the nature of an explanatory "theory." Interpretation in this sense includes the "filling in" of certain data (from the top down) which seems to be "missing" at some moment in the text as well as the construction of macro-propositions which are *about* the text though not strictly *in* it, or denoting it. Structures that are achieved in cognition cannot be reduced to a list of phenomenal forms or cues. We demonstrate our knowledge of narration, of "how to go on," by interpreting, by going on.

The notion of levels, I believe, provides a way of escaping a simple structuralism as well as a strict empiricism, because comprehension is not made to depend upon a few basic surface units, or "cues," which may be endlessly combined in strings through addition and subtraction. Some aspects of narrative *can* profitably be analyzed in this way, but the notion of levels brings with it the relationships of embedding and hierarchy, which, in turn, provide mechanisms for a fundamentally different kind of contribution to human cognition than laws of addition and subtraction, or the rules of branching networks. A higher level, acting like an exemplar or guiding procedure, may constrain, but does not determine, the organization of data rising from below, or arriving from other sources. Thus "levels" are a way of talking about flexibility, complexity, and efficiency in modeling a situation – how different processes interact and how data is discarded, compared, and integrated.[58] In this sense, a set of levels may be thought of as a "vertical" partitioning of data that operates simultaneously with a "horizontal" segmentation across a specified range of knowledge. Moreover, since a lower level depends upon the working assumptions of *all* of the levels above it, each step down the hierarchy increases the number of assumptions that must be made and narrows the range of knowledge available to the spectator. Thus the hierarchy of levels may be seen as a set of probabilities that predicts the likelihood of hypotheses. For example, unless there is evidence to the contrary, an image is more likely to be interpreted as "objective" (i.e., nonfocalized) than "subjective" (externally or internally focalized) because fewer assumptions are necessary.

A hierarchy of levels also helps to explain what Richard Gerrig calls "anomalous suspense" (a person may continue to feel suspense while reading a story even though he or she has read the story many times) and "anomalous replotting" (a person may wish for a different outcome even though he or she knows the plot).[59] Since these responses may occur in reading either nonfiction (e.g., history or biography) or fiction, the explanation must lie partly in the dual nature of narrative: the *declarative* knowledge of narrative (given through a narrative schema) depends upon an awareness of the *contingency* of cause and effect chains – that is, depends upon a person's ongoing assessment of the probabilities which govern the grouping of events – while the *procedural* knowledge of narrative (given through narration) is stratified into *levels*, allowing a person to respond to the contingency of cause and effect chains in multiple ways. Thus a reader's participation in narrative is not limited to the binary choice of whether to know, or not to know, but may assume more complex nuances within a range of epistemological contexts each of which, in turn, defines a limited form of contingency.

One should not think that analyzing narration as a series of levels implies that the narrations must be consistent or assembled into a single hierarchy (see fig. 8).[60] For example, Tzvetan Todorov asserts that narrations may interact in three fundamental ways through linking, alternating, or embedding and thus may be seen rhetorically as repetitive, progressive, antithetical, complementary, parallel, nested, and so forth.[61] Presumably, levels may also be overlapping, deceptive, contradictory, ambiguous, implicit, and uncertain. The next three chapters will examine some arrangements of narrations from simple to complex in particular films.

A comprehensive description of narrative

I am now in a position to summarize three concepts of narrative theory that have traditionally been viewed as fundamental: point of view, omniscience, and narrative. These characterizations will be basic enough to allow competing narrative theories to develop and elaborate the concepts in different ways. Formulating general definitions will also allow us to compare a variety of narrative theories and evaluate the particular decisions each theory must make about methodology.

Narrative *point of view* is the relationship between *any pair* of levels of narration, not necessarily adjacent. The relationship between a pair of levels may

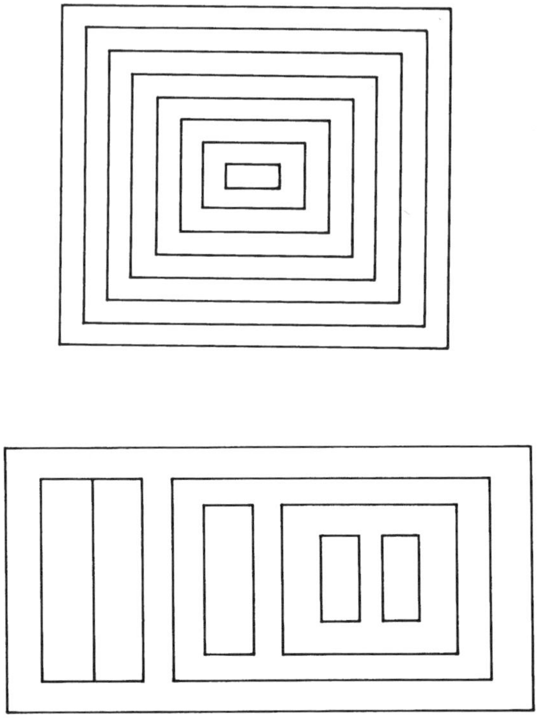

Figure 8 a & b Simple and complex configurations of narration
Figure 8a is a box diagram showing a hierarchical arrangement of the eight levels of narration of figure 1. Figure 8b is a box diagram showing one of many possible nonhierarchical arrangements of the levels of narration in a text. Each level is shown as a box. A level is represented as being subordinate to another level by being enclosed within a box.

be analyzed in various ways.[62] Even so, point of view is only a partial description of the movement of narration through a text. For example, although the choice of a particular point of view is frequently analyzed in terms of the information which is thereby suppressed, other effects – such as the overall management and delay of enigmas, the arrangement of action sequences, and soliciting the reader's, or spectator's, interest – are more global in nature and are best analyzed when narration is considered as an interlocking system of many levels.

Narrative *omniscience* refers to any one of the higher levels of narration. The level may be relatively explicit (e.g., intrusive commentary) or implicit (e.g., implied authorial evaluation). The highest level of narration – that which frames all the other levels but which cannot itself disclose its own framing – is simply everything the reader, or spectator, comes to know about the structure of the text and provides a reference point from which to measure any other level. Omniscience does not mean that the reader finally knows all, or that there is an author/narrator who knows all, but merely refers to the reader's toleration of a boundary or *limit* to what finally can be known *in* the text.[63] This boundary, in a more or less arbitrary manner, usually attempts to dissipate the desire to know more. Just as a narrative schema attempts to shape causality on both large and small scales to achieve a closure effect, so narration typically seeks a measure of completeness, an "omniscience effect." For example, to narrate the "end" of a story one must do more than merely stop: an appropriate ending normally requires a point of overview from which the previous knowledge that has been gained by the reader is shown to have been acquired through a comprehensive power to know. Of course, even the most explicit assertion that a power to know *is* comprehensive is still not an explicit assertion of its own power to know.

I conclude by offering a characterization of film narrative which draws upon topics discussed in this and previous chapters.

> Film *narrative* is a way of understanding data under the illusion of *occurrence*; that is, it is a way of perceiving by a spectator which organizes data as if it were witnessed unfolding in a temporal, spatial, and causal frame. In understanding a film narrative, a spectator employs top-down and bottom-up cognitive processes to transform data on the *screen* into a *diegesis* – a world – that contains a particular *story*, or sequence of events.
>
> "Story" data takes two forms: declarative knowledge ("what" happens) and procedural knowledge ("how" it is witnessed and known).
>
> 1 Declarative knowledge is generated by a *narrative schema* ("abstract," "orientation," "initiating event," etc.) which yields a series of episodes collected as a focused causal chain (as opposed to a "heap," "catalogue," "unfocused chain," etc.). An experience of time emerges as data is processed and associated, that is, as the spectator *reorders* fragments on the screen (creating such story relationships as temporal continuity, ellipsis, overlap, etc.). Different experiences of time ("description," "duration," "causal implication," "order") are produced according to the complexity of juxtaposition allowed by the particular method (heap, catalogue, episode, etc.) being used to associate data. These temporal experiences related to the story may reinforce, oppose, or be variously integrated with screen time.
>
> An experience of space, too, emerges as data is processed and associated, creating such story relationships as spatial chains,

gaps, and reversals that in turn may reinforce, oppose, or be variously integrated with the two-dimensional space of the screen.

Focused causal chains are not just sequences of paired story events in time and space, but embody a desire for pairing events and the power to make pairs. Narrative causes ("remote," "intervening," "enabling," etc.) are thus principles of explanation, or criteria for grouping elements, which are derived from cultural knowledge as well as from physical laws: the human plans, goals, desires, and routines – realized in action sequences – which are encouraged, tolerated, or proscribed by a community.

2 Procedural knowledge is generated by a *narration* (or narrational schema) which yields a series of levels, or epistemological boundaries ("disparities"), associated with such nominal agents as narrators, actors, and focalizers. Acts of witnessing by these agents (similar to the spectator's acts of perceiving) function as explicit frames of reference for declarative knowledge. Several levels may operate simultaneously with varying degrees of compatibility and explicitness producing multiple descriptions of the data.

Procedural knowledge is limited to specific epistemological domains but the domains may be connected to one another. For instance, an event may appear to the spectator as if it were being directly witnessed ("scene"), or alternatively the event may appear in the second degree as merely referred to, or "mentioned," by a witness ("summary").[64] This is a simple illustration of the recursive nature of narration: a given level – describing how an object is being perceived – may itself be dramatized and become an object of perception, that is, become declarative and known through another (higher-level) procedure, one step more distant, which merely "mentions" the object. Hence a common structure for narration is hierarchical where one subject-object pair (describable in a temporal, spatial, and causal frame of reference) becomes the embedded object of another (more powerful) subject in a higher frame of reference. Levels may be linked, alternated, or embedded, and may assume a variety of rhetorical functions.

As a medium, film is a distinctive collection of techniques for representing time, space, and causality on the screen. Normally these techniques (e.g., sound and picture editing, camera movement, and *mise-en-scène*) should be understood not as conveying a "meaning" in themselves, but as "instructions" relating to procedures and rules used by a spectator in constructing a set of interrelationships. Such

> procedures are neither true nor false, but are measured only by their success or failure with respect to some goal.
>
> By contrast, the declarative knowledge being produced by a spectator is true or false about the story world and may also be converted into propositions which the spectator believes to be true or false about his or her own, ordinary world. The operation of this latter type of reference, and its relationship to story and screen, is governed by a theory of *fiction* (see chapter 7).

The concepts in these general definitions must be supplemented, interpreted, and refashioned in accordance with the aims of particular narrative theories. Take, for example, my claim that narrative is a way of understanding data under the "illusion of occurrence." One way to interpret "illusion of occurrence" would be to seize upon the word "illusion" and argue that the perceptual illusions presented on the screen (e.g., of three-dimensional depth and motion) are the basis for cognitive *delusions* in which a spectator mistakes narrative patterns for the real world, or else imagines himself or herself within the story world. In this interpretation, narrative would be seen as attempting to psychologically baffle or transport the perceiver.

Another way of interpreting "illusion of occurrence" would be to emphasize the word "occurrence," embracing Arthur Danto's formulation of narrative as

> an account in which the *general* knowledge of what *kind* of thing must have happened [under a known general law] is replaced by the *specific* knowledge of what *specific* thing, of the required kind, *in fact* occurred.[65]

Narrative in Danto's view is the end result of substituting concrete instances into laws covering causal interactions. Danto's formulation explains why one cannot argue with the logic of a fictional narrative by simply asserting that a given event "didn't happen." The reason is that a narrative explanation of data *begins* with a representation of space and time, begins with "what happened" as a premise for its instantiation of general laws. One can disagree with the general law which seems to be at work, or with its application, but not with "what happened," for that is a category mistake. Danto's concern – narratives constructed by historians is thus doubly constrained: specific events occurring in the real world must be collected and then subsumed under one or more master narratives of greater generality.

Not all theories make the kinds of distinction I have used above in my general definition of narrative. Nevertheless I believe that my distinctions will be useful in evaluating how a concept is functioning within a particular theory. I also believe that many basic concepts (e.g., realism, time, editing, the camera, space, causality, voice, text) should be broken up into components and redefined according to their top-down and bottom-up aspects as well as their declarative and procedural aspects. The result will be a new complexity for some familiar concepts, but a better fit with the powers of narrative.

Five types of narrative theory

Narrative is enormously complicated even when we set aside its exchange value as a manufactured object in a community and concentrate on its use value as a psychological object for a perceiver. Many theories of narrative may be constructed by beginning at different points, highlighting different aspects of the phenomenon, and ignoring others. Roughly speaking, I believe that one can mark out five recent types of narrative theory using the above general definition of narrative as a frame of reference.[66] The five types of theory differ in the relative weight they assign to various aspects of narrative and especially in how they draw the line between declarative and procedural knowledge and the importance they assign to sensory knowledge. Without denying the sophistication and subtlety of individual theories, I will refer to the types broadly as being distinguished by an emphasis on plot, style, communication, reception, or the human drives.

One type of theory concentrates on the developmental logic of that "series of events" which is collected into a focused causal chain. This aspect of narrative organization may be termed the "plot." Vladimir Propp broke it down into a set of minimal actions each of which was further classified as a particular "function," conceived as "an act of a character, defined from the point of view of its significance for the course of the action." Propp insisted that the study of *what* is done in a narrative should precede "questions of who does it and how it is done."[67] An important result of research based on this type of narrative theory emphasizing plot was that different actions in diverse stories could be shown to perform *similarly*, that is, to have the same "function" in producing the coherence of the events. For example, Propp argues that identical functions underlie each of the following events producing a powerful similarity among them in spite of the fact that they come from different stories.

1 A tsar gives an eagle to a hero. The eagle carries the hero away to another kingdom.
2 An old man gives Sucenko a horse. The horse carries Sucenko away to another kingdom.
3 A sorcerer gives Ivan a little boat. The boat takes Ivan to another kingdom.
4 A princess gives Ivan a ring. Young men appearing from out of the ring carry Ivan away into another kingdom.[68]

In a classic study, Propp found that in a hundred Russian folktales, there were only thirty-one functions and that while some of them could be omitted in particular stories, they almost always occurred in the same order in all the stories. The idea of a fixed set of functions in an unvarying order helps to explain some of the underlying similarities that may be perceived among certain groups of stories. In this way, "plot" becomes a theoretical and abstract concept capable of explaining a range of data, including the data of stories not yet invented.[69] Plot theories of narrative, though, have little to say about procedural knowledge and narration. Only a few of Propp's functions touch on the issue of the regulation and distribution of knowledge in a text; hence, his method will be inadequate for analyzing plots that depend on complex enigmas, psychological attitudes, or subtle shifts in perception and awareness.[70] At best, plot theories are confined to the aspect of narrative that I have called nonfocalized narration.

A second type of theory concentrates on style, on how the devices and techniques which are *specific*, or intrinsic, to a given medium operate to convert a "plot" into a "story." Style in film is conceived as a relatively autonomous system comprised of a set of uniquely cinematic techniques. However, defining the differences between plot and story, and the interactions between them that betray style at work, is a most delicate task. According to David Bordwell's definition, plot is at one remove from what is visibly and audibly present in the film before us; it includes certain inferences about narrative events as well as certain nondiegetic material bearing upon those events. Story is at a further remove from plot; it is a mental reconstruction of some of the events of narrative which are not witnessed by the spectator, though it also includes what is explicitly presented. For example, explicit events presented out of order in the plot are reordered by the spectator and supplemented by inferred events in constructing the story. However, Bordwell says that in some cases (a particular shot, or scene) the differences between plot and story vanish.[71] This raises a question: what is the appropriate temporal scale with which to measure plot and how does the spectator know what is appropriate? For instance, are both shots of an eyeline match part of the plot, or only the shot on the screen? Clearly, the notion of plot here is much more intricate and powerful than envisioned by the first type of theory discussed above. Plot has become more than a simple analysis of character action; it is now part of a larger cognitive process *intermediate* between the phenomenal text (which includes aspects of "style") and the "story" as mentally completed by the spectator (with all of its many implications). The concept of plot now carries great weight and has become a fulcrum for the explanation of narrative comprehension in terms of a "style." Indeed when this stylistic account of narrative is itself viewed as an Aristotelian narrative with a beginning in phenomenal form, a middle in plot, and an end in story, one may glimpse the true importance of "plot" as that "middle term" which separates style from story – preserving the integrity of each – while explaining the transformation of first into last.[72]

A second crucial problem for a narrative theory emphasizing style is to draw a firm distinction between the aesthetic and the nonaesthetic (the "practical") so that the effects of "style" – the particular use of materials and techniques that are deemed unique to a given art medium – may be better isolated. Kristin Thompson, building upon the work of the Russian formalists, asserts the importance of "art" as follows:

> The nature of practical perception means that our faculties become dulled by the repetitive and habitual activities inherent in much of daily life. Thus art, by renewing our perceptions and thoughts, may be said to act as a sort of mental exercise, parallel to the way sports is an exercise for the body.[73]

Thompson approves Victor Shklovsky's pronouncement that the "purpose of art is to impart the *sensation* of things as they are perceived, and not as they are *known*."[74] Art is a ceaseless and never-ending struggle to "defamiliarize" the familiar.[75] Thus it may be that Russian formalism, as one stylistic theory of narrative, has no need for a theory of interpretation separate from a theory of the sensation of things as they are perceived. The emphasis on sensation here recalls Bertrand Russell's "knowledge by acquaintance" from which he derives all other knowledge (e.g., "knowledge by description," or "knowing that").[76] Russell argues that "knowledge by acquaintance" includes an acquaintance with all the sense-data of things and with oneself (memory, introspection) as well as with certain *universals* (e.g., qualities like redness, spatial and temporal relations, and logical universals like resemblance). Russell also argues that the notion of knowledge by acquaintance is fully compatible with ontologies based upon materialism, idealism, or dualism; that is, a strong form of empiricism is not a necessary consequence of this type of knowledge. It would seem that something akin to knowledge by acquaintance is the epistemology underlying Russian formalism and its varieties. Consistent with the idea that acquaintance is *logically prior* to all other forms of knowledge and reasoning, Thompson, along with David Bordwell, is able to forcefully argue that the goal of narrative criticism is not to uncover meanings or connotations, or to produce interpretations, but to analyze the actual patterns of the specific and concrete devices in each art medium that engage our perception of narrative.[77] This bold attempt to rethink the role of interpretation, and our interaction with the knowledge produced by narrative, will no doubt attract considerable comment.

A third type of theory treats narrative itself as a general, transcendent sort of medium – as a discourse or speech act – which is superimposed upon specific media like film and literature. This approach concentrates on how the techniques of "narration" (e.g., knowing how to do things with words or pictures) function as a general means of "communication," much like ordinary language and rhetoric, in altering and conveying a pre-existent story (setting, character, action, theme) for a spectator or reader. Narration in this sense is not confined to, or derived from, "aesthetic" discourse, but rather is powerfully connected to human goals and the exchange of information. As discussed earlier, works by Susan Lanser, Seymour Chatman, Mary Louise Pratt, and Wolfgang Iser illustrate the approach.[78]

The most recent approaches to narrative comprehension continue to focus on "narration," and "knowing how," but have shifted the attention from authors and narrators toward the reader – toward the reception of narrative and its immediacy for a reader.[79] What are the conditions which make possible a reading? How is sense made by the reader? In what ways does a reader imagine and construct authors and narrators? "Our easiest approach to a definition of any aspect of fiction," says E.M. Forster, "is always by considering the sort of demand it makes on the reader." In the reception approach, discovering "messages" from an author becomes less important than studying the psychology of a reader and how he or she is engaged by/in a text. For example, suspense, mystery, and surprise might be defined according to a reader's response to what he or she knows relative to what a particular character knows; or, a genre might be defined according to a reader's hesitation between two competing interpretations.[80] Reception theories may also define a reader's "horizon of expectation" in historical or sociological terms. These theories mark a return to the perceptual processes that were important to the Russian formalists even though they never developed a detailed theory of perception.[81] Nevertheless, reception theories differ strikingly from style and communication theories across a range of basic philosophical beliefs concerning the nature of meaning.[82]

A reception theory may make use of linguistic methods without thereby being committed to the assumptions underlying a communication theory. Recall that for Metz the spectator's perception of film *imagery* was a "spontaneous perception" of a "potential linguistic focus."[83] This notion may be developed in several different ways by a reception theory. For example, language may be connected to a theory of "inner speech" activated in a film spectator (conceived as either preconscious speech or conscious pre-speech);[84] or, it may be connected to a theory of the ordinary ways we create and exchange verbal reports about visual experiences. One need not posit an author, or delivery man, against which to measure the discovery of subvocal or vocal meanings. David Alan Black has created from these kinds of ideas virtually a new area of film study which he calls a theory of "synopsis." He argues that particular films are understood as narratives, and function within political settings, according to certain highly condensed verbal summaries we make of them.

> [R]ather than saying that a film shows us something . . . we have reason to want to say – however circuitous it may sound – that the

> viewing of the film has authorized us to *say*, to relate, that we have seen something: in fact, that we have seen something said, related.[85]

Black's novel theory and terms are meant to describe at the same moment both the reception of film narrative through what can be said of it, and the limitations imposed on its comprehension by languages already established and spoken in society.

A fifth type of narrative theory is related to reception theories, but asserts that the cognitive abilities of a reader used in producing various types of knowledge do not exhaust what is at work in responding to a narrative. There are forces "driving" cognition itself. Prominent among the class of so-called drive theories is psychoanalysis. It begins with the assumption that the instinctual drives are defined as *mental representations* of stimuli originating within the organism; that is, it is assumed that the human body creates representations not just of the external world but also of various internal, physiological states.[86] Internal and external representations jostle and intermix, and are not always clearly distinguishable or conscious: what is seen in the external world, especially, may have an origin from within – may be dictated by desire or fear. The study of human *memory* thus becomes critical because in storing and interconnecting information, it may erase such traits as the "source" of the information when assigning it a new meaning within a mental structure. Since "consciousness" is a relatively high-level form of awareness with severe capacity limitations (similar to the restrictions on short-term memory), it cannot be a full measure of what we know or why we act.

Like other types of theory applied to narrative texts, psychoanalysis may seize upon one or another aspect of the narrative phenomenon. It may, for instance, interpret the "plot" as a set of symptoms or distorted symbols analogous to a patient's dream; or, more fundamentally, it may challenge the very idea that a "story" underlies a plot. Jonathan Culler argues, for example, that studying the formal relations between story and plot neglects the insights offered through Freudian mechanisms, like deferred action. (Deferred action involves experiences and memories that are revised at a later date, acquiring new meanings to fit new circumstances or a later stage of psychic development.[87]) The operation of such Freudian mechanisms makes it "difficult to establish a bedrock of events which then get reordered by narrative; for narrative ordering may be what constitutes key events as events."[88] Furthermore, unconscious desires and fantasies, may construct a "plot" by concealing and repressing other plots. These ideas hint that the "narration" we imagine in a narrative may be interpreted in terms of a "primary process" of human thought governed by the pleasure principle (and anxiety) and not just as an aspect of the preconscious-conscious system governed by the reality principle and rationality, i.e., a "secondary process" perfectly generating an underlying, coherent "story."[89] Narration in this deeper psychoanalytic sense engages a reader in bringing forth unconscious (infantile) wishes and conflicts as well as provoking the reader *to react to* what is brought forth, or merely threatened (or possibly threatened!) to be brought forth, in his or her interactions with the text. A psychoanalytic approach stresses that the spectator's conscious understanding of a text is inseparable from his or her often unconscious memories and feelings. Under psychoanalysis the narrative object becomes fully as dense, complex, and contradictory as the human mind.

One of the difficulties a drive theory encounters in explaining narrative is that there is little agreement on which psychic mechanisms are pertinent, how they function, how they may be represented, and when they may appear in a text. Furthermore, unconscious drives, or "instincts," are contradictory by definition because they spring from unresolved tensions which must be repressed – desires that have been driven out of conscious experience (under the influence of the "reality principle"). Contradiction in its many guises is crucial to a psychoanalytic theory of narrative for it testifies to the actions of the unconscious. Thus the critic must search for the structure of narrative in unlikely places (or at several strata of human thought). The critic must boldly read against the grain, searching for the *non*literal, the counterintuitive, and for what is *not* said and *not* shown (i.e., repressed, forgotten, distorted, or disowned).[90] The critic looks for what is incompatible in the text (i.e., for evidence of conflict and anxiety) and hence he or she must strive to disunify what appears to be complete. This remains true even if the human drives are rendered as explicit themes in the form of *declarative* knowledge (e.g., films about psychoanalysis like *Freud, Spellbound*, and *Secrets of a Soul*) because the drives will continue to operate as (contradictory) *procedural* principles for the generation of the textual material. Psychoanalysis thus acknowledges a limit to what can be made explicit and coherent in a text as well as a limit to the types of knowledge humans can acquire about the psyche. At the center of the psychoanalytic method is a search for what is invisible and implicit and what may never be known. Such material of the irrational provides few landmarks for the analyst. Nevertheless I believe that cognitive psychology, like other reception theories, needs a drive theory. I also believe that psychoanalysis needs a more complete theory of the secondary process. Whether cognitive psychology and psychoanalysis need each other, however, is still another question.

Our perception of events in a story occurs within a variety of epistemological boundaries set by the levels of a narration which we initially believe are "in" a text that is "out there," rather than also in our own perceptions and imaginings. A narrative theory, too, initially classifies human experiences by setting boundaries on our thinking about objects that exist "out there." It specifies what will count as a narrative; what psychological effects may be produced by it; the possible uses, social value, and aesthetics of narrative; and how a history of narrative should be written. As such, however, a given theory is responding to some of our deepest beliefs about human beings and the nature of society, and reveals not only a narrative artifact, but also how we are thinking about the working of the human mind.

Notes

1 I have added the bottom two levels and have renamed several of Lanser's levels consistent with my terminology; for example, Lanser's "public" and "private" narrators become "nondiegetic" and "diegetic" narrators. I have also made other changes, most notably reversing Lanser's levels of "focalizer" and "character" consistent with my revised definition of "focalization." See Susan Sniader Lanser, *The Narrative Act: Point of View in Prose Fiction* (Princeton, N.J.: Princeton University Press, 1981), chap. 3, "From Person to Persona: The Textual Voice," esp. pp. 131–48.

2 My definition of a text is meant to rule out, for example, such objects as trees and tables, as well as a book being used to patch a hole in the roof.

3 Roland Barthes, "An Introduction to the Structural Analysis of Narrative," trans. by Lionel Duisit, *New Literary History*, vol. 6, no. 2 (Winter 1975), p. 261 (Barthes's emphases).

4 On the "biographical legend," see David Bordwell, *Ozu and the Poetics of Cinema* (Princeton, N.J.: Princeton University Press, 1988), "A Filmmaker's Legend," pp. 5–7, and *The Films of Carl-Theodor Dreyer* (Berkeley: University of California Press, 1981), "An Author and His Legend," pp. 9–24. On authorship generally, see *Theories of Authorship: A Reader*, ed. by John Caughie (London: Routledge & Kegan Paul, 1981) and Stephen Crofts, "Authorship and Hollywood," *Wide Angle*, vol. 5, no. 3 (1983), pp. 16–22.

5 See my discussion of the paradoxical statement, "I am lying" in *Point of View in the Cinema: A Theory of Narration and Subjectivity in Classical Film* (New York and Berlin: Mouton, 1984), pp. 2–5, 172–3, 182–4. The analysis of narration into "levels," each with a nominal subject, is one way of talking about how a text as a whole may represent a "splitting of the subject."

6 Recall that a narrative schema organizes causal patterns in order to make important, and make relevant, our already existing interests and activities. Hitchcock promises such an organization and solicits our attention. Hitchcock's opening statement is based upon pressing together two familiar metaphors: fact is stranger than fiction (but otherwise is like it), and life is (like) a story. His opening, "And yet . . .", inaugurates the complex interplay between the probable and the improbable, nonfiction and fiction, nonnarrative and narrative that is held together by the metaphors.

7 See Marshall Deutelbaum, "Finding the Right Man in *The Wrong Man*," in *A Hitchcock Reader*, ed. by Marshall Deutelbaum and Leland Poague (Ames: Iowa State University Press, 1986), pp. 207–18.

8 Initially the distant figure walks toward the camera but then stops, plants his feet squarely, and begins to speak. The figure has not really come any closer to us nor can we see him any better. Why has he moved at all? By moving he has demonstrated that he is *facing us directly* and has emphasized that we are being specially addressed as extra-fictional spectators. By pointing his gigantic shadow into the camera, he has drawn attention to himself and demonstrated that his role will be active. Characters in the story, however, will not look directly into the camera and speak to us in this way (addressing us as "you"). Certainly there are conventions involved here, but more importantly the conventions are being used to draw epistemological boundary lines within this particular text. Also, the shot

permits us to indulge in *stylistic metaphors*, if we wish, by, for example, relating the size of Hitchcock's shadow to an otherworldly power to create; or, by relating the shadow to a presumed, and prior, "first cause" of the story who is dimly seen as a figure that breaks the light and has the power to "shed light" on (enlighten, illuminate) matters.

9 After the end title of *The Wrong Man* a final title appears:

> We are grateful to Mr. Sherman Billingsley for his gracious cooperation in permitting scenes of this picture to be photographed at the Stork Club in New York City.

This title amounts to a final assertion by an extra-fictional narration that what we have seen is true by virtue of being filmed on location. The Hitchcock "I" is now hidden behind a "we."

10 Figure 2 is taken from Ray Jackendoff, *Consciousness and the Computational Mind* (Cambridge, Mass.: MIT Press, 1987), p. 169. Jackendoff uses the figure in discussing David Marr's theory of vision.

11 In chapter 6, I will analyze in detail how an implicit narration is created from elements that are missing from the explicit narrations of *Letter from an Unknown Woman*. Also relevant to the concept of implicitness is the general issue of the separation of material and structure which is discussed in chapter 5.

12 In chapter 2, I examined the relation of screen and story space in the context of another sort of "perception of a misperception" that concerned a husband spying on his wife in Hitchcock's *The 39 Steps*.

13 Hitchcock qualified his dislike for *The Wrong Man* by saying, "But I did fancy the opening of the picture because of my own fear of the police. I also liked the part where the real culprit is discovered just as [Henry] Fonda is praying. Yes, I liked that ironic coincidence." François Truffaut, *Hitchcock* (New York: Simon & Schuster, rev. edn 1984), p. 243.

14 For various definitions of the implied author, see, e.g., Wayne C. Booth, *The Rhetoric of Fiction* (Chicago: University of Chicago Press, 1961), pp. 67–77; Shlomith Rimmon-Kenan, *Narrative Fiction: Contemporary Poetics* (New York: Methuen, 1983), pp. 86–9, 101–4; Seymour Chatman, *Story and Discourse: Narrative Structure in Fiction and Film* (Ithaca, N.Y.: Cornell University Press, 1978), pp. 147–51, and *Coming to Terms: The Rhetoric of Narrative in Fiction and Film* (Ithaca, N.Y.: Cornell University Press, 1990), chaps 5 and 6, "In Defense of the Implied Author" and "The Implied Author at Work," pp. 74–108; Marjet Berendsen, "The Teller and the Observer: Narration and Focalization in Narrative Texts," *Style*, vol. 18, no. 2 (Spring 1984), pp. 146–8; Sarah Kozloff, *Invisible Storytellers: Voice-Over Narration in American Fiction Film* (Berkeley: University of California Press, 1988), pp. 80–1, 109, 117–26; Edward Branigan, "Diegesis and Authorship in Film," *Iris 7*, vol. 4, no. 2 (Fall 1986), pp. 52–3. Gérard Genette has argued that the concept of an implied author serves no purpose; *Narrative Discourse Revisited*, trans. by Jane E. Lewin (Ithaca, N.Y.: Cornell University Press, 1988), pp. 135–50.

15 Christian Metz, *Film Language: A Semiotics of the Cinema*, trans. by Michael Taylor (New York: Oxford University Press, 1974), chap. 2, "Notes Toward a Phenomenology of the Narrative," pp. 20–1 (Metz's emphases except for the final phrase; footnote omitted). See also Metz, "The Impersonal Enunciation, or the Site of Film (In the margin of recent works on enunciation in cinema)," *New Literary History*, vol. 22, no. 3 (Summer 1991), pp. 747–72.

16 See Branigan, *Point of View*, pp. 172–3, 182–4. For more on objectivity and uncertainty, see chapter 6 below.

17 Some speech-act theories of fiction allow several narrations to exist simultaneously by recognizing that a text is composed of "layers" whereby an author "delegates" responsibility for making assertions to "substitute" speakers who contest with one another in an environment of "simultaneous" utterances. See Marie-Laure Ryan, "Fiction as a Logical, Ontological, and Illocutionary Issue," *Style*, vol. 18, no. 2 (Spring 1984), esp. pp. 135–8.

18 On the integration of bottom-up and top-down perceptual processes through the opening music of *The Wrong Man*, compare the discussion of the "integrated spatial match" in *The 39 Steps* in chapter 2, and the discussion of the creation of an inverted pyramid of narrations in the opening of *Hangover Square* in chapter 5.

The key issue in the credit sequence of *The Wrong Man* concerns types of narration, and contexts of perception, not, as Deutelbaum believes, the "temporal vagueness" of the music – which is not vague – nor the "legibility" of the shots which are perfectly clear ("Finding the Right Man in *The Wrong Man*," pp. 214–15). In general, the spectator is *revising* hypotheses and searching for a fit, not making "mistakes" or being "misled." The analyst's choice of a theory of reading (by hypothesis, or by error) leads to larger theoretical issues. See Edward Branigan, "The Spectator and Film Space – Two Theories," *Screen*, vol. 22, no. 1 (1981), pp. 55–78.

19 Compare the notion of a chameleon text with the discussion of "double causal motivation" in chapter 1. My use of the notion of a chameleon text differs from that of Robert Stam and Ella Shohat; see "*Zelig* and Contemporary Theory: Meditation on the Chameleon Text," *Enclitic* 17/18, vol. 9, nos. 1–2 (1987), pp. 185–6.

20 David Bordwell, "Happily Ever After, Part II," *The Velvet Light Trap* 19 (1982), p. 5. See generally Roger Seamon, "The Story of the Moral: The Function of Thematizing in Literary Criticism," *The Journal of Aesthetics and Art Criticism*, vol. 47, no. 3 (Summer 1989), pp. 229–36.

21 The concept of nondiegetic narration also explains why we know what happens in the story world *after* this particular story is finished and as a "new" story in that world is beginning. Just prior to the end title of *The Wrong Man*, the following title appears:

> Two years later, Rose Balestrero walked out of the sanitarium – completely cured.
>
> Today she lives happily in Florida with Manny and the two boys . . . and what happened seems like a nightmare to them – but it did happen . . .

Because of its nondiegetic position, the narration may pronounce Rose Balestrero "completely cured" and summarize character beliefs today ("seems like a nightmare to them"). Since the new story is beginning "today," it cannot yet be narrated and so the nondiegetic narrator must fall silent.

22 What will count as "explicit" rather than "implicit," or indeed as "non-existent," haunts theories of narrative and cannot be defined without reference to the theory as a whole. Rimmon-Kenan's six "degrees of perceptibility" of the narrator illustrate some of the issues; see *Narrative Fiction*, pp. 52, 88–9, 96–100, 108. Cf. Gérard Genette's notion of the "pseudo-diegetic" in *Narrative Discourse: An Essay in Method*, trans. by Jane E. Lewin (Ithaca, N.Y.: Cornell University Press, 1980), pp. 236–7. The pseudo-diegetic is analyzed by David Alan Black in "Genette and Film: Narrative Level in the Fiction Cinema," *Wide Angle*, vol. 8, nos. 3/4 (1986), pp. 19–26.

Is it possible for a story to have *no* narrator, or is the narration merely covert? This question leads to a theory's basic grounding in rationalism or empiricism. Cf. Rimmon-Kenan, *Narrative Fiction*, pp. 88 n. 4 and 96 n. 9 with Branigan, *Point of View*, pp. 168–71. See also Dorrit Cohn, "Signposts of Fictionality: A Narratological Perspective," *Poetics Today*, vol. 11, no. 4 (Winter 1990), pp. 794–8; and p. 109 above. Chapter 6 will address the issue of explicit versus implicit in the context of "objective" narrations.

23 Stephen Heath distinquishes five modes of characterization in film: agent, character, person, image, and figure. "Film and System: Terms of Analysis," Part II, *Screen*, vol. 16, no. 2 (Summer 1975), pp. 102–7.

24 *Movies On TV: 1982–1983 Edition*, ed. by Stephen H. Scheuer (New York: Bantam, 9th rev. edn 1981), p. 741. A character's speech on thought is nonfocalized when it is rendered in a highly abbreviated form. For example, in the sentence, "Manny decided to take the train home," no details are provided about how the decision was reached; the decision is merely reported as an action. For Genette, such speech or thought is *narratized* (narrated, narrativized). See *Narrative Discourse*, pp. 170–1. Cf. the examples discussed on pp. 168–9 above.

25 See Edward Branigan, "Point of View in the Fiction Film," *Wide Angle*, vol. 8, nos. 3/4 (1986), pp. 6–7.

26 Some narrative theorists refer to the distinction between representing an experience as intersubjective versus representing it as private as an opposition between "voice" – literally, whose words do we hear? – and "point of view."

27 I am not using the concept of "identification" in its full psychological sense of "identification with." Making the levels of narration more precise is not yet a theory of a spectator's fascination with character and story.

28 Hitchcock has discussed the techniques he used to portray events through the viewpoint of Manny. Hitchcock's memory of some of the scenes is not entirely accurate but nonetheless is revealing about external focalization:

> The whole approach is subjective. For instance, they've slipped on a pair of handcuffs to link him [Manny] to another prisoner. During the journey between the station house and the prison, there are different men guarding him, but *since he's ashamed*, he keeps his head down, staring at his shoes, so we never show the guards. From time to time one of the handcuffs is opened, and we see a different wrist. In the same way, during the whole trip, we only show the guards' feet, their lower legs, the floor, and the bottom parts of the doors.
>
> (Truffaut, *Hitchcock*, p. 239, my emphasis.)

For another example of external focalization, see p. 78 above, figs 15 and 16, panels 3–8 of *Nick Fury*.

29 On the various ways in which events may be externally and internally focalized through character, and on the conventions of subjectivity in film, see Branigan, *Point of View*, chaps 4–6.

30 Stephen Heath, for example, asserts that

> Point of view . . . depends on an overlaying of first and third person modes. There is no radical dichotomy between subjective point-of-view shots and objective non-point-of-view shots; the latter mode is the continual basis over which the former can run in its particular organization of space, its disposition of the images.
>
> ("Narrative Space" in *Questions of Cinema* (New York: Macmillan, 1981), p. 48. See also pp. 51, 54.)

31 *Wild Strawberries* creates its effects by defining, and then subverting, a single hierarchy of narrations. However, as suggested by figure 26, narrations may be arranged in more complex ways. Depictions of memory that are more complex and radical than *Wild Strawberries* may be found in *Life is a Dream* (Ruiz, 1986), *Distant Voices, Still Lives* (Davies, 1988), and *Sans Soleil* (Marker, 1983). I will discuss the latter film in chapter 7.

32 For Genette, the sudden transgression of a boundary between two levels of the narration would be a metalepsis and is related to paralepsis and paralipsis (i.e., exceeding, or else withholding, information called for by the logic of a given focalization). In general, such a transgression is called an "alteration" or "infraction." See *Narrative Discourse*, pp. 234–7, 194–8. The permeability of narrational boundaries has been addressed by theorists in a variety of ways. David Bordwell speaks of the "degree" of communicativeness of a narration *with respect to* a given "range" and "depth" of knowledge. Didier Coste defines the "informative performance" of a "voice" based on a relationship between "cognitive competence" and "informative competence." Finally, William F. Edmiston analyzes Genette's paralipsis as a "hyper-restriction"; that is, a narration that falsely represents itself as too restrictive to convey certain important information. Presumably, the opposite case would be termed a *hypo*-restriction which would be applied to the situation where a nominal restriction is briefly *exceeded* (thus providing more information than is allowed by the given restriction). The terms proposed by Bordwell, Coste, and Edmiston give the analyst a way of comparing the source of information that is named in the text with the actual inferences that the reader is able to make.

The general problem being addressed by these terminologies concerns issues of the segmentation and large-scale form of narration, local changes in narration (e.g., intrusions, transitions), and the ways in which a given narration may be emphasized, defied, or concealed. In deciding whether to analyze a segment as the momentary transgression of a single narration (e.g., a hyper- or hypo-restriction), or instead as the alternation of two distinct narrations, the analyst will need to weigh such factors as the suddenness, duration, relevance, and saliency of a change in the information against the scope of the analysis. Note also that similar issues arise in assessing the function of a "character" in a narrative: a character may know "too little" or "too much" (e.g., by speaking more than he or she knows – dramatic irony – or by being in the perfect place at the perfect time). As Genette notes, "Narrative always says less than it knows, but it often makes known more than it says" (p. 198). Compare the issues discussed on p. 170 above; compare also the notion of a "hyperdiegetic" narration on p. 189 above. See generally Bordwell, *Narration in the Fiction Film* (Madison: University of Wisconsin Press, 1985), pp. 57–61; Coste, *Narrative as Communication* (Minneapolis: University of Minnesota Press, 1989), pp. 178–9; Edmiston, "Focalization and the First-Person Narrator: A Revision of the Theory," *Poetics Today*, vol. 10, no. 4 (Winter 1989), p. 741.

33 In a study of fifty-three languages representing fourteen different language stocks from all the major parts of the world, Ake Viberg found that all the verbs of perception of the five senses (sight, hearing, touch, taste, smell) could be classified according to whether they indicated an activity of a subject, an experience of a subject, or the subject itself as an object to be perceived. The following is an example of these three possibilities for verbs of sight:

1 Peter *looked at* the birds.
2 Peter *saw* the birds.
3 Peter *looked* happy (cf.: Peter is *good-looking*).

An example for verbs of hearing:

1 Peter *listened to* the birds.
2 Peter *heard* the birds.
3 Peter *sounded* happy.

A number of important syntactic, morphological, and semantic characteristics common to all fifty-three languages can be explained using this approach. "The Verbs of Perception: A Typological Study" in *Explanations for Language Universals*, ed. by Brian Butterworth, Bernard Comrie, and Osten Dahl (New York: Mouton, 1984), pp. 123–62. Compare also the two, or perhaps three or four, types of verbs that state narrative predications discussed in chapter 1 above (e.g., the modes "to be," "to go," "to stay").

Reformulating this tripartite division of the verbs of perception in order to match the types of perceiving and knowing characteristic of *narration* would result in three sorts of subject (i.e., a subject in one of three possible narrative roles): actor, focalizer, and narrator, respectively. The reason that I treat the third case above (i.e., where a subject becomes an object to be perceived by another, unidentified subject) as analogous to narration involving a narrator, rather than narration involving an actor/agent or a focalizer, is that I interpret sentences like 3 as containing an implicit and undefined perceiver who becomes, in effect, the justification for our interpretation of the sentence as a statement *about* what could be seen (or heard), a perceptual judgment that has been rendered *about* something that has been objectified for someone (and for us). Thus:

3 Peter *looked* happy [to *someone* who looked at, or saw, or could have looked at, or could have seen, him and consequently would have been in a position to make the judgment about him and "narrate" it for us].

Positing someone as an implicit "narrator" who reports an event, then, is shorthand for saying that we are seeing what is, or could be, *seen to be*. The context for the "seeing" (which need not be literal) is not defined, leaving merely the judgment. For more discussion of "objective" narration, see chapter 6.

34 Cf. Mieke Bal, "The Narrating and the Focalizing: A Theory of the Agents in Narrative," *Style*, vol. 17, no. 2 (Spring 1983), pp. 243–5. I have reversed the positions that Bal assigns to actors and focalizers because I have restricted focalization to characters.

35 Focalization is not defined by the binary contrasts of either recounting versus enacting nor telling versus showing. See Bordwell, *Narration in the Fiction Film*, pp. 77–80; and chaps 1 and 2 on mimetic and diegetic theories of narration. Focalization is also not defined by speaking versus seeing. See William Nelles, "Getting Focalization into Focus," *Poetics Today*, vol. 11, no. 2 (Summer 1990), pp. 366–8. George M. Wilson shows the logical absurdities which result when a film image is deemed to be literally spoken by a narrator as a "speech-act" or "visualized" as a mental image. *Narration in Light; Studies in Cinematic Point of View* (Baltimore: Johns Hopkins University Press, 1986), chap. 7, "On Narrators and Narration in Film," pp. 126–44. Furthermore, the above contrasts are singularly misleading about many other aspects of the narrative process.

36 See, e.g., Genette, *Narrative Discourse*, pp. 188–94; Mieke Bal, *Narratology: Introduction to the Theory of Narrative*, trans. by Christine van Boheemen (Toronto: University of Toronto Press, 1985), pp. 100–26; Rimmon-Kenan, *Narrative Fiction*, pp. 71–85; Lanser, *The Narrative Act*, pp. 37–8, 141–8, 212–14; Berendsen, "The Teller and the Observer," pp. 140–58; Edmiston, "Focalization and the

First-Person Narrator," pp. 729–44; Nelles, "Getting Focalization into Focus," pp. 365–82; Steven Cohan and Linda M. Shires, *Telling Stories: A Theoretical Analysis of Narrative Fiction* (New York: Routledge, 1988), pp. 94–104.

37 Bal, *Narratology*, pp. 100–18.

38 Seymour Chatman, "Characters and Narrators: Filter, Center, Slant, and Interest-Focus," *Poetics Today*, vol. 7, no. 2 (1986), esp. pp. 193–7. For an illustration of these concepts, see Chatman, "Who Is the Best Narrator? The Case of *The Third Man*," *Style*, vol. 23, no. 2 (Summer 1989), pp. 183–96.

39 Genette, *Narrative Discourse*, pp. 188–94. Genette's "external focalization" also differs from my use of the concept. For Genette, it refers to a nonpsychological ("behaviorist") rendering of character from an external position. This seems to be what I have referred to as "nonfocalization." Genette also distinguishes among fixed, variable, and multiple focalization. However these categories exist only at a global level of the text and result from particular patterns of change in internal focalization.

40 Lanser, *The Narrative Act*, cf. p. 96 with p. 85. In Lanser's version of figure 1, the diagonal line above each sender on the left is labelled "status"; the diagnonal line below each sender becomes a dotted line and is called "stance"; and a new horizontal dotted line is drawn between each sender and receiver, and called "contact." Status describes the speaker's right to communicate: the authority, competence, and credibility which the communicator is conventionally and personally allowed by a linguistic community. Stance describes the speaker's ideological and psychological attitudes toward the message he or she is uttering. Contact describes the speaker's physical and psychological relationship to the audience. Lanser, *The Narrative Act*, pp. 64–77, 84–97, 145, 223–5.

41 Barthes, "An Introduction to the Structural Analysis of Narrative," p. 260 (Barthes's emphases).

42 Dudley Andrew, *Concepts in Film Theory* (New York: Oxford University Press, 1984), p. 81; but cf. pp. 44, 48, 92, 138, 167–71.

43 Chatman, *Story and Discourse*, p. 28. Chatman also says, "Narratives are communications, thus easily envisaged as the movement of arrows from left to right, from author to audience" (p. 31; and see his diagram of narrative structure on p. 267).

44 James L. Kinneavy, *A Theory of Discourse: The Aims of Discourse* (New York: W.W. Norton & Co., 1971), p. 19. Other formulations of a communication theory may be found in Didier Coste's *Narrative as Communication*; Roman Jakobson, "Linguistics and Poetics" in *The Structuralists: From Marx to Lévi-Strauss*, ed. by Richard and Fernande de George (Garden City, N.Y.: Doubleday, 1972), esp. pp. 89–97; and Umberto Eco, *A Theory of Semiotics* (Bloomington: Indiana University Press, 1976), pp. 32–47, 139–42.

45 Roland Barthes, *S/Z*, trans. by Richard Miller (New York: Hill & Wang, 1974), p. 151 (Barthes's emphasis); see also pp. 10–11, 41–2. Barthes transforms the notion of "voice" into a "code" that "de-originates" the utterance (p. 21). See generally Barthes, "The Death of the Author" in *Image – Music – Text*, trans. by Stephen Heath (New York: Hill & Wang, 1977), pp. 142–8; *The Pleasure of the Text*, trans. by Richard Miller (New York: Hill & Wang, 1975); "To Write: An Intransitive Verb?" in *The Structuralist Controversy: The Languages of Criticism and the Sciences of Man*, ed. by Richard Macksey and Eugenio Donato (Baltimore: Johns Hopkins University Press, 1972), pp. 134–45.

46 Jonathan Culler, "Problems in the Theory of Fiction," *Diacritics*, vol. 14, no. 1 (Spring 1984), pp. 5–6.

47 Bordwell, *Narration in the Fiction Film*, p. 62 (Bordwell's emphasis). See also n. 22 above.

48 See, e.g., Noam Chomsky, *Reflections on Language* (New York: Pantheon, 1975), p. 69 ("Communication is only one function of language, and by no means an essential one."); Michael J. Reddy, "The Conduit Metaphor – A Case of Frame Conflict in Our Language about Language" in *Metaphor and Thought*, ed. by Andrew Ortony (New York: Cambridge University Press, 1979), pp. 284–324; William Frawley, *Text and Epistemology* (Norwood, N.J.: Ablex, 1987); Ann Banfield, *Unspeakable Sentences: Narration and Representation in the Language of Fiction* (London: Routledge & Kegan Paul, 1982). Alain Robbe-Grillet argues that communication metaphors and anthropomorphisms encourage a false metaphysics; "Nature, Humanism, Tragedy" in *For A New Novel: Essays on Fiction*, trans. by Richard Howard (New York: Grove, 1965), pp. 49–75. But see Mark Johnson, *The Body in the Mind: The Bodily Basis of Meaning, Imagination, and Reason* (Chicago: University of Chicago Press, 1987).

49 Cf. Friedrich Nietzsche, *Beyond Good and Evil: Prelude to a Philosophy of the Future*, trans. by Walter Kaufmann (New York: Vintage, 1966), sects 16 and 17.

50 I will readdress the question of using anthropomorphic metaphors to describe narration when we consider the holistic theories of Telotte, Sobchack, and Kawin in chapter 5 and the concept of an invisible observer in chapter 6. Cf. George Lakoff and Mark Johnson's general discussion of "orientational metaphors" and the "canonical person" in *Metaphors We Live By* (Chicago: University of Chicago Press, 1980), pp. 14–21, 41–5, 132–8, 160–2, and see David Bordwell, *Making Meaning: Inference and Rhetoric in the Interpretation of Cinema* (Cambridge, Mass.: Harvard University, 1989), chap. 7, "Two Basic Schemata," sect. "Making Films Personal," pp. 151–68. For detailed arguments about the communication metaphor as applied to film narrative, see, e.g., Branigan, *Point of View*, pp. 8–9, 14, 39–40, 59, 194–5; Seymour Chatman's review of this book in *Film Quarterly*, vol. 40, no. 1 (Fall 1986), pp. 45–6; my reply to the review and his response in *Film Quarterly*, vol. 41, no. 1 (Fall 1987), pp. 63–5; Sarah Kozloff's review of Bordwell's *Narration in the Fiction Film* in *Film Quarterly*, vol. 40, no. 1 (Fall 1986), pp. 43–5; Chatman's review of this book in *Wide Angle*, vol. 8, nos. 3/4 (1986), pp. 139–41; and Bordwell's reply (unpublished).

51 See Wallace Martin, *Recent Theories of Narrative* (Ithaca, N.Y.: Cornell University Press, 1986), p. 156. On the search for an intermediate position, see also Robert Burgoyne, "The Cinematic Narrator: The Logic and Pragmatics of Impersonal Narration," *Journal of Film and Video*, vol. 42, no. 1 (Spring 1990), pp. 3–16.

52 Shlomith Rimmon-Kenan adopts Chatman's communication model for narrative but excludes the implied author and the implied reader from the communication situation even though she stresses that these two constructs remain essential to an analysis of a reader's comprehension of narrative fiction. In addition, she includes the narrator and the narratee as constitutive, not just optional, elements in the communication situation; *Narrative Fiction*, pp. 2–4, 86–9. Chatman has responded with some changes to his model; *Coming to Terms*, p. 218 n. 29.

53 Robert de Beaugrande, *Text, Discourse, and Process: Toward a Multidisciplinary Science of Texts* (Norwood, N.J.: Ablex, 1980), p. 125 (Beaugrande's emphases except for the word "how"); cf. his list of ten universals of language and twenty-one cognitive skills in processing texts, pp. 125–6, 278–9.

54 See note 13 above.

55 Scheuer (ed.) *Movies On TV*, p. 741.

56 On the theoretical status of verbal descriptions of pictorial data, see especially David Alan Black, *Narrative Film and the Synoptic Tendency* (Ph.D. diss.: New York University, 1988).

57 In arguing against Genette's theory of focalization, Mieke Bal notes that "the nonchalant use of a preposition is enough to overturn a theory," "The Narrating and the Focalizing," p. 241. In my arguments I have tried to be sensitive to the nuances of such prepositions as over, at, with, through, into, in, and about. In chapters 6 and 7, I will explore the nuances of definite and indefinite articles in relation to narrative.

58 Cf. Marie-Laure Ryan, "Stacks, Frames and Boundaries, or Narrative as Computer Language," *Poetics Today*, vol. 11, no. 4 (Winter 1990), pp. 873–99. As an example of how differing levels of representation operate in perception, consider that our perception of a visual object, say, on a motion picture screen is initially dependent on our *angle* of view while higher-level recognition of the "same" object (e.g., our memory of it) is *not* dependent on *that* point of view and, moreover, may be translated into other, nonvisual epistemological schemes (and thus may be stored and retrieved in quite different formats under different "views"). Of course, we have no awareness at all of some levels and processes of perception; for example, we lose all awareness of an image in its initially inverted, curvilinear, and tiny state within the retina. I believe that the above sorts of considerations also govern higher-level cognitive processes like narrative comprehension when it, too, is seen as multi-layered. Cf. the discussion of some remarkable facts about narrative comprehension on pp. 14–15.

59 Richard J. Gerrig, "Reexperiencing Fiction and Non-Fiction," *The Journal of Aesthetics and Art Criticism*, vol. 47, no. 3 (Summer 1989), pp. 277–80.

60 Figure 8b is based on box diagrams showing the relationships of various narrations in Maturin's *Melmoth the Wanderer* and Longus's *Daphnis and Chloe*; Joseph Kestner, "Secondary Illusion: The Novel and the Spatial Arts" in Jeffrey R. Smitten and Ann Daghistany (eds), *Spatial Form in Narrative* (Ithaca, N.Y.: Cornell University Press, 1981), pp. 111, 115. Marvin Minsky contrasts a hierarchy with a "heterarchy" that is organized as a series of cross-connected rings and loops. *The Society of Mind* (New York: Simon & Schuster, 1986), p. 35.

61 Tzvetan Todorov, "Categories of the Literary Narrative," trans. by Ann Goodman, *Film Reader* 2 (1977), cf. p. 29 with p. 21; *Introduction to Poetics*, trans. by Richard Howard (Minneapolis: University of Minnesota Press, 1981), pp. 52–3.

62 The concept of "point of view" is misleading in that it suggests that there is a single principle (a "point") that accounts for the unity of a perceptual judgment (a "view"), rather than a series of relationships spanning a range of mental activities. For example, Seymour Chatman argues that "point of view" should be analyzed in terms of four variables: centrality (the relative importance of an entity to the cause-effect chain); filter (the represention of a perception, a "consciousness of"); slant (the representation of an attitude); and finally, the reader's interest-focus. See Chatman, "Characters and Narrators," and *Coming to Terms*, chap. 9, "A New Point of View on 'Point of View,' " pp. 139–60.

In the case of film, Jacques Aumont also finds four aspects to point of view: the point from which a gaze originates, i.e., the position of the camera; the spatial perspective in which an event is represented, i.e., the particular way in which an illusion of depth is created on the screen; the "narrative" point of view which is, in turn, comprised of three additional places from which a gaze originates – from the character, auteur, and spectator; and finally, the mental attitude (e.g., an intellectual, moral, or political attitude) that conveys the narrator's judgment on the event. Aumont believes that the history of narrative cinema (as well as perhaps the history of film theory) is one of the discovery and fixing of "the rules of correspondence" among these four aspects of point of view. "The Point of View," trans. by Arthur Denner, *Quarterly Review of Film and Video*, vol. 11, no. 2 (1989), pp. 2–3.

63 Branigan, *Point of View*, pp. 40–2, 46, 48–9, 68 n. 18, 120 n. 22, 171–3, 182.

64 For further discussion of "scene" and "summary," see chapter 5.

65 Arthur C. Danto, *Narration and Knowledge* (including the integral text of *Analytical Philosophy of History*) (New York: Columbia University Press, 1985), p. 238 (Danto's emphases except for the word "specific").

66 I have recast Wallace Martin's description of four varieties of narrative theory along somewhat different lines using different terms. I add a new, fifth major type and relate his fourth type of theory to topics discussed in his chapter 7 rather than to his choice which is chapter 6; see *Recent Theories of Narrative*, pp. 107–11. Dudley Andrew proposes eight types of narrative theories in *Concepts in Film Theory*, pp. 81–8.

67 Vladimir Propp, *Morphology of the Folktale*, trans. by Laurence Scott, rev. and ed. by Louis A. Wagner (Austin: University of Texas Press, 2nd edn 1968), pp. 20 and 21 (emphases omitted from both quotes).

68 Propp, *Morphology of the Folktale*, pp. 19–20.

69 In film studies, Propp's approach has been applied in especially novel and provocative ways to define three types of plot in the Western genre, Frederick Wiseman's documentary films, the Japanese "Sword Film," and an underlying plot for the films of Yasujiro Ozu. See Will Wright, *Six Guns and Society: A Structural Study of the Western* (Berkeley: University of California Press, 1975), pp. 40–9, 64–9, 99–113; Bill Nichols, *Ideology and the Image: Social Representation in the Cinema and Other Media* (Bloomington: Indiana University Press, 1981), pp. 212–16; David Desser, *The Samurai Films of Akira Kurosawa* (Ann Arbor, Mich.: UMI Research Press, 1983), pp. 48–51; and David Bordwell, *Ozu and the Poetics of Cinema*, pp. 56–64.

On Propp's theory and its relatives, see David Bordwell, "ApProppriations and ImProppRieties: Problems in the Morphology of Film Narrative,". *Cinema Journal*, vol. 27, no. 3 (Spring 1988), pp. 5–20; and Wallace Martin, *Recent Theories of Narrative*, pp. 88–98. For a recent application to film narrative, see Richard Abel, "*Notorious*: Perversion par Excellence" in *A Hitchcock Reader*, ed. by Marshall Deutelbaum and Leland Poague (Ames: Iowa State University Press, 1986), pp. 162–69.

For extensions of Propp's method into other areas of study, see Claude Lévi-Strauss, *Structural Anthropology*, trans. by Claire Jacobson and Brooke Grundfest Schoepf (Garden City, N.Y.: Doubleday, 1967) and Claude Bremond; "The Logic of Narrative Possibilities," *New Literary History*, vol. 11, no. 3 (Spring 1980), pp. 387–411. See generally, Jonathan Culler, *Structuralist Poetics: Structuralism, Linguistics and the Study of Literature* (Ithaca, N.Y.: Cornell University Press, 1975).

70 Five of Propp's thirty-one functions touch on the manipulation of character knowledge: reconnaissance (4), delivery of information (5), deception by villain (6), recognition of hero (27), and exposure of villain (28). These five, however, seem even less important when Propp lists all 151 elements of the wondertale. Propp, *Morphology of the Folktale*, Appendix I, pp. 119–27 (elements 37, 41, 43, 143, 145).

71 On the distinction between plot and story, cf. Bordwell, *Narration in the Fiction Film*, pp. 50–7, 77–88, 77 n. 6, with Bordwell and Kristin Thompson, *Film Art: An Introduction* (New York: McGraw-Hill, 3rd edn 1990), pp. 55–8, 85–6. For an examination of how the definition of plot responds to the underlying assumptions of a narrative theory, see Ruth Ronen, "Paradigm Shift in Plot Models: An Outline of the History of Narratology," *Poetics Today*, vol. 11, no. 4 (Winter 1990), pp. 817–42.

72 On the general function of a "middle term" in explaining change within a three-term narrative sequence, see Danto, *Narration and Knowledge*, pp. 233–56. Danto argues that the logic of narrative is *identical* to the logic of *any* causal explanation (e.g., he says, an account of the movement of billiard balls) and is also closely related to a deductive argument. For Danto, narrative constitutes a fundamental form of knowledge and is the basis for all historical explanation. His ideas would seem to be in accord with Bordwell and Thompson's general definition of narrative which is powerful enough to describe both a novel and the motions of a planet orbiting the sun. Bordwell and Thompson define narrative as "a chain of events in cause-effect relationship occurring in time and space." *Film Art*, p. 55 (emphasis omitted). One should not believe, however, that such a theory of narrative is necessarily empiricist, or depends on a positivist theory of language. See Danto, *Narration and Knowledge*, chaps 3–6.

The footnote would not be complete without placing Danto's book between Edward W. Said's *Beginnings: Intention and Method* (New York: Basic Books, 1975) and Frank Kermode's *The Sense of an Ending: Studies in the Theory of Fiction* (New York: Oxford University Press, 1967). Despite their selective emphases, it seems to me that each of these three books reasserts, at least as a first approximation, the essential unity and closure that we expect from a "narrative."

73 Kristin Thompson, *Breaking the Glass Armor: Neoformalist Film Analysis* (Princeton, N.J.: Princeton University Press, 1988), chap. 1, "Neoformalist Film Analysis: One Approach, Many Methods," p. 9; see also pp. 21, 27, 32, 36, 43. Basic assumptions of Russian Formalism are described by Thompson in *Eisenstein's Ivan the Terrible: A Neoformalist Analysis* (Princeton, N.J.: Princeton University Press, 1981), esp. chap. 1, pp. 8–60; on narrative, pp. 37–46. See also Herbert Eagle's introductory essay in *Russian Formalist Film Theory*, ed. by Herbert Eagle (Ann Arbor, Mich.: University of Michigan Press, 1981), pp. 1–54, and Peter Steiner, *Russian Formalism: A Metapoetics* (Ithaca, N.Y.: Cornell University Press, 1984).

74 Thompson, *Breaking the Glass Armor*, p. 10 (my emphases); cf. p. 7.

75 Russian formalism may have no need for a theory of fiction (and belief) separate from a theory of narrative because of its emphasis on the dulling and repolishing of human perception that is posited as distinct from a specific language or communication faculty (which would involve reference and knowing).

76 Bertrand Russell, *The Problems of Philosophy* (London: Oxford University Press, 1972), pp. 43–59, 108–9; *Mysticism and Logic and other Essays* (London: George Allen & Unwin, 1949), chap. 10, "Knowledge by Acquaintance and Knowledge by Description," pp. 209–32.

77 Thompson, *Breaking the Glass Armor*, pp. 12–15, 21. See David Bordwell, *Making Meaning*. Noël Carroll introduces four distinctions which appear to address epistemological issues: "knowing that," "believing that," "seeing that," and "seeing how." The distinctions, however, are drawn in such a manner that problems of knowledge, interpretation, and narration are reduced to aspects of *style* and to a perceiver's acquaintance with the sensuous surface of film. See Carroll, "Buster Keaton, *The General*, and Visible Intelligibility" in *Close Viewings: An Anthology of New Film Criticism*, ed. by Peter Lehman (Tallahassee: Florida State University Press, 1990), pp. 132–3.

78 In setting up a communication theory of narrative, Lanser and Chatman attempt to incorporate the work of the Russian formalists who developed what I have termed a style-based theory of narrative while Pratt and Iser attack the formalists. See, e.g., Lanser, *The Narrative Act*, p. 32 n. 27; Chatman, *Story and Discourse*, pp. 15–22; Mary Louise Pratt, *Toward a Speech Act Theory of Literary Discourse*

(Bloomington: Indiana University Press, 1977), pp. 67–78; Wolfgang Iser, "Narrative Strategies as a Means of Communication" in *Interpretation of Narrative*, ed. by Mario J. Valdes and Owen J. Miller (Toronto: University of Toronto Press, 1978), pp. 102–7.

79 See, e.g., Martin, *Recent Theories of Narrative*, chap. 7, "From Writer to Reader: Communication and Interpretation," pp. 152–72; Horst Ruthrof, *The Reader's Construction of Narrative* (London: Routledge & Kegan Paul, 1981); and especially Janet Staiger, *Interpreting Films: Studies in the Historical Reception of American Cinema* (Princeton, N.J.: Princeton University Press, 1972). For brief overviews of some of the issues, see Sarah Ruth Kozloff, "Narrative Theory and Television," and Robert C. Allen, "Reader-Oriented Criticism and Television" in *Channels of Discourse: Television and Contemporary Criticism*, ed. by Robert C. Allen (Chapel Hill: University of North Carolina, 1987), pp. 42–112.

Since I have formulated the basic issues and concepts of film narrative against the backdrop of the cognitive abilities of a reader, my general approach in this book would fit into this fourth class of theories emphasizing the reception of narrative.

80 E.M. Forster, *Aspects of the Novel* (New York: Harcourt, Brace & Co., 1927), p. 158. On suspense, mystery, and surprise, see chapter 3 above; on a genre defined by the duration of a reader's uncertainty, see Tzvetan Todorov, *The Fantastic: A Structural Approach to a Literary Genre*, trans. by Richard Howard (Ithaca, N.Y.: Cornell University Press, 1975), p. 25.

81 An exception is the Russian formalist Boris Eikhenbaum who developed a perceptual theory based on "inner speech." See note 84 below.

82 See, e.g., Richard Shusterman, "Interpretation, Intention, and Truth," *The Journal of Aesthetics and Art Criticism*, vol. 46, no. 3 (Spring 1988), pp. 399–411. More polemical is Bill Nichols, "Form Wars: The Political Unconscious of Formalist Theory," *The South Atlantic Quarterly*, vol. 88, no. 2 (Spring 1989), pp. 487–515.

83 Metz, *Film Language*, p. 21; more fully quoted in the text above at note 15.

84 See, e.g., Paul Willemen, "Cinematic Discourse: The Problem of Inner Speech," *Screen*, vol. 22, no. 3 (1981), pp. 63–93; Sergei Eisenstein, *The Film Sense*, trans. by Jay Leyda (New York: Harcourt, Brace & World, 1947), esp. part I, "Word and Image," pp. 1–65. See also Nelson Goodman, *Of Mind and Other Matters* (Cambridge, Mass.: Harvard University Press, 1984), chap. 1, sects 5 and 6, "Can Thoughts Be Quoted?" and "On Thoughts Without Words," pp. 19–28; Nelson Goodman and Catherine Z. Elgin, *Reconceptions in Philosophy and Other Arts and Sciences* (Indianapolis: Hackett, 1988), chap. 5, "Sights Unseen," pp. 83–92.

85 David Alan Black, *Narrative Film and the Synoptic Tendency*, p. 142 (Black's emphasis).

86 See F. Xavier Plaus, "Freudian Drive Theory and Epistemology," in *The Psychology of Knowing*, ed. by Joseph R. Royce and William W. Rozeboom (New York: Gordon & Breach, 1972), pp. 413, 420, 424.

87 In deferred action, or deferred revision, sensory material stored in memory is subject always to being recalled, repressed, or drastically reinterpreted in light of new circumstances including the maturation of the organism. Through deferred action, original stimuli stored in memory may produce entirely new feelings not experienced originally (guilt, anxiety, pleasure). Effects of the "present" may not be determined, much less known, until later. The temporality of the human psyche is thus much more complex than the temporality of initial stimuli. See J. Laplanche and J.-B. Pontalis, *The Language of Psycho-Analysis*, trans. by Donald Nicholson-Smith (New York: W. W. Norton & Co., 1973), "Censorship,"

"Deferred Action," "Phantasy," and "Secondary Revision," pp. 65–6, 111–14, 314–19, and 412.

88 Culler, "Problems in the Theory of Fiction," p. 3. See also Culler, "Fabula and Sjuzhet in the Analysis of Narrative: Some American Discussions," *Poetics Today*, vol. 1, no. 3 (1980), pp. 27–37; Peter Brooks, *Reading for the Plot: Design and Intention in Narrative* (New York: Alfred A. Knopf, 1984), chaps 1, 4, 10; and Eric S. Rabkin, "Spatial Form and Plot" in Smitten and Daghistany, *Spatial Form in Narrative*, pp. 83, 90.

89 By contrast, Kristin Thompson argues that the unconscious level of mental processes is largely an unnecessary construct for criticism. "For the neoformalist critic, conscious processes are usually the most important ones, since it is here that the artwork can challenge most strongly our habitual ways of perceiving and thinking and can make us aware of our habitual ways of coping with the world. In a sense, for the neoformalist, the aim of original art is to put any or all of our thought processes onto this conscious level." Thompson also discusses the specific failings of psychoanalytic criticism; *Breaking the Glass Armor*, pp. 27–8.

90 See E. Ann Kaplan's "Introduction: From Plato's Cave to Freud's Screen" in *Psychoanalysis & Cinema*, ed. by E. Ann Kaplan (New York: Routledge, 1990), pp. 1–23. For an example of reading against the grain, see Stuart Marshall's discovery of three contradictory views of female sexuality at work in the representation of the character Adrienne Fromsett in *Lady in the Lake*, quoted in note 32 in chapter 5 below.

Recall in the context of a counterintuitive reading, the discussion of Alan Williams's "four films," the spectator's systematic "forgetting," and the dyad "transparency-invisibility" in chapter 3. The fact that some things have slipped from consciousness explains the attraction of such concepts as "suture" and "excess" for psychoanalytic criticism. On suture, see note 27 in chapter 2 above; on excess, see note 4 in chapter 2 above. Marshall draws on suture to explain the "failure" of *Lady in the Lake; "Lady in the Lake*: Identification and the Drives," *Film Form*, vol. 1, no. 2 (Autumn 1977), pp. 38, 42.